FILM
AWARDS

Volume One
1927/28 – 1959

About the Author

Brian Lindsay was awarded a PhD from the University of New South Wales for his thesis "Darkening Frontier, Vanishing Outback: Film, Landscape and National Identities in Australia and the United States". His articles about the Academy Awards have appeared in *The Sydney Morning Herald* and *The Australian*. Passionate about film and theatre history, he lives in Sydney, Australia with his partner, Simon.

His previous publication, *Category Fraud*, examined how studios have gamed the Oscar nominations for decades by campaigning for lead performances to be nominated in the supporting categories, and argued that it was past time the Academy reformed its rules to end the practice and restore integrity to the Oscars. *Category Fraud* was published by Tranter Ward Books in 2016.

The second volume of *Film Awards: A Reference Guide to US & UK Film Awards*, the only film awards reference book to cover the annual awards season category by category, will be published by Tranter Ward Books in 2018.

FILM
AWARDS

A Reference Guide to
US & UK Film Awards

Volume One
1927/28 – 1959

Brian Lindsay

Tranter Ward Books

Tranter Ward Books
Sydney NSW Australia
www.tranterward.com

First Edition 2017

ISBN: 978-0-9804909-4-7

This book previously appeared under the title
Reel Winners: Volume One 1927/8-1959 with the ISBN: 978-0-9804909-3-0

Cover design by Simon Moore, Elton Ward Creative

A catalogue record for this book is available from the National Library of Australia

With thanks to Stephen

Introduction

Each year the Academy Awards ceremony is the culmination of a season of award presentations by critics' associations, industry guilds and other prestigious organisations. As the season unfolds, debate invariably unfolds as to whether each set of accolades portend Oscar glory or are merely curious anomalies.

There are numerous books and websites that diligently list the various nominees and winners, many providing commentary on which films were favoured by the critics and which swept the Globes on the way to the Oscars. Without exception, they chronicle the annual awards season the same way, taking each set of awards in turn – the New York Film Critics' Circle winners, then the National Board of Review winners, then the Golden Globe Award nominees and winners, and so forth, concluding with the Academy Awards.

It's only on rare occasions, however, that we want an overview of an entire awards season or even a snapshot of all the winners of the Los Angeles Film Critics' Association prizes from a given year. More often, we reach for such reference books because, at that moment, we are interested in a certain film or a particular performance. Having just watched *All About Eve*, for example, you're curious to see how Bette Davis fared during that year's awards season. Which groups nominated her legendary performance? Who was she up against? Which accolades did she win? Who did she lose out to? When you have such questions, this is the book to grab.

Film Awards takes a fresh and long overdue approach to the annual awards season: category by category. No more looking up the Best Actress winner from one critic's group, then turning the page to look up the winner from a different critic's group later in that season, then flicking to another page to find out who was nominated for the Golden Globes, and then finally turning to yet another page and scanning through a list of all the Academy Award nominees to find out who was in contention for the Oscar. In this book, the nominees and winners for Best Actress from all the major awards groups in a given year are listed together in one quick-reference table on the same page. At a glance, you can see which awards Bette Davis won for *All About Eve*, who she was nominated alongside and to whom she lost.

Reference tables are compiled in *Film Awards* for Best Picture, Director, Actor, Actress, Supporting Actor and Supporting Actress. In this first volume, covering the years 1927/8 through to 1959, the tables include the nominees and winners of the Academy Awards, Golden Globe Awards, British Academy Awards, Directors Guild of America Awards, New York Film Critics' Circle Awards and National Board of Review Awards where relevant in each instance (depending on which year the awards commenced and in which categories they were presented). As the Hollywood Foreign Press Association does not have comprehensive records for this early period, the lists of Golden Globe Awards nominees are as complete as possible. Information about major film festival prize winners are not included as only a small number of selected candidates are eligible rather than all the films released throughout the year as is the case with the major annual awards.

The reputation of a film can diminish or become enhanced with the passage of time. In 2012, for example, leading film critics and academics polled by the British Film Institute's Sight & Sound magazine selected Alfred Hitchcock's thriller *Vertigo* as the greatest film of all time. The film did not, however, win any Best Picture prizes in the year of its original release. It was not even nominated for the top prizes at the Academy Awards, Golden Globes or BAFTAs. In 1958, reaction to *Vertigo* ranged from mixed to dismissive. The New York Times called it "clever [but] devilishly far-fetched" and remarked "there is a big hole – a big question-mark – at a critical point. It will stop you, if you're a quick thinker. But try not to be and enjoy the film". Variety, meanwhile, said it was "uneven" and "too long and too slow" and declared "it's questionable whether that much time should be devoted to what is basically only a psychological murder mystery". To better understand why certain films and performances garnered awards recognition while others were overlooked, *Film Awards* quotes from leading film critics in the United States, the United Kingdom and Australia to reveal the critical opinion contemporaneous to each film's initial release. Such quotes are reproduced with original spellings.

Throughout the book, films are referred to by the title under which they were originally released in their country of origin. Alternate titles by which a film was known in the United States are included in parentheses.

References to directors and performers in the index relate only to instances when the individual was an awards season contender. For example, only instances when Olivia de Havilland is listed or referred to as a winner, nominee or contender for Best Actress or Best Supporting Actress appear in the index. Other incidental references to her in the book, such as when she was a presenter of the Best Actor statuette or was the star of a Best Picture nominee are omitted.

Film Awards has been designed to place the annual Oscar winners for Picture, Director and Acting into historical context alongside the other winners and nominees from that season as well as the opinions of the leading newspaper and magazine film critics of the day. Hopefully it will be an interesting and informative companion as you discover (or rediscover) the lauded films and performances of the years 1927 to 1959.

Abbreviations

AMPAS	Academy of Motion Picture Arts and Sciences
BAFTA	British Academy of Film and Television Awards
DGA	Directors Guild of America
HFPA	Hollywood Foreign Press Association
NBR	National Board of Review

CIN	Cinema
FM	Film Monthly
Esq	Esquire
FQ	Film Quarterly
FSp	Film Spectator
FW	Film Weekly
HCN	Hollywood Citizen News
HRp	Hollywood Reporter
HRv	Hollywood Review
HSp	Hollywood Spectator
HT	Herald Tribune
LHE	Los Angeles Herald-Express
MFB	Monthly Film Bulletin
N&D	Night & Day
NBR Mag	National Board of Review Magazine
NYDN	New York Daily News
NYer	The New Yorker
NYT	The New York Times
PP	Photoplay
S&S	Sight & Sound
SMH	The Sydney Morning Herald
Sp	The Spectator
TT	The Times
V	Variety

Note on income figures quoted for Best Picture Academy Award nominees:
Figures quoted are for United States theatrical rental receipts during period of original release.

BEST PICTURE

ACADEMY AWARDS

(Outstanding Production)

The Racket
  (Caddo, Paramount, 84 mins BW,
  1 Nov 1928, 1 nom)

Seventh Heaven
  (Fox, 110 mins BW,
  6 May 1927, 6 noms)

• *Wings*
  (Paramount, 139 mins BW,
  12 Aug 1927, 2 noms)

(Artistic Quality of Production)

Chang
  (Paramount, 69 mins BW,
  3 Sep 1927, 1 nom)

The Crowd
  (M-G-M, 104 mins BW,
  18 Feb 1928, 2 noms)

• *Sunrise*
  (Fox, 95 mins BW,
  23 Sep 1927, 4 noms)

In the Academy's first year, the Board of Judges (chosen by the Academy's founder, M-G-M boss Louis B. Mayer) selected two films for prizes which are now considered the forebears of the Best Picture award.

For Most Outstanding Production the Academy honoured *Wings*, a silent film about two American World War One pilots in love with the same girl. The film had been a box office hit as audiences flocked to see what The New York Times had called "amazing air duels".

Also considered for the award were two other popular successes: the crime hit *The Racket* (NYT "one of the most entertaining pictures in quite a time") and the romance *Seventh Heaven* (NYT "grips your interest from the very beginning"; TT "incredibly sentimental as it is, it is often very moving").

For the Artistic Quality award the Board initially chose *The Crowd*, a bleak drama about a New York couple struggling to survive in the modern city. The New York Times had called it "a substantial and worthy pictorial feature" and "a powerful analysis" and Film Spectator said it was "one of the finest and most worthy motion pictures ever made." However, Variety described it as "a drab actionless story of ungodly length and apparently telling nothing." Although it was an M-G-M film, Mayer agreed with the latter assessment and pressured the Board until it changed its choice and instead honoured the Fox film *Sunrise*. The first US film by internationally acclaimed director F.W. Murnau, *Sunrise* had been a commercial and critical success (NYT "remarkable"; V "a distinguished contribution to the screen"; TT a "remarkable achievement"; SMH "among the most remarkable films that have ever been flashed on the screen"). The other film considered for the prize was *Chang*, an acclaimed semi-documentary nature feature about elephants in Thailand (V "a remarkable moving picture"; TT "one of the exceptional rewards of film-going"; SMH "impressive").

Two important films were awarded special awards and not considered for the Academy's top two prizes. The first talking picture, *The Jazz Singer*, was given a special award as "the pioneer outstanding talking picture, which has revolutionized the industry". Meanwhile, Charlie Chaplin was given a special award for *The Circus*, which had divided critics (NYT "a little disappointing"; V "Chaplin's best"; TT "at least the equal of anything Mr Chaplin has done"; SMH "does not seem to be particularly entertaining").

Overlooked by the Academy were the two films for which Emil Jannings won the Best Actor award. The New York Times called *The Way of All Flesh* "compelling" and "a great artistic triumph". Variety, meanwhile, described *The Last Command* as "exceptional". Both films were included by The New York Times on its annual end of year top ten list along with *Chang*, *Wings*, *Seventh Heaven*, *Sunrise*, and *The Circus*.

Two other notable films were ignored by the Academy in its first year: Fritz Lang's science fiction film *Metropolis* (NYT "a remarkable achievement" and "a technical marvel" but "soulless" and "extravagantly theatric"; V "nothing of the sort has ever been filmed before ... positively overwhelming. From a photographic and directorial standpoint it is something entirely original"; PP "a great spectacle"; FSp "extraordinary"; SMH an "intellectual triumph"); and *Dawn*, the controversial British film about Edith Cavell, the nurse who was executed by the Germans in the First World War for assisting escaped British prisoners of war in Belgium (NYT a "sad and painful chronicle" which is "the outstanding achievement to come from Great Britain").

Wings and *Sunrise* shared the honour of being Best Picture in the first year but because Most Outstanding Production was the last award presented at the banquet, newspapers such as The Times reported that "the outstanding picture of the year was declared to be *Wings*." Consequently, today *Sunrise* remains largely overshadowed.

BEST DIRECTOR

ACADEMY AWARDS
(Drama)
• **Frank Borzage for *Seventh Heaven***
Herbert Brenon for *Sorrell and Son*
King Vidor for *The Crowd*

ACADEMY AWARDS
(Comedy)
• **Lewis Milestone for *Two Arabian Knights***
Ted Wilde for *Speedy*
[NOTE: nominee Charles Chaplin for *The Circus* was not considered after the
Board of Judges decided to present him with a special award]

In its first year, the Academy gave two Best Director awards, distinguishing for
the only time between dramas and comedies. With Charlie Chaplin's name
removed from consideration for the award in the comedy category following the
decision by the Board of Judges to present him with a special award, Lewis
Milestone won for *Two Arabian Knights* which The New York Times called "a
genuinely clever comedy" which he had "expertly handled".

The award in the drama category should arguably have gone to the great
German director F.W. Murnau for *Sunrise*, the first Hollywood production for
the maker of the silent classics *Nosferatu* and *Faust* (NYT "Murnau shows
himself to be an artist in camera studies, bringing forth marvellous results"; V
he displays "a gift or a genius for broad effects"; FSp "inspired"). Surprisingly,
however, Murnau was not even considered for the prize.

Also overlooked were: Harry d'Abbadie d'Arrast for *Serenade* (NYT "a
brilliantly directed picture"); Alan Crosland for *Glorious Betsy* (NYT "Crosland
is to be congratulated on his direction of this film. It is his outstanding pictorial
achievement. The narrative flows gently and there is always a measure of
suspense"); Fritz Lang for the science fiction drama *Metropolis* (NYT "the
various ideas have been spliced together quite adroitly"); Josef von Sternberg
for *The Last Command*, one of the films for which Emil Jannings received the
inaugural Best Actor statuette; and Herbert Wilcox for the biographical drama
Dawn (NYT "Wilcox tells his gruesome story with proper suspense and he
depicts adroitly the dread of discovery").

Instead the main contenders for the prize in the drama category were King
Vidor for *The Crowd* (NYT "Vidor's imaginative direction" is "inspired") and
Frank Borzage for the popular *Seventh Heaven* (NYT Borzage "has given to it

all that he could put through the medium of the camera"; FSp "sympathetic direction"). Both men's films were mentioned in consideration for the Academy's Best Picture honours but neither won. The third nominee was Herbert Brenon for the drama *Sorrell and Son* (NYT "Brenon soon becomes entangled in a maze of movieisms from which he rarely extricates himself").

In the end, Borzage was selected as the Academy's choice in the drama category. Both he and Milestone would win the Best Director prize again within five years.

BEST ACTOR

ACADEMY AWARDS

Richard Barthelmess as 'Nickie Elkins' in *The Noose* and as 'The Patent Leather Kid' in *The Patent Leather Kid*

• **Emil Jannings as 'Gen. Dolgorucki (Grand Duke Sergius Alexander)' in *The Last Command* and as 'August Schiller' in *The Way of All Flesh***

[NOTE: nominee Charles Chaplin as 'Charlie, a tramp' in *The Circus* was not considered after the Board of Judges decided to present him with a special award]

In *The Circus*, Charlie Chaplin again played the character of the little tramp that he had popularised with numerous shorts and feature films over many years. A hit with audiences, his performance also garnered praise from critics (NYT "Chaplin never fails to tickle one's fancy") and was short-listed for the Academy's Best Actor award. In the end, however, he was not considered for the statuette. His name was later withdrawn when the Board of Judges decided to present him with a special honour.

That left two contenders for the prize. The first was Richard Barthelmess, one of the Academy's founding members and the biggest box office star of the year. Known for his tendency to overact at times, Barthelmess was named for his portrayals of a prizefighter in *The Patent Leather Kid* (NYT "there is not a single flaw in his acting throughout"; V "perfect") and an alleged murderer in *The Noose* (NYT "Barthelmess is not always at his best in the picture"; SMH "weak").

The other nominee was Emil Jannings, the German actor who in silent movies such as *Faust* had established himself as one of the world's greatest actors. He was considered for his first two performances in American films: as a bank clerk who has a disastrous affair in *The Way of All Flesh* (NYT "perfect", "never falters in his delineation of the character", "a painstaking performance"; V "a fine piece of acting and holds a wealth of detail"; FSp "superb"); and as a former Russian general reduced to being a film extra in *The Last Command* (NYT "a brilliant performance in which there is a wealth of imagination").

Overlooked by the Academy were: Al Jolson in the first talking picture *The Jazz Singer*; Charles Farrell in *Seventh Heaven*; Lionel Barrymore in both *Sadie Thompson* (NYT "shares honors with Miss Swanson ... plays the part in a singularly gifted fashion") and in *The Lion and the Mouse* (NYT "splendid acting"); his brother John Barrymore in *Tempest* (NYT "remarkable"; PP "excellent"); Lon Chaney in both *Mr Wu* (NYT "excellent"; TT "undeniably good"; SMH "fine acting" by Chaney "at his best") and *The Unknown* (NYT

"Chaney really gives a marvelous idea of the Armless Wonder, for to act in this film he has learned to use his feet as hands when eating, drinking and smoking"); Rudolph Schildkraut in *A Ship Comes In*; and Conrad Veidt in the 1924 German film *Orlacs Hände (The Hands of Orlac)* (V a "masterly characterization").

In the opinion of most film historians, the greatest sin of omission was the Academy's failure to nominate comedian Buster Keaton for either his performance as the son of a river boat captain in *Steamboat Bill Jr.* or his turn as a freshman trying unsuccessfully to impress the girl he loves in *College*. Reviews at the time, however, were unkind. Of *Steamboat Bill Jr.,* The New York Times opined, "Buster Keaton's latest attempt to make the millions laugh is a sorry affair … Mr Keaton preserves his stoicism, but while watching this film one feels that one looked rather like Mr Keaton the greater part of the time, which is probably not exactly what Mr Keaton was aiming for." The paper was equally dismissive of *College* declaring, "Keaton himself strives to be funny, but his actions are so frightfully absurd."

Eager to gain international prestige and avoid accusations of favouring its own members, the Academy gave Jannings the first Best Actor award. However, the actor was not at the banquet to collect the prize. Knowing that he would not be able to work in English-language talking pictures because of his heavy German accent he had returned to his homeland in early 1929. His biggest success after the Oscar was as the university professor whose life is ruined by his infatuation with a nightclub singer in the 1930 German film *Der Blaue Engel (The Blue Angel)* with Marlene Dietrich.

When the Nazi regime came to power in Germany, Jannings made a series of anti-Semitic propaganda films which resulted in his professional black-listing by the Allies after the war.

1927/28

BEST ACTRESS

ACADEMY AWARDS
Louise Dresser as 'Mamma Pleznick' in *A Ship Comes In*
• **Janet Gaynor as 'Diane' in *Seventh Heaven*, as 'Angela' in *Street Angel*
and as 'The Wife' in *Sunrise***
Gloria Swanson as 'Sadie Thompson' in *Sadie Thompson*

Louise Dresser was the Academy Award's first surprise nominee. She was considered for her performance as a Polish immigrant in *A Ship Comes In* about which The New York Times wrote "Dresser gives an earnest portrayal as the mother but her actions, due to the direction, are far too slow." Dresser was not a big star and many were surprised to see her name on the shortlist ahead of other more established actresses, particularly as she only had a supporting role in the film.

Mary Pickford, arguably the biggest star in the American silent film industry and the only woman among the Academy's founding members, was overlooked for her last silent, *My Best Girl* (NYT "Pickford's acting is, as usual, delightful. She reflects sincerity and earnestness in her joy and sadness").

Also passed over were: the Swedish star Greta Garbo whose appearance in *Love*, a film version of Leo Tolstoy's tragedy 'Anna Karenina', had divided critics (NYT "outshines any other performance she has given to the screen ... singularly fine acting"; TT "Garbo's Anna has nothing of the temperamental complexity which gives to Tolstoy's story its inward conflict"); the popular Mexican star Dolores del Rio for three lauded performances in *Resurrection* (NYT "few screen actresses have ever given as fine a performance in a role as difficult"), *The Gateway of the Moon* (NYT "excellent acting") and *Ramona* (NYT "an achievement. Not once does she overact"; V "overacts markedly throughout"); Eleanor Boardman in the critically acclaimed drama *The Crowd* (NYT "amazingly appealing ... the spark of genuine interest in the role is discernible in all that Miss Boardman does"); and the British actress Sybil Thorndike in *Dawn* (NYT "a sterling and dignified impersonation of Edith Cavell"; SMH "superbly acted").

The two actresses who really vied for the first Best Actress award were the two biggest female box office stars of the year. Silent veteran Gloria Swanson had a huge box office hit with *Sadie Thompson*, an adaptation of the play 'Rain' by W. Somerset Maugham, and had been widely praised for her performance in the title role (NYT "exceptionally clever" ... shows "genuine ability and imagination" with her best performance to date; V "exceptionally played"; TT "excellent").

The award, however, went to a 22-year-old newcomer, Janet Gaynor, for her acclaimed performances in three commercial hits. The Times applauded her "unquestionably great acting" as the young wife of an unfaithful farmer plotting her murder in *Sunrise*. The New York Times wrote that her performance as a Parisian waif in *Seventh Heaven* "is true and natural throughout ... never once does she falter in her difficult task of reflecting the emotions of the character she portrays". And finally, The New York Times said that as a circus performer in her final silent, *Street Angel*, she was "especially fine".

Gaynor became a popular star in talking pictures. She was nominated again in 1937 for her performance in the original film version of *A Star is Born*.

BEST PICTURE

ACADEMY AWARDS

Alibi
(Art Cinema, UA, 90 mins BW, 20 Apr 1929, 3 noms)

• *The Broadway Melody*
(M-G-M, 110 mins BW & C, 1 Feb 1929, 3 noms)

The Hollywood Revue
(M-G-M, 116 mins BW & C, 23 Nov 1929, 1 nom)

In Old Arizona
(Fox, 95 mins BW, 20 Jan 1929, 5 noms)

The Patriot
(Paramount, 113 mins BW, 1 Sep 1928, 5 noms)

In its second year, the Academy embraced five popular and acclaimed American films. Of the hit crime thriller *Alibi*, starring Chester Morris, The New York Times said there are "genuine thrills in the latest talking crook melodrama". The hugely successful *The Broadway Melody*, a musical about two sisters in search of fame starring former silent star Bessie Love, had been called "absorbing" by the Sydney Morning Herald. The New York Times recommended the all–star M-G-M comedy and musical revue *The Hollywood Revue* as "brimming over with good fun and catchy music" while Variety though it was the "top novelty film" to date. The first outdoor talkie *In Old Arizona* was a hit with audiences, and the historical drama *The Patriot*, starring Emil Jannings, had been embraced by critics (NYT "this motion picture is indeed a credit to the screen … there is, as a matter of fact, hardly a flaw to be found in the whole picture … a gripping piece of work with subtle touches"; V has "a valid claim to greatness"). All five nominees were American studio productions and were all, at least in part, talkies.

Several notable American films were overlooked including: *The Letter* (V "gripping"); *The Shopworn Angel* (NYT "unusually fine and convincing"; V "a glamorous gem"); *Madame X* (NYT "extraordinarily poignant"; V "pictures of this calibre and their makers are entitled to untold commendation"); *The Docks of New York* (NYT "the picture as a whole is good"); and *Show People* (NYT "clever … a hardy satire").

Although now considered by historians as a silent cinema masterpiece, the Lillian Gish vehicle *The Wind* was not well received at the time of its release and was ignored by the Academy (NYT "Yesterday's rain was far more interesting than the Capitol Theatre's current offering, *The Wind* … invariably seems like a sham").

The most glaring omission from the list considered by the Board, however, was foreign. The Academy did not bestow a single nomination on what was arguably the most acclaimed film of the year, the French silent film *La Passion de Jeanne d'Arc (The Passion of Joan of Arc)* which chronicled the trial and execution of Joan of Arc. The New York Times included it on its 1928 Top Ten list and enthusiastically called it "an impressive" and "singularly arresting and original film" and a "remarkable example of cinematic work" which was "a production of unequalled artistry." The FM called it a "masterpiece" that was "one of the grandest of all motion pictures." Despite the glowing notices, the film was overlooked for the Oscars.

In the end the Board was not left with a difficult choice. Having been pressured out of giving the previous year's top prize to M-G-M's *The Crowd*, they honoured the same studio's technically innovative, extravagantly expensive and enormously popular talkie, *The Broadway Melody*.

Tragically, no print of *The Patriot* is known to have survived to the present today.

1928/29

BEST DIRECTOR

Lionel Barrymore for *Madame X*
Harry Beaumont for *The Broadway Melody*
Irving Cummings for *In Old Arizona*
• **Frank Lloyd for *The Divine Lady***
    also nominated for *Drag* and for *Weary River*
Ernst Lubitsch for *The Patriot*

The New York Times praised Danish director Carl Dreyer for his "imaginative camera work and direction" for the French silent film *La Passion de Jeanne d'Arc (The Passion of Joan of Arc)*. Film Monthly said his work was "brilliant." Despite the acclaim, Dreyer was not nominated for the Best Director award.

Also overlooked were both Clarence Brown for his direction of the Greta Garbo silent *A Woman of Affairs* (NYT "Brown has handled this production imaginatively") and Josef von Sternberg for *Docks of New York* (NYT "has directed the play with tact and an eye to minute details").

Although his film is now considered a masterpiece, Victor Sjöström's *The Wind* was not received well by critics at the time of its release and his work was ignored by the Academy. Although respected as a genius, Erich von Stroheim's infamous directorial excesses made him numerous enemies in Hollywood, particularly among the powerful studio producers. Unsurprisingly, he too was bypassed for *The Wedding March*.

Instead, the nominees for Best Director of the year were: Harry Beaumont for *The Broadway Melody* (V "excellent direction"); renowned theatre actor Lionel Barrymore for *Madame X*; Ernst Lubitsch for the acclaimed drama *The Patriot* (NYT "through Lubitsch's skillful guidance it seems quite natural"); and Frank Lloyd for three films he directed for the small studio First National – *The Divine Lady* (NYT "an ambitious and handsome production"), *Weary River* and *Drag*. The reviews of the latter were generally negative while those for *Weary River* were mixed (NYT "banal" and "hopeless hodge–podge", suffers from a "lack of imagination and suspense"; V "one of the thoroughly fine films of the current season" and a credit to all concerned, particularly Lloyd; SMH "dull").

The Academy's Board of Judges selected Lloyd as the year's winner but not for all three films for which he had been nominated. He won the statuette solely for his efforts on *The Divine Lady*. Inappropriately, Lloyd was himself on the Board of Judges. Like each of the previous year's Best Director winners, Lloyd would go on to win the Best Director award again within five years.

1928/29

BEST ACTOR

ACADEMY AWARDS
George Bancroft as 'Jim Lang' in *Thunderbolt*
• **Warner Baxter as 'The Cisco Kid' in *In Old Arizona***
Chester Morris as 'Chick Williams' in *Alibi*
Paul Muni as 'Joseph Douglas, aka James Dyke' in *The Valiant*
Lewis Stone as 'Count Pahlen' in *The Patriot*

If he had not returned to Germany at the advent of talking pictures in Hollywood, the first Best Actor Academy Award winner, Emil Jannings, may have been nominated again for he received some of the best reviews of his career for his portrayal of the mad Tsar Paul I of Russia in *The Patriot*. Variety described his performance as "magnificent" while The Sydney Morning Herald said that "his acting has never before been so powerful". The New York Times raved "superlatives flow to one's mind as one thinks of his depiction of Czar Paul's different moods without borrowing any tricks that he has previously displayed in other screen efforts. There is here not the slightest sign of overacting and yet Mr Jannings has probably attacked the most difficult role of his career ... he submerges his whole being in the character ... and in the last moments of fear Mr Jannings brings to the screen something that is unrivalled ... [he] dominates the whole picture."

Instead it was Jannings' co–star who was nominated for the Oscar. Lewis Stone "gives a balanced and polished performance" wrote Variety. "Superb" said Photoplay. The New York Times considered his performance to be "capital". Tragically, no print of *The Patriot* is extant so the acclaimed performances of Jannings and Stone appear to be lost forever.

The other four contenders for the award were all nominated for playing criminals.

The surprise nominee was George Bancroft for his portrayal of a prisoner in Sing Sing awaiting execution in *Thunderbolt*. The New York Times has been very negative about the film saying there is "nothing edifying about this production". In contrast, the paper had commended him for giving "a good performance as a blustering, carefree stoker" in the drama *The Docks of New York*.

Also nominated for playing a prisoner awaiting execution was the great Yiddish theatre actor Muni Weisenfreund, appearing under his new screen name Paul Muni. He "brings to his role a wealth of humanity. He registers splendidly with utter naturalness" wrote Variety of Muni's portrayal in the prison drama *The Valiant*. The New York Times said he was "splendid".

1928/29

Chester Morris was mentioned by the Academy for his work as a gangster in the hit crime talkie and Best Picture nominee *Alibi*.

Finally, Warner Baxter made the list for his role in the first talking picture made on location, the Western *In Old Arizona*. Baxter played the Mexican outlaw–hero 'The Cisco Kid'. Variety called his portrayal "a great screen performance", The New York Times said it was "capable work" and FM called him "compelling". Actor–director Raoul Walsh had intended to play the part himself but was injured in a car accident.

Absent from the Academy's short-list were the year's best comedic performances, including Buster Keaton in *The Camerman* and William Haines in *Show People* (NYT "a restrained performance").

For his performance in *In Old Arizona* it was Baxter who became the first American to win the Best Actor Oscar.

BEST ACTRESS

ACADEMY AWARDS
Ruth Chatterton as 'Jacqueline' in *Madame X*
Betty Compson as 'Carrie' in *The Barker*
Jeanne Eagels as 'Leslie Crosbie' in *The Letter*
Corinne Griffith as 'Emma Hart (Lady Hamilton)' in *The Divine Lady*
Bessie Love as 'Hank Mahoney' in *The Broadway Melody*
• **Mary Pickford as 'Norma Besant' in *Coquette***

A founder of both United Artists and the Academy, and known as 'America's Sweetheart', Mary Pickford was the biggest silent movie star in American films but she feared her popularity would not survive her transition to talking pictures. Her first talkie was *Coquette*, a film version of a play written for Helen Hayes. Variety said that "Pickford gives an excellent performance as the little southern flirt who throws her home town into a turmoil which ends in tragedy" while The New York Times said that her "fine" performance saved an otherwise poor film. In London, however, The Times was less kind saying that "her acting is more open than usual to criticism."

Despite mixed reviews *Coquette* was her most successful film ever. Having played innocent adolescent girls throughout most of her career, Pickford had cut off her famous girlish curls and sported a stylish new bob haircut in *Coquette* in which she played an adult role. Audiences were fascinated by the transformation. Even before production had begun, Pickford was determined to crown her new screen image and her new career in talking movies with an Oscar statuette. Shortly after the nominations were announced, she invited the entire Board of Judges over to their home for tea. Her eventual selection as Best Actress was so controversial that the Board was abolished the following year in favour of voting by the membership. Despite winning the Oscar, she never enjoyed great success in the talkies after the novelty of *Coquette*. She retired from the screen in 1933.

Three actresses gave performances that earned more acclaim from critics: Jeanne Eagels as a murderess in *The Letter* (V "an acting triumph"; SMH "brilliant"; FM "the most brilliant performance" in talking pictures); Ruth Chatterton as a woman defended in a murder trial by the son she gave up as an infant in *Madame X* (NYT "the outstanding achievement of the picture ... she portrays the emotional spells of the saddened woman with intelligence and artistry"; V there is "not a flaw in her performance"; SMH she "portrays with wonderful conviction the gradual hardening of the woman's character"); and Corsican actress Maria Falconetti in the silent film *La Passion de Jeanne d'Arc (The Passion of Joan of Arc)* (NYT a "gifted performance ... the acting of Maria

Falconetti as Jeanne is the paramount feature of this production ... it is doubtful whether any other actress could have given such an inspired performance ... Falconetti is superb"). Chatterton and Eagels (who had died of a heroin overdose in October 1929) were nominated for the Academy Award, but Falconetti was overlooked.

The performance of Lillian Gish in *The Wind*, which is today acclaimed as one of the greatest portrayals in American silent cinema, did not impress critics at the time and was ignored by Oscar voters. Similarly, poor reviews probably encouraged the Academy's Board of Judges to overlook Greta Garbo for her performances in *The Divine Woman* (NYT "occasionally given to overacting ... does not compel the admiration she elicited by her fascinating portrayal in *Love*") and *A Woman of Affairs* for which she is today lauded by historians. Marion Davies, who was never taken seriously in Hollywood, was also bypassed for her work in the satire *Show People*.

Many historians argue that Betty Compson ought to have been recognised for *The Docks of New York* (NYT "plays the part of Sadie well") rather than for her turn in *The Barker*, but critics at the time were sold on her performance in the latter film (NYT "gives a sterling performance").

1929/30

BEST PICTURE

ACADEMY AWARDS
• *All Quiet on the Western Front*
   (Universal, 131 mins BW, 27 Apr 1930, 4 noms)
The Big House
   (Cosmopolitan, M-G-M, 84 mins BW, 25 Jun 1930, 4 noms)
Disraeli
   (Warner Bros., 90 mins BW, 2 Oct 1929, 3 noms)
The Divorcee
   (M-G-M, 83 mins BW, 19 Apr 1930, 4 noms)
The Love Parade
   (Paramount, 107 mins BW, 19 Nov 1929, 6 noms)

In its first two years, the Academy gave Best Picture awards to popular films ahead of more critically acclaimed contenders, choosing mainstream fare over artistic or political entrants. The same cannot be said of its choice in 1929/30. *All Quiet on the Western Front*, a film adaptation of Erich Maria Remarque's anti-war novel, was internationally acclaimed as a masterpiece. The New York Times called it "trenchant and imaginative", "a notable achievement, sincere and earnest, with glimpses that are vivid and graphic" and "a memorable piece of work." Variety said it was "a harrowing, gruesome, morbid tale of war, compelling in its realism, bigness and repulsiveness ... a very great talking picture." Film Spectator hailed it as "the greatest motion picture ever made ... stunning, moving" while Cinema called it "magnificent" and "superb." In London, The Times commented that "as a film of war it is unsurpassed" while in Australia The Sydney Morning Herald simply called it "a magnificent production."

Of the other nominees, critics had commended *Disraeli* (V "vivid and appealing"), *The Big House* (NYT "realistic", "thrilling") and *The Love Parade* (NYT "charming"; V "a fine, near-grand entertainment"). Only the M-G-M melodrama *The Divorcee* had received negative reviews from critics. While the cast of *All Quiet on the Western Front* were passed over for Oscar consideration, the stars of these other four Best Picture nominees were all included on the Academy's short-lists.

Included on The New York Times list of the year's ten best films, but overlooked by the Academy, were Greta Garbo's first talkie *Anna Christie* (FSp "superb") and the thriller *Bulldog Drummond* (NYT "the happiest and most enjoyable entertainment").

The sound version of Alfred Hitchcock's British drama *Blackmail* was praised by Variety as "a picture which does not lose any film technique and gains effect from dialog" and as such one that "comes near to being a landmark." Photoplay called the film "splendid". But it too was ignored by the Academy. Also bypassed was the drama *Applause* which had performed poorly at the box office.

Film historians argue that the most egregious omission from the slate of Best Picture nominees was G.W. Pabst's drama *Die Büsche der Pandora (Pandora's Box)* starring American actress Louise Brooks as a woman who destroys the lives of the men who fall in love with her. Rediscovered by cineastes in the 1970s, it is now considered a masterpiece. In 1929, however, it was screened in the United States only in a censored version with an altered ending and did not impress the critics. The New York Times dismissed it as "seldom interesting" and "a disconnected melodramatic effusion".

The film omitted from the Academy's shortlist that had the strongest reviews at the time of its release was King Vidor's all African-American musical *Hallelujah*, about a cotton picker turned preacher who struggles against his own vices. Although Variety questioned its appeal to America's white audiences, it still considered *Hallelujah* "a big, entertaining picture" and "an artistic success." Film Spectator said it was "a magnificent achievement." The Times described it as "one of the few American contributions to the development of the film as an art distinct from a form of entertainment" while Sight & Sound called it "a definite artistic landmark." The New York Times rated it one of the year's ten best films. Despite such acclaim and a Best Director nod for Vidor, the film was not among the nominees for Best Picture of the year.

1929/30

BEST DIRECTOR

ACADEMY AWARDS
Clarence Brown for *Anna Christie* and for *Romance*
Robert Z. Leonard for *The Divorcee*
Ernst Lubitsch for *The Love Parade*
• Lewis Milestone for *All Quiet on the Western Front*
King Vidor for *Hallelujah*

The acclaim for Lewis Milestone's *All Quiet on the Western Front* was so strong there was never any doubt he would win his second Best Director award at the third Oscar ceremony in late 1930. The New York Times wrote "Milestone has used his fecund imagination [while] still clinging loyally to the incidents of the book". In the paper's opinion, "often the scenes are of such excellence that if they were not audible one might believe that they were actual motion pictures of activities behind the lines, in the trenches, and in No Man's Land".

Milestone won his second statuette over a field comprised of candidates recognised for many of the year's noted directorial achievements. Clarence Brown was mentioned for directing Greta Garbo's first talking pictures, *Anna Christie* (NYT "depicts [the story] with marked ability") and *Romance*. Ernst Lubitsch received his second nomination for directing *The Love Parade*, a Best Picture nominee, which The New York Times had described as "a finely directed film." Only Robert Z. Leonard among the nominees had been included for a film that had received universally negative notices, the M-G-M release *The Divorcee* starring Norma Shearer. And even then, Leonard's work had fared better than either his cast or the film. The New York Times had concluded "it is a competently acted production, with good direction in some of its scenes".

The main challenger to Milestone was another nominee from the Academy's first year. King Vidor made the list for the all African–American musical *Hallelujah*. Variety enthused "Vidor has accomplished his greatest work."

The notable omissions from the list of contenders included: Victor Fleming for the western *The Virginian* (V "a great directorial job"); Alfred Hitchcock for the sound version of the thriller *Blackmail*; James Whale for the British war film *Journey's End* (NYT "Whale has worked wonders"); Dorothy Arzner for *Sarah and Son* (NYT "intelligently directed"); and G.W. Pabst for *Die Büsche der Pandora (Pandora's Box)* (NYT "there are several adroitly directed passages").

Despite negative reviews and poor box office figures at the time of its release, many film historians argue that Rouben Mamoulian ought to have been short-listed for the drama *Applause* (NYT "commits the unpardonable sin of being far too extravagant").

BEST ACTOR

ACADEMY AWARDS
• **George Arliss as 'Prime Minister Benjamin Disraeli' in** *Disraeli*
    also nominated as 'The Rajah of Rukh' in *The Green Goddess*
Wallace Beery as 'Butch Schmidt' in *The Big House*
Maurice Chevalier as 'Pierre Mirande' in *The Big Pond* and as 'Count Alfred'
    in *The Love Parade*
Ronald Colman as 'Bulldog Drummond' in *Bulldog Drummond* and as 'Michel
    Oban' in *Condemned*
Lawrence Tibbett as 'Yegor' in *The Rogue Song*

The most critically acclaimed film of the year was the anti-war drama *All Quiet on the Western Front*. Although the film won both the Best Picture and Best Director awards – the first to be so honoured by the Academy – its young star, Lew Ayres, was not nominated for his performance as the young German soldier disillusioned by his experiences in the trenches of the First World War (FSp played the part "intelligently and impressively"). Louis Wolheim was also overlooked for his supporting part in the film (FSp "superb"; CIN a "particularly fine performance").

Instead, the surprise nominee in the Best Actor category was Lawrence Tibbett, the star baritone of New York's Metropolitan Opera who made his film debut in *The Rogue Song* (a film which unfortunately now exists only as a soundtrack recording). The New York Times was very positive about Tibbett's talent as a singer and Variety called the film a "one–man–picture", but no–one gave him much of a chance of winning the Academy's prize against four screen stars nominated for lauded performances in the year's most acclaimed films.

Charismatic French star Maurice Chevalier had received positive reviews for his performance as the young man courting Claudette Colbert's character in *The Big Pond* and more particularly as the amorous nobleman in the Best Picture nominee and box office hit *The Love Parade* (NYT "whether he is speaking or singing, makes every utterance count for its full worth"). The Academy cited him for both portrayals.

Also nominated was Wallace Beery, whose performance as a rebellious prisoner in the Best Picture nominee *The Big House* had earned him praise from the critics. The New York Times, for example, commended him on an "outstanding performance." Overlooked for a nomination, however, was Beery's co-star and one of the previous year's Best Actor nominees, Chester Morris (who also starred in *The Divorcee* opposite Best Actress winner Norma Shearer).

The New York Times called Englishman Ronald Colman's turn as a detective–adventurer in *Bulldog Drummond* a "matchless so far as talking pictures are concerned" and Photoplay called it "the best talkie performance to date ... superb". Variety, meanwhile, said he delivered a "likeable performance" as a French prisoner in *Condemned*. The Academy mentioned him for both portrayals.

Another Englishman nominated for two performances was the internationally renowned stage and silent screen actor George Arliss, who made his debut in talking pictures by recreating two of his silent film roles. Arliss filmed *The Green Goddess* first and gave what The New York Times later called "his usual polished performance", however the star thought that *Disraeli* would be a better talking picture debut and arranged to have it released first. The New York Times considered it Arliss' best performance, while The Times wrote "we have nothing but praise for the full and sensitive interpretation which Mr Arliss has given us." The Sydney Morning Herald said his portrayal was "a triumph ... worthy of the highest praise."

The Academy agreed and named Arliss the Best Actor of the year for his performance as former British Prime Minister Benjamin Disraeli, making him the first Englishman to win the award. Arliss was not at the ceremony in the Ambassador Hotel as he was enjoying a holiday in France. The statuette was accepted on his behalf by Darryl F. Zanuck, the head of productions at Warner Bros.

Over the remaining seven years of his career Arliss was a popular box office star and received considerable praise from critics, particularly for his other portrayals of historical figures in such films as *Voltaire*, *House of Rothschild* and *Cardinal Richelieu*. Despite such successes, however, he was never again nominated for the Best Actor award. He returned to England in 1935 and retired from the screen two years later to care for his ailing wife, the actress Florence Montgomery.

BEST ACTRESS

ACADEMY AWARDS

Nancy Carroll as 'Hallie Hobart' in *The Devil's Holiday*

Ruth Chatterton as 'Sarah Storm' in *Sarah and Son*

Greta Garbo as 'Anna Christie' in *Anna Christie* and as 'Rita Cavallini' in *Romance*

• **Norma Shearer as 'Jerry' in *The Divorcee***

    also nominated as 'Lucia "Lally" Marlett' in *Their Own Desire*

Gloria Swanson as 'Marion Donnell' in *The Trespasser*

The abolition of the Board of Judges and the introduction of voting by the Academy's membership following the previous year's choice of Mary Pickford as Best Actress did not free the awards of controversy – and again it was the Best Actress award that was the focus of allegations of favouritism. The winner was Norma Shearer, wife of M-G-M's young 'wunderkid' producer Irving G. Thalberg, the studio's top female star and one of the most popular actresses of the day. Shearer was nominated for her performances in two showcase vehicles, *The Divorcee* and *Their Own Desire*.

The New York Times was negative about *The Divorcee* calling it "a competently acted production", but did say "Shearer does all that is possible in the circumstances with her role" as a woman who has an affair when she discovers that her husband has been unfaithful, and then leads a promiscuous life after they divorce. The paper considered her character to be the only "real" one in the movie while Variety thought her performance was "good". There had been a similar critical response to *Their Own Desire*. The New York Times called it "a film with excellent photography and competent acting" in which Shearer "played charmingly" the lead role. Although never confirmed, there were many reports that studio executives had pressured employees to vote for Shearer.

Ironically, Shearer's best reviews were for her performance in another film released prior to those for which she was mentioned by the Academy. Variety praised her for doing "extremely well with the heroine" in *The Last of Mrs Cheyney*, while The New York Times said she was "remarkably good."

There had been greater critical acclaim for nominee Gloria Swanson's portrayal in her first talkie, *The Trespasser*, in which she also proved that she could sing. The New York Times said she gave a "better performance" than in *Sadie Thompson* (for which she had been nominated two years earlier), while The Times said that she "makes the picture" and "proves how fluent a mastery she has obtained of the sound medium."

1929/30

Critics also praised Greta Garbo for mastering talking pictures with her turn in *Anna Christie* (FSp "magnificent"; Cinema "extremely good") and she was recognised with a nomination from the Academy. Overlooked, however, was Garbo's co-star, Marie Dressler, who garnered even stronger reviews than the Swedish legend. The New York Times said it was "far and away her outstanding film characterization". Variety, meanwhile, opined she had proven herself "an actress with an affecting knack of genuine pathos" and The Times said that she had "carried off the honours."

The New York Times said that nominee Ruth Chatterton gave "another splendid performance" in *Sarah and Son*, while Variety commented that in *The Devil's Holiday* nominee Nancy Carroll was "nothing less than a revelation ... here is no pretty–faced ingenue but a genuine trouper with imagination and power. She is entirely persuasive."

The notable omissions from the Academy's list of nominees were Nina Mae McKinney, one of the African–American stars of King Vidor's acclaimed musical *Hallelujah* (V "natural, convincing and unbelievably good"; FSp "superb") and Helen Morgan as a burlesque queen in *Applause* (NYT "does remarkably well"). Although now celebrated by film historians, Louise Brooks was snubbed for her work in *Die Büsche der Pandora (Pandora's Box)*. The film was not widely seen in the United States and Brooks was *persona non grata* in Hollywood at the time.

Despite strong competition, the Queen of M-G-M, Norma Shearer, was named the Best Actress of the year by the Academy at its third banquet in November 1930. Shearer was said to have appeared almost overwhelmed when she received the statuette.

BEST PICTURE

ACADEMY AWARDS
• *Cimarron*
   (RKO Radio, 131 mins BW, 9 Feb 1931, 7 noms)
East Lynne
   (Fox, 72 mins BW, 16 Feb 1931, 1 nom)
The Front Page
   (Caddo, United Artists, 101 mins BW, 4 Apr 1931, 3 noms)
Skippy
   (Paramount, 85 mins BW, 25 Apr 1931, 4 noms)
Trader Horn
   (M-G-M, 101 mins BW, 23 May 1931, 1 nom)

Three of the year's most expensive, acclaimed and popular films were nominated for Best Picture in the Academy's fourth year.

The M-G-M adventure *Trader Horn*, which had been partly filmed in Africa, had been called a "shrewdly fashioned jungle melodrama" in which "thrilling realism is spliced cleverly with rugged fiction" by The New York Times, and "one of the most remarkable travel films in the history of the screen" by The Sydney Morning Herald.

Meanwhile, Variety described Fox's production of the tragic melodrama *East Lynne* as "an excellent piece of work" and "a screen drama of strength and charm." The New York Times, meanwhile, considered it be a "handsome production".

Even more popular with audiences was RKO's *Cimarron*, an historical epic about the foundation of Oklahoma, starring Richard Dix and Irene Dunne. The New York Times called the film "graphic and engrossing" while Variety said it was "an elegant example of super film making" and Photoplay hailed it as "one of the year's best." Overseas, The Sydney Morning Herald described it as "striking" and "spectacular", but in London, The Times was less enthusiastic saying that despite an "impressive" opening the film was flawed by an "unsatisfactory ending."

Cimarron led the Oscar field with a record tally of seven nominations when the Academy Award nominations were announced (it was the first film ever mentioned for all five of the top awards). *East Lynne* and *Trader Horn*, however, were not nominated in any other category and consequently the main challengers to *Cimarron* were two other popular hits: Lewis Milestone's comedy about a Chicago newspaper office *The Front Page* (NYT "witty", "fast-paced"; V "very entertaining"; SMH "extraordinary") and *Skippy*, a film version of a popular children's comic-strip serial (NYT "endowed with wholesome amusement and affecting tenderness"). The stars and directors of both films received Oscar nominations.

Among the films overlooked for the top award were two major M-G-M productions that had been box office hits despite negative reviews. The New York Times called the latest vehicle for Greta Garbo, *Inspiration*, in which she appeared opposite Robert Montgomery and Lewis Stone, "sadly unconvincing" with "uninspired" performances. An "unimaginative production" of a "lurid, implausible affair" was how the same paper described *A Free Soul*, the studio's attempt to re-create the success of *The Divorcee*. Norma Shearer starred, this time opposite Lionel Barrymore. Variety called it "an ungainly rambling and preposterous theme, awkwardly brought to the screen." Among the other popular movies to be ignored were the horror film *Dracula* (NYT "best of the many mystery films") and the gangster sensation *Little Caesar* (V "gripping and interesting"). Both are now considered landmark cinema classics.

Several acclaimed films were also passed over by the Academy. The most glaring omission was the latest film by Charlie Chaplin, *City Lights*, which was a box office hit despite the public's bias against silent films. It was included by The New York Times on its list of the year's ten best films. Also on the list was *Abraham Lincoln*, D.W. Griffith's latest epic which Variety called "more than an outstanding classic of sound pictures ... a startlingly superlative accomplishment." Josef von Sternberg's German hit *Der Blaue Engel (The Blue Angel)* and his Hollywood film *Morocco*, which both starred Marlene Dietrich, were each passed over (even though von Sternberg and Dietrich both received nominations for the latter). Also ignored was the prison drama *The Criminal Code*, directed by Howard Hawks.

On Oscar night, *Skippy*'s Norman Taurog was an upset winner in the Best Director category, and Dix and Dunne missed out on the acting awards. The pre-ceremony favourite *Cimarron* nevertheless emerged as the winner of the Best Picture prize.

BEST DIRECTOR

ACADEMY AWARDS
Clarence Brown for *A Free Soul*
Lewis Milestone for *The Front Page*
Wesley Ruggles for *Cimarron*
• **Norman Taurog for *Skippy***
Josef von Sternberg for *Morocco*

The New York Times said that Clarence Brown brought *A Free Soul* "awkwardly" to the screen, but he made the Oscar list for a second consecutive year despite such negative reviews.

Also appearing on the ballot once again was Lewis Milestone, who had collected his second Best Director statuette the previous year. Milestone received an unprecedented third nomination for the comedy *The Front Page* for which The Times in London commended him for his "excellent" use of the original stage material.

Nominated for the first time were: Wesley Ruggles for the popular Western *Cimarron* (NYT "most intelligently directed"); Norman Taurog for *Skippy*; and Josef von Sternberg for *Morocco* (NYT "expertly directed").

Interestingly von Sternberg received better reviews for his earlier German drama *Der Blaue Engel (The Blue Angel)* which was released in the United States in the wake of the box office success of *Morocco* (NYT "direction is infinitely superior to that of *Morocco*"; FM "brilliantly directed").

Missing from the list of nominees were W. S. Van Dyke for Best Picture nominee *Trader Horn* (NYT has "succeeded in conveying a keen sense of danger") and previous Oscar winner Frank Lloyd for Best Picture nominee *East Lynne* (NYT "vastly superior to anything he had done in several years"). Also overlooked were: Charlie Chaplin for *City Lights* (NYT "a film worked out with admirable artistry"); Tod Browning for *Dracula*; Archie Mayo for *Svengali* (NYT "knowledgeful supervision" of some of "the most striking and interesting camera feats ever accomplished in a film"); William Wellman for *The Public Enemy*; and Howard Hawks for *The Criminal Code* (NYT "Hawks's direction for the most part [is] intelligent and firm [but] there are occasional sequences which he spoils by extravagant ideas or by leaving too little to the imagination").

Heading into the Oscar ceremony Ruggles was considered the strong favourite for the Oscar given his film's status as the frontrunner for Best Picture. In an upset, however, the winner was 32-year-old Taurog. He remained the youngest winner of the Best Director Oscar for over eighty years until the victory of Damien Chazelle for *La La Land*.

1930/31

BEST ACTOR

• **Lionel Barrymore as 'Stephen Ashe' in** *A Free Soul*
Jackie Cooper as 'Skippy Skinner' in *Skippy*
Richard Dix as 'Yancey Cravat' in *Cimarron*
Fredric March as 'Tony Cavendish' in *The Royal Family of Broadway*
Adolphe Menjou as 'Walter Burns' in *The Front Page*

The frontrunners for the Best Actor Oscar were 53-year-old acclaimed theatre star Lionel Barrymore and 10-year-old newcomer Jackie Cooper. Mentioned two years earlier as Best Director for *Madame X*, Barrymore became the first person nominated in different categories when he was short-listed for the Best Actor prize for his performance as drunken lawyer in *A Free Soul*. The New York Times wrote, "Barrymore does all that is possible with his role ... his is the only characterization that rings true ... steals whatever honors there may be" while in Australia, The Sydney Morning Herald declared that he "furnishes an excellent study, natural as well as consistent". Jackie Cooper also made Oscar history when he was named for his portrayal of the popular comic-strip character Skippy Skinner in *Skippy*. He remains the youngest Best Actor nominee in history and was the first to be nominated for a performance in a film directed by a relative (his uncle Norman Taurog). The New York Times thought his work was "extraordinarily natural" and "truly remarkable" while Variety thought he "could not be improved upon".

Also earning nominations were: former silent screen star Richard Dix as a pioneer in the popular Western *Cimarron* (NYT "a fine impersonation of Cravat"); Adolphe Menjou as a newspaper editor in *The Front Page* (a role he inherited after the sudden death during rehearsals of Louis Wolheim) (NYT "excellent"; V "standout performance"); and Fredric March as a famous theatre actor in *The Royal Family of Broadway*.

Interestingly, March's character was a spoof of nominee Lionel Barrymore's young brother, John Barrymore, who was overlooked despite giving two of the year's most acclaimed performances. The New York Times praised his portrayal of Captain Ahab Ceeley in *Moby Dick* (a remake of his 1926 silent *The Sea Beast* and a very loose adaptation of Herman Melville's classic novel), while the same paper later wrote that his "imaginative and forceful portrayal" in *Svengali* "surpasses anything he has done for the screen." Variety called his performance in the latter "sterling."

Glaring omissions from the list of nominees were: Edward G. Robinson as a gangster in *Little Caesar* (NYT "wonderfully effective"; V "entirely convincing"; Life "exceptionally fine"); Charlie Chaplin in *City Lights* (NYT "hilarious"); Bela Lugosi in *Dracula*; and previous winner Emil Jannings as a literature professor in the German hit *Der Blaue Engel (The Blue Angel)* (NYT "exceptionally fine"; SMH "sterling"; FM "brilliant").

Other well reviewed performances included: Charles Bickford's dual performances as a man accused of murder and the policeman tracking him down in *River's End*; James Cagney as a hoodlum in *The Public Enemy* (NYT "remarkably lifelike portrait … interesting"); previous nominee Lawrence Tibbett in *The Prodigal*; and Walter Huston as an attorney-general turned prison warden in *The Criminal Code* (NYT "another sure and strong characterization").

Barrymore was the clear favourite for the prize and duly won the honour. Despite acclaimed performances over the next decade he was never again nominated.

1930/31

BEST ACTRESS

ACADEMY AWARDS
Marlene Dietrich as 'Amy Jolly' in *Morocco*
• **Marie Dressler as 'Min' in *Min and Bill***
Irene Dunne as 'Sabra Cravat' in *Cimarron*
Ann Harding as 'Linda Seton' in *Holiday*
Norma Shearer as 'Jan Ashe' in *A Free Soul*

M-G-M sought to recreate the success of the previous year's success *The Divorcee* with another melodrama, *A Free Soul*. The film was a box office success but received weak reviews. The film failed to make the list of Best Picture candidates, but earned nominations for its director and for stars Lionel Barrymore and Norma Shearer. The inclusion of the previous year's Best Actress winner was a surprise as her performance had been poorly reviewed. The New York Times thought she was "unsuited" to the role of the socialite who refuses to marry, while The Sydney Morning Herald said that she failed to make "a wholly artificial character appear plausible." Shearer was the first person to receive a third nomination in the acting categories.

The favourite for the Best Actress statuette was another of M-G-M's popular stars, 62-year old Marie Dressler. She was included on the ballot for her performance as the tough owner of a waterfront hotel who struggles to protect the future of the girl she has raised since infancy in the hit *Min and Bill*, a role written especially for her. While The New York Times praised her "good performance", Variety raved that "no other woman anywhere could have played Miss Dressler's role convincingly at all" and lauded her "excellent balance of pathos and comedy." Her nomination came a year after she had almost stolen *Anna Christie* from Greta Garbo.

Also nominated for the Best Actress award were screen newcomer Irene Dunne for *Cimarron* (NYT "excellent"; V "does nicely enough"; SMH "admirable") and two actresses who had given acclaimed performances in films other than those for which they were nominated. German star Marlene Dietrich was mentioned for her first Hollywood film, *Morocco*, even though she received much stronger reviews for her earlier German hit *Der Blaue Engel (The Blue Angel)*. The New York Times said that her "exceptionally fine performance" was better than her turn in *Morocco* and Variety agreed commenting "she more definitely impresses in this one." Young star Ann Harding was nominated for *Holiday* (NYT "graceful") even though she received raves for her portrayal of Lady Isabella Carlyle in the box office hit and Best Picture nominee *East Lynne*. Of her work in *East Lynne*, The New York Times said that her "impressive performance ... captures one's full attention." Variety called her performance "outstanding", The Times said it was "remarkable" and The Sydney Morning Herald said that her "excellent acting" had made the character "a genuine figure."

Overlooked for the prize were: Barbara Stanwyck in *The Miracle Woman* (NYT a "clever performance"); May Robson in *The She-Wolf* (NYT "gives a vigorous and impressive portrayal of a crafty, domineering and parsimonious feminine financier"); Ruth Chatterton for her dual roles as mother and daughter in *The Right to Love* (NYT "extremely clever"); the inaugural winner Janet Gaynor as a cabaret singer in *The Man Who Came Back* (NYT "an exhibition of really fine acting"); Virginia Cherrill for her film debut in Charlie Chaplin's *City Lights* (NYT "charmingly impressive"); Ina Claire in *The Royal Family of Broadway* (NYT "ably portrayed"); and Joan Crawford in *Dance, Fools, Dance* as a socialite who becomes a newspaper reporter after her family loses its fortune in the stock market crash (NYT "Crawford's acting is still self-conscious, but her admirers will find her performance well up to her standard").

Among the notable performances in supporting roles to be ignored were Sylvia Sidney as the poor factory worker in *An American Tragedy* (NYT "earnest") and Edna May Oliver in *Cimarron* (NYT "furnishes some really clever comedy").

On the night, Dressler was the winner. The popular actress was to be a major contender for the Best Actress award again the following year.

BEST PICTURE

ACADEMY AWARDS

Arrowsmith
  (Goldwyn, United Artists, 108 mins BW, 26 Dec 1931, 4 noms)
Bad Girl
  (Fox, 90 mins BW, 13 Aug 1931, 3 noms)
The Champ
  (M-G-M, 87 mins BW, 21 Nov 1931, 4 noms)
Five Star Final
  (First National, 89 mins BW, 11 Sep 1931, 1 nom)
• *Grand Hotel*
  (M-G-M, 112 mins BW, 12 Apr 1932, 1 nom)
One Hour With You
  (Paramount, 80 mins BW, 23 Mar 1932, 1 nom)
Shanghai Express
  (Paramount, 84 mins BW, 17 Feb 1932, 3 noms)
The Smiling Lieutenant
  (Paramount, 88 mins BW, 22 May 1931, 1 nom)

The most anticipated film of the year was M-G-M's all-star drama *Grand Hotel* which featured Greta Garbo, Lionel and John Barrymore, Joan Crawford and Wallace Beery. The film was a critical and popular hit which Photoplay said was "magnificent" and which The New York Times called "a production thoroughly worthy of all the talk it has created". Surprisingly, however, the film was nominated for Best Picture but no other awards. The newspaper drama *Five Star Final* and the hit musical comedies *Our Hour With You* (NYT "excellent") and *The Smiling Lieutenant*, one of The New York Times Top Ten of the year, were similarly nominated for Best Picture and in no other categories.

The most nominated films of the year were *Arrowsmith* and *The Champ*. Based on Sinclair Lewis' novel, *Arrowsmith* was popular with audiences and critics. The New York Times considered it an "intelligent and forceful" and "highly praiseworthy" film and declared it one of the year's ten best. The tearjerker *The Champ*, directed by King Vidor, was also a huge box office success, teaming two of the previous year's big stars, Wallace Beery (*Min and Bill*) and Jackie Cooper (*Skippy*), as a washed-up fighter and his son.

Also included in the Best Picture category was *Shanghai Express* (PP "fascinating"), which reteamed Josef von Sternberg and Marlene Dietrich a year after they had scored Oscar nominations for *Morocco* and enjoyed box office success and critical acclaim with *Der Blaue Engel (The Blue Angel)*. Completing the field of candidates was *Bad Girl*, a small romantic film about a struggling young couple which had been an unexpected hit with audiences and had appeared on The New York Times list as one of the year's ten best. *Bad Girl* won the Best Director award for Frank Borzage.

The Academy overlooked two hit horror films: *Dr Jekyll and Mr Hyde* (NYT a "tense and shuddering affair ... blood-curdling") for which Fredric March won the Best Actor statuette; and *Frankenstein* (V "a new peak in horror"). Both films had been selected by The New York Times as among the year's ten best movies.

The Academy also passed over: *Private Lives*, a version of Noel Coward's play starring Norma Shearer; *The Guardsman*, for which Alfred Lunt and Lynn Fontanne were both nominated in the acting categories, and which Variety had called a "flawless" and "sophisticated study of back stage characters"; the pacifist film *The Man I Killed* starring Lionel Barrymore (NYT "ironic, sentimental post-war film"; V "well made ... artistically there is much in the film's favor"); and the gangster film *Scarface: The Shame of a Nation* starring Paul Muni (S&S "brilliant"). Both *Private Lives* and *The Guardsman* had appeared on The New York Times top ten list.

Once again, several notable foreign films were ignored. There were no nominations for: *Michael and Mary*, the British film version of A. A. Milne's play about a couple trying to keep their bigamous marriage a secret (NYT "an entertainment of considerable fervour and beauty"); *Sturme der Leidenschaft (Tempest)* starring Emil Jannings which Variety called "the most powerful and realistic film yarn in years" which was "so strong that it is impossible not to be impressed"; or the anti-war film *Les Croix de Bois (Wooden Crosses)* which The New York Times labelled "one of the great films in motion picture history" and "a masterpiece of realism and simplicity".

Although well regarded by film historians, *What Price Hollywood?* was not well received by film critics at the time and was unsurprisingly bypassed by Academy voters as a result. The New York Times conceded that it was "not all bad" saying that it was "very amusing" in parts, but was unimpressed overall.

Prior to the Oscar ceremony, Variety predicted a triumph for *Arrowsmith*. Instead, on the night the all-star hit *Grand Hotel* won a second Best Picture statuette for M-G-M. Some observers expressed disapproval of the choice. The Los Angeles Times, for example, commented that *Grand Hotel* had won because it filled "the requirements of bigness."

BEST DIRECTOR

ACADEMY AWARDS
• **Frank Borzage for** *Bad Girl*
King Vidor for *The Champ*
Josef von Sternberg for *Shanghai Express*

The New York Times praised English director Edmund Goulding for "an excellent piece of work" in directing the all-star cast of M-G-M's *Grand Hotel*. Yet Goulding was a notable omission from the Academy's Best Director category. Surprisingly, John Ford, the director of the other main Best Picture contender *Arrowsmith*, was also overlooked.

Consequently, it seemed that the award might go to King Vidor, receiving his third nomination as Best Director in five years for his work on the box office hit and Best Picture nominee *The Champ*. The New York Times had praised him for his "expert direction."

Also nominated was the very first Best Director winner Frank Borzage for *Bad Girl* (NYT "deft direction") and one of the previous year's nominees, Josef von Sternberg, for *Shanghai Express* (NYT "the best picture Josef von Sternberg has directed").

Not considered for the award were: James Whale for the horror film *Frankenstein* (V "subtle handling of the subject"; PP "magnificent" direction; SMH "excellently produced"); Sidney Franklin for both *The Guardsman* and *Private Lives* (NYT "excellent" direction); Rouben Mamoulian for *Dr Jekyll and Mr Hyde* (NYT film "is pictured with an excellent cunning"); Howard Hawks for *Scarface: The Shame of a Nation*; Ernst Lubitsch for *The Man I Killed* (NYT "further evidence of Mr Lubitsch's genius"); Raymond Bernard for *Les Croix de Bois (Wooden Crosses)*; and Robert Siodmak for *Sturme der Leidenschaft (Tempest)*.

As Oscar night approached it was Borzage that observers picked as the favourite (ahead of von Sternberg and then Vidor) and at the ceremony in November 1932, the Academy honoured him with his second Best Director statuette.

BEST ACTOR

ACADEMY AWARDS
• **Wallace Beery as 'Andy "The Champ" Purcell' in *The Champ***
Alfred Lunt as 'The Actor' in *The Guardsman*
• **Fredric March as 'Dr Henry Jekyll/Mr Hyde' in *Dr Jekyll and Mr Hyde***

Lionel Barrymore, the previous year's Best Actor, gave acclaimed performances in *The Man I Killed* (NYT "an unexcelled performance"; V "superb") and in *Grand Hotel* (NYT "superb"; V "inspired"; SMH "makes a masterpiece of this difficult part"). Despite the acclaim, he did not receive a nomination.

The other three previous Best Actor winners were also overlooked: Emil Jannings was ignored for *Sturme der Leidenschaft (Tempest)* (NYT "thoroughly convincing"); Warner Baxter was passed over for reprising his Oscar-winning role in the sequel *The Cisco Kid* (NYT "excellent"); and George Arliss was overlooked for *Alexander Hamilton* (NYT "a fine, sensitive portrayal"; TT "a distinguished piece of work"; SMH "a fascinating study").

Several stars of Best Picture nominees were also left out of consideration: Maurice Chevalier for *The Smiling Lieutenant* (NYT "clever acting"); James Dunn for *Bad Girl* (NYT a "thoroughly human performance"); Edward G. Robinson for *Five Star Final* (NYT "strong"); and Ronald Colman for *Arrowsmith* (SMH "superb").

Also overlooked were: Boris Karloff for *Frankenstein* (SMH "splendidly acted"); Paul Muni in the controversial gangster drama *Scarface: The Shame of a Nation* (NYT "compelling"; PP "one of the finest characterizations the screen has ever seen"); and Cedric Hardwicke for the British drama *Dreyfus* (NYT "impressive"; TT "without a trace of false sentiment he conveys the innocence and the pathos of the man").

Theatre star Alfred Lunt earned a nomination for his talking picture debut in *The Guardsman* opposite his wife, Best Actress nominee Lynn Fontanne. Lunt had played the role on Broadway in 1924. The race for the statuette, however, was seen as contest between two previous nominees.

Fredric March was mentioned for his dual roles as the title characters in *Dr Jekyll and Mr Hyde*. The New York Times praised him for a "stellar performance" while The Sydney Morning Herald lauded his "powerful acting" and commented that he drew "the contrasting characters with great skill." Variety, meanwhile, commended him for "an outstanding bit of theatrical acting." Interestingly, March turned in another praised dual performance that year as twin brothers in *Strangers in Love* (NYT an "excellent performance"; V "one of his best performances to date").

Wallace Beery received his second nomination for his portrayal of an alcoholic former boxer in *The Champ* opposite one of the previous year's nominees, Jackie Cooper. The NYT noted their "clever acting" while Variety called Beery's acting "studied" and "understanding" and Cooper's "inspired". The Sydney Morning Herald said Cooper was "phenomenal" and lauded Beery as "remarkably convincing".

Variety predicted a win for Beery, however on the night Norma Shearer revealed the winner to be March who thanked his make-up artist Wally Westmore "for the greater measure of my success." Later in the evening it was discovered that Beery had come within one vote of March. Consequently, Academy President Conrad Nagel declared a tie and Beery was also presented with an award. It remains the only time that the Best Actor award has been shared.

BEST ACTRESS

ACADEMY AWARDS
Marie Dressler as 'Emma (Thatcher Smith)' in *Emma*
Lynn Fontanne as 'The Actress' in *The Guardsman*
• **Helen Hayes as 'Madelon Claudet' in *The Sin of Madelon Claudet***

Critics lauded the Swedish star Greta Garbo for four different performances that were eligible for Academy Award consideration in 1931/32 and yet she was overlooked for them all. It had been widely expected that she would receive a nomination for *Grand Hotel* (NYT "stunning") but she was ignored by the Academy. She also failed to earn a mention for her portrayals in *Susan Lenox: Her Rise and Fall* (NYT "compelling"; V "another impressive portrait"), the box office hit *Mata Hari* (NYT "brilliant") and *As You Desire Me* (NYT "as brilliant as anything she has accomplished in her long list of film roles"; V "Garbo's performance is always absorbing, vivid in its acting and compelling in its appeal").

Garbo was not the only actress snubbed by the Academy in the year it reduced the number of nominees from five to three. Also overlooked were: Joan Crawford in *Grand Hotel* (NYT "splendid"); previous winner Norma Shearer in *Private Lives*; previous winner Janet Gaynor (again opposite Charles Farrell) in *Delicious* (NYT an "appealing performance"; SMH "a triumph"); Miriam Hopkins for her supporting performance in *Dr Jekyll and Mr Hyde* (NYT "Hopkins does splendidly"; S&S "a remarkable tour de force"); Marlene Dietrich in *Shanghai Express* (NYT "impressive"); previous nominee Ruth Chatterton in *Tomorrow and Tomorrow* (V "flawless"); and Barbara Stanwyck in *The Miracle Woman* (NYT a "clever performance").

Although her performance is today championed by many film historians, critics at the time of the film's release were mixed in their view of Constance Bennett in *What Price Hollywood?*. For example, the New York Times opined, "Miss Bennett yells quite a bit in the more hysterical of the scenes but performs creditably elsewhere."

Nominated ahead of these established screen actresses, were theatre stars Helen Hayes and Lynn Fontanne, and the previous year's Oscar winner Marie Dressler.

Fontanne was named for her talking picture debut in *The Guardsman* opposite her husband, Best Actor nominee Alfred Lunt, in a role that she had played on Broadway in 1924.

Dressler received her second nomination for her performance as a housekeeper who marries her employer in *Emma*. The New York Times said that she "contributes another sterling portrayal, possibly her best" with "one of the finest character studies that has come to the screen." While Variety had been negative about the film, it praised Dressler's "astonishing ability to command conviction."

Dressler may have won a second consecutive award if it had not been for the acclaimed portrayal of a self-sacrificing mother by Hayes in her screen debut in *The Sin of Madelon Claudet*. The New York Times raved about her "superb portrayal in a difficult role" while Variety declared that she "should receive all the credit" for the film's success. In Australia, The Sydney Morning Herald said "the character of Madelon is drawn with vividly realistic strokes by Miss Hayes" in a "fine performance." The film was such a success that Hayes was quickly cast opposite Ronald Colman in *Arrowsmith* which earned her further positive reviews later in the year (V "an enlightening and natural performance") and became a Best Picture nominee.

Hayes was heavily favoured to win and on the night Lionel Barrymore presented her with her first Academy Award (she would win a second as Best Supporting Actress in 1970). Apparently, she had polled more votes than Dressler and Fontanne combined. One of Broadway's most respected stars, Hayes had played the lead role in *Coquette* on stage prior to the property becoming an Oscar-winning vehicle for Mary Pickford.

BEST PICTURE

ACADEMY AWARDS

• *Cavalcade*
  (Fox, 110 mins BW, 5 Jan 1933, 4 noms)
A Farewell to Arms
  (Paramount, 80 mins BW, 9 Dec 1932, 4 noms)
42nd Street
  (Warner Bros., 89 mins BW, 9 Mar 1933, 2 noms)
I am a Fugitive from a Chain Gang
  (Warner Bros., 93 mins BW, 19 Nov 1932, 3 noms)
Lady for a Day
  (Columbia, 88 mins BW, 7 Sep 1933, 4 noms)
Little Women
  (RKO Radio, 117 mins BW, 16 Nov 1933, 3 noms)
The Private Life of Henry VIII
  (London Films, United Artists, 97 mins BW, 13 Oct 1933, 2 noms)
She Done Him Wrong
  (Paramount, 66 mins BW, 9 Feb 1933, 1 nom)
Smilin' Through
  (M-G-M, 98 mins BW, 24 Sep 1932, 1 nom)
State Fair
  (Fox, 80 mins BW, 27 Jan 1933, 2 noms)

BOARD OF REVIEW
  (1932) I am a Fugitive from a Chain Gang
  (1933) Topaze

In late 1932, the National Board of Review named the acclaimed drama *I am a Fugitive from a Chain Gang* as its choice as Best Picture of the year. The New York Times had called it "a stirring picture" while Variety said it was "a picture with guts" which "grips with its stark realism and packs lots of punch." In London, The Times labelled it "an intensely exciting film." Over a year later, it was one of an unprecedented ten films nominated for the Best Picture Oscar. It was an early front-runner despite the omission of Mervyn LeRoy from the Best Director category.

The other three main contenders were the films with the most nominations. Paramount and Fox both harboured hopes of winning a Best Picture award for the first time since the inaugural Oscar ceremony 1929: Paramount with *A Farewell to Arms*, a version of Ernest Hemingway's novel directed by Frank Borzage (NYT "too much sentiment"; V "powerful" and "engagingly realistic") and Fox with *Cavalcade*, an American film version of the hit Noel Coward play, which had been filmed in London with a British cast (NYT "affecting and impressive"; PP "outstanding"; TT "intensely moving" and "the best film of English life that has ever been made"). Columbia, meanwhile, hoped to collect a prestigious Best Picture statuette for the first time for Frank Capra's *Lady for a Day* (NYT "a merry tale with touches of sentiment").

Also nominated for Best Picture were: *Little Women* (Life "one of the finest pictures ever made"); the comedy *State Fair* starring Janet Gaynor; and the British picture *The Private Life of Henry VIII*, which was the first foreign film nominated for the Academy's top prize (NYT "brilliant"; V "a fine piece of work"). All three had appeared on the New York Times list of the year's ten best films.

The surprise omission from the Best Picture category was the all-star *Dinner at Eight* with which M-G-M had hoped to recreate the success of *Grand Hotel*. It had also been on The New York Times list, as had *A Bill of Divorcement*, *Berkeley Square* (V "imaginative, beautiful and well handled"; SMH "a picture of unusual distinction") and *The Invisible Man* (NYT "remarkable"; V "new and refreshing").

Also overlooked were: the Ernst Lubitsch film *Trouble in Paradise* (NYT "a shimmering, engaging piece of work ... effective entertainment"); the Greta Garbo vehicle *Queen Christina* (NYT "a skillful blend of history and fiction ... an easy flowing romance"; *The Emperor Jones* which starred Paul Robeson in a version of the Eugene O'Neill play (NYT "distinguished"; V "ranks high in cinematic achievement"); *King Kong* (NYT "fantastic"; V "highly imaginative"; SMH "spectacular"); *Topaze* which was the NBR's choice for Best Picture of 1933 (NYT "an agreeable and effective film"); *Rasputin and the Empress* which starred Lionel, John and Ethel Barrymore and had divided the critics (NYT "engrossing and exciting"; V "a long-winded affair ... at no times gripping"; SMH "dreary"); and Fritz Lang's acclaimed 1931 German film *M* which was released in the US in April 1933 (NYT "a strong cinematic work"; V "extraordinary ... constantly compelling").

Variety predicted that *Cavalcade* would win and on the big night the trade paper was proved correct. *Cavalcade* won narrowly ahead of *A Farewell to Arms* and *Little Women*.

BEST DIRECTOR

ACADEMY AWARDS
Frank Capra for *Lady for a Day*
George Cukor for *Little Women*
• **Frank Lloyd for *Cavalcade***

Frank Borzage, the previous year's Best Director winner, received good reviews from critics for *A Farewell to Arms*, an adaptation of Ernest Hemingway's wartime novel about a soldier and a nurse (NYT "occasional excellent directorial ideas"; V "particularly high" standard of direction; SMH "brilliant direction"). Despite a Best Picture nomination for the film, however, Borzage did not receive another Oscar nomination in the Best Director category.

The directors of two of the other major Best Picture contenders were also overlooked. Mervyn LeRoy was snubbed for *I am a Fugitive from a Chain Gang* (NYT "several sequences are worked out with genuine suspense") and Alexander Korda was bypassed for *The Private Life of Henry VIII* (V "a splendid job").

James Whale and Rouben Mamoulian were both ignored for the second year in a row, this time for *The Invisible Man* and *Queen Christina* respectively. Robert Z. Leonard, meanwhile, was overlooked for *Strange Interlude* (NYT "brilliantly directed"). Also left off the list were: Fritz Lang for *M* (V "a very great artistic success"; PP "superbly done"); Ernst Lubitsch for *Trouble in Paradise*; and the collaborative efforts of Merian C. Cooper and Ernest B. Schoedsack for the enormously popular *King Kong*.

Instead nominations went to George Cukor for *Little Women*, Frank Capra for *Lady for a Day* (V "smartly directed") and previous Best Director Oscar winner Frank Lloyd for *Cavalcade* (V "will get all sorts of eulogies and artistic praise"). All three films were Best Picture nominees.

Capra was the favourite and Variety's predicted winner. On the night, however, Capra was the runner-up. For the second year in a row the Best Director prize went to a previous winner with Frank Lloyd collecting his second award in five years.

1932/33

BEST ACTOR

ACADEMY AWARDS
Leslie Howard as 'Peter Standish' in *Berkeley Square*
• **Charles Laughton as 'King Henry VIII' in *The Private Life of Henry VIII***
Paul Muni as 'James Allen' in *I am a Fugitive from a Chain Gang*

The year after his acclaimed performance in *Scarface: The Shame of a Nation* had been overlooked, Paul Muni was the early favourite for the Best Actor award at his second nomination (he had been considered for the award in the Academy's second year for his performance in the silent film *The Valiant*). Up against two Englishmen, the American star was initially considered a certain winner for his lauded portrayal of an innocent man brutalised by the criminal justice system after a wrongful conviction in the acclaimed drama and Best Picture nominee *I am a Fugitive from a Chain Gang* (NYT "a convincing and earnest performance"; V "superb"; TT "a performance which makes up in intensity what it lacks in range and flexibility"; SMH "impressive").

The two Englishmen were Leslie Howard and Charles Laughton. Howard was nominated for recreating his stage success as a man transported back through time in *Berkeley Square* (NYT "it is doubtful whether he has ever given so impressive and imaginative a performance"; V "as near perfection as can be hoped for in a screen characterization"; SMH "plays the part with beautiful naturalism and restraint"). He had also appeared opposite Norma Shearer in the Best Picture nominee *Smilin' Through* (NYT "splendid").

The acclaimed theatre actor Laughton made his Hollywood screen debut in late 1932 as the submarine captain insanely jealous of his wife (played by Tallulah Bankhead) in *Devil and the Deep* (NYT "excellent") and earned praise in the supporting role of the Roman Emperor Nero in D. W. Griffith's epic *The Sign of the Cross* (V an "exceptional performance"). It was for his portrayal of King Henry VIII in Alexander Korda's British film *The Private Life of Henry VIII*, however, that he received his strongest reviews and earned his first Oscar nomination (NYT "reveals his genius as an actor"; TT "astonishing"; SMH "a phenomenal piece of acting").

Overlooked for the prize were: John Barrymore for three lauded performances in *A Bill of Divorcement*, *Topaze* (NYT "lends no little artistry to the role"; SMH "splendid") and *Reunion in Vienna* (NYT "a brilliant portrayal"); Gary Cooper in *A Farewell to Arms* (NYT "an earnest and splendid portrayal"; SMH "fine acting"); Spencer Tracy in *The Power and the Glory*; previous Oscar winner George Arliss in *Voltaire* (NYT "a thoroughly intriguing portrait"; V "an artistic performance"); Hungarian actor Peter Lorre for his screen debut as the child murderer in the German thriller *M* (NYT "most convincing", "remarkably fine acting"; V "outstanding", a "flawless performance"); Paul Robeson as the ambitious Brutus Jones in a film version of Eugene O'Neill's *The Emperor Jones* (NYT "a most compelling portrayal"; V a "triumph"; SMH "brilliant"); and Groucho Marx for the comedy *Duck Soup*.

Muni was the front-runner for the award until just prior to the ceremony when Variety predicted a win for Hollywood outsider Laughton. On the night, an absent Laughton was named the year's Best Actor. He was the first person to win an Academy Award for a performance in a foreign film.

1932/33

BEST ACTRESS

ACADEMY AWARDS
• **Katharine Hepburn as 'Eva Lovelace' in** *Morning Glory*
May Robson as 'Apple Annie' in *Lady for a Day*
Diana Wynyard as 'Jane Marryot' in *Cavalcade*

The young Broadway star Katharine Hepburn made her film debut in October 1932 in *A Bill of Divorcement* and stole the film from co-star John Barrymore. The New York Times wrote "Hepburn's portrayal is exceptionally fine ... one of the finest seen on the screen." Variety commented "the stand-out here is the smash impression made by Katharine Hepburn", while in Australia The Sydney Morning Herald described her performance as a "spectacular" debut that was "memorable for its realism, its force, and its sheer brilliance." She received equally strong reviews for her portrayal of Jo March in *Little Women* (NYT a "talented character study"; V "creates a new and stunningly vivid character"; TT "a delightfully vivid and sensitive piece of portraiture"; SMH "a fresh and stimulating performance"), however it was for her turn as a stage-struck young actress in her third film, *Morning Glory*, that she received her first Academy Award nomination. Hepburn "triumphantly confirms her versatility" wrote The Sydney Morning Herald of her turn in *Morning Glory*, while The New York Times said she gave "an ingratiating portrayal".

Despite the acclaim, Hepburn was not the favourite for the Oscar. She was a film industry outsider who was rumoured to have disdain for both Hollywood and the Academy Awards. Local sentiment favoured a win by the 75-year-old Australian-born actress May Robson for her acclaimed performance in Frank Capra's sentimental hit *Lady for a Day* (NYT "splendid"; V "remarkable"; PP "unforgettable"; Life "simply superb"). Robson played 'Apple Annie', an alcoholic bag-lady transformed into a society matron by gangsters in order to receive her estranged daughter and her fiancé. Bette Davis reprised the role in Capra's 1961 remake (entitled *Pocketful of Miracles*) but did not earn a mention from Oscar voters.

Lauded performances by several established actresses were overlooked for Oscar consideration. Greta Garbo was snubbed for her performance in *Queen Christina* (NYT "a performance which merits nothing but the highest praise ... she handles some of the reticent levity in a superb fashion"; SMH "magnificent") while Oscar winners Janet Gaynor, Norma Shearer, Marie Dressler and Helen Hayes missed out for their respective roles in *State Fair* (NYT "her best performance in talking pictures"), *Strange Interlude* (NYT "excels [over] anything she has done hitherto"), *Tugboat Annie* (NYT "Dressler is admirable, giving a genuinely human touch to her role") and *A Farewell to Arms* (S&S "moving"). Also overlooked were: Henrietta Crosman for her lauded work as an embittered mother in John Ford's *Pilgrimage* (NYT "a triumph"; V "compelling"); Marlene Dietrich for *Blonde Venus* (NYT a "good portrait"); and Kay Francis in *One-Way Passage* (NYT a "capable performance"). Although the film was included among the Best Picture contenders, Mae West was snubbed for her starring turn in *She Done Him Wrong*.

Nominated instead was English actress Diana Wynyard for her screen debut in the Best Picture winner *Cavalcade*. "Wynyard is excellent as Jane Marryot," wrote the New York Times, "She portrays her role with such sympathy and feeling that one scarcely thinks of her as an actress." Variety agreed calling her performance "impressive" and "exceptional."

Variety tipped Robson to win but on the night, in what the Los Angeles Times considered a surprise, it was Hepburn who was named by the Academy as the year's Best Actress. It was the first of a record four statuettes she would receive in the category during her career.

BEST PICTURE

ACADEMY AWARDS

The Barretts of Wimpole Street
  (M-G-M, 110 mins BW, 28 Sep 1934, 2 noms)
Cleopatra
  (Paramount, 102 mins BW, 16 Aug 1934, 5 noms)
Flirtation Walk
  (First National, 97 mins BW, 28 Nov 1934, 2 noms)
The Gay Divorcee
  (RKO Radio, 104 mins BW, 12 Oct 1934, 5 noms)
Here Comes the Navy
  (Warner Bros., 87 mins BW, 21 Jul 1934, 1 nom)
The House of Rothschild
  (20th Century, United Artists, 94 mins, BW & C, 14 Mar 1934, 1 nom)
Imitation of Life
  (Universal, 111 mins BW, 23 Nov 1934, 3 noms)
• *It Happened One Night*
  (Columbia, 105 mins BW, 22 Feb 1934, 5 noms)
One Night of Love
  (Columbia, 84 mins BW, 6 Sep 1934, 6 noms)
The Thin Man
  (M-G-M, 93 mins BW, 29 Jun 1934, 4 noms)
Viva Villa
  (M-G-M, 115 mins BW, 10 Apr 1934, 4 noms)
The White Parade
  (Fox, BW, 9 Nov 1934, 2 noms)

BOARD OF REVIEW – *It Happened One Night*

M-G-M sought to emulate some of the success of the previous year's Best Picture winner, *Cavalcade*, by casting Oscar winners Norma Shearer, Fredric March and Charles Laughton in *The Barretts of Wimpole Street*, a film about the romance of English poets Elizabeth Barrett and Robert Browning. Both popular and acclaimed (NYT "a distinguished film") the film was voted Best Picture by four hundred film critics in a poll conducted by Film Daily, although it was not included by The New York Times on its annual list of the year's ten best. The film was a Best Picture nominee but its chances were undermined by the omission of Sidney Franklin from the Best Director category.

Exclusion from the acting and directing categories similarly seemed to limit the chances of other nominated dramas: Cecil B. DeMille's epic *Cleopatra* and the tear-jerker *Imitation of Life* (NYT "a dignified and sombre chronicle") which both starred Claudette Colbert; *The House of Rothschild* which featured George Arliss (NYT one of the ten best of the year; V "a fine picture"); and *Viva Villa* which starred Wallace Beery (V "impressive"; SMH "one of the notable productions of the year").

The film with the most nominations was the popular musical *One Night of Love* which Variety called "surprisingly effective and entertaining". The New York Times described it as "an enjoyable light diversion" and included the film on its list of the year's ten best films.

Also nominated was the very successful Fred Astaire and Ginger Rogers film *The Gay Divorcee* (NYT "glimmering... gay in its mood and smart in its approach ... the source of a good deal of innocent merriment") and the patriotic musical *Flirtation Walk*, directed by Frank Borzage (NYT "a pleasant conventional comedy"). The year's most commercially successful musical, however, the operetta *The Merry Widow* starring Maurice Chevalier, was a surprise omission. The New York Times had declared it to be "a witty and incandescent rendition" of the operetta by Franz Lehar.

The biggest shock exclusion from the list of candidates was the hit screwball comedy *Twentieth Century* starring John Barrymore. Also left off the list was Josef von Sternberg's *The Scarlet Empress*, which bemused and divided critics. The New York Times called it "a ponderous, strangely beautiful lengthy and frequently wearying production ... strictly not a dramatic photoplay at all but a succession of over-elaborated scenes, dramatized emotional moods and gaudily plotted visual excitements." Ultimately, the paper declared "the verdict has to be in the negative".

Included ahead of them were the acclaimed comedies *The Thin Man* (NYT "an excellent combination of comedy and excitement"; V "entertaining"; TT a successful combination of "exciting adventure with genuine comedy") and Frank Capra's *It Happened One Night* (NYT "a screen feast" and a "merry romance"; Sp "spirited and delightful"). Capra's film ended the year as its biggest box office hit and appeared on The New York Times list of the year's ten best films.

Two months before the Oscars, the NBR chose *It Happened One Night* as its Best Picture and Variety subsequently predicted an Oscar win for Capra's comedy. At the Academy's seventh ceremony, *It Happened One* Night swept the top five categories winning statuettes for Best Adapted Screenplay, Best Actor, Best Actress, Best Director and Best Picture. It was the first film to be so honoured – and the achievement would not be equalled for another forty years.

The Academy subsequently revealed that in the voting for the Best Picture award M-G-M's *The Barretts of Wimpole Street* had ranked a distant second in the voting, while *One Night of Love* polled third.

1934

BEST DIRECTOR

ACADEMY AWARDS
• **Frank Capra for *It Happened One Night***
Victor Schertzinger for *One Night of Love*
W. S. Van Dyke for *The Thin Man*

Overlooked for an Oscar nomination two years earlier, Sidney Franklin seemed certain to be recognised in 1934 for his direction of M-G-M's prestigious costume drama *The Barretts of Wimpole Street*. The film received a Best Picture nomination but Franklin was once again passed over. Nominated instead were the directors of three other Best Picture contenders.

The musical comedy *One Night of Love* had been an unexpected box office success and surprisingly earned more nominations than any other film. Among them was a mention for Victor Schertzinger whom Variety said directed the film "splendidly." W. S. Van Dyke earned his first Oscar nomination for the popular hit *The Thin Man* which combined screwball comedy with murder mystery, while Frank Capra received his second consecutive Best Director nomination for another screwball comedy, *It Happened One Night*, which The Times said had been "intelligently directed."

Howard Hawks, the director of the year's other acclaimed screwball comedy, the hugely popular *Twentieth Century*, was overlooked two years after he had been snubbed for his direction of the controversial gangster drama *Scarface: The Shame of a Nation*. Also overlooked were: Ernst Lubitsch for *The Merry Widow* (NYT "excellent … his sense of humor is impeccable and his taste is faultless"); Josef von Sternberg for *The Scarlet Empress* (NYT has "sacrificed story, characterization and life itself to his own hungry and unreasonable dreams of cinema greatness … has even accomplished the improbable feat of smothering the enchanting Marlene Dietrich under his technique"); and Victor Schertzinger for the musical *One Night of Love*, the year's most nominated Oscar contender (NYT "has handled this amiable narrative in a sympathetic and imaginative manner".)

Capra, who had been very disappointed not to have won the previous year for *Lady for a Day*, was an almost unbackable favourite in 1934. He easily outpolled the other contenders to collect the first of his three Oscars as Best Director of the year.

BEST ACTOR

ACADEMY AWARDS
• **Clark Gable as 'Peter Warne' in *It Happened One Night***
Frank Morgan as 'Alessandro, Duke of Florence' in *The Affairs of Cellini*
William Powell as 'Nick Charles' in *The Thin Man*

The year after winning the Best Actor Oscar, Charles Laughton was again a major contender for the statuette as the cruel and callous father of Elizabeth Barrett in M-G-M's all-star period drama *The Barretts of Wimpole Street*. The New York Times said he was "superb" while Variety lauded his "outstanding screen portrait". S&S meanwhile commended his "fine character study". In a major surprise, however, Laughton did not receive a nomination from the Academy.

Another glaring omission was John Barrymore's self-parody in Howard Hawks' screwball comedy *Twentieth Century*. The New York Times said that as a vain producer Barrymore was "in fine fettle" and acted "with such imagination and zest that he never fails to keep the picture thoroughly alive." The paper declared his work to be "his best performance since the one he gave in the film *Reunion in Vienna*". In London, The Times called his performance "a glorious, noisy, and extravagant satire."

Also overlooked for a nomination were three previous Oscar winners: George Arliss for his dual roles in the Best Picture nominee *The House of Rothschild* (NYT "outshines any performance he has contributed to the screen"; V "superb"); Warner Baxter in *Stand Up and Cheer* (NYT "excellent"); and Wallace Beery (again opposite Jackie Cooper) as Long John Silver in *Treasure Island* (NYT "does extraordinarily well").

Academy voters also passed over: English actor Robert Donat in *The Count of Monte Cristo* (NYT "adds a welcome modern touch to the great chronicle with the cool and even-tempered brilliance of his performance"; TT "excellent"); French-Canadian actor Matheson Lang in the British drama *Channel Crossing* (NYT "a thoroughly expert characterization"; SMH "impressive"); and French actor Maurice Chevalier in *The Merry Widow* (NYT "he has never been better in voice nor charm").

The surprise contender in the field of three nominees was Frank Morgan who was recognised for recreating a role he had played on stage. He "runs away with the film" said Variety of Morgan's supporting role as a scatter-brained Duke in *The Affairs of Cellini*. (NYT "the brunt of the comedy is shouldered by Mr Morgan, who is at the peak of his form"). Several observers had expected a nomination for the film's star, Oscar winner Fredric March.

While Barrymore was snubbed, the Academy nominated the stars of the year's two other hit screwball comedies: William Powell for *The Thin Man* (NYT "in his element"); and Clark Gable for Frank Capra's *It Happened One Night* which was the year's most commercially successful film. Gable earned praised for his performance in the part of the journalist falling in love with a runaway heiress on a bus trip, a role that had been turned down by Robert Montgomery. He was lauded as "excellent" by The New York Times and The Times noted that his portrayal demonstrated "a sensitiveness and understanding hitherto absent from his acting." Later in the year Gable showed his versatility with a contrasting performance as a doctor in *Men in White* which Variety praised as an "excellent job."

Variety predicted a win for Gable and on the night the star narrowly outpolled Morgan to collect the Oscar. He would be nominated again for the award the following year and for his most famous performance as Rhett Butler in *Gone with the Wind* in 1939, but on neither occasion would he secure a second statuette.

1934

BEST ACTRESS

• **Claudette Colbert as 'Ellie Andrews' in *It Happened One Night***
Grace Moore as 'Mary Barrett' in *One Night of Love*
Norma Shearer as 'Elizabeth Barrett' in *The Barretts of Wimpole Street*

After years of complaining about the poor parts that she was being given at Warner Bros., Bette Davis convinced Jack Warner to loan her to RKO to star opposite Leslie Howard in *Of Human Bondage*, a film version of W. Somerset Maugham's novel. She stole the film and earned the year's strongest reviews. The New York Times lauded her "enormously effective portrayal" while Variety said she "plays her free 'n' easy vamp too well. She's totally unsympathetic if, perhaps, honest with her emotions." In London, The Times said she had given "an alarmingly realistic portrait" and The Spectator said she was "wickedly good." The Sydney Morning Herald said she was "perfect" in an "excellent performance." Life magazine wrote that Davis had given "probably the best performance ever recorded on screen by a U.S. actress." Many in Hollywood believed that Davis was certain to win the 1934 Best Actress award. When the nominations were announced, however, there was an outcry: Davis was not on the list. It was rumoured that Warner was determined that Davis should not win for a rival studio's film and had pressured Warner Bros. contract players not to vote for her.

Nominated ahead of Davis were previous winner Norma Shearer, opera star Grace Moore and the French-born actress Claudette Colbert for performances in Best Picture nominated films. Shearer earned an unprecedented fourth nomination for her portrayal of the English poet Elizabeth Barrett in M-G-M's *The Barretts of Wimpole Street* (NYT "a brave and touching piece of acting"; V "at all times sincerely convincing"; TT "plays the part with sensitiveness and intelligence"). Moore was a nominee for her turn in the year's most nominated film, the box office hit *One Night of Love* (NYT "proves herself to be quite an expert comedienne"; V "splendid"; Sp "her acting is quite undistinguished") while Colbert received her first Best Actress nomination for playing the runaway heiress in Frank Capra's *It Happened One Night*, the favourite for the Best Picture award. The New York Times had praised Colbert for giving "an engaging and lively performance." The role had been turned down by Myrna Loy, Constance Bennett, Miriam Hopkins and Margaret Sullavan. Ironically, Warner had also refused Columbia's request to borrow Davis for the part.

Of the three nominees Colbert was the favourite. She had also appeared in two other Best Picture nominees: *Cleopatra* (NYT "looks even more attractive than usual ... speaks her lines with the necessary confidence ... and when the chance is offered for a little comedy she acquits herself cleverly"); and *Imitation of Life* (NYT "plays the leading role with her usual charm and intelligence")

Due to the outcry over Davis' exclusion, the Academy changed the voting rules to allow members to ignore the chosen nominees and 'write-in' the name of any other performers. Consequently, Davis still had a chance to win the statuette as did other candidates such as: Myrna Loy for *The Thin Man*; Constance Bennett for her dual roles in *Moulin Rouge* (NYT "shines as a comedienne"); Ann Harding for *The Fountain* (NYT "gives a definite and sincere characterization"); Diana Wynyard for *One More River* (NYT "gives a stirringly sincere personation"); French actress Valentine Tessier for the French film version of *Madame Bovary* (V "arresting"); Carole Lombard for *Twentieth Century* (NYT "gives an able portrayal"); Greta Garbo for *The Painted Veil* (NYT "triumph", "superb"); African-American actress Louise Beavers for her arguably supporting role in *Imitation of Life* (NYT "capable"; V her "performance is masterly"; S&S "heart-rendering performance"; Life "perfect"); and Polish-born Elisabeth Bergner for two British films, the historical *Catherine the Great* (NYT "a clever portrayal") and the romance *Ariane* (NYT "compelling").

Despite the decision to allow write-ins Variety predicted a win for Colbert. The star herself was not so confident, however. Certain of a Davis victory, she decided not to attend the ceremony. Moore and Shearer likewise elected to stay at home. Davis later wrote in her memoirs, "The air was thick with rumors. It seemed inevitable that I would win the coveted award. The press, the public and the members of the Academy who did the voting were sure I would win!" But on the night, Variety was proven correct. Colbert was named Best Actress ahead of Shearer and Davis. Contrary to newspaper reports at the time, Academy records show that Davis outpolled Moore.

Colbert's win helped *It Happened One Night* to an historic sweep of the top awards, but did not settle the affair of Davis' exclusion from the list of official nominees. The drama would have a major impact on the Best Actress category the following year.

1935

BEST PICTURE

ACADEMY AWARDS

Alice Adams
(RKO Radio, 99 mins BW, 14 Aug 1935, 2 noms)

Broadway Melody of 1936
(M-G-M, 102 mins BW, 20 Sep 1935, 3 noms)

Captain Blood
(Warner Bros.-Cosmopolitan, 119 mins BW, 28 Dec 1935, 2 noms)

David Copperfield
(M-G-M, 130 mins BW, 18 Jan 1935, 3 noms)

The Informer
(RKO Radio, 91 mins BW, 9 May 1935, 6 noms)

Les Miserables
(20th Century, UA, 108 mins BW, 20 Apr 1935, 4 noms)

Lives of a Bengal Lancer
(Paramount, 109 mins BW, 11 Jan 1935, 7 noms)

A Midsummer Night's Dream
(Warner Bros.-First National, 132 mins BW, 30 Oct 1935, 2 noms)

• *Mutiny on the Bounty*
(M-G-M, 132 mins BW, 8 Nov 1935, 8 noms)

Naughty Marietta
(M-G-M, 105 mins BW, 29 Mar 1935, 2 noms)

Ruggles of Red Gap
(Paramount, 90 mins BW, 8 Mar 1935, 1 nom)

Top Hat
(RKO Radio, 101 mins BW, 6 Sep 1935, 4 noms)

NEW YORK – *The Informer*
BOARD OF REVIEW – *The Informer*

Many of the year's most acclaimed films were among the twelve movies nominated for the Best Picture Oscar in 1935. In his review in The New York Times in January, Andre Sennwald had described *David Copperfield*, an adaptation of the Charles Dickens novel, as a "gorgeous photoplay" and a "genuine masterpiece". Sennwald continued, "It is my belief that this cinema edition of 'David Copperfield' is the most profoundly satisfying screen manipulation of a great novel that the camera has ever given us." A few months later, Sennwald called *The Informer* "an astonishing screen drama ... at the same time a striking psychological study of a gutter Judas and a rawly impressive picture of the Dublin underworld during the Black and Tan terror". In November, Sennwald declared the historical drama *Mutiny on the Bounty* to be "as savagely exciting and rousingly dramatic a photoplay as has come out of Hollywood in recent years … it is superlatively thrilling." Variety, meanwhile, had called the military adventure picture *Lives of a Bengal Lancer* "an exceptional film". All four were mentioned by the Academy as were the well-reviewed *Alice Adams* (NYT "splendid"), *Les Miserables* (NYT "magnificent") and *Ruggles of Red Gap* (NYT "rapturously funny").

A surprise nominee was *Captain Blood* which premiered at the end of the year and starred Errol Flynn and Olivia de Havilland together for the first time (TT "a tolerable film" with cardboard characters but "lavish and unusually convincing" battle scenes).

Also included was the expensive *A Midsummer Night's Dream* about which The Times had been extremely negative: "the play is cut to ribbons," it complained, "all the more important passages of poetry are omitted". The New York Times, meanwhile had described it as "a work of high ambitions and unflagging interest" despite "its flaws".

These movies were nominated at the expense of several lauded films. Alfred Hitchcock's *The 39 Steps* had been praised on both sides of the Atlantic (NYT "one of the most fascinating pictures of the year"; TT "a first-rate film") but both it and Hitchcock's *The Man Who Knew Too Much* were ignored, as was James Whale's *Bride of Frankenstein* which Variety had labelled "an imaginative and outstanding film." Also overlooked were: the British film *The Scarlet Pimpernel*; the Marx Bros comedy *A Night at the Opera* (NYT "the loudest and funniest screen comedy of the Winter season"); the W. C. Fields vehicle *The Man on the Flying Trapeze* (NYT "although it is marred by that cheapness of manufacture which we have come to expect in Mr Fields' picture, [it] provides some of the richest humor that has reached the screen in months"); and – despite the first ever campaign by a studio – the M-G-M film *Ah, Wilderness!*, an adaptation of the work by Eugene O'Neill (NYT "splendid").

The Best Picture contest was between the $2million M-G-M all-star blockbuster *Mutiny on the Bounty* and the RKO Radio box office dud *The Informer* which had been filmed in just 18 days at one tenth of its rival's cost. *The Informer* was embraced by the critics with prizes from the NBR and the newly formed New York critics circle (who voted for it unanimously). At the Oscars, it won awards for Screenplay, Director and Actor. The Hollywood-based Academy, however, gave its top award to the film described by Variety as "Hollywood at its very best", *Mutiny on the Bounty*. It was the only statuette the film won.

BEST DIRECTOR

ACADEMY AWARDS
• **John Ford for** *The Informer*
Henry Hathaway for *Lives of a Bengal Lancer*
Frank Lloyd for *Mutiny on the Bounty*

NEW YORK – John Ford – *The Informer*

Alfred Hitchcock received some of the year's best reviews for two of his British films: his first version of *The Man Who Knew Too Much* and *The 39 Steps* (NYT "a master of shock and suspense, of cold horror and slyly incongruous wit, he uses his camera the way a painter uses his brush, stylizing his story and giving it values which the scenarists could hardly have imagined"). Despite this, neither film earned Hitchcock a Best Director nomination, even though he was the runner-up for the New York critics' prize (and had actually led after the first round of voting).

Also overlooked by the Academy in spite of good reviews were: Richard Boleslawski for *Les Miserables* (NYT "in a work which represents the perfect collaboration of many talents, it is difficult to award the laurel adequately. But we can come pretty close by applauding Richard Boleslawski for his direction"); George Stevens for *Alice Adams* (NYT "the film is a triumph, too, for its director"); and James Whale for *Bride of Frankenstein* whom The New York Times congratulated for "another excellent job".

The three men who were nominated for the Best Director Oscar were the directors of the year's three main Best Picture contenders. Henry Hathaway had been praised by Variety for skillfully blending "the comedy shading and heavy melodramatic yarn" in *Lives of a Bengal Lancer* while double Best Director Oscar winner, Frank Lloyd, was credited by The New York Times for "a distinguished job" in handling the M-G-M epic *Mutiny on the Bounty*, and John Ford was enthusiastically praised by the same paper for his "bold and smashing skill" and his "shrewd and sensitive direction" of *The Informer*. "Within his obvious limitations," said The New York Times, "Mr Ford has achieved one of the finest dramas of the year."

On Academy Awards night, the runners-up were Hathaway and, due to the write-in rule and a campaign by studio head Jack Warner, Michael Curtiz for *Captain Blood*. The Oscar, however, went to Ford who thus became the first person to win prizes from the New York critics and the Academy in the same year.

1935

BEST ACTOR

ACADEMY AWARDS
Clark Gable as 'Fletcher Christian' in *Mutiny on the Bounty*
Charles Laughton as 'Capt. William Bligh' in *Mutiny on the Bounty*
• **Victor McLaglen as 'Gypo Nolan' in *The Informer***
Franchot Tone as 'Roger Byam' in *Mutiny on the Bounty*

**NEW YORK – Charles Laughton – *Mutiny on the Bounty* and *Ruggles of
Red Gap***

Charles Laughton received the year's strongest reviews from critics for performances in three films: as the title character in *Ruggles of Red Gap*, as Javert in *Les Miserables* and as Captain Bligh in *Mutiny on the Bounty*. The Times called Laughton's comic portrayal of Ruggles "an astonishing tour de force" and considered him the stand-out in *Les Miserables*. The New York Times, meanwhile, called his performance as Javert in *Les Miserables* a "distinguished" performance which ought to be regarded as "one of the great screen portraits". The New York Times described his turn as Captain Bligh as a "fascinating and almost unbearable portrait … he plays it perfectly" while Variety said he was "magnificent" and The Sydney Morning Herald called him "remarkably forceful." Laughton was named Best Actor by the New York critics and almost won the honour unanimously. A single vote, however, was cast in favour of Victor McLaglen's portrayal of a man who betrays his friend in *The Informer*. McLaglen was lauded by critics for his performance. Variety said he was "completely convincing", while The New York Times called him "brilliant" and said "he makes something stark and memorable" out the film's central character.

The two Englishmen were the main contenders for the Oscar and were both nominated. Included on the Oscar list with them were Laughton's *Mutiny on the Bounty* co-stars: the previous year's Best Actor Oscar winner Clark Gable and Franchot Tone who had a supporting role in the film (and who had also starred in *Lives of a Bengal Lancer* and in *Dangerous* opposite Best Actress winner Bette Davis). The two American co-stars were nominated ahead of several highly-praised performances by both American and foreigners.

Variety called German actor Conrad Veidt "inspired" and "superb" in the 1933 British film *The Wandering Jew* while The New York Times praised his "moving portrayal" and said his work was "perfectly attuned to each of the four phases of his wanderings and conveying, by delicate implication, the changes in the character during the intervening centuries … [he is] the life and essence of the film". The same paper, meanwhile, called Frenchman Maurice Chevalier "excellent" in dual roles in *Folies Bergere*. Four Englishmen also impressed the critics with performances in British movies: Ronald Colman in *Clive of India*; Robert Donat in *The 39 Steps* (NYT "excellent"); Leslie Howard in *The Scarlet Pimpernel* (NYT "superb ... it is a temptation to say that Leslie Howard's newest performance is also his best"; and Cedric Hardwicke in *Nell Gwyn* (NYT "superb").

The work of several Americans was also ignored by the Academy. Previous winner Fredric March earned praise for his turn in *Les Miserables* (NYT "distinguished ... flawless ... strong and heartbreaking", he reveals himself as "a screen player of enormous resource") while Paul Muni was lauded for his part in *Black Fury* (NYT "magnificently performed") and W. C. Fields earned acclaim for his turn in *The Man on the Flying Trapeze* (NYT "one of his most important screen triumphs ... asserts his battered ego in one of the most satisfying scenes in recent motion picture history"). Critics were also enthusiastic about W. C. Fields and 15-year old Mickey Rooney for their supporting performances in *David Copperfield* and *A Midsummer Night's Dream*, respectively. In The New York Times, Andrew Sennwald had enthused, "Being himself generally a spiritual descendant of Mr Micawber, W. C. Fields manages with the greatest of ease to become on with his illustrious predecessor according to the directions laid down in the test of Dickens". Sennwald subsequently labelled Rooney's work to be "remarkable".

Decades later, meanwhile, audiences continue to be charmed by Fred Astaire's charismatic performance and seemingly-effortless dancing in *Top Hat*, and by the comic brilliance of Groucho Marx in *A Night at the Opera*. More impressed by drama, the Academy overlooked both.

Laughton's chances of winning the Oscar in 1935 were probably compromised by the fact he had won the Best Actor award only two years earlier. It was 49-year old McLaglen who won the statuette. The award helped him gain credibility in the industry as a leading man. Surprisingly, Academy records reveal Muni was a close runner-up as a write-in candidate.

1935

BEST ACTRESS

ACADEMY AWARDS
Elisabeth Bergner as 'Gemma Jones' in *Escape Me Never*
Claudette Colbert as 'Dr Jane Everest' in *Private Worlds*
• **Bette Davis as 'Joyce Heath' in *Dangerous***
Katharine Hepburn as 'Alice Adams' in *Alice Adams*
Miriam Hopkins as 'Becky Sharp' in *Becky Sharp*
Merle Oberon as 'Kitty Vane' in *The Dark Angel*

NEW YORK – Greta Garbo – *Anna Karenina*

The year after being snubbed for *Of Human Bondage*, Bette Davis won the Best Actress Oscar. She had not, however, received particularly strong reviews for her award-winning performance in *Dangerous*. The New York Times said she had failed to "match the grim standard" of her earlier portrayal, while Variety said her performance was "fine on the whole, despite a few imperfect moments." Both publications thought she had given a better performance earlier in the year in *Bordertown* – Variety thought her turn equal to her work in *Of Human Bondage*, while The New York Times said that she was "impressive" in "a fine and uncommonly honest performance." Davis conceded that her Oscar was a consolation prize and Katharine Hepburn had deserved the honour for *Alice Adams* (NYT "a performance which will rank with her finest work on screen").

At the end of the year, Hepburn was the runner-up for the inaugural Best Actress prize from the newly formed New York Film Critics Circle. The winner was Greta Garbo who had received strong reviews for her performance as the title character in *Anna Karenina*, a part which she had played less than a decade before in a silent version. "There is no flaw to be found in her current rendition of the love-wracked Russian girl," said Variety. "A delicate and restrained performance" wrote The Times.

Despite this honour, and the box office success of her film, the Swedish star was once more overlooked by the Academy. Davis and Hepburn were nominated but Garbo was snubbed in favour of Elisabeth Bergner, the previous year's winner Claudette Colbert, Merle Oberon and – most surprisingly – Miriam Hopkins. For her turn as the title character in the first Technicolor movie, *Becky Sharp*, Hopkins had received a negative response from critics (NYT "indifferently successful"; Variety "lacking"; Sp "indecisive acting").

Ordinarily, with Garbo ignored, Hepburn might have become the first actress to win a second award. Instead the previous year's turmoil saw Davis win her first Oscar.

BEST PICTURE

ACADEMIC AWARDS

ACADEMY AWARDS

Anthony Adverse
(Warner Bros., 139 mins BW, 12 May 1936, 7 noms)
Dodsworth
(Goldwyn, UA, 101 mins BW, 23 Sep 1936, 7 noms)
• *The Great Ziegfeld*
(M-G-M, 176 mins BW, 8 Apr 1936, 7 noms)
Libeled Lady
(M-G-M, 98 mins BW, 9 Oct 1936, 1 nom)
Mr Deeds Goes to Town
(Columbia, 115 mins BW, 16 Apr 1936, 5 noms)
Romeo and Juliet
(M-G-M, 125 mins BW, 3 Sep 1936, 4 noms)
San Francisco
(M-G-M, 115 mins BW, 26 Jun 1936, 6 noms)
The Story of Louis Pasteur
(Warner Bros., 87 mins BW, 9 Feb 1936, 4 noms)
A Tale of Two Cities
(M-G-M, 128 mins BW, 25 Dec 1935, 2 noms)
Three Smart Girls
(Universal, 84 mins BW, 1 Jan 1937, 3 noms)

NEW YORK – *Mr Deeds Goes to Town*
BOARD OF REVIEW – *Mr Deeds Goes to Town*

For a second year running the New York critics and the NBR agreed on the year's best picture: *Mr Deeds Goes to Town* (NYT "another shrewd and lively comedy"; TT "one of the events of the film year"; HSp "brilliant"; Sp "a comedy quite unmatched"). Chosen as one the year's best by the NYT the film was a frontrunner for the top Oscar.

The runner-up for the New York prize was Fritz Lang's *Fury* (NYT "the finest original drama the screen has provided this year ... it is almost flawless"; SMH a "shattering spectacle ... brilliant"). Variety said it was "certain for celluloid honours" while in The Spectator Graham Greene called the drama about mob violence "astonishing ... the only film I know to which I have wanted to attach the epithet of 'great'." Despite the acclaim, the film was overlooked by the Academy for a Best Picture nomination.

Also ignored were: Charlie Chaplin's *Modern Times* (NYT A "comic feast"; V "great fun"); *These Three* (NYT "absorbing"); the hit musical *Show Boat* (NYT "excellent"; V "a smash"); the British drama *The Passing of the Third*

Floor Back (NYT "excellent"); and the French winner of the New York award for Best Foreign Film *La Kermesse Héroïque (Carnival in Flanders)* (NYT "an outstanding picture by any standards ... the film has achieved a delicate balance between broad farce and subtle humor which makes it one of the most refreshing and witty pictures of the year"; S&S a "masterpiece"; CA "superb"). Despite receiving nominations in six categories, including Best Director and all four acting categories, *My Man Godfrey* was not nominated (NYT "the daffiest comedy of the year").

Although acclaimed by film historians decades later, *Swing Time* starring Fred Astaire and Ginger Rogers had not impressed film critics. "We left the theatre feeling definitely let down," wrote Frank S. Nugent in The New York Times. "The picture is good, of course. It would have to be with that dancing ... But after *Top Hat*, *Follow the Fleet*, and the rest, it is a disappointment." Although nominated for Best Dance Direction and Best Original Song, the film was not short-listed by the Academy for Best Picture.

The most nominated films, each short-listed for seven statuettes, were: *Anthony Adverse* (NYT "a bulky, rambling and indecisive photoplay"; HSp "one of the finest things the screen has done"; Life "a great picture"); *Dodsworth* (NYT "excellent"; V "superb"); and *The Great Ziegfeld* (NYT "fragmentary" and "confused" but "impressive"; V "outstanding"). Also named were: *The Story of Louis Pasteur* (NYT "excellent"; V "splendid"); *Romeo and Juliet* (Sp "unimaginative ... a little banal"); *A Tale of Two Cities* (NYT "a screen classic"); and *San Francisco* (HSp "a great achievement").

Variety predicted a win for *San Francisco*, which had become a huge box office success, but industry sentiment suggested a close contest between *Mr Deeds Goes to* Town and *The Great Ziegfeld*. Desperate to win acclaim for his costly musical, L. B. Mayer struck a deal with Jack Warner. Both studio bosses directed their contractees to vote for *The Great Ziegfeld* as Best Picture and for Paul Muni in Warner Bros.' *The Story of Louis Pasteur* as Best Actor.

On Academy Awards night, *The Great Ziegfeld* was declared the winner by a narrow margin over *The Story of Louis Pasteur*. The controversial win was openly criticised in the media. In The Spectator, Graham Greene called the winner "the longest and ... silliest, vulgarest, dullest novelty of the season." Slamming the film as "an atrocious production" and "a picture false in biography", the HCN meanwhile condemned the Academy's choice by declaring "a truer demonstration of the stupidity and rank barbarism of these times had never been more ably given."

BEST DIRECTOR

ACADEMY AWARDS
• **Frank Capra for *Mr Deeds Goes to Town***
Gregory LaCava for *My Man Godfrey*
Robert Z. Leonard for *The Great Ziegfeld*
W. S. Van Dyke for *San Francisco*
William Wyler for *Dodsworth*

NEW YORK – Rouben Mamoulian – *The Gay Desperado*

Rouben Mamoulian won the New York critics' Best Director prize for the musical *The Gay Desperado* (NYT "a first-rate musical comedy") on the tenth ballot ahead of Austrian director Fritz Lang for his acclaimed drama *Fury* (NYT "brilliantly directed"; V "masterfully guided"; Sp an "extraordinary achievement: no other director has got so completely the measure of his medium"). Surprisingly both were overlooked by the Academy.

Also excluded from contention were: Charlie Chaplin for *Modern Times*; James Whale for *Show Boat* (NYT "not merely a screened concert … has a rhythmic pace and a balanced continuity of movement which is as exceptional as it is welcome"); and the 1936 Venice Film Festival winner, Jacques Feyder for *La Kermesse Héroïque (Carnival in Flanders).* Also passed over were the directors of two of the main Best Picture contenders, William Dieterle for *The Story of Louis Pasteur* (NYT "gifted direction") and Mervyn LeRoy for *Anthony Adverse* (V "a topnotch job"; HSp "a triumph … no picture ever has been given better direction"; Life "great and intelligent direction").

Variety predicted that William Wyler would win for *Dodsworth* (HSp "a beautiful job, one that finally establishes young Wyler's right to recognition as one of Hollywood's really great directors") in a close race over Frank Capra for *Mr Deeds Goes to Town* (HSp "inspired") and Robert Z. Leonard for the expensive spectacle *The Great Ziegfeld.* Many thought Wyler's chances would be boosted by the additional acclaim he had earned for helming *These Three* (NYT "superb direction").

The Best Director category did prove a close contest, but not with the result that Variety expected. Capra, the President of the Academy, was named Best Director for the second time in three years by a narrow margin over W. S. Van Dyke for *San Francisco*, a hit film about the 1906 earthquake. Capra proved a popular choice. In London, The Times exclaimed, he "certainly deserves a second award for giving us *Mr Deeds Goes to Town*".

1936

BEST ACTOR

ACADEMY AWARDS
Gary Cooper as 'Longfellow Deeds' in *Mr Deeds Goes to Town*
Walter Huston as 'Sam Dodsworth' in *Dodsworth*
• **Paul Muni as 'Louis Pasteur' in *The Story of Louis Pasteur***
William Powell as 'Godfrey Parke' in *My Man Godfrey*
Spencer Tracy as 'Father Mullin' in *San Francisco*

NEW YORK – Walter Huston – *Dodsworth*

The year after he nearly won the Best Actor Academy Award as a write-in candidate, Paul Muni was an early favourite for the prize for portraying the famous French scientist Louis Pasteur in the drama *The Story of Louis Pasteur* (NYT "brilliant", a "sensitive characterization"; SMH "quiet but convincing representation"). The film was released in February, a month prior to the Oscar ceremony at which Muni had almost caused a sensational upset for his performance in *Black Fury*.

Also released in February was *Modern Times*, a comedy starring Charlie Chaplin which he had also written and directed. It was his first screen appearance in five years and Frank S. Nugent in The New York Times remarked that Chaplin remained "a master of pantomime" and that "time has not changed his genius". Variety declared *Modern Times* was "Chaplin at his best" and in Australia, The Sydney Morning Herald concurred opining Chaplin is "better than ever before".

As the year progressed, further contenders emerged with claims for the Best Actor statuette.

In March Jean Hersholt's performance in *Country Doctor* was lauded by critics (V "an excellent job of complete conviction"; SMH "extraordinary insight and sympathy ... a splendid character study"), while in April, Gary Cooper earned mixed reviews for *Mr Deeds Goes to Town* (V "too scatterbrained"; HSp "brilliant") and William Powell appeared in the box office hit *The Great Ziegfeld* (he also appeared that year in the Best Picture nominees *Libeled Lady* and *My Man Godfrey*).

One of Powell's *Libeled Lady* co-stars, Spencer Tracy, became a contender in June with his acclaimed performance in *Fury* (NYT "splendidly performed ... utterly convincing"; V "Tracy gives his top performance"; SMH "brilliant"). He also earned praise for his supporting performance as a priest in *San Francisco* (NYT "another brilliant portrayal"). The New York Times said he was "heading surely toward an award for the finest performances of the year."

1936

Late in the year four previous Best Actor winners earned positive citations: Fredric March appeared in *Anthony Adverse* (NYT "thoroughly spiritless"; V "convincing"); Lionel Barrymore portrayed President Jackson in *The Gorgeous Hussy*; Victor McLaglen starred in *The Magnificent Brute* (NYT "a blusteringly perfect performance"); and Charles Laughton played the title role in *Rembrandt* (V "Laughton is far from satisfactory"; TT "impressive"; SMH "convincing").

Another contender emerged at the end of the year when the New York critics chose Walter Huston on the fifth ballot ahead of Tracy, for the recreation of his 1934 stage success in *Dodsworth*. Huston was the first American to win a New York critics' acting prize.

The Academy short-listed Cooper, Huston, Muni, Powell and Tracy. Surprisingly Powell was mentioned for *My Man Godfrey* rather than Best Picture favourite *The Great Ziegfeld*. As a result of a push by M-G-M, Tracy appeared on the ballot for his supporting turn in the expensive blockbuster *San Francisco* rather than for his acclaimed turn in the leading role in the drama *Fury*.

As the first man to earn a third nomination and the winner of the 1936 Venice Film Festival prize, Muni remained the favourite for the Oscar. Concerned about Huston's win on the east coast and by Tracy's growing popularity, studio boss Jack Warner made a deal with M-G-M's Louis. B. Mayer in which they directed their contractees to vote for M-G-M's *The Great Ziegfeld* as Best Picture and for Muni in the Best Actor category for Warner's *The Story of Louis Pasteur*.

On the big night, Muni won the Oscar. Academy records reveal that it was Cooper rather than Huston who came second in the voting. "I will try and continue to work to make myself worthy of the Academy's high and meaningful honour," Muni said. He was a major contender for the golden statuette again the following year.

1936

BEST ACTRESS

ACADEMY AWARDS
Irene Dunne as 'Theodora Lynn' in *Theodora Goes Wild*
Gladys George as 'Carrie Snyder' in *Valiant is the Word for Carrie*
Carole Lombard as 'Irene Bullock' in *My Man Godfrey*
• **Luise Rainer as 'Anna Held' in *The Great Ziegfeld***
Norma Shearer as 'Juliet Capulet' in *Romeo and Juliet*

NEW YORK – Luise Rainer – *The Great Ziegfeld*

In autumn 1936, Norma Shearer's husband, producer Irving G. Thalberg, died of pneumonia at the age of just 36. A few months later, his distraught widow received a record fifth Academy Award nomination for playing Shakespeare's teenage heroine in *Romeo and Juliet*, a project that Thalberg had put together especially for her. Shearer's short-listing by the Academy came in spite of generally poor reviews on both sides of the Atlantic. The New York Times had lamented that she was "not at her best" while TT concluded that "the art of getting rhythm and music into Shakespeare's lines eludes her". Nonetheless, Shearer was considered by many to be a frontrunner for the statuette.

The other main contender was Austrian newcomer Luise Rainer for *The Great Ziegfeld*. Although really a supporting performance, Rainer left a major impression with the famous telephone scene in which she congratulates her former husband on his second marriage. The New York Times considered her "inclined to emotional excesses that are not entirely justified and frequently were extremely trying" but the majority of critics were positive. At the end of the year she was named Best Actress by the New York critics.

The inclusion of Rainer in the Best Actress stakes contributed to the exclusion of *The Great Ziegfeld*'s notional leading actress, Myrna Loy (who played Ziegfeld's actress wife Billie Burke, herself a Best Supporting Actress Oscar nominee in 1938) for her comic turn in the comedy *Libeled Lady*. Loy's co-star, Jean Harlow, was also overlooked. The New York Times considered Loy and Harlow and co-stars William Powell and Spencer Tracy as "just about as perfect a light-comedy foursome as you will encounter anywhere". The most surprising omission, however, was New York runner-up Ruth Chatterton as a social-climbing wife in *Dodsworth* (NYT "one of her best" performances).

Also passed over were: Elisabeth Bergner for playing Rosalind in a British film version of the Shakespeare comedy *As You Like It* (NYT "her finest performance"; SMH "poor"); Frances Farmer for dual roles in *Come and Get It* (SMH "excellent"); Françoise Rosay in *La Kermesse Héroïque (Carnival in*

Flanders) (V "exceptionally fine"); Merle Oberon in *These Three* (NYT "gives one of her finest performances"); Rosalind Russell in *Craig's Wife* (NYT "a viciously eloquent performance); previous winner Katharine Hepburn in *Sylvia Scarlett* (NYT "Hepburn is at her best"); and 1935 Best Actress champ Bette Davis in *The Petrified Forest* (NYT "demonstrates that she does not have to be hysterical to be credited with a grand portrayal").

Nominated ahead of these women were: popular stage actress Gladys George for the tearjerker *Valiant is the Word for Carrie* (NYT "the stage's most charming gift to the screen this year"; SMH "struggles"); Carole Lombard for *My Man Godfrey* (NYT "she rises beautifully to the role"); and Irene Dunne, who received her second mention by the Academy, for playing a small-town woman who secretly writes a steamy bestseller in the comedy *Theodora Goes Wild* (TT "does one of the best pieces of work in her career", "emerges as an accomplished exponent of comedy"). Dunne had also garnered praised for the musical *Show Boat* (NYT "splendid"; V "superb").

Variety predicted that a sympathy vote would take Shearer to an historic second win. Other observers favoured Rainer, and a few predicted that a close contest between them would see Lombard emerge victorious. Hoping to boost the profile of his new star, studio boss Louis B. Mayer directed M-G-M contractees to vote for Rainer instead of Shearer, the studio's reigning star.

Shearer made her first public appearance since Thalberg's death at the Academy Awards ceremony, but did not collect an unprecedented second statuette for acting. Instead, Rainer became the first person to win acting awards from both the New York critics' circle and the Academy. A year later, it would be Rainer who herself would make Oscar history by collecting a second golden statuette in the acting categories.

1936

BEST SUPPORTING ACTOR

ACADEMY AWARDS
Mischa Auer as 'Carlo' in *My Man Godfrey*
• **Walter Brennan as 'Swan Bostrum' in *Come and Get It***
Stuart Erwin as 'Amos Dodd' in *Pigskin Parade*
Basil Rathbone as 'Tybalt' in *Romeo and Juliet*
Akim Tamiroff as 'Gen. Yang' in *The General Died at Dawn*

"Critics were generally of the opinion that Spencer Tracy would have won if he had been nominated for Supporting Actor for *San Francisco*" wrote the HCN after the actor left the 1936 Oscar ceremony without the recognition many had predicted for him. Eager to establish him as a star, M-G-M had promoted his performance in the Best Actor category rather than for the newly created Best Supporting Actor prize. Tracy was among the nominees for Best Actor and was consequently excluded from the inaugural Best Supporting Actor category.

Ironically, one of the nominees for the award was named for a top-billed performance in a leading role: Stuart Erwin in the musical comedy *Pigskin Parade* (NYT a "topnotch comic … plays [his] scenes for all they are worth"). Also nominated were: Mischa Auer in *My Man Godfrey*; Walter Brennan as the honest Swede in *Come and Get It* (NYT "faultless"; V "guilty of exerting too much pressure now and then"; SMH close to "dominating the film"); Akim Tamiroff in *The General Died at Dawn* (NYT "perfect"; V "exceptional"; TT "both alarming and subtle"; SMH "unconvincing"); and Basil Rathbone as Tybalt in *Romeo and Juliet* (NYT "a perfect devil of a Tybalt … no possible fault there"; TT "excellent").

Overlooked were: Eugene Pallette in *My Man Godfrey*; Frank Morgan in *The Great Ziegfeld* (NYT "splendid"); Edmund Gwenn in *Sylvia Scarlett* (NYT "excellent"); Donald Crisp in *The White Angel*; Paul Robeson in *Show Boat*; Claude Rains in *Anthony Adverse* (V "splendid"; HSp "admirable"); and Fritz Leiber as Dr Charbonnet in *The Story of Louis Pasteur* (NYT "outstanding"). Although his work is well-regarded decades later, critics were unkind about Oscar Homolka's portrayal of South African President Paul Kruger at the time of the release of the historical biopic *Rhodes*. The New York Times, for example, dismissed his work as "little better than a caricature, played with overdone make-up and ridiculously slow timing, the latter, apparently, a result of faulty direction".

With Tracy out of contention, Variety correctly predicted a win for Brennan. It was the first of his record three Best Supporting Actor statuettes.

1936

BEST SUPPORTING ACTRESS

ACADEMY AWARDS
Beulah Bondi as 'Rachel Jackson' in *The Gorgeous Hussy*
Alice Brady as 'Angelica Bullock' in *My Man Godfrey*
Bonita Granville as 'Mary Tilford' in *These Three*
Maria Ouspenskaya as 'Baroness von Obersdorf' in *Dodsworth*
• **Gale Sondergaard as 'Faith Paleologue' in *Anthony Adverse***

Two teenagers received strong praise for their performances in the drama *These Three*: 14-year old Bonita Granville and 13-year old Marcia Mae Jones. Variety called their work "inspired" and The Sydney Morning Herald commented that as the malevolent student who spreads scandalous lies about her teachers Granville was "only too credible" and Jones was "equally striking." The Spectator wrote "never before has childhood been represented so convincingly ... the lying sadistic child is suggested with quite shocking mastery by Bonita Granville ... [while] Marcia Mae Jones gives an almost equally fine performance." The New York Times said "the honors really belong to Bonita Granville" and while Jones was overlooked, Granville made the Academy's list.

Also nominated were: Beulah Bondi as the pipe-smoking wife of President Jackson in *The Gorgeous Hussy* (V "particularly clever"; SMH "could not be faulted"); Alice Brady in *My Man Godfrey* (NYT plays her character "magnificently"); and for their screen debuts, Maria Ouspenskaya in *Dodsworth* (TT "extremely well-acted"; HSp "outstanding") and Gale Sondergaard as the scheming housekeeper in *Anthony Adverse* (SMH "brilliant").

Overlooked were: Dennie Moore for her uncredited screen debut in *Sylvia Scarlett*; Edna May Oliver as the nurse in *Romeo and Juliet* (NYT "droll, wise impish in her humor ... she is grand"); and Josephine Hutchinson for her performance as Marie Pasteur in *The Story of Louis Pasteur* (NYT "splendid").

Initially, the Academy and the Hollywood film community at large, took the view that the new supporting categories were for featured artists and contract players rather than established or rising stars. It was likely for this reason that the Academy excluded Jean Arthur from consideration for her supporting turn in *Mr Deeds Goes to Town*.

Variety predicted a close race between Ouspenskaya and Sondergaard and on the big night it was Sondergaard who became the first winner of the Academy Award for Best Supporting Actress.

1937

BEST PICTURE

ACADEMY AWARDS

The Awful Truth
(Columbia, 91 mins BW, 21 Oct 1937, 6 noms)

Captains Courageous
(M-G-M, 115 mins BW, 25 Jun 1937, 4 noms)

Dead End
(Goldwyn, United Artists, 93 mins BW, 24 Aug 1937, 4 noms)

The Good Earth
(M-G-M, 138 mins BW, 29 Jan 1937, 5 noms)

In Old Chicago
(20th Century Fox, 96 mins BW, 15 Jan 1938, 6 noms)

• *The Life of Emile Zola*
(Warner Bros., 116 mins BW, 2 Oct 1937, 10 noms)

Lost Horizon
(Columbia, 138 mins BW, 1 Sep 1937, 7 noms)

One Hundred Men and a Girl
(Universal, 85 mins BW, 17 Sep 1937, 5 noms)

Stage Door
(RKO Radio, 92 mins BW, 8 Oct 1937, 4 noms)

A Star is Born
(Selznick International, 111 mins, 22 Apr 1937, 7 noms)

NEW YORK – *The Life of Emile Zola*
BOARD OF REVIEW – *Night Must Fall*

The early favourite for Best Picture of 1937 was *The Good Earth* starring the previous year's Best Actor and Best Actress Academy Award winners Paul Muni and Luise Rainer as Chinese peasants. The New York Times called the film "superb ... one of the finest things Hollywood has done this season or any other" while Variety considered it "a remarkable screen production" that was "impressive" but "sometimes ponderous". In London, The Times thought it was "impressive ... but lacking" the force of the original novel, while in Australia the Sydney Morning Herald simply said it was "a great picture."

Included along with *The Good Earth* on the annual New York Times list of the year's best films were: Frank Capra's *Lost Horizon* (NYT "outstanding"; SMH "a masterpiece"; Sp "disappointing"); *A Star is Born* (V "a smash which unquestionably will rate among the half dozen best of the season"; SMH "an outstanding film"); *Make Way for Tomorrow* (V "gripping"; SMH "one of the most striking films of the year"; CA "one of the finest things Hollywood has done this year"); *Captains Courageous* (SMH "a beautiful and stirring screen classic"); *They Won't Forget* (NYT "a brilliant sociological drama"; SMH "masterful … leaves an impression seldom created by a picture"; S&S "excellent"); *The Life of Emile Zola* (NYT "the finest historical film ever made"; V an "outstanding achievement"); and *Stage Door* (NYT "a brilliant picture").

The Academy nominated all of these films with the exception of *They Won't Forget* and Leo McCarey's drama *Make Way for Tomorrow*. Included on the short-list instead were: McCarey's comedy *The Awful Truth* (NYT "one of the more laughable screen comedies of 1937 … original and daring"); the historical spectacle *In Old Chicago* (S&S "impersonal and strangely unmoving"; HRp "one of the greatest works of screen art ever presented … magnificent"); and, most unexpectedly, *One Hundred Men and a Girl* starring Deanna Durbin.

Overlooked by the Academy were: Alfred Hitchcock's *Sabotage (The Woman Alone)* (NYT "a masterly exercise in suspense"); the musical *Maytime* (NYT "the most entrancing operetta the screen has given us"); *The Hurricane* (HRp "a great picture", "compelling"); the French drama *Mayerling*, winner of the New York critics' Best Foreign Film award (NYT "it is impossible to remain aloof, to regard the romance dispassionately … there is no resisting the fire that players, writer and director have struck from the screen"); and the German film *Der Herrscher (The Ruler)* (V "outstanding").

The Academy also failed to include in the Best Picture line-up, the film that would prove to be the most popular box office hit of the following year. Premiering in Los Angeles just prior to Christmas was the first animated feature, Disney's *Snow White and the Seven Dwarfs* (NYT "altogether captivating ... a classic"; V "absorbing ... the film approaches real greatness"; SMH "brilliant ... will stir the imagination of all who see it", "a more beautiful or fascinating production could not be visualised"). Nominated only for Best Score, the film was recognised with a special honorary award the following year.

At the end of the year, the NBR and the New York critics selected different films as Best Picture for the first time. The NBR named the box office disappointment *Night Must Fall*, a stage-play adaptation starring Robert Montgomery which was not nominated for the Academy's top prize (TT "a thoroughly exciting film"; V "tedious, slow and even dull in spots"). The New York critics, meanwhile, chose the biographical picture *The Life of Emile Zola* on the second ballot, ahead of *Captains Courageous* and *The Good Earth*.

The three main contenders for the New York critics' award were also the three frontrunners for the Best Picture Oscar. With a record ten nominations, *The Life of Emile Zola* was considered the slight favourite over M-G-M's expensive version of *The Good Earth*. On the big night, the biopic won Warner Bros. a Best Picture statuette for the first time. The film also made history as the first named Best Picture by both the New York critics' circle and the Academy.

BEST DIRECTOR

ACADEMY AWARDS
William Dieterle for *The Life of Emile Zola*
Sidney Franklin for *The Good Earth*
Gregory LaCava for *Stage Door*
• **Leo McCarey for *The Awful Truth***
William Wellman for *A Star is Born*

NEW YORK – Gregory LaCava – *Stage Door*

Having been overlooked for the previous year's Best Picture runner-up *The Story of Louis Pasteur*, William Dieterle was favoured to take home the statuette for his latest biographical film, *The Life of Emile Zola* (NYT "Dieterle's majestic direction"; V "excellently balanced") which was also the year's most nominated film. Dieterle's main challengers appeared to be Sidney Franklin for *The Good Earth*, the early Best Picture frontrunner, and Gregory LaCava who had been named Best Director by the New York critics for *Stage Door* on the first ballot.

Also in contention for the Academy Award were William Wellman for *A Star is Born* (NYT "Wellman's direction is expert"; SMH "directed by William Wellman with an unerring instinct for genuine dramatic effect") and Leo McCarey for the battle of sexes comedy *The Awful Truth*.

Overlooked for nominations were: George Cukor for *Camille* (NYT "under his benign handling [the film] is not the reverentially treated museum we half expected to see"): Fritz Lang for *You Only Live Once* (NYT "Lang's direction is his usual brilliant compound of suspense and swift action"); Alfred Hitchcock for *Sabotage (The Woman Alone)* (SMH "excellent … this is real genius in direction"); Henry King for *In Old Chicago* (NYT "inspired"); Anatole Litvak for the French tragedy *Mayerling* (NYT "superb"); and, for the second year in a row, Mervyn LeRoy, this time for *They Won't Forget* (NYT "remarkably skillful direction"; SMH "directed by Mervyn LeRoy with a brilliance that verges on genius"). Perhaps the most unexpected absentee from the ballot, however, was Victor Fleming for the Best Picture contender *Captains Courageous* for which Spencer Tracy won the Best Actor award (NYT "admirable direction").

In a major upset on Oscar night, the winner was McCarey for *The Awful Truth*. He accepted the statuette but politely told the Academy, "Thanks, but you gave it to me for the wrong picture!" McCarey had been disappointed his other 1937 release, the family drama *Make Way for Tomorrow* for which The New York Times had praised him for "brilliant direction" had been ignored and for years he maintained that he deserved his first Oscar for *Make Way for Tomorrow*.

1937

BEST ACTOR

ACADEMY AWARDS
Charles Boyer as 'Napoleon Bonaparte' in *Conquest*
Fredric March as 'Norman Maine' in *A Star is Born*
Robert Montgomery as 'Danny' in *Night Must Fall*
Paul Muni as 'Emile Zola' in *The Life of Emile Zola*
• **Spencer Tracy as 'Manuel' in *Captains Courageous***

NEW YORK – Paul Muni – *The Life of Emile Zola*

Paul Muni, the previous year's winner, was favoured to win the prize again when he became the first man to receive a fourth nomination. He made the list for the biographical drama *The Life of Emile Zola,* which dramatised the French novelist's part in the scandalous Dreyfus affair (NYT "without doubt, the best thing he has done"; TT "magnificent"; Esq "another great characterization"). Like *The Story of Louis Pasteur* for which he had triumphed the previous year, the film was directed by William Deiterle. Muni also garnered praise that year for his performance as a Chinese peasant in another major Best Picture contender *The Good Earth*, a role played on stage by Claude Rains (NYT "flawless"; V "splendid"; SMH "magnificent in an astoundingly realistic and consistent study").

Among the acclaimed performances overlooked by Academy voters were: Cary Grant in *The Awful Truth*; Ronald Colman in *Lost Horizon* (NYT "there is nothing but unqualified endorsement here of Mr Colman"); Henry Fonda for *You Only Live Once* (V "brilliant"); Basil Rathbone as a murderous husband in *Love From a Stranger* (V "excellent"); Claude Rains as the ambitious district attorney in *They Won't Forget* (NYT "chief credit must go ... to Mr Rains, for his savage characterization of the ambitious prosecutor"; SMH "superb"); Paul Robeson in the British drama *Jericho*; Oscar Homolka in *Sabotage (The Woman Alone)* (NYT "superb ... the perfect tool for Hitchcock's deliberate tempo"; V "a stand-out"; SMH "powerful"); Harry Baur's portrayal of the mad Emperor Rudolph II of Bohemia in the Czech film *Le Golem (The Golem)* (V "a genuinely outstanding performance. It is among the top acting jobs of all time"; TT "magnificent"); and the first Best Actor winner Emil Jannings in the German film *Der Herrscher (The Ruler)*, for which he won the 1937 Venice Best Actor prize.

Previous Oscar winner, Fredric March, earned his third nomination for *A Star is Born* (SMH "vivid and poignant"; NBR Mag "magnificent") while Spencer Tracy made the list for a second year in a row as a Portuguese fisherman in

78

Captains Courageous despite mixed reviews (NYT "seemed curiously unconvincing in the beginning ... but made the part his in time"; SMH "magnificent portrayal"). The President of the SAG, Robert Montgomery, was also a surprise nominee for his against-type portrayal of a whistling murderer in *Night Must Fall* (TT plays the part "with remarkable skill"; SMH "a complete success"). The final nominee was French star Charles Boyer who was mentioned for the expensive drama *Conquest* (NYT "does not fire the imagination").

Interestingly, many historians contend that March and Boyer merited their nominations for performances in other films released that same year: March in the screwball comedy *Nothing Sacred* and Boyer for the acclaimed French tragedy *Mayerling* (NYT "matchless ... never been better"; V "superb"; TT "perfect").

At the end of the year, the New York critics' circle, who had passed over Muni the previous year for his Oscar-winning turn, gave him their Best Actor prize, thus consolidating his chance of an historic second Oscar statuette. Despite the critics' award, Muni believed that nobody could win consecutive Academy Awards and did not campaign.

On the night, the winner was Tracy who had been the runner-up for the New York critics' prize for the second year in a row and who had expressed great surprise that he had even been nominated.

Ironically, Muni's belief that winning consecutive Oscar statuettes was impossible was dramatically shown to be unfounded. That same year Luise Rainer won her second consecutive Best Actress trophy. The very next year Tracy himself would collect another Best Actor award. Muni would make the Oscar lists once more, in 1957.

BEST ACTRESS

ACADEMY AWARDS
Irene Dunne as 'Lucy Warriner' in *The Awful Truth*
Greta Garbo as 'Marguerite' in *Camille*
Janet Gaynor as 'Vicki Lester' in *A Star is Born*
• **Luise Rainer as 'O-Lan' in *The Good Earth***
Barbara Stanwyck as 'Stella Dallas' in *Stella Dallas*

NEW YORK – Greta Garbo – *Camille*

In the six years since she had been nominated for her first two talking pictures, Greta Garbo had been repeatedly snubbed by the Academy. Her performances in *Grand Hotel*, *Queen Christina* and *Anna Karenina* (for which she won the inaugural New York critics' circle prize) were not even recognised by the Academy with Best Actress nominations.

In January 1937, she appeared as the tragic Marguerite Gautier in *Camille*, a version of Alexandre Dumas' play "La Dame aux Camelias". In The New York Times, Frank S. Nugent called her work "eloquent, tragic, yet restrained", "incomparable" and "brilliant". He praised her "perfect artistry" and "complete command of the role", concluding that "Camille is Garbo's best performance". *Camille* became Garbo's most successful at the box office and garnered her rave reviews (LHE "Hollywood's greatest dramatic actress in her greatest dramatic role"; V "Garbo has never done anything better"; TT "brilliant"; SMH "a striking portrayal ... if any have never fully realised what a great emotional actress Greta Garbo is, her performance in Camille should convince them").

Garbo received further praise for her performance as the Polish patriot, Countess Marie Walewska in the historical drama *Conquest* (NYT "stilted"; V "splendid"; TT "a moving and sensitive portrayal"). Soon after its release, she became the first person to win a second prize from the New York critics when she won their Best Actress award for the second time in three years. When she was included on the Academy's short-list she became an almost unbackable favourite to finally claim an Oscar statuette.

Previous Oscar winner Katharine Hepburn, the runner-up for the New York critics prize, was overlooked by the Academy for her performance as a wealthy socialite determined to become an actress in *Stage Door* as was her co-star Ginger Rogers in the role of a struggling actress (SMH her "portrayal has many facets, and each one is brilliant"). In The New York Times, Frank S. Nugent had commented, "Miss Hepburn and Miss Rogers, in particular, seemed to be acting so far above their usual heads that, frankly, we hardly recognized them."

1937

Also overlooked were: Sylvia Sidney in Fritz Lang's *You Only Live Once* (NYT "poignantly real"); Beulah Bondi as the old woman in Leo McCarey's drama *Make Way for Tomorrow* (NYT "superb performance": V "standout", "clever character work"; TT "superlatively fine performance"; Esq "couldn't be surpassed"); French actress Danielle Darrieux in *Mayerling* (V "superb"; SMH "so moving"); Flora Robson as Queen Elizabeth I in *Fire Over England* (NYT "a colourful interpretation"; SMH "impressive" with "moments of sheer magnificence"); Anna Neagle as Queen Victoria in *Victoria the Great* (NYT "Neagle's performance is one of those rare gems of a screen year"; V "an unwavering performance"; HSp "magnificent"); Carole Lombard in the comedy *Nothing Sacred*; the late Jean Harlow for her final performance in *Saratoga*; and previous winner Bette Davis as a prostitute in *Marked Woman*, for which she won the Best Actress prize at the 1937 Venice Film Festival (NYT "her best performance since ... *Of Human Bondage*"; V "her performance here is also rife with subtleties of expression and gesture which fellow performers will recognize and give due credit").

Making the Academy's list alongside Garbo were: the very first Best Actress winner Janet Gaynor as the rising Hollywood starlet in *A Star is Born* (SMH "excellent"); Irene Dunne in the screwball comedy *The Awful Truth* (S&S "a really witty and intelligent performance"); Barbara Stanwyck as the self-sacrificing mother in *Stella Dallas* (NYT "portrayal as courageous as it is fine"; V her "top acting performance"; SMH "outstanding ... a poignant performance"; HSp "brilliant ... a sensitive, beautifully shaded characterization"); and the previous year's Best Actress Oscar winner Luise Rainer as a Chinese peasant in *The Good Earth*, a role played on stage by the popular Russian theatre actress Alla Nazimova (NYT "Rainer is tragically real" and "splendid"; TT "singularly impressive" and "genuinely moving"; SMH "Rainer submits one of the greatest portraits in the history of the screen"; HRp "compelling")

In a major upset on Oscar night, the strength of Rainer's performance saw her outpoll Garbo for the Best Actress prize and become not only the first person to win a second Oscar for acting but the first to do so with consecutive victories.

Married to screenwriter Clifford Odets, Rainer made a handful of further Hollywood films over the next couple of years, including *The Great Waltz* in 1938. She made fewer appearances during the war years before suddenly retiring at just thirty-three years of age in 1943. She was never again nominated for an Oscar.

BEST SUPPORTING ACTOR

ACADEMY AWARDS
Ralph Bellamy as 'Daniel Leeson' in *The Awful Truth*
Thomas Mitchell as 'Dr Kersaint' in *The Hurricane*
• **Joseph Schildkraut as 'Capt. Alfred Dreyfus' in *The Life of Emile Zola***
H. B. Warner as 'Chang' in *Lost Horizon*
Roland Young as 'Cosmo Topper' in *Topper*

In reviewing Frank Capra's *Lost Horizon*, several critics singled out the supporting performances of Sam Jaffe as the High Lama (V "capital"; SMH "the finest portrayal in the picture ... slightly sentimentalised .... [but] amazingly realistic") and Thomas Mitchell as the fugitive (NYT a "grand performance"; SMH "excellent"). Surprisingly, however, it was H. B. Warner who garnered a nomination from the Academy for his turn as one of the lamas. Oscar voters overlooked Jaffe entirely, but Mitchell was recognised for his acclaimed performance in another film released that year – as the doctor in the action drama *The Hurricane* (SMH "stands out"; HRp "a notably veracious and sympathetic portrait").

Similarly, while reviews of the screwball comedy *Topper* had praised Eugene Pallette for his performance as the house detective (V "splendid"; SMH "excellent"), the Academy instead nominated Roland Young for his performance in the film's leading role of the banker whose life is transformed by a pair of ghosts (NYT "responsible for whatever success ... [the] film enjoys"; SMH "superb").

The most surprising omission from the ballot paper was Walter Connolly for his role as the uncle in the prestige drama *The Good Earth* (V "a sparkling job"). Also neglected were: Henry Daniell as the jilted lover in *Camille* (V "a performance of unusual interest"); Anton Walbrook for his portrayal of Prince Albert in the British historical drama *Victoria the Great* (NYT "brilliant interpretation of the misunderstood Prince"; V "superb", "he delineates his character flawlessly"; TT "original and accomplished study"); Clinton Rosemund as the terrified janitor in *They Won't Forget* (S&S "tragic and sincere study ... superb"); and Humphrey Bogart as a gangster returning home in *Dead End*.

Nominated along with Mitchell, Warner and Young were Ralph Bellamy for his turn as the slow-witted boyfriend of Irene Dunne's character in the comedy *The Awful Truth* and Joseph Schildkraut for his portrayal of the unjustly persecuted Jewish army officer Captain Alfred Dreyfus in *The Life of Emile Zola* (V "outstanding").

Industry insiders declared Bellamy and Warner to be the two frontrunners for the award and consequently one of the other candidates chose to take the advice of his agent and stay home and rest rather than attend the banquet and prize-giving ceremony. As a result, when Austrian-born Schildkraut was named as the winner, Academy officials had to telephone the actor at home and have him rush into the ceremony and collect the statuette. Schildkraut's chances may well have been helped by the success of his film, which subsequently won the Best Picture Oscar.

Schildkraut was never nominated by the Academy again, despite earning widespread acclaim and a Golden Globe nomination as Best Actor (Drama) for reprising his stage success as the father of Anne Frank in *The Diary of Anne Frank* in 1959.

1937

BEST SUPPORTING ACTRESS

ACADEMY AWARDS
• **Alice Brady** as 'Molly O'Leary' in *In Old Chicago*
Andrea Leeds as 'Kaye Hamilton' in *Stage Door*
Anne Shirley as 'Laurel Dallas' in *Stella Dallas*
Claire Trevor as 'Francey' in *Dead End*
May Whitty as 'Mrs Bramson' in *Night Must Fall*

Gale Sondergaard was a surprise omission from the Best Supporting Actress category the year after she had won the inaugural award. She was considered by The New York Times to be the only praise-worthy part of the remake of *Seventh Heaven* (NYT "outstanding") and had been lauded by critics as the wife of Captain Dreyfus in the Best Picture winner *The Life of Emile Zola* (V "outstanding"; Esq "splendid") which had garnered more nominations than any other release that year.

Also overlooked were: Dorothy Peterson as a gangster's secretary in *Her Husband Lies*; both Constance Collier as an ageing Shakespearian actress (SMH "splendid piece of acting") and Lucille Ball as the girl with lumberjack boyfriends in *Stage Door*; Barbara O'Neil as the stepmother in *Stella Dallas* (V "excellent"; SMH "outstanding portrayal"); Suzy Prim in *Mayerling*; Marjorie Main as a gangster's mother in *Dead End* (NYT "memorable"); and Maria Ouspenskaya as the senile mother of Countess Marie Walewska in *Conquest*.

Although O'Neil was not considered for the award, Anne Shirley's acclaimed performance as the daughter in *Stella Dallas* did earn the 20-year old a nomination (NYT "flawless"; V "excellent"; TT "in a trying part, is sensitive and expressive"; SMH "wonderful"). Also nominated for the first time were: Claire Trevor for playing a prostitute in *Dead End* (NYT "memorable"); Andrea Leeds for playing a young actress desperate for the lead role in a new Broadway play in *Stage Door* (NYT "the real discovery of the picture"; TT "has the inspiration of genius … plays the part with a beautiful sense of tragedy"); and May Whitty for recreating her stage role as the wheelchair-bound old lady charmed and then terrified by a murderer in *Night Must Fall* (V "excellent"; TT "admirable").

The winner was the only one of the nominees to have previously made the Academy's lists. The year after being mentioned for *My Man Godfrey*, Alice Brady was named Best Supporting Actress for playing an Irish pioneer mother in the disaster drama *In Old Chicago* (V "outstanding", "compelling and sincere"; SMH "fine and restrained"; HSp "a thoughtful, human and appealing performance").

1937

Brady was unable to attend the Oscar ceremony at the Biltmore Hotel in Los Angeles because she had a broken ankle. When she was announced as the winner an unidentified man accepted the award, ostensibly on her behalf. When Brady later told Academy officials that she had sent no representative and that she had never received her award, a replacement was organised and presented to her a fortnight later.

Tragically Brady died of cancer at the age of forty-seven just eighteen months after receiving her Academy Award. Her final screen appearance was in *Young Mr Lincoln* released in 1939.

BEST PICTURE

ACADEMY AWARDS
The Adventures of Robin Hood
   (20th Century Fox, 102 mins, 11 Feb 1938, 4 noms)
Alexander's Ragtime Band
   (20th Century Fox, 105 mins BW, 19 Aug 1938, 6 noms)
Boys' Town
   (M-G-M, 96 mins BW, 9 Sep 1938, 5 noms)
The Citadel
   (M-G-M, 110 mins BW, 3 Nov 1938, 4 noms)
Four Daughters
   (Warner Bros., 90 mins BW, 9 Aug 1938, 5 noms)
La Grande Illusion (Grand Illusion)
   (R.A.O., 111 mins BW, 12 Sep 1938, 1 nom)
Jezebel
   (Warner Bros., 103 mins BW, 10 Mar 1938, 5 noms)
Pygmalion
   (M-G-M, 89 mins BW, 3 Mar 1939, 4 noms)
Test Pilot
   (M-G-M, 118 mins BW, 22 Apr 1938, 3 noms)
• *You Can't Take It With You*
   (Columbia, 126 mins BW, 1 Sep 1938, 7 noms)

NEW YORK – *The Citadel*
BOARD OF REVIEW – *The Citadel*

For the third time in four years, the New York critics and the NBR chose the same winner: King Vidor's *The Citadel*, an adaptation of the ground-breaking novel by A. J. Cronin which had become a best-seller the previous year. When the film opened in early November, Frank S. Nugent declared in The New York Times that the film was "one of the most satisfying screen dramas of the year" and "one of the great events of the season". The Hollywood Reporter, meanwhile, said *The Citadel* was "a fine, exciting and dramatic picture". The film was among ten short-listed by the Academy for the Best Picture statuette.

The New York critics and the NBR also agreed on their selection of Jean Renoir's anti-war film *La Grande Illusion (Grand Illusion)* as the Best Foreign-Language Film. An unexpected success at the box office in the United States, the film won praise from The New York Times as "a strange and interesting film" and from Variety as "an artistically masterful feature". When the nominees for the Academy Awards were announced, *La Grande Illusion (Grand Illusion)* became the first non-English language film ever nominated as Best Picture.

The other nominees included: another British-based M-G-M production adapted from a recently lauded piece of literature, *Pygmalion* (NYT "a grand show"; TT "extraordinarily amusing"; S&S "not a very good film"); the Civil War drama *Jezebel* (NYT "interesting"; V "engrossing"; HRp "exceptional"); the aviation drama *Test Pilot* starring Clark Gable (NYT "spectacular"); the Irving Berlin tribute *Alexander's Ragtime Band* (NYT "the best musical show of the year"); *Four Daughters* (NYT "a charming, at times heartbreakingly human, little comedy"); *Boys' Town* (NYT "great" but undermined by "the embarrassing sentimentality of its closing scenes"); *The Adventures of Robin Hood* (NYT "it leaps boldly to the forefront of this year's best"; V "cinematic pageantry at its best"); and Frank Capra's comedy *You Can't Take It With You*, which was based on the hit Pulitzer Prize-winning play (NYT "a grand picture"; TT "unusually good"; SMH "brilliant").

While *La Grande Illusion (Grand Illusion)* made the short-list, Academy voters ignored *Un Carnet de Bal (Life Dances On)*, the winner of the Best Picture prize at the 1937 Venice Film Festival (NYT "a brilliant mosaic of drama and comedy"; TT "brilliant", "entrancing"; SMH "absorbing", "brilliant"; S&S an "artistic triumph"; N&D "a film which must be seen").

Also overlooked were: *Three Comrades* (NYT "a superlatively fine picture, obviously one of 1938's best ten"; V "dull"); *Angels with Dirty Faces* (NYT "engrossing and vivid"); *Marie Antoinette* (V "approaches real greatness"; S&S "long, slow and frequently tedious"); and two British films – *Owd Bob (To the Victor)* (NYT "admirable") and Alfred Hitchcock's *The Lady Vanishes* (NYT "brilliant", "devilishly clever"; TT "absorbing and extraordinarily exciting").

Arguably, the most notable omission was *Algiers* (NYT "first-rate entertainment … a fascinating drama … few films this season, or any other, have sustained their mood so brilliantly … clearly one of the most interesting and absorbing dramas of the season").

Although considered a cinematic classic by film historians, the screwball comedy *Bringing Up Baby* was not well-received by critics upon its release (NYT "a farce which you can barely hear above the ominous tread of deliberative gags … after the first five minutes we were content to play the game called 'the cliché expert goes to the movies'") and was a failure at the box office. Unsurprisingly, it was shunned by the Academy.

While many favoured *The Adventures of Robin Hood* for the Best Picture award (and indeed it won more Oscars than any other film that year), it was the Capra comedy that emerged as the Best Picture winner (it had gone into the ceremony as the film with the most nominations). Although *You Can't Take It With You* had not been included on The New York Times list of the year's ten best films, S&S had called it "brilliant" and "without any reservation" the best film of the year. The Academy apparently agreed.

BEST DIRECTOR

ACADEMY AWARDS
• **Frank Capra for *You Can't Take It With You***
Michael Curtiz for *Angels with Dirty Faces*
Michael Curtiz for *Four Daughters*
Norman Taurog for *Boys' Town*
King Vidor for *The Citadel*

NEW YORK – Alfred Hitchcock – *The Lady Vanishes*

When Frank Capra received a record fourth nomination as Best Director for the comedy *You Can't Take It With You*, the popular President of both the Academy and the Directors Guild was the favourite to win an unprecedented third statuette.

His main challengers were King Vidor, who also received a record fourth nod, for the New York and NBR Best Picture winner *The Citadel* and Michael Curtiz who became the first person to receive two Best Director nominations in the same year when he was named for the gangster drama *Angels with Dirty Faces* and the Best Picture nominee *Four Daughters*. Curtiz had also directed the Best Picture nominee and box office hit *The Adventures of Robin Hood*.

The surprise double citation for Curtiz excluded several of the year's most acclaimed directors from the ballot. The most notable omissions were Alfred Hitchcock, the first British winner of the New York Best Director award, for *The Lady Vanishes* (V "admirable direction"; TT "his touch has never been surer nor his power to hold our attention more complete"; SMH "brilliant") and William Wyler for *Jezebel*, the Civil War drama for which Bette Davis and Fay Bainter both won Oscars (NYT "admirably directed"; TT "has proved himself a director of imagination"). In her autobiography, Davis wrote: "The thrill of winning my second Oscar was only lessened by the Academy's failure to give the directorial award to Willie. He made my performance ... It was all Wyler."

Also by-passed were: previous winner Frank Borzage for *Three Comrades* (NYT "magnificently directed"); John Cromwell for *Algiers* (NYT "one of the finest directorial jobs"); Howard Hawks for *Bringing Up Baby*; Julien Duvivier for *Un Carnet de Bal (Life Dances On)* (NYT "unerringly directed"; TT "has throughout handled his material with delicacy and charm"; SMH "has directed this film with great imagination"); and Jean Renoir for Best Picture nominee *La Grande Illusion (Grand Illusion)* (V "imaginative direction").

Despite handling one of the year's most acclaimed films, Vidor went unrewarded for the fourth time. In contrast, Capra – whose film won the Best Picture award – became the first person to win a third Best Director Oscar.

1938

BEST ACTOR

ACADEMY AWARDS
Charles Boyer as 'Pepe Le Moko' in *Algiers*
James Cagney as 'Rocky Sullivan' in *Angels with Dirty Faces*
Robert Donat as 'Andrew Manson' in *The Citadel*
Leslie Howard as 'Professor Henry Higgins' in *Pygmalion*
• **Spencer Tracy as 'Father Flanagan' in *Boys' Town***

NEW YORK – James Cagney – *Angels with Dirty Faces*

James Cagney was named Best Actor by the New York Film Critics Circle and was a strong favourite for the Academy Award for his performance as a gangster who feigns cowardice as he goes to his execution in *Angels with Dirty Faces* (NYT "at his best"). The other main contender was the runner-up for the New York prize and the previous year's Oscar winner – Spencer Tracy – who became the first person to earn three consecutive nominations for acting with his turn in *Boys' Town* (NYT "perfection itself").

Also nominated were: Charles Boyer for his part as a jewel thief in *Algiers*, a role played the previous year by Jean Gabin (V "an interesting portrait"; TT "sympathetic and persuasive"); Robert Donat for his work as the young doctor in the New York and NBR Best Picture choice *The Citadel* (V "excellent ... a most seasoned performance of high excellence"; SMH "brilliant"; S&S "beautifully acted"; HRp "splendid"); and Leslie Howard for his performance as Professor Henry Higgins in a film version of *Pygmalion* which he co-directed and for which he won the Best Actor award at the 1938 Venice Film Festival (V "excellent").

Overlooked for the award were Walter Huston in *Of Human Hearts* (NYT "superb"), Errol Flynn for both *The Adventures of Robin Hood* and *The Dawn Patrol*, Cary Grant for the comedy *Bringing Up Baby*, and three British actors: previous Best Actor winner Charles Laughton in *Vessel of Wrath (The Beachcomber)* (NYT "brilliant"; V "another enthralling performance"; S&S "marvellously acted"), Ronald Colman in *If I Were King* (V "excellent") and Scottish actor Will Fyffe for the British film *Owd Bob (To the Victor)* (NYT "remarkably adept performance").

For the fourth year in a row the Academy disagreed with the east coast critics. Passing over the favourite Cagney, they handed Tracy his second consecutive Best Actor statuette. He was the first man to win a second Best Actor statuette from the Academy.

1938

BEST ACTRESS

ACADEMY AWARDS
Fay Bainter as 'Hannah Parmalee' in *White Banners*
• **Bette Davis as 'Julie Marston' in *Jezebel***
Wendy Hiller as 'Eliza Doolittle' in *Pygmalion*
Norma Shearer as 'Queen Marie Antoinette' in *Marie Antoinette*
Margaret Sullavan as 'Pat Hollmann' in *Three Comrades*

NEW YORK – Margaret Sullavan – *Three Comrades*

Margaret Sullavan became the first American to win the New York Film Critics Circle's Best Actress award for her performance as a young woman who dies from tuberculosis in *Three Comrades*. In The New York Times, Frank S. Nugent applauded Sullavan's work declaring "hers is a shimmering, almost unendurably lovely performance". In Australia, The Sydney Morning Herald concurred saying she "plays her part to perfection". Variety, however, dissented opining that her portrayal was "confused". Sullavan was a frontrunner for the Academy's award with her first (and only) nomination.

Another strong candidate was English actress Wendy Hiller, runner-up for the New York award, for her turn as Eliza Doolittle in *Pygmalion* (NYT "Hiller is a discovery", "flawless", "perfect"; V "Hiller carries off a difficult part faultlessly"; TT "remarkable skill"; SMH "remarkable"; S&S "brilliantly successful"). The HSp commented Hiller "is so outstanding, so far above the average and better-than-average run of Hollywood performances, that she merits filmdom's highest award."

Fay Bainter made Academy Awards history when she became the first performer nominated in both acting categories in the same year. She received a Best Actress nomination for her turn as the kindly housekeeper in *White Banners* (V "moving"; SMH "magnificent", "compelling", "superb"), but was considered a better chance of collecting the Best Supporting Actress award for *Jezebel*.

Also considered only an outside chance was previous winner Norma Shearer who made the list for a record sixth (and final) time for her portrayal of the ill-fated Queen in *Marie Antoinette* (NYT "it would not be fair to assume that any other screen actress could have made this particular Antoinette more real than she has done"). Shearer had received the Best Actress award at the 1938 Venice Film Festival for her performance.

The winner, however, was Bette Davis who collected her second Best Actress Oscar for her performance in *Jezebel* as a scandalous and feisty Southern debutante during the Civil War. The role had been played on stage by Miriam

Hopkins and both she and Ruth Chatterton were considered for the film version before Davis was cast. In London, The Times said "Davis is one of the few actresses on the screen who is not content with an insipid naturalism, but who sets herself out consciously and deliberately to act ... it is because she realises this that Julie takes on an animation, a contradictory, wilful existence of her own, which is very rare indeed on the screen." In Australia, The Sydney Morning Herald said that Davis was "quite remarkable" in "another triumph." Film Weekly lauded her portrayal as "vivid and inspiring", while The Hollywood Reporter said she was "brilliant." Davis had also earned praise for her very different performance as the wife of a writer in *The Sisters* (NYT "a particularly lovely performance"; V "one of her most scintillating performances"; Life "extraordinary grace, sensitivity and distinction").

The most surprising exclusion from the list of nominees was previous winner Katharine Hepburn. She had earned plaudits from critics for recreating the role in *Holiday* for which Ann Harding had been Oscar-nominated in 1930/31 (V "her acting is delightful and shaded with feeling and understanding") but had divided critics with her comic turn in *Bringing Up Baby* (NYT "a role which calls for her to be breathless, senseless, and terribly, terribly fatiguing. She succeeds, and we can be callous enough to hint it is not entirely a matter of performance"; V "one of her most invigorating screen characterizations").

Also overlooked were: Danish actress Aino Taube for the Swedish drama *En Saga* (NYT "excellent"); Elsa Lanchester, the wife of previous Best Actor Oscar winner Charles Laughton, for *Vessel of Wrath (The Beachcomber)* (NYT "brilliant"; S&S "superb"); and Rosalind Russell for the Best Picture nominee *The Citadel* (HRp "splendid").

The victory for Davis marked the second year in a row in which an actress collected a second Best Actress statuette. The feat would not be achieved again for over a decade.

BEST SUPPORTING ACTOR

ACADEMY AWARDS
• **Walter Brennan as 'Peter Goodwin' in** *Kentucky*
John Garfield as 'Mickey Borden' in *Four Daughters*
Gene Lockhart as 'Regis' in *Algiers*
Robert Morley as 'King Louis XVI of France' in *Marie Antoinette*
Basil Rathbone as 'King Louis XI of France' in *If I Were King*

For his screen debut in a supporting role as the cynical student in *Four Daughters*, John Garfield polled third in the New York critics' vote for Best Actor. The New York Times called his performance "brilliant" and said that he stole the movie. Variety called his work "forceful," commenting that "he threatens to throw the picture out of focus by drawing too much interest." The 25-year old was the favourite for the Oscar against previous winner Walter Brennan as the old horse-breeder in *Kentucky* (V "vivid and convincing"; SMH "magnificent", "the highlight of the film"), Gene Lockhart as a police informer in *Algiers*, and Robert Morley and previous nominee Basil Rathbone as French Kings in *Marie Antoinette* (S&S "memorable") and *If I Were King* (SMH "a brilliant study of sardonic eccentricity"), respectively. Rathbone had also impressed as the Sherriff of Nottingham in *The Adventures of Robin Hood*.

The surprise omissions from the category were Mickey Rooney for *Boys' Town* and Ralph Richardson for *The Citadel* (HRp "a knockout"). Other omissions included: Joseph Calleia in *Algiers*; Pierre Blanchar in *Un Carnet de Bal (Life Dances On)* (TT "unforgettable realism and terrible conviction"; SMH "unforgettable"); Charles Ruggles in *Bringing Up Baby*; Charles Coburn in *Vivacious Lady* (V "excellent"); Roland Young in *The Young in Heart* (V "brilliant"); Donald Crisp in *Jezebel* (HRp "excellent"); and Claude Rains as King John in *The Adventures of Robin Hood*.

The Academy also shunned Erich von Stroheim, the former silent film director then working in France as a virtual exile from Hollywood, for his work in *La Grande Illusion (Grand Illusion)* (SMH "the finest performance of his career"; S&S "excellent"). The New York Times, had remarked his "appearance as von Rauffenstein reminds us again of Hollywood's folly in permitting so fine an actor to remain idle and unwanted."

On Oscar night, in a major upset, the Best Supporting Actor statuette was presented to Brennan (who had also earned praise for his supporting turn in *The Texans*). It was his second trophy in three years making him the first person to win two Oscars in the supporting categories. He would win an unprecedented third Best Supporting Actor Oscar just two years later.

1938

BEST SUPPORTING ACTRESS

ACADEMY AWARDS
• **Fay Bainter as 'Aunt Belle Massey' in** *Jezebel*
Beulah Bondi as 'Mary Wilkins' in *Of Human Hearts*
Billie Burke as 'Miss Emily Kilbourne' in *Merrily We Live*
Spring Byington as 'Penny Sycamore' in *You Can't Take It With You*
Miliza Korjus as 'Carla Donner' in *The Great Waltz*

In 1938, the experienced Broadway stage veteran Fay Bainter became the first person to receive nominations in both the leading and supporting acting categories in the same year. Consequently, she became the favourite to win the supporting prize for her performance as the title character's aunt in *Jezebel* (SMH "presents a superbly witty and sympathetic character"; HRp "excellent").

The other main contenders were Spring Byington as the ditzy play-writing mother in the Best Picture winner *You Can't Take It With You* (NYT "delightful") and previous nominee Beulah Bondi in the arguably leading role of the wife of a frontier preacher in *Of Human Hearts* (NYT "a superb performance"; V "convincing acting"). Bondi had also earned praise for her supporting role in *Vivacious Lady* (NYT "excellent").

Also nominated were opera star Miliza Korjus for her only screen performance as the woman who tries to seduce Johann Strauss in the historical melodrama *The Great Waltz* (NYT "sings her waltzes well enough") and Billie Burke for her eccentric socialite in the comedy *Merrily We Live* (SMH "Burke has a part which few actresses could play with such a delightfully light touch while infusing it with personality"). Burke, who had been portrayed by Myrna Loy in the 1936 Best Picture *The Great Ziegfeld*, also earned praise for her part in *The Young in Heart* (V "brilliant").

Absent from the ballot were May Robson in the comedy *Bringing Up Baby* and May Whitty for the Alfred Hitchcock thriller *The Lady Vanishes*.

On Oscar night, as expected, double nominee Bainter lost the Best Actress contest to her *Jezebel* co-star Bette Davis, but was named as the year's Best Supporting Actress. She was nominated for a third time, in 1961, for her performance as the grandmother in a film version of Lillian Hellman's *The Children's Hour*.

BEST PICTURE

ACADEMY AWARDS

Dark Victory
(Warner Bros., 104 mins BW, 22 Apr 1939, 3 noms)
• *Gone with the Wind*
(Selznick/M-G-M, 222 mins, 15 Dec 1939, 13 noms)
Goodbye, Mr Chips
(M-G-M, 114 mins BW, 28 Jul 1939, 7 noms)
Love Affair
(RKO Radio, 87 mins BW, 16 Mar 1939, 6 noms)
Mr Smith Goes to Washington
(Columbia, 125 mins BW, 19 Oct 1939, 11 noms)
Ninotchka
(M-G-M, 110 mins BW, 3 Nov 1939, 4 noms)
Of Mice and Men
(United Artists, 106 mins BW, 30 Dec 1939, 4 noms)
Stagecoach
(United Artists, 96 mins BW, 2 Mar 1939, 7 noms)
The Wizard of Oz
(M-G-M, 111 mins BW & C, 25 Aug 1939, 6 noms)
Wuthering Heights
(Goldwyn, United Artists, 103 mins BW, 13 Apr 1939, 8 noms)

NEW YORK – *Wuthering Heights*
BOARD OF REVIEW – *Confessions of a Nazi Spy*

Film historians have long regarded 1939 as the golden year of old Hollywood, and so it is unsurprising that some of the most acclaimed productions of the studio era were nominees for the Best Picture Oscar that year. They included: the Bette Davis tear-jerker *Dark Victory* (V "intense"); the sentimental drama *Goodbye, Mr Chips* (NYT "a serene, heart-warming and generally satisfying film"; SMH one of the screen's "finest masterpieces"); the romance *Love Affair* (NYT "extraordinarily fine", "a glowing and memorable picture"; HRp "impressive"); Frank Capra's patriotic political drama *Mr Smith Goes to Washington* (NYT "brilliant", "a stirring and even inspiring testament to liberty and freedom", "one of the best shows of the year"; V "absorbing", "one of the finest and consistently interesting dramas of the screen"; SMH "one of the screen's most distinguished productions"; Sp "a great film"); the Greta Garbo comedy *Ninotchka* (NYT "one of the sprightliest comedies of the year"; Sp "enchanting"); the literary adaptation *Of Mice and Men*; the Western *Stagecoach* (V "sweeping and powerful drama of the American frontier"; HSp "superb

94

entertainment"); the fantasy adventure *The Wizard of Oz* (NYT "delightful"; V "unique and highly entertaining"; HSp "a cinematic masterpiece"); and the prestigious literary adaptation *Wuthering Heights* (NYT "a strong and sombre film ... unquestionably one of the most distinguished pictures of the year"; V "an artistic success"; TT "praiseworthy").

Leading this field of acclaimed movies, however, was the Civil War epic *Gone with the Wind* which was released late in the year and quickly became the biggest box office money-earner of all time. In The New York Times, Frank S. Nugent called it "a great show" and "the greatest motion mural we have seen and the most ambitious film-making venture in Hollywood's spectacular history." Variety declared it to be "one of the truly great films" while The Sydney Morning Herald concluded that it was "superb" and although "the film has it flaws ... it re-creates with high bravado, the pageant and the tragedy of the American Civil War". The Academy recognised the historical epic with a record thirteen Oscar nominations in twelve categories.

The biggest surprise omission from the Best Picture category was the all-female drama *The Women* (NYT "marvellous"; V "one of the smash hits of the season"). Also passed over were: the musical *Let Freedom Ring* (V "momentous"; TT "little more than a well-organised musical comedy"); the adventure film *Gunga Din* (NYT "splendid"; V "spectacular"); the historical drama *Juarez* (NYT "with all its faults, still must be rated a distinguished, memorable and socially valuable film"); the British film *Four Feathers*; the historical drama *Stanley and Livingstone* (V "absorbing"); and Alfred Hitchcock's *Jamaica Inn* (V "gripping").

Also noticeably absent from the Academy's short-list was the film that the NBR selected as the Best Picture of the year, the drama *Confessions of a Nazi Spy* (V "significant"; TT "remarkable"; SMH "uncompromising"). It is worth noting that the NBR made their choice prior to the release of *Gone with the Wind*.

The New York critics' circle was divided between *Mr Smith Goes to Washington* and *Gone with the Wind*. They were unable to separate the two films after twelve ballots and, rather than declaring a tie, surprisingly compromised on *Wuthering Heights*. These three films were the most Oscar nominated films of the year.

On awards night, the result of the Best Picture contest was never in doubt. While Clark Gable was surprisingly outpolled for the Best Actor award, there was no upset for the top prize. The epic *Gone with the Wind* became the first colour film named Best Picture, crowning a record tally of eight Academy Awards.

BEST DIRECTOR

ACADEMY AWARDS
Frank Capra for *Mr Smith Goes to Washington*
• **Victor Fleming for *Gone with the Wind***
John Ford for *Stagecoach*
Sam Wood for *Goodbye, Mr Chips*
William Wyler for *Wuthering Heights*

NEW YORK – John Ford – *Stagecoach*

The directors of five of the year's Best Picture nominees were short-listed by the Academy for the Best Director award with previous winners Frank Capra and John Ford quickly emerging as the frontrunners. The popular Capra was the first person to receive a fifth Best Director Oscar nomination for *Mr Smith Goes to Washington* (NYT "has paced it beautifully and held it in perfect balance"), while Ford became the first person to win a second Best Director award from the New York critics for *Stagecoach* (NYT "in one superbly expansive gesture ... John Ford has swept aside ten years of artifice and talkie compromise and has made a motion picture that sings a song of camera"; HRp "brilliant").

The darkhorse seemed to be William Wyler for *Wuthering Heights* (NYT "magnificent"; V "direction by William Wyler is slow and deliberate, accenting the tragic features of the piece"; NBR Mag "superb"). Also nominated were Victor Fleming for *Gone with the Wind* and Sam Wood for *Goodbye, Mr Chips* (SMH "magnificently" directed). Wood was also one of the directors who had replaced Fleming on the Civil War epic after he had suffered a nervous breakdown. Initially, Fleming was considered only a slim chance for the award as the film was seen primarily as the work of producer David O. Selznick.

Overlooked for the award were: Fleming for *The Wizard of Oz*; New York prize runner-up Ernst Lubitsch for *Ninotchka*; previous winners Leo McCarey for *Love Affair* (V "excellent") and Lewis Milestone for *Of Mice and Men* (V "skillful"); Alfred Hitchcock for *Jamaica Inn*; Henry King for *Stanley and Livingstone* (V "excellent"); Edmund Goulding for *Dark Victory*; and George Cukor for *The Women* (HSp "extraordinarily clever").

As the Oscars approached, many in Hollywood began to hear rumours that Selznick was taking too much credit for *Gone with the Wind* and that his relentless hounding of Fleming had resulted in the director's breakdown. The subsequent sympathy and the near total domination of the Oscars by the box office sensation, helped Fleming to narrowly out-poll the other nominees and claim the Best Director award.

1939

BEST ACTOR

ACADEMY AWARDS
• **Robert Donat as 'Charles Chipping' in** *Goodbye, Mr Chips*
Clark Gable as 'Rhett Butler' in *Gone with the Wind*
Laurence Olivier as 'Heathcliff' in *Wuthering Heights*
Mickey Rooney as 'Mickey Moran' in *Babes in Arms*
James Stewart as 'Jefferson Smith' in *Mr Smith Goes to Washington*

NEW YORK – James Stewart – *Mr Smith Goes to Washington*

Like most people, producer David O. Selznick was certain that Clark Gable would win a second Best Actor award for his performance as Rhett Butler in the box office record-breaker *Gone with the Wind* (NYT "almost as perfect at the grandstand quarterbacks thought he would be"; V "a forceful impersonation").

A few observers, however, defied the prevailing wisdom and predicted a win by either James Stewart, who had won the New York critics' circle prize for his turn as a naïvely honest Senator in *Mr Smith Goes to Washington* (NYT "a joy"), or Englishman Robert Donat, one of the previous year's nominees, as the dedicated English school teacher in *Goodbye, Mr Chips* (NYT "incredibly fine"; TT "competent" but "strangely superficial", "nondescript and dull"; SMH "astonishingly realistic"; HSp "a remarkable demonstration of powerful and understanding characterization"). Donat had been the runner-up to Stewart for the New York critics' Best Actor prize.

Also nominated were 19-year old Mickey Rooney as a young vaudeville showman in *Babes in Arms* (V "provides one of the most extensive performances ever given on the screen") and English stage star Laurence Olivier for his lauded portrayal of Heathcliff in the literary adaptation *Wuthering Heights* (NYT "brilliant"; V "a fine portrayal as the moody, revengeful lover"; TT "impressive"; SMH "remarkable"; NBR Mag "one of the screen performances that has to be called great"). Rooney, Stewart and Olivier were all first-time Oscar nominees.

The most surprising omission of the year was Henry Fonda who received plaudits from reviewers for his portrayal of Abraham Lincoln in John Ford's *Young Mr Lincoln*, a drama about the future President's early life as a struggling young lawyer (NYT "his performance kindles the film, making it a moving unity, at once gentle and quizzically comic"; V "impressively realistic"; TT "a very elaborate piece of acting", "convincing"; HSp "masterly"; Sp "a fine performance"). Fonda had also earned praise for his turn as the assistant in *The*

Story of Alexander Graham Bell, for which Don Ameche was overlooked for the Best Actor Oscar (SMH "fine").

French star Charles Boyer failed to gain a third consecutive nomination for his part in Best Picture nominee *Love Affair* (NYT "superb"), despite nominations for both Irene Dunne and Maria Ouspenskaya. Another French actor, Harry Baur, who had been overlooked two years earlier in *Le Golem (The Golem)*, was also passed over. The New York Times said that Baur's performance as the controversial monk in *Rasputin* "belongs to the great performances of the screen" while Variety said "Baur brings probably his most powerful characterization to the screen." Nikolai Cherkasov was also ignored for his title performance in Sergei Eisenstein's Russian epic *Aleksandr Nevsky (Alexander Nevsky)* (V "a performance not easily forgotten").

Charles Laughton, the 1935 Best Actor Oscar winner was passed over for his part in Alfred Hitchcock's *Jamaica Inn* (Sp "superb"). The 1936 Best Actor Oscar winner Paul Muni was overlooked for his portrayal of the titular Mexican leader in *Juarez* (TT "very impressively portrayed") and Spencer Tracy, the Best Actor Oscar winner of the previous two years, was denied the chance of making it three wins in a row when the Academy chose not to nominate his portrayal of Stanley in *Stanley and Living*stone (V "outstanding"; SMH "succeeds admirably"; S&S "magnificent").

Also overlooked were: Paul Lukas for the NBR's choice for Best Picture of the year *Confessions of a Nazi Spy* (SMH "brilliant"); John Garfield for *They Made Me a Criminal* (NYT "carries the show along"; V "a stunning performance"); and James Cagney for *The Roaring Twenties* (NYT "if it also seems to be good entertainment, credit it to James Cagney in another of his assured portrayals of a criminal career man"). Although The New York Times thought Sam Jaffe "should be a serious contender for the best performance of the year" for his fourth-billed performance of the title character in *Gunga Din*, he too was missing from the Academy's short-list.

On 29 February 1940, it was Donat who emerged as an upset winner, outpolling Stewart (with Gable third) for the Best Actor Oscar. He was the only one of the nominees absent from the ceremony at Los Angeles' Ambassador Hotel. His award was accepted on his behalf by presenter Spencer Tracy. Donat never made the Academy's lists again despite a series of strong performances in British films during the 1950s including *The Winslow Boy*, *The Magic Box* and as the aged mandarin, his final screen role, in *The Inn of the Sixth Happiness* (for which he received a Golden Globe nomination).

Peter O'Toole received a Best Actor nomination thirty years later when he took on the role of 'Mr Chips' in a musical remake of *Goodbye, Mr Chips*. His interpretation of the part, however, did not earn him a Best Actor statuette.

1939

BEST ACTRESS

ACADEMY AWARDS
Bette Davis as 'Judith Traherne' in *Dark Victory*
Irene Dunne as 'Terry McKay' in *Love Affair*
Greta Garbo as 'Lena Yakushova' in *Ninotchka*
Greer Garson as 'Katherine Ellis' in *Goodbye, Mr Chips*
• **Vivien Leigh as 'Scarlett O'Hara' in *Gone with the Wind***

NEW YORK – Vivien Leigh – *Gone with the Wind*

"Bette Davis won an Academy award last year for her performance in *Jezebel*, a spottily effective film," wrote Frank S. Nugent in The New York Times in April 1939, "Now it is more than ever apparent that the award was premature. It should have been deferred until her *Dark Victory* arrived ... Miss Davis is superb". Davis' performance in the role of the dying socialite which Tallulah Bankhead had played in an unsuccessful stage version five years earlier and which had once been touted as a screen vehicle for Greta Garbo, earned her some of the best reviews of her career. Variety said Davis appeared "in a powerful and impressive role, which will be mentioned in nominations for top performances of the year" and lauded her for "a sincere and realistic performance". In London, The Times said the film was "a real opportunity to display her versatility and her capacity for treating quite different emotions with the same convincing candour" while in Australia, The Sydney Morning Herald wrote "Davis compels close attention to every expression and mood of her character". The NBR Magazine, meanwhile, said she was "genuinely human and moving ... she has never before seemed to be so entirely inside a part, with every mannerism and physical aspect of her suited to its expression".

Davis was praised a few weeks later for her supporting role in *Juarez* and then a few months later for her turn as a self-sacrificing mother in the box office hit *The Old Maid* (NYT "a poignant and wise performance"; V "a strong portrayal"; TT "a serious and often affecting study"). At the end of the year she impressed again as Queen Elizabeth I in *The Private Lives of Elizabeth and Essex* (V "persuasive and compelling" ... "will catch attention and approval from audiences and critics"; TT "she makes one believe in her Elizabeth ... undeniably most impressive").

Four lauded performances in box office successes only a year after winning her second Best Actress Oscar made Davis a serious contender for the award again in 1939 and in the end she was defeated by only a narrow margin. The winner was a young English actress in a role that Davis had thrown away her chance to play: Vivien Leigh as Scarlett O'Hara in the epic historical melodrama *Gone with the Wind*. Leigh became the second actress to collect prizes from both the New York critics and the Academy with a critically acclaimed performance as the tempestuous southern belle. The New York Times declared, Leigh is "so perfectly designed for the part by art and nature that any other actress in the role would be inconceivable ... [she is] the pivot of the picture". Variety, meanwhile, lauded her for "a brilliant performance ... of wide versatility" and The Times said she "acts with genuine gusto and sustained vitality". In Australia, The Sydney Morning Herald said "Leigh could scarcely have been bettered".

Also nominated (for the final time) was Greta Garbo, runner-up for the New York prize for her comic turn as a Russian agent in the comedy *Ninotchka* (NYT "Garbo's delightful debut as a comedienne ... [is] superb"; V "excellent"; TT "splendid"; SMH "a definite success"). Irene Dunne received her fourth nomination for *Love Affair* (NYT "superb"; V "excellent") and Irish actress Greer Garson made the list for her well-reviewed screen debut as the kindly wife in *Goodbye, Mr Chips*, even though hers was only a supporting role with limited screen time (TT "beautifully played"; SMH "magnificent"; HSp "screen acting rarely equalled").

Garson's surprise nomination came ahead of: Jean Arthur in *Mr Smith Goes to Washington* (NYT "tosses a line and bats an eye with delightful drollery"; V "excellent"; SMH "brilliant"); Judy Garland in *The Wizard of Oz*; previous winner Norma Shearer in *The Women* (NYT "one of the best performances she has given"; V "sparkling"); Merle Oberon as Cathy in the literary adaptation *Wuthering Heights* (NYT "brilliant ... has perfectly caught the restless changeling spirit of the Bronte heroine"; V "excellent"; TT "artificial"); Elisabeth Bergner as twins in *Stolen Life* (S&S "two brilliant performances"); previous winner Claudette Colbert in *Zaza* (V "a sincere and scintillating portrayal of the frivolous and tempestuous Zaza"); and Swedish newcomer Ingrid Bergman in *Intermezzo: A Love Story* (V "convincing, providing an arresting performance").

Leigh was the first English actress to win the Academy's Best Actress award. She would earn the prize again in 1951 for playing another southern belle in *A Streetcar Named Desire*.

1939

BEST SUPPORTING ACTOR

ACADEMY AWARDS
Brian Aherne as 'Emperor Maximilian von Hapsburg' in *Juarez*
Harry Carey as 'President of the U. S. Senate' in *Mr Smith Goes to Washington*
Brian Donlevy as 'Sgt. Markoff' in *Beau Geste*
• **Thomas Mitchell as 'Doc Boone' in *Stagecoach***
Claude Rains as 'Sen. Joseph Paine' in *Mr Smith Goes to Washington*

Two years after being unsuccessfully nominated for *The Hurricane*, Thomas Mitchell was the strong favourite for the Best Supporting Actor award for his performance as a drunken doctor in John Ford's *Stagecoach* (SMH "outstanding"; HRp "superb"). Mitchell had also been praised for his appearances in two other 1939 Best Picture nominees, Frank Capra's *Mr Smith Goes to Washington* (as a newspaperman) and *Gone with the Wind* (as Scarlett O'Hara's father), as well as in the popular drama *Only Angels Have Wings* and *The Hunchback of Notre Dame*.

Harry Carey and Claude Rains (NYT "splendid") made the list for their performances in *Mr Smith Goes to Washington*, as did Brian Donlevy for his turn as a sadistic sergeant in *Beau Geste* and Brian Aherne for his portrayal of the Emperor Maximilian in *Juarez* (V "excellent"; TT "makes the Emperor ... a most dignified and humane character"; SMH "the one piece of acting that holds the film together"; NBR Mag "remarkably effective").

The most surprising omission from the category was Henry Hull, whose performances in *Jesse James* (V "Hull's brilliant performance as the country editor is a standout") and *Spirit of Culver* were both lauded by critics. Also overlooked were: Mitchell's *Stagecoach* co-star Donald Meek; Paul Henreid as the German instructor in *Goodbye, Mr Chips* (NYT "splendid"); Vincent Price as the weak Duke of Clarence in *Tower of London* (V "excellent"); and Henry Travers in *Stanley and Livingstone* (TT "a skillful and moving portrait of the British Consul in Zanzibar").

On Oscar night Mitchell won the Oscar and modestly thanked the Academy saying, "I didn't think I was that good!" Despite other lauded performances such as those in the Best Picture Oscar nominees *Wilson*, *It's a Wonderful Life* and *High Noon*, he never made the Academy's lists again.

BEST SUPPORTING ACTRESS

ACADEMY AWARDS
Olivia de Havilland as 'Melanie Hamilton' in *Gone with the Wind*
Geraldine Fitzgerald as 'Isabella Linton' in *Wuthering Heights*
• **Hattie McDaniel as 'Mammy' in *Gone with the Wind***
Edna May Oliver as 'Mrs Sarah McKlennar' in *Drums Along the Mohawk*
Maria Ouspenskaya as 'Grandmother Marnet' in *Love Affair*

Hattie McDaniel became the first African-American nominated for an Academy Award in any category when her performance as Scarlett O'Hara's maid servant in *Gone with the Wind* was recognised. The New York Times said that of the film's cast McDaniel, a veteran of such films as *Alice Adams*, *Show Boat* and *Libeled Lady*, was "best of all, perhaps, next to Miss Leigh." The NBR Magazine said her portrayal was "magnificently played", while in London, The Times said that she "almost acts everybody else off the screen." The popular actress was the unbackable favourite to win the award.

McDaniel's co-star Olivia de Havilland made the Oscar lists for the first time for her turn as Melanie (NYT "a gracious, dignified, tender gem of characterization"), while Edna May Oliver received her only nomination for portraying a widowed pioneer in *Drums Along the Mohawk*. Geraldine Fitzgerald also received her only nomination, recognised for her performance as Heathcliff's wife in *Wuthering Heights* (NYT "flawless"; V "impressive"; NBR Mag "brilliant" and "heart-breaking"). Critics also praised Fitzgerald's turn as the best friend in *Dark Victory* (NYT "a sentient and touching portrayal"; V "fine"). Previous nominee Maria Ouspenskaya rounded out the list with her turn as the kindly grandmother in *Love Affair* (HRp "superb").

Overlooked were: Binnie Barnes as a saloon singer in love with Doc Holiday in *Frontier Marshal*; both Joan Crawford and Rosalind Russell (NYT "flawless"; V "a highlight characterization"; SMH "overacts") in *The Women*; Gladys George in *The Roaring Twenties* (NYT "has breathed poignance into the stock role of the night club hostess"); Flora Robson in *We Are Not Alone*; Claire Trevor in *Stagecoach*; and the final performance of the 1937 Best Supporting Actress winner, the late Alice Brady in *Young Mr Lincoln*. Greer Garson's debut screen performance in the supporting role of a schoolteacher's wife in *Goodbye, Mr Chips* was recognised in the Best Actress category.

On Oscar night, McDaniel claimed the award and became the first African-American Oscar winner. It would be nearly a quarter of a century before a second African-American won an Oscar in one of the acting categories.

1940

BEST PICTURE

ACADEMY AWARDS

All This, and Heaven Too
(Warner Bros., 141 mins BW, 13 Jul 1940, 3 noms)

Foreign Correspondent
(United Artists, 120 mins BW, 16 Aug 1940, 6 noms)

The Grapes of Wrath
(20th Century Fox, 128 mins BW, 15 Mar 1940, 7 noms)

The Great Dictator
(United Artists, 126 mins BW, 15 Oct 1940, 5 noms)

Kitty Foyle
(RKO Radio, 108 mins BW, 27 Dec 1940, 5 noms)

The Letter
(Warner Bros., 95 mins BW, 22 Nov 1940, 7 noms)

The Long Voyage Home
(United Artists, 105 mins BW, 8 Oct 1940, 6 noms)

Our Town
(United Artists, 90 mins BW, 13 Jun 1940, 6 noms)

The Philadelphia Story
(M-G-M, 112 mins BW, 1 Dec 1940, 6 noms)

• *Rebecca*
(Selznick, United Artists, 130 mins BW, 12 Apr 1940, 11 noms)

NEW YORK – *The Grapes of Wrath*
BOARD OF REVIEW – *The Grapes of Wrath*

The year after a Technicolor film won the Best Picture Oscar for the first time, the Academy short-listed ten black-and-white films – all of which were Hollywood studio productions. The favourite was the critically acclaimed *The Grapes of Wrath* (NYT a "screen classic", "honest and powerful", "one of the few great sociological motion pictures of all time"; V "an absorbing, tense melodrama, starkly realistic"; TT "powerful"; S&S "splendid"; NBR Mag "magnificent"). Based on the novel by John Steinbeck and directed by John Ford, the film chronicled the experience of a family displaced by the Depression. It was named Best Picture by the NBR and a week later by the New York critics, making it the fourth film in six years to be honoured by both groups. The Academy nominated it for seven awards.

The other main contender for the top Oscar was the year's most nominated film, Alfred Hitchcock's *Rebecca*, an adaptation of the popular novel by Daphne du Maurier (NYT "an altogether brilliant film, haunting, suspenseful, handsome"; V "an artistic success", "one of the finest production efforts of the past year"; SMH "outstanding"). The film, which received eleven nominations, was produced by David O. Selznick, winner of the 1939 Best Picture award for *Gone with the Wind*.

Other films directed by John Ford and Alfred Hitchcock were also nominated for the Oscar: Ford's sea epic *The Long Voyage Home* which was the runner-up for the New York critics' prize (NYT "a masterpiece of stark, vivid, realism"; V "fails to fill requirements for general audience appeal") and Hitchcock's espionage thriller *Foreign Correspondent* (HRp a "masterpiece"; V "breath-taking", "suspenseful and highly exciting"; TT "first-rate"). Also included were two films directed by Sam Wood, *Kitty Foyle* and *Our Town* (NYT "profound and deeply compassionate"; V "excellent"), and two films starring Bette Davis, *All This, and Heaven Too* (V "excellent", "film theatre at its best", "compelling entertainment") and *The Letter* (NYT "a superior melodrama"; V "suspenseful"). Also nominated were Charlie Chaplin's first full talkie *The Great Dictator* (NYT "magnificent", "truly superb"; V "extremely entertaining"; S&S "wonderful) and the comedy *The Philadelphia Story* (S&S "sophisticated comedy in its best sense"; V "a winner").

Surprisingly overlooked by the Academy were two pictures selected by The New York Times for its annual top ten list: *Pride and Prejudice* (NYT "one of the most charming and elegant costume pictures ever made"; V "possesses little of general interest"; TT "high-spirited entertainment"); and *The Great McGinty* (NYT "the best comedy-satire of the year"). Also omitted were: the comedy *His Girl Friday* (NYT "a bold-faced reprint of what was once – and still remains – the maddest newspaper comedy of our times"); *The Howards of Virginia* (NYT "a master work", "one of the best historical pictures to date"); the acclaimed anti-Nazi drama *The Mortal Storm* (V "exciting", "a film that demands universal screening in American theatres"; TT "exciting"; SMH "extraordinarily vivid", "magnificently idealistic film"); the 1938 French comedy *La Femme du Boulanger (The Baker's Wife)* which both the NBR and the New York critics named as the year's best foreign film (NYT "outstanding"); and the British colour fantasy *The Thief of Bagdad* which won more Oscars in 1940 than any other film (NYT "beguiling and wondrous", "truly exciting entertainment"; V "one of the most colorful, lavish and eye-appealing spectacles ever screened"). The Academy also passed over the year's two Disney animated features: *Pinocchio* (NYT "delightful"; S&S "breath-taking", "remarkable"); and *Fantasia* (NYT "spectacular"; HSp "extraordinary", "superb entertainment").

Although Ford once again won the Best Director Oscar, the Academy named *Rebecca* as the year's Best Picture. It was Selznick's second Best Picture statuette in a row and was the only Hitchcock film to win the Best Picture Academy Award.

1940

BEST DIRECTOR

ACADEMY AWARDS
George Cukor for *The Philadelphia Story*
• **John Ford for *The Grapes of Wrath***
Alfred Hitchcock for *Rebecca*
Sam Wood for *Kitty Foyle*
William Wyler for *The Letter*

NEW YORK – John Ford – *The Grapes of Wrath* and *The Long Voyage Home*

John Ford, the 1935 Best Director Oscar winner, received enthusiastic praise from film critics for two films in 1940: *The Grapes of Wrath*, an adaptation of the John Steinbeck novel (NYT "brilliant", "magnificent") and *The Long Voyage Home*, adapted from four short plays by Eugene O'Neill about the lives of men at sea (NYT "magnificent"; V "a directorial achievement"; TT "admirable"). For his dual achievements, Ford was named Best Director by the New York critics for a record third time in six years. When the Academy nominated him for *The Grapes of Wrath* he became a strong favourite to win the Oscar as well.

Ford had been a nominee the previous year for *Stagecoach* and two other directors were also nominated for the second consecutive year: Sam Wood for the Best Picture nominee *Kitty Foyle* and William Wyler for the melodrama *The Letter*. Wyler had also directed *The Westerner* that year, for which Walter Brennan won his third Oscar, while Wood had earned strong reviews for his handling of the Best Picture contender *Our Town* (HRp "brilliantly directed").

Also mentioned was George Cukor for the comedy *The Philadelphia Story* for which James Stewart won the Best Actor award.

The only first-time nominee in the category was British director Alfred Hitchcock who was considered for *Rebecca*, the year's most nominated film (V "inspired direction"; TT "has certainly done his best"). He had also directed the espionage thriller *Foreign Correspondent* (HRp "an individual triumph for Mr Hitchcock"). Both films were Best Picture nominees.

The most surprising omission from the category was Charlie Chaplin for the satire *The Great Dictator* which was nominated for the Best Picture award and for which Chaplin was mentioned for the Best Actor prize.

Also overlooked were: Howard Hawks for the comedy *His Girl Friday*; previous winner Frank Borzage for the anti-Nazi propaganda drama *The Mortal Storm* (V "one of his best directorial jobs"); Preston Sturges for *The Great McGinty* (NYT directed "with remarkable skill"); King Vidor for *Northwest*

Passage (V "masterful"); and Anatole Litvak for the Best Picture nominee *All This, and Heaven Too* (V "outstanding").

Thorold Dickinson was ineligible for his direction of the British thriller *Gaslight* (V "excellent direction") because it was not released in the United States until 1952 (eight years after the release of M-G-M's Oscar-winning Hollywood remake).

At the Academy Awards banquet, Ford, the only nominee not present, was named Best Director for the second time, while Hitchcock's film won the Best Picture Oscar. Although he would be nominated another four times, Hitchcock never took home the statuette. In contrast, Ford collected a third Best Director award the very next year, and then a record fourth in 1952.

1940

BEST ACTOR

ACADEMY AWARDS
Charles Chaplin as 'a Jewish barber' and 'Adenoid Hynkel, Dictator of
 Tomania' in *The Great Dictator*
Henry Fonda as 'Tom Joad' in *The Grapes of Wrath*
Raymond Massey as 'Abraham Lincoln' in *Abe Lincoln in Illinois*
Laurence Olivier as 'Maxim de Winter' in *Rebecca*
• James Stewart as 'Mike Connor' in *The Philadelphia Story*

NEW YORK – Charles Chaplin – *The Great Dictator*

The year after he was overlooked for playing President Abraham Lincoln in John Ford's *The Young Mr Lincoln*, Henry Fonda was a strong favourite for the Best Actor Oscar for his portrayal of a displaced Oklahoma sharecropper during the Depression in another Ford drama, *The Grapes of Wrath* (NYT "flawless").

The other main contender for the prize was James Stewart who had been the runner-up to Robert Donat for the Oscar the previous year. Stewart received his second consecutive nomination for playing a fast-talking reporter in *The Philadelphia Story* (NYT "brilliant"), a role which Katharine Hepburn had originally wanted for Spencer Tracy. Although his part was arguably a supporting role, Stewart had also been lauded for two leading performances, both opposite Margaret Sullavan, in the romantic drama *The Shop Around the Corner* (V "outstanding characterization") and the anti-Nazi film *The Mortal Storm* (V "excellent" SMH "remarkably sensitive").

Laurence Olivier also received a second consecutive Best Actor Oscar nomination, named for the year's most nominated film, Alfred Hitchcock's *Rebecca* (V "an impressionable portrayal"). The role had been turned down by Ronald Colman.

Also nominated, for the second (and final) time, was New York critics winner Charlie Chaplin for his dual performances as a Jewish barber and a fascist dictator in the satirical *The Great Dictator* (NYT "superb", "displays his true genius"; TT "incomparable"). Chaplin was overlooked for the Best Director award, even though the film, his first full talkie, was a Best Picture nominee.

The fifth nominee was Raymond Massey who was recognized for his portrayal of President Abraham Lincoln in *Abe Lincoln in Illinois* (S&S "uncanny ... a really miraculous job").

The nomination of Stewart possibly contributed to the exclusion of the leading actor in *The Philadelphia Story*, Cary Grant, who had also starred in *His Girl Friday* (NYT "splendid, except when he is being consciously cute") and had received a mixed critical response for his turn in the historical drama *The Howards of Virginia* (NYT "major disappointment"; V "a robust, convincing performance"). The most surprising oversight, however, was Edward G. Robinson's acclaimed performance in *Dr Erlich's Magic Bullet* as the 19th Century German scientist (V "one of the most distinguished performances in the star's lengthy career").

Also left out of consideration were: Francis Lederer as a German-American drawn to Nazism during a visit to Germany in *The Man I Married* (NYT "excellent"); Brian Donlevy in the comedy *The Great McGinty* (NYT "masterful"; V "excellent"); previous Best Actor Oscar winner Spencer Tracy in *Northwest Passage* (V "brilliantly impressive"); Brian Aherne in *My Son, My Son* (V "impressively outstanding"); and Charles Boyer as a French aristocrat in *All This, and Heaven Too* (V "one of his best performances"; TT "subtle"). The acclaimed performance of Walter Brennan in *The Westerner* was included in the supporting category.

The performance of Anton Walbrook was ineligible for a nomination for his acclaimed performance in the British thriller *Gaslight* as the film was not released in the USA until 1952, eight years after the Hollywood remake had garnered seven Oscar nominations, including a nomination for Charles Boyer in the role Walbrook had played in the British version.

Stewart was the only nominee to attend the Oscar banquet, although he said he was not confident as even he had voted for Fonda. When Alfred Lunt opened the envelope to reveal the evening's final winner, however, it was Stewart's name inside. "I want to assure you that this is a very, very important moment in my life" he told the audience.

Stewart would receive a further three Best Actor Oscar nominations over the following twenty years, but never won a second award. Fonda would see his daughter win two Best Actress Oscars before he finally won a statuette with his second nomination in 1981, forty-one years after he had first made the Academy's lists.

1940

BEST ACTRESS

ACADEMY AWARDS
Bette Davis as 'Leslie Crosbie' in *The Letter*
Joan Fontaine as 'Mrs de Winter' in *Rebecca*
Katharine Hepburn as 'Tracy Lord' in *The Philadelphia Story*
• **Ginger Rogers as 'Kitty Foyle' in *Kitty Foyle***
Martha Scott as 'Emily Webb' in *Our Town*

NEW YORK – Katharine Hepburn – *The Philadelphia Story*

Hoping to recreate the publicity he had enjoyed with the prolonged casting search for the role of 'Scarlett' in *Gone with the Wind*, producer David O. Selznick hyped the search of an actress to play the title role in *Rebecca*. Vivien Leigh, Loretta Young, Margaret Sullavan, Anne Baxter and Olivia de Havilland were all considered but in the end the part went to de Havilland's younger sister, Joan Fontaine. Variety said her performance as Daphne du Maurier's frightened heroine was "excellent" and she was considered a strong chance for the Best Actress Oscar with her first nomination.

The other Oscar favourite was previous winner Katharine Hepburn in her comeback from being labelled by critics in 1938 as 'box office poison'. She had won her only New York Film Critics Circle Best Actress award for reprising her stage success as a spoiled socialite on the verge of a second marriage in the comedy *The Philadelphia Story* (NYT "brilliant").

The year after she narrowly missed out on a third Best Actress Oscar, Bette Davis earned a third consecutive nomination for playing the murderess in *The Letter*, the role for which Jeanne Eagels had been nominated in 1928/29. Davis was also lauded for her tragic governess in the Best Picture nominee *All This, and Heaven Too* (V "in none of her recent films has she approached her work in Heaven").

The other two candidates were both first-time nominees recognised for films directed by Sam Wood. Ginger Rogers, who had given up her successful dance career opposite Fred Astaire to concentrate on dramatic roles, was mentioned for her love-struck secretary in *Kitty Foyle* (V "a strong dramatic portrayal"). She had also been praised for her starring turn in *Primrose Path*. Martha Scott earned her (only) nomination for her screen debut in *Our Town* – a reprisal of her Broadway role as the daughter of a newspaper editor (NYT "vibrant"; V "a sincerely warm portrayal"). She had also won acclaim for *The Howards of Virginia* (NYT "excellent").

1940

It was the second year in a row that all five of the Best Actress nominees appeared in films that were nominated for the Best Picture Oscar.

The most surprising exclusion from the category was Rosalind Russell's acclaimed turn as a reporter in *His Girl Friday*. The New York Times wrote "If Rosalind Russell doesn't cop all votes for the best screen comedienne of this year, it certainly won't be her fault".

Also overlooked were: the previous year's winner Vivien Leigh for the remake of *Waterloo Bridge* (NYT "remarkable", "superb"; V "demonstrates outstanding ability", "strongly persuasive and sympathetic"; SMH "succeeds"); Greer Garson as Jane Austen's heroine Elizabeth Bennett in *Pride and Prejudice* (TT "outstandingly good"); Olivia de Havilland as a violinist in *My Love Came Back* (V "excellent"); Constance Bennett in *The Man I Married* (V "excellent"); and Margaret Sullavan for both *The Shop Around the Corner* (NYT "reminds us she still is one of our most piquant and delightful screen ladies"; V "outstanding characterization") and *The Mortal Storm* (V "excellent" SMH "remarkably sensitive").

Meanwhile, previous Best Actress nominee Diana Wynyard was ineligible for a nomination for her acclaimed performance in the British thriller *Gaslight* (TT "particularly good") as the film was not released in the USA until 1952, eight years after Ingrid Bergman had won an Oscar for the same role in a Hollywood remake.

On Oscar night, neither Fontaine nor Hepburn claimed the Best Actress Oscar. The surprise winner was Rogers, whose role had been turned down by Hepburn prior to her defection from RKO to M-G-M. Hepburn later told reporters, "Ginger was wonderful, she's enormously talented and she deserved the Oscar." The accolade secured Rogers a series of both drama and comedy roles in prestige films, but she never again made the Academy's lists.

1940

BEST SUPPORTING ACTOR

ACADEMY AWARDS
Albert Basserman as 'Van Meer' in *Foreign Correspondent*
• **Walter Brennan as 'Judge Roy Bean' in *The Westerner***
William Gargan as 'Joe' in *They Knew What They Wanted*
Jack Oakie as 'Napaloni, Dictator of Bacteria' in *The Great Dictator*
James Stephenson as 'Howard Joyce' in *The Letter*

In 1940 Jack Oakie impressed critics and audiences with two comic performances: in *Tin Pan Alley* (NYT "steals the show"; V "a standout"); and as a dictator, based on Mussolini, in Charlie Chaplin's *The Great Dictator* (NYT "hilarious", "splendid"). The latter earned him a nomination from the Academy and he became one of the strong favourites for the Oscar. The other favoured nominee was James Stephenson as a disillusioned district attorney in *The Letter* (NYT "superb"; TT "impressive").

In a shock result, however, the winner was Walter Brennan in *The Westerner* (NYT "excellent ... one of the finest exhibits of acting seen on the screen in some time"; V "commands major attention"; TT "entertaining"). He was the first person to win a third Oscar for acting (all as Best Supporting Actor and all within five years). Brennan's performance should arguably have been considered for Best Actor and so many in the Academy and the press were not pleased with his win (the NYT called him the film's "leading player"). His victory was attributed to the influence of the thousands of extras who were eligible to vote at the time – Brennan had begun his career as an extra.

Ironically Brennan had been praised for a supporting performance in *Northwest Passage* (V "typically fine characterization") but had been overlooked. Also passed over were: Eduardo Ciannelli as a waiter in *Kitty Foyle*; Robert Young in *The Mortal Storm* (SMH "remarkably sensitive"); Frank Morgan in both *The Mortal Storm* (NYT "superior") and *The Shop Around the Corner*; Lloyd Nolan as a journalist in *The Man I Married* (NYT "believable"); Akim Tamiroff in *The Great McGinty* (NYT "surprisingly restrained and incisive"); Cedric Hardwicke in *The Howards of Virginia* (NYT "superb"); John Carradine in *The Grapes of Wrath* (V "excellent"); Otto Kruger in *Dr Erlich's Magic Bullet* (V "excellent"); Louis Hayward in *My Son, My Son* (V "a highlight"); Walter Hampden in *All This, and Heaven Too* (V "a standout"); Conrad Veidt in *The Thief of Bagdad*; and Frank Fay in *They Knew What They Wanted*.

BEST SUPPORTING ACTRESS

ACADEMY AWARDS

Judith Anderson as 'Mrs Danvers' in *Rebecca*
• **Jane Darwell as 'Ma Joad' in *The Grapes of Wrath***
Ruth Hussey as 'Elizabeth Imbrie' in *The Philadelphia Story*
Barbara O'Neil as 'Duchesse de Praslin' in *All This, and Heaven Too*
Marjorie Rambeau as 'Mamie Adams' in *Primrose Path*

Sixty-one year old Jane Darwell was the overwhelming favourite for the Best Supporting Actress Academy Award for her performance as the tough mother of a family displaced by the Depression in *The Grapes of Wrath* (NYT "flawless"). When she collected her Oscar she famously remarked "Awards are nice, but I'd much rather have a job!" Apparently, she had not worked since the film had wrapped seven months earlier. Following her win, she worked consistently for another twenty years.

Also nominated for the Oscar were: Australian-born Judith Anderson for her turn as the nasty housekeeper in *Rebecca* (NYT "splendid"); Ruth Hussey for playing the magazine photographer in *The Philadelphia Story*; Barbara O'Neil as the obsessively jealous duchess in *All This, and Heaven Too* (NYT "considerably overplays the part"); and Marjorie Rambeau as a prostitute in *Primrose Path* (V "impresses").

Rambeau's eight-year old co-star Joan Carroll was overlooked (NYT "amazing"; V "splendid portrayal") as were several actresses for performances in Best Picture nominees. Previous Best Supporting Actress Oscar winner, Gale Sondergaard, was the most surprising omission for her turn as the Eurasian wife of the murdered lover in *The Letter*, while Paulette Goddard was overlooked for *The Great Dictator* (NYT "excellent") and both previous winner Fay Bainter and Beulah Bondi were passed over for *Our Town* (V both "excellent").

Also left out of consideration were: Ruth Gordon in *Abe Lincoln in Illinois*; Ida Lupino in *They Drive By Night* (NYT "Miss Lupino goes crazy about as well as it can be done"); Anna Sten as a young Nazi woman in *The Man I Married* (NYT "natural"; V a "highlight"); Alla Nazimova in *Escape*; May Whitty in *A Bill of Divorcement* (V "commands attention"); Virginia Field in *Waterloo Bridge* (V "excellent"); both Mary Boland (V "good") and Edna May Oliver in *Pride and Prejudice*; and Helen Westley for a very brief role as the grandmother in *Lillian Russell* (SMH "outstanding").

1941

BEST PICTURE

Hoping to turn around its fortunes, the struggling studio RKO financed the directorial debut of Orson Welles, the young man whose radio version of H. G. Wells' science-fiction classic 'The War of the Worlds' had been a national sensation a few years earlier. Welles developed a film called *Citizen Kane* about a media mogul (inspired by the newspaper magnate William Randolph Hearst). The film was a massive success with critics. The New York Times enthused that it was "far and away the most surprising and cinematically exciting motion picture to be seen here in many a moon ... it comes close to being the most sensational film ever made in Hollywood", while Variety called it "a triumph." In Britain, S&S said it was "wicked, exhausting, satirical, clever" and labelled it "the best American film of 1941" while The Times described it as "brilliant" and "a film entitled to rank as a work of art." In Australia, The Sydney Morning Herald considered it "outstanding" and "a masterpiece."

At the end of the year both the NBR and the New York critics selected *Citizen Kane* as the year's Best Picture. But while critics raved, the powerful Hearst was not impressed. When RKO rejected his offer to buy and destroy all prints of the film, he used his considerable media influence to limit the film's box office distribution, cripple its commercial success and, eventually, undermine its chances of Oscar glory. The Academy nominated the film for nine awards, including mentioning Welles himself a record four times (as producer, director, actor and writer). In the end, however, perhaps fearful of Hearst's influence, the Academy backed away from giving *Citizen Kane* their top award.

With the critics' choice effectively side-lined, the contest for the Best Picture Academy Award was between *Sergeant York*, the year's biggest box office hit and most Oscar nominated film, and *How Green Was My Valley*, the latest film from John Ford. These two films had been the runners-up for the New York critics' prize (in fact *Sergeant York* had led on the first ballot). Howard Hawks' *Sergeant York* was a patriotic drama about a World War One hero played by Gary Cooper (NYT "a simple and dignified screen biography"; V "moving", "thrilling", "film biography at its best") while Ford's *How Green Was My Valley* was a sentimental drama about a struggling family in a small Welsh mining town at the turn of the century (NYT "a motion picture of great poetic charm and dignity", "outstanding", "stunning masterpiece"; V "one of the year's better films"; S&S "dull").

Many of the year's other most lauded films were also nominated including: *Suspicion*, Alfred Hitchcock's follow-up to the 1940 Best Picture winner *Rebecca* (NYT "a psychological thriller which is packed with lively suspense"; V "suspenseful drama", "vivid", "excellent"; TT "absorbing"); the film noir mystery thriller *The Maltese Falcon* (NYT "the best mystery thriller of the year"; V "intriguing and entertaining", "outstanding"; TT "sets a new and exciting standard"; S&S "the most interesting film of the season"); the melodrama *The Little Foxes*, an adaptation of the hit Broadway play by Lillian Hellman (NYT "the most bitingly sinister picture of the year", "spectacular", "extraordinarily vivid and compelling"; V "among the best vehicles to come out of Hollywood in recent years"; TT "delicately perceptive study"); *One Foot in Heaven* (NYT "one of the funniest pictures of the year … cheerful and warmly compassionate"; V "excellent"); and the comedy *Here Comes Mr Jordan* (NYer "one of the brightest comedies of the year"; NYT "one of the choicest comic fantasies of the year … rollicking entertainment").

The surprise nominees were the sentimental *Blossoms in the Dust*, which was the only colour film on the Best Picture short-list that year (NYT "a shade too much shining nobility in this film") and the romantic melodrama *Hold Back the Dawn* (NYT "an amazingly poignant picture, rich in humor, heart and subtle ironies").

The most unexpected omissions from the Academy's list were Frank Capra's *Meet John Doe* (NYT "superlative") and the Preston Sturges comedy *The Lady*

Eve (NYT "the most exquisite comedy of the year"; V "entertainment of top proportions"; SMH "hilarious").

Also overlooked were: the popular drama *The Great Lie* (V "a sophisticated drama"; SMH "substantial, emotional"); the comedy *Ball of Fire* (NYT "excellent"; SMH "grand comedy"); the British historical romance *That Hamilton Woman*; and Disney's animated family film *Dumbo*, which was named by the NYT as one of the year's ten best (NYT "a picture which touches the very heart of sentiment").

The Academy also ignored two highly-anticipated prestige studio films that had failed to impress critics: the M-G-M remake of *Dr Jekyll and Mr Hyde* starring Spencer Tracy and Ingrid Bergman (NYT "preposterous mixture of hokum and high-flown psychological balderdash"; S&S "weary remake") and Greta Garbo's final film, the comedy *Two-Faced Woman* (NYT "dull and overlong", "one of the more costly disappointments of the year").

Many observers felt that a tide of wartime patriotism would carry *Sergeant York* to a Best Picture win. However, Variety predicted that it would be narrowly outpolled by Ford's family drama. A year after failing to reward Ford's lauded picture *The Grapes of Wrath*, the Academy named *How Green Was My Valley* as the year's Best Picture.

The widely-acclaimed *Citizen Kane* was presented with only one statuette. Orson Welles and his co-writer Herman J. Mankiewicz received the Oscar for Best Screenplay.

1941

BEST DIRECTOR

ACADEMY AWARDS
• **John Ford for *How Green Was My Valley***
Alexander Hall for *Here Comes Mr Jordan*
Howard Hawks for *Sergeant York*
Orson Welles for *Citizen Kane*
William Wyler for *The Little Foxes*

NEW YORK – John Ford – *How Green Was My Valley*

For the fourth time in seven years and for the third year in a row, the New York critics named John Ford as the year's Best Director. Ford's well-reviewed handling of the family drama *How Green Was My Valley* (V "skillful") narrowly outpolled Orson Welles' acclaimed direction of *Citizen Kane* (NYT "excellent direction ... Welles has put upon the screen a motion picture that really moves ... [he has] grabbed the medium by the ears and began to toss it around with the dexterity of a seasoned veteran"; TT "masterly", "rare distinction"). For his directorial debut, Welles earned his first (and only) Best Director Oscar nomination (along with mentions for Best Picture, Actor and Screenplay). Ford was included on the Academy's list of nominees for the fourth time. Variety predicted that these two men would be the main contenders for the Oscar.

Also nominated were: Alexander Hall for the comedy *Here Comes Mr Jordan* (NYT has "the rare sense to keep the comedy where it belongs – in the characters and situations rather than in a series of double exposures"); William Wyler for *The Little Foxes* (his third consecutive nomination); and Howard Hawks for the year's most nominated film *Sergeant York*. Hawks had also handled the comedy *Ball of Fire* (NYT "Hawks has kept the whole thing moving at an accelerated pace for nigh two hours").

The most surprising exclusions from the category were Alfred Hitchcock for the thriller *Suspicion* (NYT deserves "unstinted praise") and John Huston, son of one that year's Best Actor nominees Walter Huston, for his directorial debut *The Maltese Falcon* (NYT "Huston gives promise of becoming one of the smartest directors in the field ... he has worked out his own style, which is brisk and supremely hardboiled"). Both films were Best Picture nominees, as were *Hold Back the Dawn* and *One Foot in Heaven*, whose respective directors Mitchell Leisen (S&S "superbly directed") and Irving Rapper (NYT "superb" direction) were also overlooked.

The Academy also passed over: previous Oscar winner Frank Capra for *Meet John Doe* (HSp "masterly direction"); Edmund Goulding for *The Great Lie*

(NYT "the direction of Edmund Goulding makes for class, but the story is such a trifle that it hardly seems worth the while"; S&S "directed in a masterly way"); William Dieterle for *All That Money Can Buy* (HRp "a masterly realization of a difficult and different theme"); and, for the second year in a row, Preston Sturges for the popular and critically acclaimed battle-of-the-sexes screwball comedy *The Lady Eve* (NYT "Sturges is indisputably established as one of the top one or two writers and directors of comedy working in Hollywood today"; HSp "brilliantly directed"; TT "directed with unfaltering expertness").

On Oscar night, the undermining of *Citizen Kane* by the powerful media magnate William Randolph Hearst effectively shut Welles out of serious contention (although he was presented with the statuette for Best Screenplay – the only Oscar he ever won). *How Green Was My Valley* won the Best Picture Oscar and earned Ford his third Best Director Academy Award, equalling the record set by Frank Capra in 1938. Ford's victory made him the first person to win consecutive Oscars for direction.

Eleven years later, Ford would become the first (and only) person in Oscar history to claim a fourth award as Best Director, for his handling of *The Quiet Man*.

BEST ACTOR

ACADEMY AWARDS
• **Gary Cooper as 'Alvin C. York' in *Sergeant York***
Cary Grant as 'Roger Adams' in *Penny Serenade*
Walter Huston as 'Mr Scratch' in *All That Money Can Buy*
Robert Montgomery as 'Joe Pendleton' in *Here Comes Mr Jordan*
Orson Welles as 'Charles Foster Kane' in *Citizen Kane*

NEW YORK – Gary Cooper – *Sergeant York*

Five years after finishing as runner-up to Paul Muni for the Best Actor Academy Award for his performance in Frank Capra's *Mr Deeds Goes to Town*, Gary Cooper earned plaudits from film reviewers for playing another average American guy in one of Capra's films, *Meet John Doe* (NYT "excellent"; HSp "superb"; TT "skillful"). He and his co-star Barbara Stanwyck received further praise when they reteamed later in the year in Howard Hawks' hit comedy *Ball of Fire* (TT "delightful"). Cooper's most acclaimed performance of the year, however, was as a World War One hero in Hawks' patriotic drama *Sergeant York* (NYT "holds the picture together magnificently, and even the most unfavourable touches are made palatable because of him"; V "convincing"; TT "natural"). The film was the year's biggest box office success and received more Oscar nominations than any other film that year, including a second Best Actor nod for Cooper who was strongly favoured to win, having already convincingly collected the New York critics' prize (he won on the first ballot).

Nominated alongside Cooper were Walter Huston, who received his second Best Actor Oscar nomination for portraying the Devil in *All That Money Can Buy* (NYT "excellent"; HRp "a grand job") even though he had limited screen time, and the three actors who had finished as runners-up to Cooper on the New York critics' ballot: Orson Welles, Cary Grant and Robert Montgomery. Also the runner-up for the New York Best Director prize, Welles received his (only) Oscar nomination for acting for his portrayal of a media magnate (inspired by William Randolph Hearst) in *Citizen Kane*. Grant, overlooked the previous year for *The Philadelphia Story*, was included for his performance in the melodrama *Penny Serenade*, although he had received more praise for his turn in Alfred Hitchcock's *Suspicion* opposite Best Actress winner Joan Fontaine (V "a sparkling characterization"; TT a "triumph"). Finally, having been previously nominated for playing a psychopathic serial killer (in *Night Must Fall* in 1937) Montgomery made the list a second (and final) time for portraying a boxer who dies before his time and returns to Earth in a different body in the comedy *Here*

Comes Mr Jordan (NYT "tops … keeps his place secure as one of the screen's deftest comedians"; V "excellent", "a highlight"). When the film was remade in 1978 as *Heaven Can Wait*, Warren Beatty recreated Montgomery's role and also earned a Best Actor Oscar nomination.

Previous winner Spencer Tracy was overlooked both for reprising his second Oscar-winning role as Father Flanagan in the sequel *The Men of Boys' Town* (NYT "excellent") and for taking on Fredric March's Oscar-winning role in the remake of *Dr Jekyll and Mr Hyde*, a performance that had divided critics (NYT "Tracy's portrait is not so much evil incarnate as it is the ham rampant … he is more ludicrous than dreadful … an affront to good taste rather than a serious, and thereby acceptable, study in sadism"; S&S "embarrassing"; TT "highly accomplished acting"). March himself was passed over for his performance as a Methodist minister in the Best Picture nominee *One Foot in Heaven* (NYT "truly excellent"; V "splendid") while the comic turn in *The Lady Eve* of the previous year's Best Actor favourite, Henry Fonda, also went unrecognised (NYT "excellent").

Also passed over were: 1940 Supporting Actor nominee James Stephenson's portrayal of a doctor in *Shining Victory* (NYT "truly superior performance"; V "excellent"); John Garfield as a vicious gangster in *Out of the Fog* (NYT "most convincing"); James Cagney in *Strawberry Blonde* (NYT "excellent"); Charles Boyer in *Back Street* (V "a deft and restrained portrayal"); Harry Baur for the 1938 French film *Mollenard (Hatred)* (NYT "excellent"; V "brilliant"); Tyrone Power in *Blood and Sand* (V "delivers a persuasive performance"); and Walter Pidgeon as the young minister in the Best Picture Oscar winner *How Green Was My Valley* (V "excellent").

The most surprising omission of the year, however, was Humphrey Bogart who gave acclaimed performances in both *High Sierra* (NYT "perfect"; V "fine") and as detective Sam Spade in the Best Picture nominee *The Maltese Falcon* (V "standout performance" and "an attention-arresting portrayal").

On Oscar night, Cooper was rewarded with his first Best Actor Oscar. His win made him the first man to collect prizes from the New York critics' circle and the Academy for the same performance.

1941

BEST ACTRESS

ACADEMY AWARDS
Bette Davis as 'Regina Giddens' in *The Little Foxes*
Olivia de Havilland as 'Emmy Brown' in *Hold Back the Dawn*
• **Joan Fontaine as 'Lina McLaidlaw' in *Suspicion***
Greer Garson as 'Edna Gladney' in *Blossoms in the Dust*
Barbara Stanwyck as 'Sugarpuss O'Shea' in *Ball of Fire*

NEW YORK – Joan Fontaine – *Suspicion*

The year after she had been unexpectedly outpolled for the Best Actress Academy Award for her role in the Best Picture Oscar winner, *Rebecca*, Joan Fontaine received critical acclaim for her performance as a young woman convinced that her husband is planning to murder her, in another thriller directed by Alfred Hitchcock: *Suspicion* (NYT deserves "unstinted praise", "compelling"; V "equals her highly-rating performance in *Rebecca*"; TT "acts with tact and understanding ... in a difficult part"). The New York critics named her as the year's Best Actress on the fifth ballot and for the second year in a row she was the favourite for the Oscar.

The other main contender for the Academy Award was Fontaine's older sister, Olivia de Havilland, a previous Supporting Actress Oscar nominee in 1939 for *Gone with the Wind*. De Havilland was the runner-up to Fontaine for the New York prize for her portrayal of a schoolteacher in love with a gigolo in the Best Picture nominee *Hold Back the Dawn* (NYT "excellent"; V "one of her finest jobs"; TT "plays with delightful simplicity"; S&S "quite unforgettable", "superb"). It was the first time that siblings had been nominated alongside one another and the press was fascinated by the rivalry between the sisters, who admitted that they had never been close.

Placed third behind the sisters in New York was Greta Garbo whose comic performance in her final film *Two-Faced Woman* had divided critics (NYT she "misses the satire"; V "a triumph"; TT "astonishing"). The Academy did not include the great Swedish star on its list of nominees. The Academy also overlooked Joan Crawford whose portrayal in *A Woman's Face* had similarly divided critics (NYT "seemed to lack the ability to project more than the superficial hardness of the character"; V "strongly dramatic and sympathetic"; S&S "extraordinary ... brilliantly depicted", "an amazing performance").

Also passed over for Oscar consideration were: Constance Bennett for almost upstaging Garbo in *The Two-Faced Woman* (V "tremendous"); Ida Lupino in *High Sierra* (NYT "impressive"; V "excellent"); previous winner Vivien Leigh in *That Hamilton Woman* (NYT "delightful to behold"; SMH "does some of her best work"); Margaret Sullavan in *Back Street* (V "strong and sympathetic"); Geraldine Fitzgerald in *Shining Victory* (V "excellent"); Gabrielle Dorziat in *Mollenard (Hatred)* (NYT & V "excellent"); Martha Scott in the Best Picture nominee *One Foot in Heaven* (NYT "magnificent"; V "splendid"); and Irene Dunne in *Penny Serenade*.

The Academy's short-list was also missing Mary Astor's lauded performance as a femme fatale in the Best Picture nominee *The Maltese Falcon* (NYT "well-nigh perfect"; V "skillfully etches the role of an adventuress"), although Astor was included in the Best Supporting Actress category for her work in *The Great Lie*.

Bette Davis earned praise for her work opposite Astor in *The Great Lie* (V "most persuasive"; SMH "splendid"), but it was for playing a scheming Southern belle in *The Little Foxes* (V "well-nigh flawless"; TT "succeeds") that she received her fifth (and record fourth consecutive) Best Actress nomination, just weeks after resigning from her brief term as Academy President following a major disagreement with the Board of Governors. It was the second time in three years that she had been nominated for a role originally performed on stage by Tallulah Bankhead.

Also nominated were Greer Garson (her second Best Actress nomination in three years) as the woman who runs a Texan orphanage in *Blossoms in the Dust* and Barbara Stanwyck who made the Academy's list for the second time for playing a burlesque dancer in Howard Hawks' comedy *Ball of Fire* (TT "expert"; SMH "natural", "fine"), a role turned down by the previous year's Best Actress winner Ginger Rogers. Stanwyck also earned praise from critics for starring in *Meet John Doe* (NYT & V "excellent"; HSp "superb") and *The Lady Eve* (NYT & V "excellent"; TT "amusingly right"; S&S "brilliant"; SMH "splendid").

Davis, Garson and Stanwyck, however, were all completely overshadowed by the two sisters. On Oscar night, just a year after she had first been favoured to win, 23-year old Fontaine was awarded the Best Actress Oscar and the feud between the sisters escalated as a result. They never resolved their differences, even though de Havilland herself won two statuettes within the decade.

Fontaine was the only person to win an Academy Award for a performance in a Hitchcock film.

BEST SUPPORTING ACTOR

ACADEMY AWARDS
Walter Brennan as 'Pastor Rosier Pile' in *Sergeant York*
Charles Coburn as 'John P. Merrick' in *The Devil and Miss Jones*
• **Donald Crisp as 'Mr Morgan' in *How Green Was My Valley***
James Gleason as 'Max Corkle' in *Here Comes Mr Jordan*
Sydney Greenstreet as 'Casper Gutman' in *The Maltese Falcon*

A year after unexpectedly collecting his third Best Supporting Actor Oscar, Walter Brennan was nominated for the award for the fourth (and final) time for his performance as a village pastor in the year's most Oscar nominated film, *Sergeant York* (NYT & TT "perfect"; V "splendid"). With the film favoured to win Best Picture, a fourth Oscar for Brennan seemed distinctly possible.

Brennan was nominated alongside four actors recognised by the Academy for the first time: Charles Coburn for his lead role as a millionaire pretending to be a salesman in *The Devil and Miss Jones* (V "stands out in a fine characterization"; SMH "delightful acting"); James Gleason as a boxing manager in *Here Comes Mr Jordan* (NYT "steals the film"; V a "standout"); 62-year old Sydney Greenstreet for his screen debut as an underworld figure in *The Maltese Falcon* (NYT "magnificent"; S&S "very fine performance"); and Donald Crisp as the stern father of a struggling Welsh mining family in *How Green Was My Valley* (S&S "tender and moving"; V "inspired").

Although Variety predicted a win for Gleason calling him "a cinch for best performance by a supporting actor", the Oscar went to industry veteran Donald Crisp for his turn in the year's Best Picture winner. Born in Scotland, the 60-year old Crisp had been making films in Hollywood for over three decades and told the audience at the Biltmore Hotel that "other old-timers should be given a chance and they, too, could win awards."

Despite a strong supporting performance as the title character's father in *National Velvet* a few years later and as the ruthless cattle baron in *The Man from Laramie*, Crisp never received a second nomination from the Academy.

Crisp's young co-star in *How Green Was My Valley*, Roddy McDowall, was one of those overlooked for the award (NYT "superb") as was Gleason's *Here Comes Mr Jordan* co-star Claude Rains (V a "standout") and Greenstreet's *The Maltese Falcon* co-star Peter Lorre. Also passed over were: Nigel Bruce for *Suspicion* (V "outstanding"); James Craig as a farmer in *All That Money Can Buy* (HRp "perfect"); Hay Petrie in the British film *Spellbound* (V "splendid"); and Marc Lawrence as a mute simpleton in *The Shepherd of the Hills* (V "one of the most outstanding support performances seen for months").

1941

BEST SUPPORTING ACTRESS

ACADEMY AWARDS
Sara Allgood as 'Mrs Morgan' in *How Green Was My Valley*
• **Mary Astor as 'Sandra Kovak' in *The Great Lie***
Patricia Collinge as 'Birdie Hubbard' in *The Little Foxes*
Teresa Wright as 'Alexandra Giddons' in *The Little Foxes*
Margaret Wycherly as 'Mother York' in *Sergeant York*

Mary Astor was the favourite to win the Oscar for her performance as a selfish concert pianist who allows a romantic rival (played by Bette Davis) to raise her child in *The Great Lie*, a role turned down by Geraldine Fitzgerald (S&S "outstanding"; V "scores notably"; TT "perfect"; SMH "splendidly acted", "brilliant").

Nominated for their roles in another Bette Davis vehicle, *The Little Foxes*, were Patricia Collinge (NYT "repeats her excellent stage performance"; V "stand-out", "memorable") and Teresa Wright (V "magnificent in a very difficult part"; TT "accomplished, understanding performance"). They made their respective screen debuts as the alcoholic aunt and the repressed daughter.

Variety tipped Astor to win, but it considered her main competition to be Sara Allgood and Margaret Wycherly who each received their only nominations for playing devoted mothers in the year's two main Best Picture contenders. Allgood was recognised as the mother of an impoverished Welsh mining family in *How Green Was My Valley* (NYT "excellent"; V "inspired"). Wycherley made the list as the Tennessee mother of a war hero in *Sergeant York* (S&S "unforgettable"; V a "standout").

The most surprising omission from the category was Dorothy Comingore as the suffering wife in *Citizen Kane* (SMH "outstanding"). She polled fourth in the vote for the New York Film Critics Circle Best Actress prize.

Also overlooked were: Ingrid Bergman in *Dr Jekyll and Mr Hyde* (TT "perfect"); Isobel Elsom in *Ladies in Retirement*; Peggy Ashcroft as the zany fiancée in *Quiet Wedding* (V "stands out"); and both Rita Hayworth (V "excellent") and Alla Nazimova (V "a corking performance") in *Blood and Sand*.

On Oscar night, Variety proved accurate. Astor, who had also been praised for her leading performance in *The Maltese Falcon*, was named Best Supporting Actress. She thanked two people in her speech: the composer Tchaikovsky and her co-star Bette Davis.

1942

BEST PICTURE

ACADEMY AWARDS

The Forty-Ninth Parallel (The Invaders)
(Ortus, Columbia, 104 mins BW, 15 Apr 1942, 3 noms)
Kings Row
(Warner Bros., 127 mins BW, 2 Feb 1942, 3 noms)
The Magnificent Ambersons
(Mercury, RKO Radio, 88 mins BW, 10 Jul 1942, $1.0m, 4 noms)
• *Mrs Miniver*
(M-G-M, 134 mins BW, 22 Jul 1942, $6.0m, 12 noms)
The Pied Piper
(20th Century Fox, 87 mins BW, 12 Aug 1942, 3 noms)
The Pride of the Yankees
(Goldwyn, RKO Radio, 127 mins BW, 14 Jul 1942, 11 noms)
Random Harvest
(M-G-M, 125 mins BW, 17 Dec 1942, $4.6m, 7 noms)
The Talk of the Town
(Columbia, 118 mins BW, 27 Aug 1942, 7 noms)
Wake Island
(Paramount, 87 mins BW, 11 Aug 1942, $3.5m, 4 noms)
Yankee Doodle Dandy
(Warner Bros., 126 mins BW, 6 Jun 1942, $4.7m, 8 noms)

NEW YORK – *In Which We Serve*
BOARD OF REVIEW – *In Which We Serve*

The New York Times called the British war drama *In Which We Serve* "one of the most stirring and poignant films ever made." S&S said it was "brilliant" and "the best war film so far made" while The Sydney Morning Herald described it as "one of the screen's great masterpieces." At the end of the year the New York critics and the NBR both selected *In Which We Serve* as Best Picture. It was the third year in a row that the groups had agreed and the first time a British film had been so honoured by either group. The film's Oscars chances, however, were dashed when the Academy changed its qualifying deadline from January 14 to December 31. Although already released in New York City, the film was unable to secure a qualifying run in Los Angeles in time to meet the new deadline. Consequently, it was ineligible for Oscar consideration. At the annual ceremony, the Academy presented a special certificate of achievement to Noel Coward "for his outstanding production achievement in *In Which We Serve*". Coward was the film's writer, star and co-director (along with David Lean). Twelve months later,

1942

In Which We Serve was a nominee for the 1943 Academy Award for Best Picture.

The main contenders for the 1942 Best Picture Oscar were the year's highest and third-highest box office earners: the war drama *Mrs Miniver* and the musical biography *Yankee Doodle Dandy*. Both impressed critics, audiences and Academy voters.

Mrs Miniver, a dramatisation of the impact of the war on an English family, was the year's most Oscar nominated film, the first to ever be nominated for Best Picture, Director, Actor, Actress, Supporting Actor, Supporting Actress and Screenplay. It was also the first film to garner five mentions in the acting categories. In The New York Times, Bosley Crowther called it "deeply affecting" and "the finest film yet made about the present war". He praised the "superb understatement and restraint exercised throughout" and concluded "the pulse of real humanity beats strong throughout the film". Other publications were equally enthusiastic. Variety said it was "superb" while the HSp ranked it "high on the list of the greatest achievements of the screen". In Australia, The Sydney Morning Herald called it "stirring" and "high-grade entertainment".

Also acclaimed and almost as commercially successful was *Yankee Doodle Dandy* which starred James Cagney as the patriotic vaudeville showman George M. Cohan. The New York Times declared it to be "as warm and delightful a musical picture as has hit the screen in years, a corking good entertainment and as affectionate, if not as accurate, a film biography as has ever – yes, ever – been made". The paper went on to label the film "sparkling" while Variety said it was "something to cheer about from any perspective" and "as American as the Liberty Bell". The HSp said it was "delightful".

Although *In Which We Serve* was absent from the Academy's list, another acclaimed British war film, *The Forty-Ninth Parallel (The Invaders)* was nominated (NYT "excellent", "absorbing and exciting"). Also mentioned among the contenders were the baseball biopic *The Pride of the Yankees* (NYT "a simple, tender, meticulous and explicitly narrative film"; V "stirring"), the New York Best Picture accolade runner-up *Wake Island* (NYT "vivid and honest"; S&S "the best Hollywood war film thus far"; V "magnificent") and the comedy *The Talk of the Town* (NYT "a lot of fun … is going to make a lot of people laugh and feel good").

The unexpected nominees of the year were *Kings Row* starring Ronald Reagan (NYT "gloomy and ponderous"), the Greer Garson vehicle *Random Harvest* (NYT "a strangely empty film") and *The Magnificent Ambersons*, Orson Welles' follow-up to *Citizen Kane* which had been a box office flop after the studio had seized control of the production, ordered scenes to be reshot and significantly re-edited the print. Although the version released was far from Welles' original vision, The New York Times called it a "magnificently executed" but "relentlessly sombre" film while Sight & Sound magazine declared it to be "the best American film of 1942".

Surprisingly these films were selected ahead of the popular battle-of-the-sexes comedy *Woman of the Year* (NYT "triumphant", "a cheering, delightful combination of tongue-tip wit and smooth romance, a picture of surface brilliance designed unreservedly 'pour le sport' but with enough of a homely little moral to make it quite comforting in these times"; V & TT "entertaining"; S&S "dull") and the hit romantic drama *Now, Voyager* (V "excellent").

Also overlooked were: Preston Sturges' *Sullivan's Travels* (NYT "a beautifully trenchant satire"; V "curious but effective"; S&S "grand"); the British war film *One of Our Aircraft is Missing* (NYT "finely drawn melodrama"; V "splendid"; SMH "brilliant", "astonishingly effective"); and the Disney animated film *Bambi* (NYT "is going to please a great many people"; V "Disney's biggest achievement").

Although the Ernst Lubitsch film *To Be or Not To Be* is now considered a classic, at the time of its release critics didn't quite know what to make of its blend of satire and war-time theme (NYT "jangled moods and baffling humors … too bad a little more taste and a little more unity of mood were not put in this film"; V "absorbing"). The Academy by-passed *To Be or Not To Be* for the Best Picture short-list.

On Oscar night *Mrs Miniver*, which had not received a single vote from any of the New York critics' circle as Best Picture of the year, won the Academy's top award.

1942

BEST DIRECTOR

ACADEMY AWARDS
Michael Curtiz for *Yankee Doodle Dandy*
John Farrow for *Wake Island*
Mervyn LeRoy for *Random Harvest*
Sam Wood for *Kings Row*
• **William Wyler for *Mrs Miniver***

NEW YORK – John Farrow – *Wake Island*

Having given their Best Picture prize to *In Which We Serve* ahead of *Wake Island*, the New York critics reversed the order when voting for Best Director, honouring Australian-born John Farrow ahead of the combined talents of Noel Coward and David Lean. While Farrow was subsequently nominated by the Academy, Coward and Lean were shut-out when *In Which We Serve* was unable to secure a Los Angeles release in time for Oscar consideration. Although the film was nominated in the Best Picture category the following year, Coward and Lean were overlooked.

Despite the New York prize, Farrow was not the favourite for the Academy Award. Variety predicted that William Wyler would win for the box office hit and leading Oscar contender, *Mrs Miniver*. It was Wyler's fourth consecutive Best Director nomination – an unprecedented (and as yet unmatched) streak.

Also nominated were Michael Curtiz for *Yankee Doodle Dandy*, Mervyn LeRoy for *Random Harvest*, and Sam Wood who surprisingly received his second nomination for the melodrama *Kings Row* rather than for his acclaimed handling of the biography of baseball legend Lou Gehrig, *The Pride of the Yankees* (V "an admirable directorial job"; TT "intelligent").

Overlooked for the award was Michael Powell for both his solo direction of the Best Picture nominee *The Forty-Ninth Parallel (The Invaders)* and his collaboration with Emeric Pressburger on another British war drama, *One of Our Aircraft is Missing* (S&S "masterly" direction). Also by-passed were: Ernst Lubitsch for *To Be or Not To Be* (S&S "brilliant"); George Stevens for the acclaimed comedies *The Talk of the Town* and *Woman of the Year* (NYT "has been directed by George Stevens so smoothly"); Julien Duvivier for *Tales of Manhattan*; and, for the third year in a row, Preston Sturges for *Sullivan's Travels* (NYT "artful").

On Oscar night *Mrs Miniver* was honoured with seven Academy Awards, including the Best Director prize for Wyler.

1942

BEST ACTOR

ACADEMY AWARDS
• **James Cagney as 'George M. Cohan' in *Yankee Doodle Dandy***
Ronald Colman as 'Charles Rainier' in *Random Harvest*
Gary Cooper as 'Lou Gehrig' in *The Pride of the Yankees*
Walter Pidgeon as 'Clem Miniver' in *Mrs Miniver*
Monty Woolley as 'Howard' in *The Pied Piper*

NEW YORK – James Cagney – *Yankee Doodle Dandy*

In 1942 Warner Bros. campaigned strongly for young star Ronald Reagan to be recognised by the Academy, despite indifferent reviews, for his performance as a man crippled in an accident in the small town melodrama *Kings Row* (NYT makes "only casual acquaintance with the character"). The film earned a Best Picture nomination, but despite the studio's efforts the future U.S. President's name did not appear on the Academy's short-list.

More surprisingly, previous winner Spencer Tracy was also overlooked for his performance opposite Best Actress nominee Katharine Hepburn in *Woman of the Year* (NYT "played brilliantly … is at his top form as the rugged sports columnist"; V "superb"). Also passed over were: Robert Young in *Johnny Eager* (S&S "so unexpectedly well played"); Joel McCrea in Preston Sturges' *Sullivan's Travels* (NYT "acted with eminent artistry … is more of a human character than he has ever been in a film"; S&S "excellent"; SMH "most convincing"); Jack Benny in *To Be or Not To Be* (NYT "despite a successful endeavour to alter his style, still gives too much of a Jack Benny, the radio comedian, to be just right"); and Humphrey Bogart in *Across the Pacific* (V "particularly strong and convincing"). Bogart had been the runner-up for the New York critics' prize for his performances in both *Across the Pacific* and *Casablanca*. The latter film had been released in New York City in late 1942, but did not qualify for Oscar consideration until it opened in Los Angeles in early 1943. Bogart was nominated for the Best Actor Oscar for his performance in *Casablanca* in 1943.

Nominated ahead of these contenders were: the previous year's winner Gary Cooper for his lauded portrayal of the tragic baseball legend Lou Gehrig in *The Pride of the Yankees* (NYT "superb", "excellent"; TT "persuasive"); Ronald Colman who made the list for a third time for his performance as an amnesiac aristocrat in *Random Harvest* opposite Greer Garson (V "a fine performance"; TT "extremely well-acted"); Walter Pidgeon for the year's Best Picture Oscar winner *Mrs Miniver*, also opposite Garson (NYT "exceptional"); Monty

Woolley for playing an Englishman who helps children escape from the Nazis in *The Pied Piper* (NYT "brilliant"; V "a direct, skillful and reticent performance"; SMH "ideal"); and the popular President of the Screen Actors Guild, James Cagney for his impersonation of the patriotic vaudeville legend George M. Cohan in the hit musical *Yankee Doodle Dandy* (NYT "an unbelievably faithful characterization and a piece of playing that glows with energy", "excels both in characterization and jubilant song and dance", "magnificent"; V "a personal triumph", "his top cinematic performance"; TT "the best performance of his career"; HSp "magnificent").

Many historians contend that Woolley was more deserving of his Oscar nomination for reprising his stage triumph as the curmudgeonly theatre critic in *The Man Who Came To Dinner* (NYT "his zest for rascality is delightful, he spouts alliterations as though he were spitting out orange seeds ... a more entertaining buttinsky could hardly be conceived").

Four years earlier Cagney had earned a New York critics' award and an Oscar nomination for his turn as a gangster in Michael Curtiz's *Angels with Dirty Faces*, the kind of role with which he had been largely synonymous during the previous decade. In *Yankee Doodle Dandy*, again under the direction of Curtiz, he took on a radically different part – singing, dancing and displaying his flair for comedy and charm. He was cast in the role after it had been turned down by Fred Astaire.

For his performance, Cagney became the first man to win a second Best Actor prize from the New York critics. A few months later, he was also honoured with the golden statuette by the Academy.

1942

BEST ACTRESS

ACADEMY AWARDS
Bette Davis as 'Charlotte Vale' in *Now, Voyager*
• **Greer Garson as 'Kay Miniver' in *Mrs Miniver***
Katharine Hepburn as 'Tess Harding' in *Woman of the Year*
Rosalind Russell as 'Ruth Sherwood' in *My Sister Eileen*
Teresa Wright as 'Eleanor Gehrig' in *The Pride of the Yankees*

NEW YORK – Agnes Moorehead – *The Magnificent Ambersons*

A year after Dorothy Comingore polled fourth on the New York critics' Best Actress ballot for her supporting role in Orson Welles' *Citizen Kane*, Agnes Moorehead won the prize for her acclaimed supporting performance in Welles' follow-up *The Magnificent Ambersons*. The Academy, however, recognised Moorehead's portrayal with a Supporting Actress nomination, leaving the Best Actress Oscar contest open for the New York runner-up, Greer Garson in *Mrs Miniver*.

The role of Kay Miniver, a charming English wife and mother in an idealistic village who demonstrates courage and determination as the Second World War impacts on the life of her family, was originally offered to previous Best Actress Oscar winner Norma Shearer. She declined the role, deciding to retire from the screen. Irish-born actress Greer Garson was cast instead and she earned rapturous reviews and her third Best Actress nomination in just four years (NYT "glows with compassion and womanly strength", "exceptional"; HSp "superb", "flawless"). *Mrs Miniver* was the year's most commercially successful and most Oscar-nominated film.

Also a hit with audiences and Academy voters was Garson's other vehicle that year, the romantic melodrama *Random Harvest* for which she received further critical acclaim (TT "extremely well-acted"). It too was nominated for the Best Picture Oscar. Nominated in the Best Actor category were both of Garson's co-stars – Walter Pidgeon for *Mrs Miniver* and Ronald Colman for *Random Harvest*.

Another of Garson's *Mrs Miniver* co-stars, Teresa Wright, was also a Best Actress nominee. The year after she received a Best Supporting Actress nomination for her debut in *The Little Foxes*, Wright received a double nomination: Best Supporting Actress as the daughter-in-law in *Mrs Miniver* and Best Actress as the wife of baseball great Lou Gehrig in *The Pride of the Yankees* (NYT "superb … has a lovely, gracious quality"; V "extremely well-played"; TT "plays the part to perfection").

1942

Also receiving her first Best Actress nomination, having been surprisingly overlooked two years earlier for *His Girl Friday*, was Rosalind Russell. She made the short-list for her work in *My Sister Eileen* (NYT "plays the smart sister with a delightfully dour and cynical air"; S&S "on the top of her form"; TT "rather wasted upon her part"; SMH "a sheer joy").

Two previous Best Actress Oscar winners were also considered by the Academy. Katharine Hepburn was nominated for a fourth time for her performance as a newspaper reporter opposite Spencer Tracy in the battle-of-the-sexes comedy *Woman of the Year* (NYT "brilliant" and "perfect"; V "superb"; TT "admirable") while Bette Davis received a record fifth consecutive Best Actress nomination and equalled Shearer's record six Best Actress nominations for her role as a repressed spinster transformed into an elegant and confident woman in the romantic drama *Now, Voyager* (NYT "plays the young woman, high-lighting her progress to emotional maturity with the decision and accuracy of an assured actress"; V "one of her superlative acting roles"; TT "proves herself one of the finest actresses the screen has produced"). Davis had also starred in *In This Our Life* although her work had divided critics (NYT "too mannered"; V "dramatically impressive").

Critically lauded performances by two other previous winners, however, were overlooked for the prize. Ginger Rogers' performance as a woman masquerading as a young girl in the comedy *The Major and the Minor* (NYT "a beautiful imitation", "one of the best characterizations of her career") was passed over as was Joan Fontaine's performance in *This Above All* (V "glowing, tender and enormously beguiling").

Arguably the most surprising omission from the category was the performance of Carole Lombard in *To Be or Not To Be* (NYT "very beautiful and comically adroit"; V an "acting triumph"). Lombard, married at the time to previous Best Actor Oscar winner Clark Gable, was killed in a plane crash, just prior to the completion of filming, while on a tour selling US war bonds. She was just thirty-four and many observers thought that the Academy would nominate her posthumously even though the film had received a mixed and somewhat puzzled reception from critics.

On Academy Awards night, Garson was named the year's Best Actress. She famously gave the longest acceptance speech in Oscar history – reportedly over five minutes. Following the commercial success of *Mrs Miniver* and her Oscar win, Garson became the biggest film star of the mid-1940s. She was a Best Actress nominee in each the following three years, and then once again in 1960.

1942

BEST SUPPORTING ACTOR

ACADEMY AWARDS
William Bendix as 'Aloysius' in *Wake Island*
• **Van Heflin as 'Jeff Hartnett' in *Johnny Eager***
Walter Huston as 'Jerry Cohan' in *Yankee Doodle Dandy*
Frank Morgan as 'the Pirate' in *Tortilla Flat*
Henry Travers as 'Mr Ballard' in *Mrs Miniver*

Thomas Mitchell, who won the Best Supporting Actor Oscar in 1939, received critical acclaim for three supporting performances in 1942 – as a priest in *Joan of Paris* (V "particularly strong"), as the friend of a deserter in *This Above All* and as a blackmailer in *Moontide*. S&S considered "every performance impeccable." Surprisingly, he was overlooked by the Academy as was three-time winner Walter Brennan in the Best Picture nominee *The Pride of the Yankees* (V "superb").

Also passed over for Oscar consideration were: Geoffrey Hibbert in the 1941 British drama *Love on the Dole* (S&S "inspired"); Eric Portman as a Nazi leader in the British war drama *The Forty-Ninth Parallel (The Invaders)* (NYT "especially fine"; S&S "admirable acting"); Edward G. Robinson in *Tales of Manhattan* (NYT "masterful performance"); Claude Rains in *Now, Voyager* (NYT "polished and even-tempered"); Charles Coburn as the rich uncle in *In This Our Life* (V "a spotlight performance"); and both Basil Rathbone as a blackmailer (V "exceptional") and Felix Bressart (V "superb") in *Crossroads*.

Recognized by the Academy were: William Bendix as a tough U.S. Marine in *Wake Island*; previous Best Actor nominee Walter Huston in *Yankee Doodle Dandy* (NYT "warm-hearted portrayal"); Henry Travers as the gentle railway stationmaster in the Best Picture frontrunner *Mrs Miniver* (HSp "superb", "flawless"); Frank Morgan as a dog-loving eccentric in *Tortilla Flat* (S&S "there is a touch of genius in Frank Morgan's characterization"; V "virtually swipes the picture" with "a simple, believable and extremely touching performance"; SMH "too sentimentalised"); and Van Heflin as the scholarly sidekick of a racketeer in *Johnny Eager* (S&S "superb"; V "outstanding", "delivers one of the top support performances of the year"; TT "proves that he is an actor with a future").

Many felt that Huston would be rewarded for a respected career and a lauded performance as the father of vaudeville star George M. Cohan. However, Huston would have to wait another six years before he collected a statuette from the Academy. Instead, the Oscar went to the upcoming star Van Heflin for what was only his second film appearance.

1942

BEST SUPPORTING ACTRESS

ACADEMY AWARDS
Gladys Cooper as 'Mrs Henry Windle Vale' in *Now, Voyager*
Agnes Moorehead as 'Fanny Amberson' in *The Magnificent Ambersons*
Susan Peters as 'Kitty' in *Random Harvest*
May Whitty as 'Lady Beldon' in *Mrs Miniver*
• **Teresa Wright as 'Carol Beldon' in *Mrs Miniver***

After winning the New York Film Critics Circle's Best Actress prize for her performance as the spinster aunt in Orson Welles' period drama *The Magnificent Ambersons* (NYT "splendid"; V "excellent"), Agnes Moorehead was a major contender for the Best Supporting Actress Oscar when she received her first nomination for the same portrayal.

The favourite for the award, however, was 24-year old Teresa Wright, who had garnered her second and third Oscar nominations in just two years. A year after being considered for her film debut in *The Little Foxes*, Wright was nominated as Best Actress in *The Pride of the Yankees* and as Best Supporting Actress as the title character's daughter-in-law in *Mrs Miniver* (NYT "excellent"; HSp "superb", "flawless"; SMH "almost steals the picture").

The commercial success of *Mrs Miniver*, its favouritism for the Best Picture Oscar, and Wright's double mention, combined to make her the strong frontrunner for the award and on Oscar night, she collected the Academy's Best Supporting Actress prize. Surprisingly, Wright never made the Oscar lists again despite such notable performances as the suspicious niece in *Shadow of a Doubt*, the girlfriend of a returned serviceman in the Best Picture winner *The Best Years of Our Lives* and as the mother of a young aspiring actress in *The Actress*.

Outpolled by Wright were: her 77-year old co-star in *Mrs Miniver*, May Whitty, who received her second (and final) Oscar nomination for playing the tough, aristocratic grandmother (NYT "excellent"; HSp "superb", "flawless"); Susan Peters in *Random Harvest*; and the surprise nominee Gladys Cooper, who was recognised for her performance as the heroine's arch and domineering old mother in *Now, Voyager* despite some negative and indifferent reviews (NYT "arbitrarily written and acted").

Also overlooked were: Joan Leslie as the co-star and wife of vaudeville performer George M. Cohan in the Best Picture nominee *Yankee Doodle Dandy* (NYT "excellent"); Elsa Janssen in *The Pride of the Yankees*, another Best Picture nomine (V "superb"); Janet Blair in *My Sister Eileen*; and previous winner Hattie McDaniel in *In This Our Life*.

BEST PICTURE

ACADEMY AWARDS
• *Casablanca*
  (Warner Bros., 102 mins BW, 23 Jan 1943, $4.2m, 8 noms)
For Whom the Bell Tolls
  (Paramount, 170 mins, 14 Jul 1943, $7.1m, 9 noms)
Heaven Can Wait
  (20th Century Fox, 112 mins, 11 Aug 1943, 3 noms)
The Human Comedy
  (M-G-M, 118 mins BW, 2 Mar 1943, 5 noms)
In Which We Serve
  (Two Cities, United Artists, 115 mins BW, 23 Dec 1942, $1.8m, 2 noms)
Madame Curie
  (M-G-M, 124 mins BW, 15 Dec 1943, $3.5m, 6 noms)
The More the Merrier
  (Columbia, 104 mins BW, 7 Apr 1943, 6 noms)
The Ox-Bow Incident
  (20th Century Fox, 75 mins BW, 21 May 1943, 1 nom)
The Song of Bernadette
  (20th Century Fox, 156 mins BW, 26 Jan 1944, $7.0m, 11 noms)
Watch on the Rhine
  (Warner Bros., 114 mins BW, 27 Aug 1943, 4 noms)

GOLDEN GLOBE AWARDS – *The Song of Bernadette*
NEW YORK – *Watch on the Rhine*
BOARD OF REVIEW – *The Ox-Bow Incident*

After selecting the same film as Best Picture for three years in a row, the New York critics and NBR chose different winners in 1943. The NBR selected *The Ox-Bow Incident*, William Wellman's drama about a lynch mob (NYT "is not a picture which will brighten or cheer your day ... [but] for sheer, stark drama, is currently hard to beat"; V "powerful"; S&S "a magnificent, sombre film"), while the New York critics honoured *Watch on the Rhine*, a drama starring Paul Lukas as an anti-fascist leader tracked down in the U.S. by Nazi agents (NYT "a distinguished film"; V "powerful", "enthralling entertainment", "a magnificent picture"; TT "unfailingly interesting"). Both films were included by The New York Times on its annual list of the year's ten best with the paper declaring *Watch on the Rhine* to be its "unqualified choice as the best picture of the year."

Both films were nominated for the Best Picture Academy Award, but surprisingly, were not considered by most industry observers to be frontrunners for the Oscar. The main contenders were instead the year's two most successful films at the box office: the film version of Ernest Hemingway's *For Whom the Bell Tolls* (NYT "magnificent" but "too long"; V "one of the most important pictures of all time") and the religious drama *The Song of Bernadette* (NYT "tedious and repetitious"; Time "remarkably good", "reverent, spiritually forthright, dignified"; V "absorbing, emotional and dramatic").

The Song of Bernadette was the year's most nominated film and the only one of these four main contenders to receive a Best Director nomination. It also had entered the Academy Awards contest with the advantage of claiming the inaugural Golden Globe Award for Best Picture.

Also nominated for the Best Picture Oscar was the previous year's New York and NBR prize-winner *In Which We Serve*. The drama had been widely acclaimed by critics, but had failed to qualify for Oscar consideration in 1942 when the Academy brought forward its qualification deadline and the film's distributors had been unable to open the film in Los Angeles in time (NYT "one of the most eloquent motion pictures of these or any other times"; HT "a masterpiece"; S&S "brilliant"; SMH "one of the screen's great masterpieces").

The short-list for the Best Picture Oscar also included: the wartime romance *Casablanca* (NYT "exciting and moving", "one of the year's most exciting and trenchant films"; V "splendid"; TT "at times successful"; S&S "excellent"; SMH "superb"); the melodrama *Heaven Can Wait* (V "a charming, sentimental comedy-drama"); the New York runner-up *The Human Comedy* (V "brilliant"); the biopic *Madame Curie* which reteamed Greer Garson and Walter Pidgeon, the stars of the previous year's Best Picture winner (NYT "impressive"; V "a great picture", "distinguished", "absorbing"); and the comedy *The More the Merrier* (NYT "warm and refreshing ... the year's outstanding comedy"; V "a sparkling and effervescing piece of entertainment").

The most surprising omission from the Academy's short-list was Alfred Hitchcock's small-town thriller *Shadow of a Doubt* starring the previous year's double nominee Teresa Wright (V "suspenseful"; TT "Hitchcock at his best ... excellent"). *Shadow of a Doubt* was another film that missed out on consideration the previous year following the Academy's change of qualification deadline, only to be mostly forgotten twelve months later.

Also overlooked were: the African-American musical *Cabin in the Sky* (NYT "sparkling and completely satisfying"; V "a disappointment" but still "a worthwhile picture"); the hit Irving Berlin musical *This is the Army* (NYT "captivating", "a great show"; V "dynamic"); and several films about the Second World War.

The year's unrecognised but notable war films included: Fritz Lang's drama about occupied Czechoslovakia *Hangmen Also Die* (V "a fiercely dramatic story", "forceful"); the action film *Sahara* (NYT "a tense, exciting film"; V "realistic"); the drama *Air Force* (NYT "realistic"; V "gripping, informative, entertaining, thrilling"); *The Moon is Down*, an adaptation of John Steinbeck's novel about Norway during Nazi occupation (NYT a "clear and incisive screen version ... powerful"; V "an outstanding picture of this year"); *Bataan* (V the film has "strong patriotic appeal"); and *Next of Kin*, a drama which was made as a military training film but later given a general release (NYT "a fascinating spy film, full of tense and involved intrigue ... thrilling");

On Oscar night, there was a huge upset in the Best Picture category. The popular romance *Casablanca*, which had opened in New York in November 1942 (but not given an Oscar qualifying run in a Los Angeles cinema until early 1943), was honoured with the top Oscar. Observers suggested that the limited release of the highly touted *The Song of Bernadette* hurt its chances because few of the thousands of extras – who at that time were eligible to vote – had seen it as screenings were only in prestige venues at premium prices, whereas most voters had viewed *Casablanca* at least once during its run in standard movie-houses.

The Academy's unexpected choice meant that the four main Best Picture awards – the Oscar, the Golden Globe, the New York critics' prize and the NBR honour – all went to different films. Such a split would not happen again until 1965.

1943

BEST DIRECTOR

ACADEMY AWARDS
Clarence Brown for *The Human Comedy*
• **Michael Curtiz for *Casablanca***
Henry King for *The Song of Bernadette*
Ernst Lubitsch for *Heaven Can Wait*
George Stevens for *The More the Merrier*

GOLDEN GLOBE AWARDS – Henry King – *The Song of Bernadette*
NEW YORK – George Stevens – *The More the Merrier*

Henry King was the strong favourite to win the Best Director Oscar when he received his first nomination for *The Song of Bernadette* (V "sensitively" directed). His picture was the most nominated film of the year and just weeks before the Oscar nominations had been announced, he had won the inaugural Golden Globe Award for Best Director.

Surprisingly overlooked were: William Wellman, the runner-up for the New York critics' prize, for *The Ox-Bow Incident* (NYT "has directed the picture with a realism that is as sharp and cold as a knife"; V "skillfully guided"); Herman Shumlin for *Watch on the Rhine* (NYT "beautifully directed"; V "remarkably expressive direction"); and, most unexpectedly, Sam Wood for *For Whom the Bell Tolls* (V "masterful" direction).

Also overlooked were: Fritz Lang who finished third on the New York ballot for *Hangmen Also Die* (V a "singular success"); Alfred Hitchcock for *Shadow of a Doubt* (V "typically deft"; TT "Hitchcock at his best", "excellent"); William Wellman for *The Ox-Bow Incident*; Irving Pichel for *The Moon is Down* (NYT "superlative direction"; V "superb direction"); and the team of Noel Coward and David Lean, the runners-up for the New York critics' award the previous year, for the British war drama *In Which We Serve* (TT "dexterously handled").

Nominated alongside King were: New York critics' prize winner George Stevens for *The More the Merrier* (NYT "brilliantly directed"); Ernst Lubitsch for *Heaven Can Wait* (V "skillfully handled"); Clarence Brown for *The Human Comedy* (V "exceptional" and "understanding" direction); and Michael Curtiz for the romantic drama *Casablanca* (SMH "highly disciplined handling").

At the Academy Awards ceremony, it was Curtiz who emerged as the surprise winner of the Best Director Oscar. Despite the win, Curtiz never made the Academy's lists again. He was most surprisingly overlooked for the film noir *Mildred Pierce* (a Best Picture nominee for which Joan Crawford won as Best Actress), the comedy *Life with Father* and the drama *The Breaking Point*.

BEST ACTOR

ACADEMY AWARDS
Humphrey Bogart as 'Rick Blaine' in *Casablanca*
Gary Cooper as 'Robert Jordan' in *For Whom the Bell Tolls*
• **Paul Lukas as 'Kurt Muller' in *Watch on the Rhine***
Walter Pidgeon as 'Pierre Curie' in *Madame Curie*
Mickey Rooney as 'Homer Macauley' in *The Human Comedy*

GOLDEN GLOBE AWARDS – Paul Lukas – *Watch on the Rhine*
NEW YORK – Paul Lukas – *Watch on the Rhine*

In the acclaimed drama *Watch on the Rhine* Hungarian-born actor Paul Lukas recreated his stage success as an anti-fascist leader tracked down to Washington D. C. by Nazi agents. He received plaudits from critics on both sides of the Atlantic for his performance (NYT "superb", "expertly played"; V "outstanding"; S&S "superb portrayal"). Later he was named Best Actor by the New York critics' circle and won the inaugural Golden Globe award. The double victory made him the favourite for the Oscar.

The other main contender for the Academy's prize was Humphrey Bogart who earned acclaim from film critics for performances in three films: *Sahara* (NYT "inspiring"; V an "outstanding performance"); *Action in the North Atlantic* (NYT "good and tough"; V "a sterling performance"); and *Casablanca* (NYT "of the first order … handles it credibly"; TT "gives his usually flat performance"; SMH "fine"). It was for his portrayal of a café-owner in the last of these films that he finished as the runner-up for the New York critics' prize in 1942 and earned his first Oscar nomination as Best Actor.

Previous winner Gary Cooper was mentioned for a third consecutive year (equalling Spencer Tracy's record streak) for his portrayal of Ernest Hemingway's Spanish Civil War hero in *For Whom the Bell Tolls* (NYT "superb"), while Walter Pidgeon was mentioned for a second year in a row for the biopic *Madame Curie* ("ideal"). Rounding out the category was 23-year old Mickey Rooney with his second citation as the young telegraph messenger in *The Human Comedy* (NYT "excellent"; V "shines brilliantly" in "the strongest performance of his career"; SMH "achieves virtual perfection").

The most notable omissions from consideration by Academy voters were the runner-up for the New York critics' prize Monty Woolley in *Holy Matrimony* (NYT a "beautiful representation") and Joseph Cotten as the heroine's suspected uncle in the Alfred Hitchcock thriller *Shadow of a Doubt* (NYT "plays with smooth, insinuating ease while injecting a harsh and bitter quality which nicely becomes villainy"; V "excellent"; S&S "hardly convincing").

Also overlooked were: the previous year's Best Supporting Actor Oscar winner Van Heflin as President Andrew Johnson in *Tennessee Johnson* (NYT a "carefully delineated portrait"); previous winner Robert Donat as the eponymous Prime Minister in the British biopic *The Young Mr Pitt* (NYT "conveys a sense of the icy reserve and the passionate devotion to office which characterized the great man, while also imparting to him a breadth of warm humanity"); previous winner Spencer Tracy as a war correspondent in *Keeper of the Flame* (NYT "solid performance"; V "a top performance"); John Garfield as a man hunted by undercover Nazi agents in *The Fallen Sparrow* (NYT "constantly convincing" in a "sure and responsive performance"); both Henry Fonda (NYT "cryptic and bitter") and Dana Andrews (NYT "a heart-wringing performance") in *The Ox-Bow Incident*; and both three-time Oscar winner Walter Brennan and Brian Donlevy in *Hangmen Also Die* (V both "excellent").

On Academy Awards night, Lukas was named Best Actor (ahead of Bogart and then Rooney). He was the first person to win an Oscar, Golden Globe and New York critics' prize for the same performance. Lukas was overlooked for two strong performances the following year in *Address Unknown* and *Experiment Perilous*, and never received a second nomination from the Academy.

1943

BEST ACTRESS

ACADEMY AWARDS
Jean Arthur as 'Connie Milligan' in *The More the Merrier*
Ingrid Bergman as 'Maria' in *For Whom the Bell Tolls*
Joan Fontaine as 'Tessa Sanger' in *The Constant Nymph*
Greer Garson as 'Marie Curie' in *Madame Curie*
• **Jennifer Jones as 'Bernadette Soubirous' in *The Song of Bernadette***

GOLDEN GLOBE AWARDS – Jennifer Jones – *The Song of Bernadette*
NEW YORK – Ida Lupino – *The Hard Way*

For the first time since 1937 Bette Davis was not among the Best Actress Oscar nominees. Her performance in *Old Acquaintance* (V "expertly handles ... a spotlight performance") and her turn as the wife of an anti-fascist leader in *Watch on the Rhine* (V "a performance of genuine distinction") were both overlooked. This was, however, not altogether surprising as Bosley Crowther had been scathing in The New York Times about her work in *Old Acquaintance*, writing "under the circumstances, Miss Davis' acting, in her customary style, is fluid and full of contrivance – but it doesn't mean a thing. Only when she dresses up expensively, as a fortyish woman of the world ... does character coincide with performance. Both are artificial then".

The most unexpected absentee from the Academy's short-list was Ida Lupino who won the New York critics' prize for her performance as a woman who ruthlessly schemes behind the scenes to ensure the success of her younger sister's showbiz career, in *The Hard Way* (NYT "Miss Lupino's performance as a female Svengali is etched in venom"; V "a strong portrayal"). She was the first winner of the New York critics' circle prize since Greta Garbo in 1935 to be left out of Oscar consideration.

Also passed over were: the previous year's Best Supporting Actress Oscar winner Teresa Wright as the suspicious niece in the Alfred Hitchcock thriller *Shadow of a Doubt* (NYT "Wright is aglow with maiden spirit and subsequent emotional distress"; S&S "quite outstanding"; V a "sincere and persuasive portrayal"); previous winner Katharine Hepburn as the patriot's widow in *Keeper of the Flame* (NYT "excellent"); Dorothy McGuire for reprising her successful stage role as the child bride who grows up in *Claudia* (NYT "astonishing"; V "believable and expressive"); and Ethel Waters for repeating her stage success in the all African-American musical *Cabin in the Sky* (NYT "magnificent" and "enthralling"; V "transcendent ... an overpowering accomplishment").

Nominated ahead of these actresses were: the previous year's Best Actress winner Greer Garson (who earned her third consecutive salutation from Academy members) for her portrayal of French scientist Marie Curie in *Madame Curie* (NYT "ideal"); previous Oscar winner Joan Fontaine who was runner-up for the New York critics' prize for her performance as the young woman in love with a composer in *The Constant Nymph* (NYT "another superb achievement"; V "brilliant"; TT "succeeds"); Jean Arthur who received her (only) nomination as a young woman who shares her tiny Washington D.C. apartment during the war in the comedy *The More the Merrier* (NYT "plays with spirit and with charm"; V "makes the most of what is undoubtedly the best screen role of her long Hollywood career"; SMH "an exquisite portrait"); and two Hollywood newcomers – 28-year old Swedish actress Ingrid Bergman and 24-year old Jennifer Jones.

Although Arthur, who had been overlooked for her comic performances in films such as Frank Capra's *Mr Smith Goes to Washington*, was a sentimental favourite for the Oscar, most observers predicted a contest between the two young newcomers, who were also close friends. Bergman was nominated for her role in *For Whom the Bell Tolls* (NYT "fine … perhaps a shade too gay") and had also starred in the Best Picture nominee *Casablanca*. Meanwhile, Jones was nominated for her screen debut as the young French girl who has a vision of the Virgin Mary at Lourdes in the Best Picture favourite *The Song of Bernadette*. Her performance had divided critics. Variety praised her for "an inspirationally sensitive and arresting performance" and Time described her portrayal as "one of the most impressive screen debuts in many years". In Great Britain, however, The Times dismissed her portrayal saying she did "little more than look with a wide-eyed candour and innocence."

In late January, Jones' chances received a boost when she was presented with the inaugural Best Actress Golden Globe. Soon after she was also victorious at the Academy Awards. She received further Oscar nominations in each of the next three years.

1943

BEST SUPPORTING ACTOR

ACADEMY AWARDS
Charles Bickford as 'Peyremaie' in *The Song of Bernadette*
• **Charles Coburn as 'Benjamin Dingle' in *The More the Merrier***
J. Carrol Naish as 'Giuseppe' in *Sahara*
Claude Rains as 'Capt. Louis Renault' in *Casablanca*
Akim Tamiroff as 'Pablo' in *For Whom the Bell Tolls*

GOLDEN GLOBE AWARDS – Akim Tamiroff – *For Whom the Bell Tolls*

Akim Tamiroff earned praise from critics for his performances as a drunken guerilla leader in *For Whom the Bell Tolls* (NYT "a masterpiece of dark and devious moods"; V "the best performance of his career") and as a nervous hotelkeeper in Africa in the war drama *Five Graves to Cairo* (V "a standout"). The former earned him the inaugural Best Supporting Actor Golden Globe and his second Oscar nomination.

Charles Coburn was also lauded for two supporting performances, both in Best Picture nominees: *Heaven Can Wait* (NYT "great"; V "terrific") and *The More the Merrier* (NYT "the comical crux of the film"; V "walks off with the honors"). It was for his performance as an older gentleman sharing an apartment in Washington D.C. in the latter that he made the Oscar list for the second time in three years.

Also short-listed by Oscar voters were: Charles Bickford as a priest in *The Song of Bernadette*; J. Carrol Naish as a captured Italian soldier in *Sahara* (V "a standout characterization"); and Claude Rains as a Vichy policeman in *Casablanca* (S&S "interesting performance"; SMH "delightful").

Surprisingly, the Academy did not recognise Sonny Tufts for his performance as an ex-footballer in *So Proudly We Hail!*. Tufts had placed third in the voting for the New York critics' Best Actor award and earned the best notices for the film (NYT "does wonders to give credibility and warmth to the scenes in which he plays"; V "walks off with the picture").

Also overlooked were: Hume Cronyn in *Shadow of a Doubt* (NYT "makes a modest comic masterpiece out of the character of a literal-minded fool"); Erich von Stroheim as a high-ranking Nazi officer in *Five Graves to Cairo* (NYT "terrifying"); Cedric Hardwicke as a Nazi colonel in *The Moon is Down* (V "admirable"); Harry Carey in *Air Force* (NYT "a beautiful performance"); Walter Huston in *The North Star* (NYT "excellent"); Lloyd Corrigan in *Secrets of the Underground* (V "outstanding"); and both William Eythe (V "superb") and Harry Davenport (NYT "affecting") in *The Ox-Bow Incident*.

For their roles as a cowardly collaborator and a Gestapo inspector respectively in *Hangmen Also Die*, Gene Lockhart and Alexander Granach were also by-passed even though Variety thought them both "excellent." The assessment of the reviewer in The New York Times had, however, been positive about only one of them, concluding "With the exception of Alexander Granach, who accomplishes the highly difficult task of creating character instead of a cliché as the Gestapo agent, the performance of the leading players are almost uniformly inadequate … Gene Lockhart insistently overplays in the role of the Czech traitor."

Kenneth Spencer, meanwhile, went unrecognised for his noteworthy performances as a Reverend in the musical *Cabin in the Sky* (NYT "excellent") and as a soldier in *Bataan* (V "delivers effectively").

On Oscar night, Coburn collected the Best Supporting Actor award. Official records reveal he had outpolled Tamiroff for the prize with Rains finishing in third place.

BEST SUPPORTING ACTRESS

ACADEMY AWARDS
Gladys Cooper as 'Sister Vauzous' in *The Song of Bernadette*
Paulette Goddard as 'Lt Jean O'Doul' in *So Proudly We Hail!*
• **Katina Paxinou as 'Pilar' in *For Whom the Bell Tolls***
Anne Revere as 'Louise Soubirous' in *The Song of Bernadette*
Lucile Watson as 'Fanny Farrelly' in *Watch on the Rhine*

GOLDEN GLOBE AWARDS – Katina Paxinou – *For Whom the Bell Tolls*

As the doubting Mistress of Novices in *The Song of Bernadette* Gladys Cooper received her second consecutive Supporting Actress nomination from the Academy while Anne Revere was short-listed for the same film for playing the struggling mother of the title character. Interestingly, neither actress was even mentioned by leading film critic Bosley Crowther when he reviewed the film for The New York Times.

The other nominees were: Paulette Goddard as a combat nurse in *So Proudly We Hail!* (NYT "Goddard, cast as a cut-up, plays one for all she is worth and is consequently rather incredible"); Lucile Watson as the mother of Bette Davis' character in *Watch on the Rhine* (V "incisive" and "brilliant"); and Greek actress Katina Paxinou as the fiery guerrilla leader in *For Whom the Bell Tolls* (NYT "exceptional" and "a marvel of tenderness and violence"; V "a triumph"; TT "when she is on the screen the film has force and fire").

At the end of the year, Paxinou finished runner-up for the New York critics' Best Actress prize (she had led on the first ballot) and in late January she collected the first Best Supporting Actress Golden Globe. Five weeks later she also claimed the Oscar.

Notable absentees from the Academy's ballot paper were: Joan Leslie in *The Hard Way*; Patricia Collinge in *Shadow of a Doubt* (NYT "gives amazing flexibility and depth to the role"); Agnes Moorehead in *Journey into Fear* (NYT "another exacerbating portrait"); Nova Pilbeam as a Dutch refugee in *Next of Kin*; Leticia Scury as an old Native American woman in the Mexican film *Tres Hombres en el Rio (Three Men of the River)* (V earns "top honors"); Mary Servoss as a nurse in *So Proudly We Hail!* (V "excellent"); Alexis Smith in *The Constant Nymph* (V "excellent"); Beulah Bondi as the French governess in *Watch on the Rhine* (V "excellent"); and both Margaret Wycherly as the wife of the town mayor (V "excellent") and Dorris Bowdon as the young woman whose husband is executed for killing a German officer in *The Moon is Down*.

1944

BEST PICTURE

Three films vied for the title of the Best Picture of 1944.

Paramount launched a campaign for *Going My Way*, a sentimental and highly popular drama about two inner-city priests struggling to raise funds for their parish. The film was the year's box office champion and had received mainly positive reviews from critics on both sides of the Atlantic. The New York Times has called it "one of the rare delights of the year" while Time magazine said it was "one of the year's top surprises". Variety opined that it was "a warm, human drama" but "overlong" while S&S concluded that it had "certain obvious merits marred by painful sentimentality".

David O. Selznick hoped to garner a third Best Picture honour with his latest prestige film, the home-front drama *Since You Went Away*. Critics, however, had been divided over the nearly three-hour long production (NYT "a rather large dose of choking sentiment" and "an excess of exhausting emotional detail"; V "heart-warming"; TT "excessive length").

Finally, Fox and producer Darryl F. Zanuck mounted a strong campaign for *Wilson*, their expensive colour biopic of T. Woodrow Wilson, the United States' World War One-era President (NYT "a commanding screen biography"; V "a thrilling saga"; HRp "a tremendous film achievement" that is "deserving of the warmest possible acclaim").

Surprisingly, the NBR chose none of these frontrunners for its Best Picture award, although *Going My Way* was the runner-up. On 23 December 1944, the NBR named *None But the Lonely Heart* as the year's best film (NYT "sensitive and warmly revealing and poetically lovely"). A drama about a Cockney drifter played by Cary Grant, *None But the Lonely Heart* was also listed as one of the year's ten best by The New York Times, but was surprisingly overlooked by the Academy for a Best Picture nomination.

Four days later, *Going My Way* won the New York critics' top prize on the third ballot ahead of another of The New York Times top ten films of the year, Preston Sturges' small town comedy *Hail the Conquering Hero* (NYT "riotously funny", "superlative", a "screen masterpiece", "entertaining, provocative and constructive satire"). Zanuck's *Wilson* polled third.

Going My Way followed this win a month later with a victory at the Golden Globe awards. Consequently, it became the strong favourite for the top Oscar.

In 1944, the Academy brought the Best Picture category into line with the other major categories by restricting its list of nominees to just five contenders (down from the ten of recent years). The three major contenders were all included on the list. *Going My Way* and *Wilson* each garnered ten nominations, one more than *Since You Went Away*. Instead of the by-passed NBR winner *None But the Lonely Heart* and the New York runner-up *Hail the Conquering Hero*, the Academy nominated two acclaimed studio productions: *Gaslight* (M-G-M's remake of the 1940 British thriller); and the film noir *Double Indemnity* (NYT "monotonous"; V "absorbing"; S&S "outstanding").

The shorter list of nominees meant that several films that would likely have rated a mention from the Academy were shut-out of consideration, including: the year's second biggest box office success, the musical *Meet Me in St Louis* (V "thoroughly enjoyable"); the drama *The Purple Heart* (NYT "a haunting, inspiring melodrama"); *Thirty Seconds over Tokyo* (NYT "magnificent"); and Preston Sturges' other 1944 comedy *The Miracle of Morgan's Creek* (NYT "the year's best farce"; Time "one of the most violently funny comedies, one of the most original, vigorous and cheerfully outrageous moving pictures that ever came out of Hollywood"; V "a diverting picture"; TT "often extremely funny" and "touching").

Arguably the two most high-profile omissions from the list of Best Picture Oscar nominees were Alfred Hitchcock's *Lifeboat* (NYT "a tremendously provocative film", "absorbing", "a tense and vital drama", "brilliant") and Otto Preminger's *Laura* (NYT "an intriguing melodrama"; V "a smart murder-mystery", "brilliant" and "absorbing entertainment"). Neither of these films were included, however both directors received nominations. The inclusion of Hitchcock and Preminger came at the expense of John Cromwell for *Since You Went Away* and George Cukor for *Gaslight* and their exclusion from the Best Director category significantly undermined the chances of their films in the top category as the last film to win the Best Picture Oscar when its director had been overlooked for a nomination was *Grand Hotel* in 1931/32.

1944

The failure of *Since You Went Away* to garner any of the major end of year awards, and the omission of Cromwell from the Best Director category, prompted Selznick to abandon his campaign. This left *Going My Way* and *Wilson* as the two main contenders.

On the night of the Academy's annual awards, the sentimental and popular *Going My Way* was named the winner of the Best Picture Academy Award. It was the first time since 1937 that the Academy had agreed with the New York critics as to the year's best film. The victory also made *Going My Way* the first film to win the Oscar, Golden Globe and New York critics' circle award as Best Picture.

At the time of the Oscar ceremony a sequel to *Going My Way* was already in front of the cameras. It was a Best Picture Oscar nominee the following year.

BEST DIRECTOR

ACADEMY AWARDS
Alfred Hitchcock for *Lifeboat*
Henry King for *Wilson*
• **Leo McCarey for *Going My Way***
Otto Preminger for *Laura*
Billy Wilder for *Double Indemnity*

GOLDEN GLOBE AWARDS – Leo McCarey – *Going My Way*
NEW YORK – Leo McCarey – *Going My Way*

Seven years after winning the Best Director Oscar for *The Awful Truth*, Leo McCarey was again honoured by the Academy. He won his second statuette for the year's Best Picture Oscar winner and box office champion *Going My Way*, a sentimental drama about two inner-city priests, played by Bing Crosby and Barry Fitzgerald, who both won Oscars for their performances. In the months prior to the Oscar ceremony McCarey also won the Best Director Golden Globe and the prize from the New York critics. Variety called his handling of the film "fine direction."

Many expected his main challenger for the Oscar to be Henry King for the expensive biopic *Wilson*. The previous year King had been the unsuccessful favourite for his direction of *The Song of Bernadette*. In the end, however, the runner-up for the Oscar was Billy Wilder who had received his first nomination for the film noir *Double Indemnity* (V "credit must go in large measure to Billy Wilder's direction"). The other contenders for the prize were Alfred Hitchcock, who made the Academy's list for the second time, for the drama *Lifeboat* (V "skillfully" directed; TT "subtle") and Otto Preminger for *Laura*.

A surprising omission from the category was that of John Cromwell for the Best Picture nominee *Since You Went Away*, a home-front war drama for which David O. Selznick had campaigned strongly for Oscar recognition (NYT "has directed everyone with his customary finish and style").

Also passed over for consideration were: George Cukor for the Best Picture nominee *Gaslight*; Howard Hawks for *To Have and Have Not*; previous Best Director Oscar winner Lewis Milestone for *The Purple Heart*; Fred Zinnemann for *The Seventh Cross* (V "well-directed"); Edward Dmytryk for *Murder, My Sweet* (NYT "Dmytryk's direction maintains the racy pace of the novel"); and Edward A. Blatt for *Between Two Worlds* (V "thoughtful, imaginative direction").

The most glaring absentee from the list of nominees, however was Preston Sturges. Having been overlooked in 1940 for *The Great McGinty*, in 1941 for *The Lady Eve* and in 1942 for *Sullivan's Travels*, Sturges was now excluded for two of the year's most acclaimed comedies: *Hail the Conquering Hero*, the runner-up for the New York critics' Best Picture award, and *The Miracle of Morgan's Creek*. Both had been included on The New York Times list of the year's ten best films and for his handling of them Sturges had been runner-up for the New York critics' Best Director award.

1944

BEST ACTOR

ACADEMY AWARDS
Charles Boyer as 'Gregory Anton' in *Gaslight*
• **Bing Crosby as 'Father O'Malley' in *Going My Way***
Barry Fitzgerald as 'Father Fitzgibbon' in *Going My Way*
Cary Grant as 'Ernie Mott' in *None But the Lonely Heart*
Alexander Knox as 'President T. Woodrow Wilson' in *Wilson*

GOLDEN GLOBE AWARDS – Alexander Knox – *Wilson*
NEW YORK – Barry Fitzgerald – *Going My Way*

For his portrayal of an ageing priest in the year's biggest box office success *Going My Way*, respected Irish character actor Barry Fitzgerald overwhelmingly won the Best Actor award from the New York critics on the first ballot ahead of his co-star, crooner-turned-actor Bing Crosby. The New York Times called his performance "stunning" saying it was "as fine a characterization as has ever been put upon the screen." James Agee echoed the sentiment in Time magazine calling Fitzgerald's acting "the finest, funniest and most touching portrayal of old age that has yet reached the screen." The Academy rewarded both him and Crosby with their first Best Actor nominations.

Surprisingly, Fitzgerald was also included in the Best Supporting Actor category. He remains the only person to be named in both categories for the same performance as the Academy by-laws were subsequently changed to prevent such an occurrence being repeated. The double nod, combined with his Best Supporting Actor Golden Globe win, meant that Fitzgerald became the favourite for the secondary Oscar and a non-starter in the contest for the Best Actor statuette.

Consequently, the favourite for the Oscar was Alexander Knox who won the Golden Globe award for his portrayal of the World War One-era United States President T. Woodrow Wilson in Darryl F. Zanuck's expensive biopic *Wilson*. The New York Times considered his performance to be "inspired" and "exceptional." It was his first (and only) nomination.

Also in contention were: French actor Charles Boyer, nominated for a third time, for his performance as the husband trying to send his wife insane in the thriller *Gaslight*, a role which Anton Walbrook had played in the original 1940 British version (NYT plays his role "right to the hilt"; V a "fine performance"); and Cary Grant, making the Oscar ballot for a second (and final) time, as a Cockney drifter unwilling to settle down and accept the responsibility of taking over his dying mother's business in *None But the Lonely Heart* (NYT an "exceptional characterization").

Paul Lukas, the previous year's Best Actor Oscar winner, was overlooked for his performances in both *Address Unknown* (NYT "dynamic") and *Experiment Perilous* (NYT a "skillful performance") while previous winner Spencer Tracy was also passed over for performances in the war dramas *The Seventh Cross* (NYT "splendid") and *Thirty Seconds over Tokyo* (NYT "eminently impressive").

Also left off the Academy's list were: Orson Welles in *Jane Eyre* (NYT a "ferocious performance"; V "excellent"; SMH "remarkably impressive"); previous winner Charles Laughton as a man planning to murder his domineering wife in *The Suspect* (NYT "has seldom portrayed a more likable character or performed with more restraint than he does in this picture"; V "an impeccable performance"); George Sanders in *Summer Storm* (NYT "excellent"; V "excellent"); Fred MacMurray in *Double Indemnity* (NYT "a bit too ingenuous"); John Garfield in *Between Two Worlds* (V "stands out sharply"); and Eddie Bracken in Preston Sturges' comedies *Hail the Conquering Hero* (NYT "a squarely hilarious imitation of a thunderstruck human football ... his more solemn shows of sincerity are affecting to a tearful degree") and *The Miracle of Morgan's Creek* (TT "brilliant"). Meanwhile, Dana Andrews also went unrecognised for his acclaimed performances in Otto Preminger's film noir *Laura* and Lewis Milestone's war drama *The Purple Heart* (NYT "magnificent" and "outstanding"; V "excellent").

On Oscar night, as expected, Fitzgerald won the Best Supporting Actor award. However, Crosby was surprisingly named Best Actor. He admitted that he had expected Knox to win and exclaimed, "Oh, my heavens" as he received the statuette from Gary Cooper. "I couldn't be more surprised if I won the Kentucky Derby."

At the time of the Oscar ceremony, Crosby was already reprising his role as Father O'Malley in *The Bells of St Mary's*, a sequel to *Going My Way*. For reprising his Oscar-winning performance he would be a Best Actor nominee again the following year.

BEST ACTRESS

ACADEMY AWARDS
• **Ingrid Bergman as 'Paula Alquist' in** *Gaslight*
Claudette Colbert as 'Annie Hilton' in *Since You Went Away*
Bette Davis as 'Fanny Trellis' in *Mr Skeffington*
Greer Garson as 'Susie Parkington' in *Mrs Parkington*
Barbara Stanwyck as 'Phyllis Dietrichson' in *Double Indemnity*

GOLDEN GLOBE AWARDS – Ingrid Bergman – *Gaslight*
NEW YORK – Tallulah Bankhead – *Lifeboat*

The roles of Judith Traherne in *Dark Victory* and Regina Giddens in *The Little Foxes* for which Bette Davis had earned Best Actress Oscar nominations in 1939 and 1941, had both been originated on stage by Broadway star Tallulah Bankhead (the actress whom many believe was later the model for Davis' characterization of Margo Channing in *All About Eve*). In 1944 Bankhead had her own chance at Oscar glory when she won the role of a wealthy woman stranded with other passengers and crew in a lifeboat after a German submarine attack in Alfred Hitchcock's drama *Lifeboat*. Praised by critics for her performance (NYT "extraordinarily fine"; HT an "extraordinarily versatile performance"; TT "sophisticated") she received the New York critics' prize. Surprisingly, however, her chance was thwarted when, like NY winner Ida Lupino the previous year, she did not receive an Oscar nomination. Industry observers speculated that the Broadway legend was too much of a Hollywood outsider to have garnered Oscar recognition.

The omission of Bankhead from the Academy's list of nominees left Ingrid Bergman the overwhelming favourite for the Best Actress Oscar. The previous year the young Swedish actress had received her first nomination for playing a Spanish peasant in *For Whom the Bell Tolls* and had starred in the year's Best Picture Oscar winner *Casablanca*. In 1944 she was nominated again, for playing a fragile Victorian woman whose sadistic husband is trying to send her insane in *Gaslight* (NYT "goes to pieces in a most distressing way ... [plays her role] right to the hilt"; V a "fine performance"). The role had been played four years earlier by Diana Wynyard in the original British film version. Bergman was runner-up for the New York critics' prize, losing to Bankhead on the sixth ballot, and won the Golden Globe for her performance. She was backed for the Oscar statuette by both M-G-M which had made *Gaslight*, and David O. Selznick to whom she was contracted.

1944

For the first time, all the Oscar nominees in one of the acting categories were previous nominees. Alongside Bergman were nominated Barbara Stanwyck (her third nomination) as a femme fatale plotting her husband's murder in Billy Wilder's Best Picture nominee *Double Indemnity* (NYT "gives a good surface performance of a destructively lurid female"; TT "first-rate"), and three previous Oscar winners: Claudette Colbert (her third and final nomination) in Selznick's *Since You Went Away* (NYT "excellent"); Greer Garson (her fifth nomination and her fourth consecutive nod) as the title character in *Mrs Parkington* (V "scores solidly"); and Bette Davis as a legendary beauty in *Mr Skeffington* (NYT "impressive"; V "a triumph", "her characterization is one of the best among those which have made her one of the screen's finest actresses"). With her nomination, Davis became the first person to receive a seventh Oscar nomination for acting. All her nominations had been in the Best Actress category and all had come within a decade.

Three other previous Best Actress Oscar winners were overlooked by the Academy. Despite much hype, Ginger Rogers was passed over for her largely negatively reviewed performance in the tear-jerker *Tender Comrade* (NYT "weak"; "stagy"; V "unrestrained performance") and Joan Fontaine was passed over for playing the title character in *Jane Eyre* (V "excellent"; SMH "very fine"). Katharine Hepburn, meanwhile, was left off the list for her performance as a Chinese peasant in *Dragon Seed* (V "especially effective").

Also overlooked were: Judy Garland for the hit musical *Meet Me in St Louis*; Irene Dunne in *The White Cliffs of Dover* (V "excellent"); Linda Darnell in *Summer Storm* (NYT "surprisingly adept"); Merle Oberon in *Dark Waters* (V "gives one of the best portrayals of her career"); and Anna Sten as a Russian nurse who falls for a wounded soldier in *Three Russian Girls* (NYT "strikingly effective").

There was one other, rather curious, omission from the Best Actress category. Despite having as much screen time as her co-star Claudette Colbert, the previous year's Best Actress Oscar winner Jennifer Jones, was included in the Best Supporting Actress category for her leading performance in the home-front drama *Since You Went Away*.

On Academy Awards night Bergman won her first Best Actress award (with Stanwyck polling second). At the time of her win she was filming *The Bells of St Mary's*, a sequel to the year's Best Picture Oscar winner *Going My Way*. She received a third consecutive nomination from the Academy the following year for her performance. In the decades that followed she would take home a further two statuettes, another for Best Actress and one as Best Supporting Actress.

1944

BEST SUPPORTING ACTOR

ACADEMY AWARDS
Hume Cronyn as 'Paul Roeder' in *The Seventh Cross*
• **Barry Fitzgerald as 'Father Fitzgibbon' in *Going My Way***
Claude Rains as 'Job Skeffington' in *Mr Skeffington*
Clifton Webb as 'Waldo Lydecker' in *Laura*
Monty Woolley as 'Col. Smollett' in *Since You Went Away*

GOLDEN GLOBE AWARDS – **Barry Fitzgerald** – *Going My Way*

For his lauded performance as a kindly priest in the year's biggest commercial success *Going My Way* (NYT "stunning") Barry Fitzgerald won the Best Actor prize from the New York critics and the Golden Globe award for Best Supporting Actor. Unexpectedly the Academy nominated him in both acting categories. With his co-star Bing Crosby also nominated as Best Actor, Fitzgerald became a strong favourite for the Best Supporting Actor Oscar. His chances were helped by his other strong supporting performance in *None But the Lonely Heart* (NYT "delightful and affecting").

Hume Cronyn received his first (and only) Oscar nomination for his performance as a German factory worker in *The Seventh Cross* (NYT "splendid") but his wife, Jessica Tandy (who would win the Best Actress Oscar in 1989), was not recognised for her supporting performance in the film despite equally positive reviews. Claude Rains received his third nomination when he made the lists for a second year in a row for playing the title character in *Mr Skeffington* (V "excellent") while Clifton Webb was recognised for his screen debut in *Laura* (NYT "sophistry personified … [an] incisive performance"). Monty Woolley, meanwhile, garnered his second nomination in three years for the Best Picture nominee *Since You Went Away* (NYT "makes a full-blown character of the man who comes to lodge").

Despite a strong campaign by producer David O. Selznick, Woolley's co-stars in *Since You Went Away* Joseph Cotten (NYT "droll") and Robert Walker (V "a bellringing performance") were both overlooked.

Also passed over were: Akim Tamiroff in *Dragon Seed* (TT "admirable"); Walter Slezak as the German in *Lifeboat* (V "terrific"); Cedric Hardwicke in *The Lodger* (NYT "splendid"); Sydney Greenstreet in *Between Two Worlds* (V "outstanding"); and Edward G. Robinson in *Double Indemnity* (NYT "a fine bit of characterization"; V "a strong performance"; TT "first-rate").

The most glaring omission from the category, however, was William Demarest who earned plaudits from critics for his comic portrayals in *The Great*

Moment (NYT "delightful") and both of Preston Sturges' hits that year: *Hail the Conquering Hero* (NYT "outstanding") and *The Miracle of Morgan's Creek* (Time "one of the few solid-gold pieces of screen acting in recent years").

On Oscar night, both Crosby and Fitzgerald received prizes from the Academy. Crosby won the Best Actor Oscar and Fitzgerald collected the award as Best Supporting Actor. Surprisingly, despite other acclaimed performances, most notably his roles in Jules Dassin's 1948 thriller *The Naked City* and in John Ford's 1952 drama *The Quiet Man*, Fitzgerald never again made the Academy's lists of nominees.

BEST SUPPORTING ACTRESS

ACADEMY AWARDS
• **Ethel Barrymore as 'Ma Mott' in** *None But the Lonely Heart*
Jennifer Jones as 'Jane Hilton' in *Since You Went Away*
Angela Lansbury as 'Nancy Olivier' in *Gaslight*
Aline MacMahon as 'Ling Tan's wife' in *Dragon Seed*
Agnes Moorehead as 'Aspasia Conti' in *Mrs Parkington*

GOLDEN GLOBE AWARDS – Agnes Moorehead – *Mrs Parkington*

The year after she won the Best Actress Oscar for *The Song of Bernadette*, Jennifer Jones became the first person nominated in the supporting category after having won an Oscar for a leading performance. She made the Oscar lists for the second time for her co-leading performance as the elder daughter in *Since You Went Away* (Time "a nervous, carefully studied" performance). The film's producer David O. Selznick had also mounted a major campaign for 16-year old Shirley Temple, but she was overlooked.

Also passed over for consideration by the Academy were: Lauren Bacall for her film debut in *To Have and Have Not* (NYT "she acts in the quiet way of catnip"); Geraldine Fitzgerald as the second wife of President Wilson in the Best Picture contender *Wilson* (NYT "makes a remarkably understanding woman of the second Mrs Wilson"); Sara Allgood as the woman who rents her attic to Jack the Ripper in *The Lodger* (NYT "splendid"; V "tremendously effective"); and Jessica Tandy for *The Seventh Cross* (NYT "emotionally devastating"). Tandy's husband, Hume Cronyn was nominated as Best Supporting Actor for his performance in the same film, but Tandy would have to wait until 1989 to receive her first nomination.

Nominated alongside Jones were: Angela Lansbury for her screen debut as the callous maid in *Gaslight* (NYT "interesting"); Aline MacMahon as a Chinese farmer's wife in *Dragon Seed* (NYT a "normal performance"); Agnes Moorehead (her second Oscar nomination in three years) in *Mrs Parkington* (NYT "good"); and first-time nominee Ethel Barrymore as the cancer-stricken Cockney mother in *None But the Lonely Heart* (NYT "excellent").

Moorehead won the Golden Globe, but on Oscar night the Academy Award went to 65-year old stage legend Barrymore, the younger sister of actors John and Lionel Barrymore (Lionel had won the Best Actor Oscar in 1930/31). Ethel Barrymore's performance in *None But the Lonely Heart* was her first screen role in over a decade. She would be nominated for the Best Supporting Actress Oscar a further three times over the next five years.

1945

BEST PICTURE

ACADEMY AWARDS
Anchors Aweigh
   (M-G-M, 143 mins, 19 Jul 1945, $4.7m, 5 noms)
The Bells of St Mary's
   (RKO Radio, 126 mins BW, 7 Dec 1945, $8.0m, 8 noms)
• *The Lost Weekend*
   (Paramount, 101 mins BW, 16 Nov 1945, $4.3m, 7 noms)
Mildred Pierce
   (Warner Bros., 111 mins BW, 20 Oct 1945, 6 noms)
Spellbound
   (Selznick, United Artists, 111 mins BW, 28 Dec 1945, $4.9m, 6 noms)

GOLDEN GLOBE AWARDS – *The Lost Weekend*
NEW YORK – *The Lost Weekend*
BOARD OF REVIEW – *The True Glory*

When *The Valley of Decision*, an adaptation of a popular novel by Marcia Davenport, topped the US box office M-G-M had good reason to believe that the drama would be included on the Academy's list despite an indifferent response from critics (NYT "Miss Davenport's fine American saga is barely perceived in this film, produced most extravagantly by Metro. But there is here a full romantic show"). Two of the past three box office champions had won the Best Picture Academy Award and the other had been a nominee. When the contenders were announced, however, *The Valley of Decision* was recognised only for the leading performance of Greer Garson and for its musical score by Herbert Stothart.

In its place the Academy chose another M-G-M film, the musical *Anchors Aweigh* (NYT "inventive") starring Gene Kelly and Frank Sinatra, which had finished as the year's second most successful film. A surprise nominee was the melodrama *Mildred Pierce* for which Joan Crawford was favoured to win Best Actress. Although popular, the film had not been well received by most critics (NYT "lacks the driving force of stimulating drama and its denouement hardly comes as a surprise"; TT "film falters into tediousness every now and again"; HRv "powerful", "a truly great motion picture"). The directors of both films were left out of the Best Director race.

Also nominated for the Best Picture Oscar were two films starring the previous year's Best Actress winner, Ingrid Bergman. Both earned Best Director nominations and both were commercial hits. Leo McCarey's *The Bells of St Mary's*, the sequel to the previous year's Best Picture Oscar winner, *Going My*

Way, was the top money-earner of 1946 (NYT "lacks the charm of its predecessor"; HRv "a beautiful picture of great spiritual uplift"; V "warmly sentimental") while Alfred Hitchcock's psychological thriller *Spellbound* (NYT "a rare film"; S&S "pretentious"; SMH "absorbing") finished as that year's third biggest money-earner.

The outright favourite for the Best Picture statuette, however, was Billy Wilder's *The Lost Weekend*, a critically acclaimed small-scale drama about an alcoholic. The New York Times called it "impressive", "unmercifully candid, shocking and deeply poignant" and "a shatteringly realistic and morbidly fascinating film" which "ranks with the best and most disturbing character studies ever put on the screen." The NYDN labelled it "the most daring film that ever came out of Hollywood" while Variety considered it "a particularly outstanding achievement". In London, The Times described it as "a distinguished film."

The Lost Weekend was named Best Picture of the year by the New York critics, won the top Golden Globe and was the runner-up for the NBR Best Picture prize (the NBR honoured the documentary, *The True Glory*). Days before the Oscar ceremony it was picked as the favourite by Variety even though it had garnered one nomination less than *The Bells of St Mary's*.

Several acclaimed films were not considered by the Academy. For the second year in a row the runner-up for the New York prize was overlooked: William Wellman's *The Story of GI Joe* was shut-out of contention despite strong reviews (NYT "magnificent", "hard-hitting, penetrating", "uncompromising realism"; V "superb"). Clarence Brown earned a Best Director nomination for *National Velvet* but the film was missing from the Best Picture list (NYT "fresh and delightful … should be a joy to all right-minded folks"). Similarly, Jean Renoir was included but his film, *The Southerner*, which would later win the Best Picture award at the 1946 Venice Film Festival, was passed over (NYT "rich, unusual and sensitive … a worthy addition to the year's roster of fine films"; V "trenchant realism" undermined by "morbidity").

Surprisingly, the Academy also overlooked: the family drama *A Tree Grows in Brooklyn* (NYT "a fine film", "deeply human and understanding", "vastly affecting"; V "one of the fine film dramas of the year"; SMH "a masterpiece"); Lewis Milestone's *A Walk in the Sun* (NYT "a swiftly overpowering piece of work … is unquestionably one of the fine, sincere pictures about the war"; S&S a "masterpiece"); the melodrama *Leave Her to Heaven* which proved popular despite poor reviews (NYT "a moody, morbid film … a piece of cheap fiction done up in Technicolor and expensive sets"); and *A Song to Remember*, a biopic about classical composer Frederic Chopin, which was nominated in six other categories (NYT "the effect of this picture upon the sense of sight and sound is altogether delightful … but its script is a dramatic hodgepodge, which provides absolutely no conception of the true character of the composer").

Also overlooked were: the Swiss war drama *Die Letzte Chance (The Last Chance)* (NYT "tense, exciting", "one of the best films of World War II to date"); *Pride of the Marines* (NYT "real and affecting"; V "forceful", "a significant film"); *They Were Expendable* (NYT "a stirring picture", "thrilling"); *The House on 92nd Street* (NYT "intriguing and exciting real-life drama"; V "absorbing"); the macabre thriller *The Body Snatcher* (NYT "has enough suspense and atmospheric terror to make it one of the better of its genre"); and the British films *The Life and Death of Colonel Blimp*, which had been released in the United Kingdom two years earlier (NYT "an impressive, if not always consistent, entertainment"; V "excellent") and *Blithe Spirit*, a comedy directed by David Lean (NYT "amusing spoof", "generally delightful"; TT "an entirely successful piece of entertainment").

The Academy also by-passed two notable Fritz Lang films: the thriller *The Woman in the Window* (V "a strong and decidedly suspenseful murder melodrama") and the controversial film noir *Scarlet Street* (NYT "seems a sluggish and manufactured tale, emerging much more from sheer contrivance than from the passions of the characters involved"). Released in late December, *Scarlet Street* was subject to a ban by local censor boards in several states, including New York, only to then be passed for wide release in February 1946.

On Oscar night, the Academy agreed with the New York critics for the second year in a row and selected *The Lost Weekend* as the year's Best Picture. The film collected only three statuettes, but the tally was still enough to make it the year's most honoured film.

Over the next few years Wilder's drama would be emulated by a cycle of small-budget films dealing with serious social issues, many of which would contend for Best Picture honours.

BEST DIRECTOR

ACADEMY AWARDS
Clarence Brown for *National Velvet*
Alfred Hitchcock for *Spellbound*
Leo McCarey for *The Bells of St Mary's*
Jean Renoir for *The Southerner*
• **Billy Wilder for *The Lost Weekend***

GOLDEN GLOBE AWARDS – Billy Wilder – *The Lost Weekend*
NEW YORK – Billy Wilder – *The Lost Weekend*
BOARD OF REVIEW – Jean Renoir – *The Southerner*

Three of the previous year's Best Director nominees were short-listed again for the Oscar in 1945. Leo McCarey, who had won his second Academy Award for *Going My Way*, received his third (and final) nomination for handling the sequel *The Bells of St Mary's* (HRv "superbly directed"). Alfred Hitchcock earned his third mention in just six years for the psychological drama *Spellbound* (NYT "has used some startling images to symbolize the content of dreams ... but his real success is in creating the illusion of love"). And Billy Wilder was included for the drama *The Lost Weekend* (NYT "ranks with the best and most disturbing character studies ever put on the screen ... truly a chef d'ouvre of motion picture art ... most impressive throughout the picture is the honesty with which it has been made"). All three films were considered for the Best Picture award.

Also nominated were Clarence Brown, who was short-listed for the fifth time for *National Velvet* (NYT "has kept [the picture] out in the open as much as he could and has got an air of wind-swept freedom and candor all the way through ... Brown has also drawn some excellent performances from his cast"), and French director Jean Renoir, who received his only mention from the Academy for one of his American films, *The Southerner* (NYT "has understandingly shown the pathos and humor of a year's struggle in the life of [a tenant farmer] ... Renoir has subtly combined his camera with sparse dialogue in the native idiom to tell his story simply and beautifully"). Renoir had been unexpectedly overlooked for a nomination in 1938 when his film *La Grande Illusion (Grand Illusion)* was the first foreign-language nominee for the Best Picture Oscar.

The shock omission from the category was William Wellman for his lauded direction of *The Story of GI Joe* (NYT "Wellman's approach is starkly realistic"; V "perfect"). It was the second time in three years that Wellman had been by-passed despite finishing as the runner-up for the Best Director prize from the New York critics.

Meanwhile, Fritz Lang was snubbed for both the thriller *The Woman in the Window* (NYT "nearly flawless"; V "fine") and the film noir *Scarlet Street* (NYT "has directed for dark moods, which his camera catches better than his cast").

Others excluded were: Elia Kazan for his directorial debut *A Tree Grows in Brooklyn* (NYT "Kazan has directed this picture, his first, with an easy naturalness that has brought out all the tone of real experience in a vastly affecting film"; V "admirably" directed); Tay Garnett for the year's biggest box office success *The Valley of Decision* (V "skillful direction"); previous winner Michael Curtiz for the Best Picture nominee *Mildred Pierce* (NYT "cunning" direction; V "skillfully handled"); Harold French for the British anti-Nazi drama *Mr Emmanuel* (NYT "masterful" direction); Leopold Lindtberg for the Swiss war drama *Die Letzte Chance (The Last Chance)*; Henry Hathaway for *The House on 92nd Street*; previous winner John Ford for *They Were Expendable* (V "exceptionally well directed"); and previous winner Lewis Milestone for *A Walk in the Sun* (NYT "has given a completely graphic picture of the natures and responses of the various men").

Although Variety predicted that McCarey would collect his third Oscar, the winner was Wilder (who had finished as runner-up to McCarey for the Oscar the previous year). It was Wilder's first Academy Award and the fifth year in a row that the Oscars for Best Picture and Best Director had been won by the same film.

1945

BEST ACTOR

ACADEMY AWARDS
Bing Crosby as 'Father O'Malley' in *The Bells of St Mary's*
Gene Kelly as 'Joseph Brady' in *Anchors Aweigh*
• **Ray Milland as 'Don Birnam' in *The Lost Weekend***
Gregory Peck as 'Father Francis Chisolm' in *The Keys of the Kingdom*
Cornel Wilde as 'Frederic Chopin' in *A Song to Remember*

GOLDEN GLOBE AWARDS – Ray Milland – *The Lost Weekend*
NEW YORK – Ray Milland – *The Lost Weekend*
BOARD OF REVIEW – Ray Milland – *The Lost Weekend*

Director Billy Wilder initially wanted theatre star José Ferrer to make his film debut in the role of a New York alcoholic in his drama *The Lost Weekend*, but Paramount wanted an established name for the part. Surprisingly, Wilder chose Welsh actor Ray Milland who up to that point in his career had been associated with popular but light-weight melodramas. Wilder's casting, however, proved to be inspired. The New York Times called Milland's performance "splendid" and concluded, "Milland rates top honors for a shattering performance." Variety agreed saying "his portrayal will have to be reckoned with when filmdom makes its annual awards." When the end of year accolades were presented, Milland became the first person to win all the major Best Actor honours – the Oscar, the Golden Globe and the prizes from the New York critics' circle and the NBR. He also collected the prestigious Best Actor citation from the jury at the Cannes Film Festival.

The performances of several other actors were lauded by critics in 1945, but surprisingly, all were overlooked by the Academy which instead chose a comparatively weak list of nominees.

David O. Selznick ran a strong campaign for Joseph Cotten as a shell-shocked soldier in the romantic drama *I'll Be Seeing You* (NYT "excellent", "deserves the highest honors") but he was snubbed. Also left out of consideration were: previous winner Paul Muni as the old music teacher in *A Song to Remember* (NYT "his characterization is amusing … but Mr Muni too often plays without restraint"; V "brilliant"); Felix Aylmer in the British anti-Nazi drama *Mr Emmanuel* (NYT "a performance which might be unqualifiedly recommended as one of the best we have ever seen"); Edward G. Robinson in the Fritz Lang thriller *The Woman in the Window* (NYT "a masterly performance"); Zachary Scott as the struggling farmer in *The Southerner* (NYT "excellent and outstanding ... at once restrained and powerful"); John Garfield as the injured soldier in *Pride of the Marines* (NYT "brilliant", "unqualifiedly excellent" and "impressive"; V "vivid"); Boris Karloff as the grave-robber in *The Body Snatcher* (NYT "is in there pitching with ghoulish delight"); previous winner Charles Laughton as the gentle shopkeeper in *The Suspect* (NYT "has seldom portrayed a more likable character or performed with more restraint than he does in this picture … handled with quiet innocence"); Burgess Meredith as the war correspondent in *The Story of GI Joe* (V "skillful" and "memorable"; TT "lacks depth"); Richard Conte in *A Walk in the Sun* (S&S "a dynamic portrait"); Thomas Mitchell as the prison warden in *Within These Walls* (V "excellent"); Roger Livesey in the 1943 British war propaganda film *The Life and Death of Colonel Blimp* (NYT "an ideal choice for the leading role … his transformation … is a gem of florid makeup and characterization"); and both Ewart G. Morrison and John Hoy as British officers trying to escape to Switzerland in the war drama *Die Letzte Chance (The Last Chance)* (NYT both "excellent").

Although now lauded by film historians, Edward G. Robinson's performance in Fritz Lang's controversial film noir *Scarlet Street* was not well received at the time of the film's release. Bosley Crowther wrote in The New York Times that he "performs monotonously and with little illumination of an adventurous spirit seeking air". Unsurprisingly, he was ignored by the Academy.

Chosen by the Academy were: Gene Kelly as a sailor on shore leave in the musical *Anchors Aweigh*, a Best Picture nominee; rising star Cornel Wilde as composer Frederic Chopin in the biopic *A Song to Remember* (NYT "Wilde is not called upon to demonstrate much acting ability"); the previous year's Best Actor Oscar winner Bing Crosby for reprising his award-winning role as a Catholic priest in the sequel *The Bells of St Mary's*, despite poor reviews (HRv "a very bad, very hokey performance"; TT "has lost his way"); and newcomer Gregory Peck as a missionary in *The Keys of the Kingdom* (NYT "fine"; V "excellent"). Wilde had appeared in the box office hit *Leave Her to Heaven*, while, in his first year on the screen, Peck had also starred in the year's biggest box office hit, *The Valley of Decision* (NYT "quietly commanding"; V "standout"), and Alfred Hitchcock's *Spellbound* (NYT "his performance, restrained and refined, is precisely the proper counter to Miss Bergman's exquisite role").

Despite his Oscar win, Milland was rarely given major film roles in mainstream Hollywood productions. Of his later screen roles he is probably best remembered for playing the husband who tries to have his wife murdered in Alfred Hitchcock's thriller *Dial M for Murder* and for his turn as the snobbish father of Ryan O'Neal's character in *Love Story*. He never again made the Academy's lists.

BEST ACTRESS

ACADEMY AWARDS
Ingrid Bergman as 'Sister Benedict' in *The Bells of St Mary's*
• **Joan Crawford as 'Mildred Pierce' in *Mildred Pierce***
Greer Garson as 'Mary Rafferty' in *The Valley of Decision*
Jennifer Jones as 'Singleton' in *Love Letters*
Gene Tierney as 'Ellen Berent' in *Leave Her to Heaven*

GOLDEN GLOBE AWARDS – Ingrid Bergman – *The Bells of St Mary's*
NEW YORK – Ingrid Bergman – *The Bells of St Mary's* and *Spellbound*
BOARD OF REVIEW – Joan Crawford – *Mildred Pierce*

The three previous Best Actress Oscar winners were among the Best Actress nominees in 1945.

Greer Garson, the 1942 winner and now the most popular actress in America, was nominated, for a record-equalling fifth year in a row, for her performance as a housemaid in love with her employer's son in *The Valley of Decision*, the year's biggest box office hit (NYT "Garson's performance is generally one of fine attitudes, more photogenic than incisive, but that's what her audiences like"; V "superb"; TT "delightful").

Despite polarising critics, Jennifer Jones, the 1943 winner, was nominated, for a third time, as an amnesiac in *Love Letters* (NYT "whatever reputation as an actress Jennifer Jones may have got for herself in *The Song of Bernadette* is likely to suffer a terrible dent as the result of her fatuous performance in *Love Letters*"; V "brilliant").

Ingrid Bergman, the previous year's winner, made the short-list, for a third year in a row, as a nun in the biggest box office hit of 1946, *The Bells of St Mary's*. She was considered a strong chance to repeat her victory (NYT "perfect"; HR "magnificent", "probably the single greatest performance that any actress in motion pictures has ever given"; TT "never succeeds"). Bergman also appeared as the psychiatrist in *Spellbound* (NYT "exquisite", "played expertly"; V "a beautiful characterization").

The fourth nominee was Gene Tierney who earned her (only) nomination as the paranoid and jealous wife in the second biggest box office hit of 1946, *Leave Her to Heaven* (NYT "Tierney's petulant performance ... is about as analytical as a piece of pin-up poster art ... strictly one-dimensional",").

Overlooked in favour of Tierney were: previous winner Ginger Rogers in *I'll Be Seeing You* (NYT "excellent"); Greta Gynt in *Mr Emmanuel* (NYT "exquisite and disturbing"); previous winner Joan Fontaine in her first comic role in *The*

Affairs of Susan (V "impressive"); Dorothy McGuire for both *A Tree Grows in Brooklyn* (SMH "exceptional") and *Enchanted Cottage* (V "outstanding"); Deborah Kerr for the British films *The Life and Death of Colonel Blimp* (NYT "remarkable") in which she played three different roles, and *Vacation from Marriage* (V "outstanding"); and Peggy Ann Garner for *A Tree Grows in Brooklyn* (NYT "a truly surpassing little actress").

The most surprising omission was Bette Davis as the teacher in *The Corn is Green*, a role played on stage by Ethel Barrymore (V "one of her best", a "great sympathetic impact"; TT "Davis has never been better").

Although now lauded by film historians, Joan Bennett's performance in Fritz Lang's controversial film noir *Scarlet Street* was not well received at the time. Bosley Crowther wrote in The New York Times that she was "static and colorless, completely lacking the malevolence that should flash in her evil role". She was ignored by the Academy.

Joan Crawford was the fifth actress included on the Academy's list. In the decade since she had been by-passed for *Grand Hotel*, Crawford had been written off as a has-been. For playing the self-sacrificing mother in *Mildred Pierce*, however, she earned both critical plaudits and her first Oscar nomination (NYT "sincere and generally effective"; V "reaches the peak of her acting career"; NYDN "the best performance of her career"; TT "acts with an inward tenseness which never degenerates into a tiresome intensity"). Crawford's publicist had begun campaigning for the Oscar before filming had even been completed.

The NBR prize went to Crawford, but in New York the comeback star finished as runner-up to Bergman, who was cited for both *The Bells of St Mary's* and *Spellbound* (Kerr finished third). Bergman then also won the Best Actress prize at the Golden Globe Awards, making her both the first person honoured with a second Globe for acting and the first person to win back-to-back Globes in the same category (she had won the previous year for *Gaslight*).

Despite Bergman's New York and Globe victories, Variety predicted an Oscar win for Crawford. Too nervous to attend, she feigned illness to stay at home and listen to the ceremony on the radio. When Charles Boyer opened the final envelope of the evening and revealed that Crawford had been chosen as the year's Best Actress, the film's director, Michael Curtiz, accepted the statuette and rushed it to her home. Crawford posed in bed with her Oscar for news–photographers.

The win revived Crawford's career and she was nominated as Best Actress by the Academy twice more over the next seven years for her performances as a murderous schizophrenic in *Possessed* and as a playwright with a younger husband in *Sudden Fear*. To her great disappointment, however, she was overlooked for her performance in *What Ever Happened to Baby Jane?*.

1945

BEST SUPPORTING ACTOR

ACADEMY AWARDS
Michael Chekhov as 'Dr Alex Brulow' in *Spellbound*
John Dall as 'Morgan Evans' in *The Corn is Green*
• **James Dunn as 'Johnny Nolan' in *A Tree Grows in Brooklyn***
Robert Mitchum as 'Lt Walker' in *The Story of GI Joe*
J. Carrol Naish as 'Charley Martin' in *A Medal for Benny*

GOLDEN GLOBE AWARDS – J. Carrol Naish – *A Medal for Benny*

Two years after being unsuccessfully nominated for the Best Supporting Actor
Oscar, J. Carrol Naish won a Golden Globe for his performance as the father of
an unlikely war hero in the comedy *A Medal for Benny*, and was once more
included on the Academy's list of contenders (NYT "exceptional"). Naish also
earned praise during the year for his turn as the unhelpful neighbour in the drama
The Southerner (NYT a "vigorous characterization").

Mentioned alongside him were four first-time nominees: Russian actor
Michael Chekhov, a nephew of the great playwright Anton Chekhov, in Alfred
Hitchcock's *Spellbound* (NYT "excellent"; V "fine"; SMH "stands out"); John
Dall as a Welsh miner studying for a university scholarship in *The Corn is Green*
(NYT "a shade too theatric"); James Dunn as an alcoholic father in *A Tree Grows
in Brooklyn* (NYT "beautifully played ... with a deep and sympathetic
tenderness"; V "excellent"; TT "cannot make [the role] persuasive"; SMH
"Dunn's acting is a work of art"); and Robert Mitchum, in his first major role,
as a war-hardened officer in *The Story of GI Joe* (NYT & V "excellent").
Surprisingly, Mitchum's nomination proved to be the only one he ever received
from the Academy.

Mitchum's co-star Freddie Steele was also praised for his turn in *The Story
of GI Joe* (NYT "excellent" and "well balanced"), but he did not make the
Academy's list. Similarly, Chekov's co-star Leo G. Carroll was passed over for
his part in *Spellbound* (V "outstanding").

Arguably the most egregious omission, however, was the performance of
Anton Walbrook as the German army officer in *The Life and Death of Colonel
Blimp*. In The New York Times, critic Thomas M. Pryor had declared,
"Walbrook gives a completely winning performance as the Prussian officer".

Also overlooked were: previous winner Donald Crisp as the father of a keen
young equestrian in *National Velvet* (NYT "splendid"); Dane Clark as the Jewish
soldier in *Pride of the Marines* (NYT "unqualifiedly excellent ... vivid");
Herbert Marshall in *Enchanted Cottage* (V "excellent"); Raymond Massey in

The Woman in the Window (NYT "excellent"; V "outstanding"); George Sanders in *The Picture of Dorian Gray* (NYT "gives the only commendable performance"); Romano Calò in his final screen appearance as the priest in *Die Letzte Chance (The Last Chance)* (NYT "particularly notable"); and 11-year old Richard Lyon in *The Unseen* (NYT "superb").

Mitchum had been the runner-up for the New York critics' Best Actor prize, but Variety predicted that the Oscar race would be a close contest between Chekhov and Naish. Surprisingly, none of these three actors emerged as the winner. When Van Heflin opened the envelope at Grauman's Chinese Theatre in Hollywood on Oscar night it was Dunn who received the prize. He never earned a second nomination from the Academy.

1945

BEST SUPPORTING ACTRESS

ACADEMY AWARDS
Eve Arden as 'Ida' in *Mildred Pierce*
Ann Blyth as 'Veda Pierce' in *Mildred Pierce*
Angela Lansbury as 'Sybil Vane' in *The Picture of Dorian Gray*
Joan Lorring as 'Bessie Watty' in *The Corn is Green*
• **Anne Revere as 'Mrs Brown' in** *National Velvet*

GOLDEN GLOBE AWARDS – **Angela Lansbury** – *The Picture of Dorian Gray*

For the second year in a row David O. Selznick campaigned strongly for the inclusion of Shirley Temple as a Best Supporting Actress nominee, this time for *I'll Be Seeing You* (NYT "splendid"). For the second year in a row his efforts were in vain.

Also overlooked were: Jeanne Crain in *Leave Her to Heaven* (NYT "colorless and wooden"; V "excellently done"); Joan Carroll as one of the children in *The Bells of St Mary's* (HRv "the best supporting performance seen so far this year"); Marie Blake as a telephone operator in *Between Two Women* (NYT "commendable"); Rosamund Jones in the British war film *The Way to the Stars (Johnny in the Clouds)*; Donna Reed in *They Were Expendable* (NYT "extraordinarily touching"); Betty Field as the wife of a struggling cotton farmer in *The Southerner* (V "fine"); Gladys Cooper in *Love Letters* (V "impressive"); Jessica Tandy in *The Valley of Decision*; and both Josephine Hull and Jean Adair as the murderous sisters in Frank Capra's adaptation of the hit stage comedy *Arsenic and Old Lace* (NYT "they're delightful in their roles").

The most egregious omission from the Academy Award ballot, however, was Margaret Rutherford for her memorable turn as the spiritual medium in the British comedy *Blithe Spirit* (NYT "played with robust good nature"; V "acting honours go to Margaret Rutherford ... no one else could ever be as good").

Anne Revere earned her second Oscar nomination in three years for her performance as the kind-hearted mother of a talented and ambitious young rider in *National Velvet* (NYT "splendid"; V "restrained and excellent") while 20-year old Angela Lansbury was mentioned for the second year in a row for *The Picture of Dorian Gray* (V "registers strongly and very sympathetically"). Eve Arden and 17-year old Ann Blyth (NYT "quite incredible"; V "scores dramatically"; TT "disturbingly convincing") received their (only) nominations for *Mildred Pierce* as the title character's best friend and spoilt daughter respectively, while another 17-year old, Joan Lorring, scored her (only) nomination as the young temptress in *The Corn is Green* (NYT plays it "on the dubious side of farce"; TT "brilliant").

Lansbury won the Golden Globe for her performance and Variety picked her as a narrow favourite for the Oscar ahead of Blyth. Unexpectedly, the winner on Oscar night proved to be the oldest of the nominees. Two years after being nominated for playing the struggling mother of Saint Bernadette of Lourdes in *The Song of Bernadette*, 42-year old Revere won for playing the kindly mother of a young female jockey in *National Velvet*. Two years later she would receive another nomination for playing the understanding mother of a journalist in *Gentleman's Agreement*.

1946

BEST PICTURE

ACADEMY AWARDS
• *The Best Years of Our Lives*
  (RKO Radio, 172 mins BW, 21 Nov 1946, $11.3m, 8 noms)
Henry V
  (Rank, Two Cities, United Artists, 135 mins, 17 Jun 1946, 4 noms)
It's a Wonderful Life
  (Liberty, RKO Radio, 130 mins BW, 7 Jan 1947, $3.3m, 5 noms)
The Razor's Edge
  (20th Century Fox, 146 mins BW, 19 Nov 1946, $5.0m, 4 noms)
The Yearling
  (M-G-M, 128 mins, 14 May 1947, $5.2m, 7 noms)

GOLDEN GLOBE AWARDS – *The Best Years of Our Lives*
NEW YORK – *The Best Years of Our Lives*
BOARD OF REVIEW – *Henry V*

Disappointed by the failure of his Oscar campaign for *Since You Went Away* two years earlier, David O. Selznick made another concerted effort to secure a third Best Picture Academy Award with *Duel in the Sun*, the first major studio Western to be filmed in colour. Hoping to recreate the success of *Gone with the Wind*, Selznick spent $7 million on the film and an unprecedented $1 million on more than eighteen months of promotion. Like its famous predecessor, the production was troubled and had no fewer than six directors. Controversial due to its sexual content, the film was a huge box office success when it went into general release in 1947 despite mostly negative reviews (NYT "spectacularly disappointing ... it is the bankroll and not the emotions by which you will be shocked"; V "daring"; TT "impressive, but never moving"). Selznick gave the film an Oscar qualifying run in Los Angeles in late December and campaigned strongly for Academy recognition. His efforts, however, were in vain. The film only received two nominations, both in the acting categories, for star Jennifer Jones and supporting player Lillian Gish.

Included ahead of Selznick's ambitious and expensive Western were four of the year's most acclaimed films and one surprise choice.

Topping the list of nominees with eight nods was William Wyler's drama about returning war veterans *The Best Years of Our Lives*. In The New York Times, Bosley Crowther enthused, "it is seldom that there comes a motion picture which can be wholly and enthusiastically endorsed not only as superlative entertainment but as food for quiet and humanizing thought". He concluded that it was the "best film this year from Hollywood". Variety, meanwhile, hailed it as "one of the best pictures of our lives" and the NYDN called it "a satisfying, heart-warming, deeply moving picture" which was the best "to come out of Hollywood since the end of the war."

Also nominated were: the family drama *The Yearling* (NYT "provides such a wealth of satisfaction as few pictures ever attain ... a cheerful and inspiring film about the coming to manhood of a youngster"; V "fine"); Frank Capra's heart-warming Christmas film *It's a Wonderful Life* (NYT "engaging"; HRp "wonderful entertainment"; TT "not a good film"); Laurence Olivier's *Henry V*, an acclaimed 1944 British film version of the historical play by William Shakespeare (NYT "a stunningly brilliant and intriguing screen spectacle"; V "striking"; S&S "a masterpiece"; HRv "a masterpiece of unexampled integrity"; Time "the movies have produced one of their rare great works of art" and "one of the great experiences in the history of motion pictures"); and, surprisingly, the melodrama *The Razor's Edge* which had received indifferent reviews but probably earned its place on the ballot due to a strong campaign by 20th Century Fox (NYT "vague and uncertain").

The unexpected inclusion of *The Razor's Edge* came at the expense of several other highly praised films such as: John Ford's Western *My Darling Clementine* (NYT "a dynamic composition ... the rich flavour of frontiering wafts in overpowering redolence from the screen"); David Lean's popular British romance *Brief Encounter* (NYT "an uncommonly good little picture ... extremely poignant"; V "intelligent, gripping"); *The Seventh Veil* (NYT "suspenseful", "intelligent and engrossing"); Alfred Hitchcock's post-war espionage thriller *Notorious* (NYT "superior", "one of the most absorbing pictures of the year"; V "terrific"); the controversial *The Postman Always Rings Twice* (NYT "a tremendously tense and dramatic show"); the musical biopic *The Jolson Story*, which earned six Oscar nominations (NYT a "gaudy fictionalization of Al Jolson's hurly-burly life ... obvious and hackneyed ... there is little or no dramatic point – and certainly no quality of character – conveyed in this fat and fatuous tale"); the thriller *The Spiral Staircase* (NYT "a creepy melodrama"; HRv "gripping, spellbinding and intensely thrilling"); the crime drama *The Killers* (NYT "a diverting picture"); the drama *Anna and the King of Siam* (NYT "worthwhile"; HRp a "magnificent spectacle"); the drama *To Each His Own* (NYT "spins dangerously on the brink of pathos but it seldom spills over into that treacherous chasm for more than a fleeting scene or two"; V a top "class emotional drama"); the film noir *The Big Sleep* (NYT "disappointing"; V "an excellent mixture of interesting characters [and] action-packed melodrama"; TT "intelligent"); and the British film *A Matter of Life and Death (Stairway to Heaven)* (NYT "wonderful", "delightful romantic fantasy") which had finished third in the voting for the New York critics' Best Picture prize.

1946

The year's two most acclaimed foreign-language movies were also overlooked by the Academy for its top prize: *Les Enfants du Paradis (Children of Paradise)* (NYT "a frequently captivating film"; V "a strange mixture of the beautiful, the esoteric and the downright dull"; S&S "important"; SMH "compassionate") and *Roma, Citta Aperta (Open City)* (NYT "overpowering realism", "unquestionably one of the strongest dramatic films yet made about the recent war", "the most intense and disturbing picture of the year"; V "excellent"; S&S "masterly production"). Each film rated a mention only in the writing categories.

Olivier's *Henry V* won the Best Picture prize from the NBR and finished as runner-up for the New York Film Critics Circle award, but its chances for winning the Oscar were significantly undermined when the Academy, fearful of a British film claiming Hollywood's coveted top prize, announced a Special Award for Olivier's combined work as actor, director and producer.

The Best Years of Our Lives was named as the year's Best Picture by the New York critics and won the Golden Globe award but was not a clear favourite for the Oscar. Variety predicted a close race between Wyler's drama and *The Yearling* which was tipped to win by the Los Angeles Times. The Hollywood Citizen News, meanwhile, passed over both and predicted a victory for Capra's *It's a Wonderful Life*.

On Oscar night, *The Best Years of Our Lives* prevailed and was named the year's Best Picture. It was the third year in a row that the Academy agreed with the New York critics.

A few months later, *The Best Year of Our Lives* was rewarded with the inaugural Best Film prize from the newly founded British Academy in London. The film subsequently finished 1947 as the year's highest money-earner at the North American box office.

1946

BEST DIRECTOR

ACADEMY AWARDS
Clarence Brown for *The Yearling*
Frank Capra for *It's a Wonderful Life*
David Lean for *Brief Encounter*
Robert Siodmak for *The Killers*
• **William Wyler for *The Best Years of Our Lives***

GOLDEN GLOBE AWARDS – Frank Capra – *It's a Wonderful Life*
NEW YORK – William Wyler – *The Best Years of Our Lives*
BOARD OF REVIEW – William Wyler – *The Best Years of Our Lives*

In 1945, for the first time, a British director was nominated for the Best Director Oscar for the handling of a British film. Surprisingly, it was not Laurence Olivier for his direction of the Best Picture nominee *Henry V* (NYT "has directed for action on a broad, spectacular scale... [but] this emphasis upon the spectacular has not absorbed Mr Olivier to the point of neglecting the subtleties and eloquences of Shakespeare's verse"; V "superb"). Instead, it was David Lean for his work on the acclaimed romantic drama *Brief Encounter*, which was a notable absentee from the top category at the Oscars (NYT "fluid direction"; V direction "of a high standard").

In the absence of Olivier, the three frontrunners for the Oscar were Clarence Brown, Frank Capra and William Wyler, who all made history as the first directors to receive a sixth Academy Award nomination: Brown for *The Yearling* (NYT "has revealed both his heart and his intelligence in keeping the whole thing restrained"); previous winner Capra for his first post-war film *It's a Wonderful Life* (HRp "Capra is at his best"); and previous winner Wyler for the year's most nominated film *The Best Years of Our Lives* (NYT "tactful and restrained direction"; NC "admirable"). It was the last time either Brown or Capra were nominated.

Unexpectedly, the final nominee was Robert Siodmak for the crime drama *The Killers* (NYT "restrained direction"). It was the only time he made the Academy's list. That year Siodmak had also directed *The Spiral Staircase* (NYT "it is quite evident by the technique director Robert Siodmak has employed to develop and sustain suspense – brooding photography and ominously suggestive settings – that he is at no time striving for narrative subtlety").

Overlooked for Oscar consideration were: Edmund Goulding for the Best Picture nominee *The Razor's Edge*; Alfred Hitchcock for the espionage thriller *Notorious* (NYT "has directed in brilliant style"; TT "admirable"; SMH "great technical skill"); Roberto Rossellini for the Italian film *Roma, Citta Aperta (Open City)*; Marcel Carné for the French drama *Les Enfants du Paradis (Children of Paradise)*; previous winner John Ford for the Western *My Darling Clementine* (NYT "can evoke fine sensations and curiously-captivating moods"); Mitchell Leisen for the melodrama *To Each His Own* (NYT "has directed the cast skillfully and his fastidious eye for detail is evident in the carefully appointed sets which reflect the various moods and circumstances of the characters"); the team of Michael Powell and Emeric Pressburger for *A Matter of Life and Death (Stairway to Heaven)*; John Cromwell for the period drama *Anna and the King of Siam* (V "intelligently handled"); and Aleksandr Stolper for the 1945 Russian drama about the Battle of Stalingrad *Dni i Nochi (Days and Nights)* (V "consistently excellent").

Capra won the Golden Globe award, but Wyler was named Best Director by both the NBR and the New York critics and on Oscar night it was he who collected his second Oscar in five years.

It was the sixth year in a row that the same film had won the Best Picture and Best Director Oscars and the third year in a row that the same director had won accolades from the New York critics and the Academy.

1946

BEST ACTOR

ACADEMY AWARDS
• **Fredric March as 'Al Stephenson' in** *The Best Years of Our Lives*
Laurence Olivier as 'King Henry V of England' in *Henry V*
Larry Parks as 'Al Jolson' in *The Jolson Story*
Gregory Peck as 'Pa Baxter' in *The Yearling*
James Stewart as 'George Bailey' in *It's a Wonderful Life*

GOLDEN GLOBE AWARDS – Gregory Peck – *The Yearling*
NEW YORK – Laurence Olivier – *Henry V*
BOARD OF REVIEW – Laurence Olivier – *Henry V*

Laurence Olivier was the early favourite to claim honours as the year's Best Actor for his performance as the title character in *Henry V*, a 1944 adaptation of the William Shakespeare play which Olivier had also produced and directed. The New York Times said his performance "sets a standard for excellence … his majestic and heroic bearing, his full and vibrant use of his voice, create a kingly figure around which the other characters rightly spin" while Variety simply called him "superb." The HRv commented that Olivier was "at once youthful and mature, straight forward and brilliant, simple and sophisticated" in his interpretation of the part of the early fifteenth century English king.

At the end of the year Olivier was named Best Actor by the NBR and convincingly won the same prize from the New York critics on the second ballot. The runner-up was previous Best Actor Oscar winner Fredric March for his acclaimed portrayal of a returning war veteran in *The Best Years of Our Lives* (NYT "magnificent … his humor is sweeping yet subtle, his irony is as keen as a knife and he is altogether genuine … this is the best acting job he has ever done"; NYDN "has never been better on the screen"; V "triumphs").

At the Golden Globe awards, the rapidly rising young American star Gregory Peck claimed the Best Actor trophy for his performance as the father of the young hero in *The Yearling* (NYT plays with "simple dignity and strength"; V "capital"). The win helped secure him a second consecutive Oscar nomination alongside Olivier (his third nomination) and March (his fourth nod – he had last been recognised for *A Star is Born* in 1937).

Also nominated were previous winner James Stewart (his third nomination) for again playing a Frank Capra hero in *It's a Wonderful Life* (NYT "does a warmly appealing job … he has grown in spiritual stature as well as in talent during the years he was in the war"; HRp "magnificent"; TT "admirable"), and Larry Parks for his impersonation of Al Jolson in the hit musical biopic *The*

Jolson Story (NYT "struts and mugs in the manner of Jolson, as a bright impersonator might do … the image at no time is equal to the vitality of the sound"; TT "well worth watching").

The inclusion of Parks and Globe winner Peck came at the expense of Tyrone Power for *The Razor's Edge* (NYT "tries exceedingly hard"; V "Power is thoroughly believable"). Twentieth Century Fox had mounted a major campaign to secure Oscar nominations for the film and its cast, particularly Power as Best Actor. Although the movie was mentioned for Best Picture and in both supporting categories, Power was overlooked. He never received a nomination from the Academy.

Also passed over were: English actor Rex Harrison, who had finished third on the New York critics' voting, for his portrayal of the King of Siam in *Anna and the King of Siam* (NYT "it is really in the performance of Rex Harrison as the king and in the cunning conception of his character that the charm of the picture lies"; V "shines"); Henry Fonda as the legendary frontier lawman Wyatt Earp in *My Darling Clementine* (NYT "quiet yet persuasive … he shows us an elemental character who is as real as the dirt on which he walks"; V "simple, sincere performance"); Cary Grant as an FBI agent in Alfred Hitchcock's espionage thriller *Notorious* (NYT plays "with surprising and disturbing clarity … exceptionally solid"; V "excellent"); Orson Welles as a Nazi war-criminal living incognito in a small American town in *The Stranger* (NYT "bad acting job"; S&S "magnificent"); John Garfield in both *The Postman Always Rings Twice* and *Humoresque*; Trevor Howard in *Brief Encounter* (NYT "thoroughly credible"); Humphrey Bogart in *The Big Sleep*; Australian actor Chips Rafferty as a cattle drover in *The Overlanders* (NYT "a cool and masterful job"); James Mason in *The Seventh Veil*; and Dana Andrews for his performance alongside March in *The Best Years of Our Lives* (NYT "incisive").

All the lauded performances by actors in foreign-language films were also left out of Oscar consideration, notably: both Marcello Pagliero (NYT "excellent", "profound"; TT "extremely well-acted") and Aldo Fabrizi (NYT "brilliant", "outstanding"; V "superb"; TT "extremely well-acted") in *Roma, Citta Aperta (Open City)*; Vladimir Solovyov in the 1945 Russian war film *Dni i Nochi (Days and Nights)* (NYT "excellent"; V "solid"); Jean Gabin in the 1941 French drama *Remorques (Stormy Waters)* (NYT "excellent"); and Jean-Louis Barrault as the famous French mime Baptiste Deburau in *Les Enfants du Paradis (Children of Paradise)* (NYT "exquisite" and "magically moody and expressive"; V "brilliantly effective"; SMH "excels").

Fearing that Olivier's English film version of *Henry V* would be the first foreign film to claim the Best Picture Oscar, the Academy announced that Olivier would receive a Special Award recognising his achievement as producer, director and actor on the film. Although his name was not removed from the ballot (as Charlie Chaplin's name had been in the first year of the awards), the Special Award meant that Olivier was no longer a serious contender.

As a result, Golden Globe winner Peck and New York runner-up March became the frontrunners for the Oscar.

At the Academy Awards ceremony, Joan Fontaine opened the evening's second last envelope to announce that March had won the statuette. March was in New York on the night of the Oscar ceremony and his statuette was accepted on his behalf by Cathy O'Donnell, one of his young co-stars.

The result made March the second man to win a second Best Actor Oscar, following Spencer Tracy's back-to-back victories in 1937 and 1938.

Two years later Olivier starred in and directed another film version of a Shakespearean play, *Hamlet*. The Academy rewarded him with the Best Actor award and a nomination as Best Director. As the film's producer, he also collected a statuette when the film was chosen as Best Picture.

March, meanwhile, received a fifth and final Oscar nomination as Best Actor five years later for his performance as the failed salesman Willy Loman in *Death of a Salesman*. His other notable performances over the next three decades in *Man on a Tightrope*, *Executive Suite*, *The Desperate Hours*, *The Man in the Gray Flannel Suit*, *Inherit the Wind*, *Seven Days in May* and *The Iceman Cometh* (his final film) were all overlooked by Academy members.

1946

BEST ACTRESS

ACADEMY AWARDS
• **Olivia de Havilland as 'Josephine Norris' in** *To Each His Own*
Celia Johnson as 'Laura Jesson' in *Brief Encounter*
Jennifer Jones as 'Pearl Chavez' in *Duel in the Sun*
Rosalind Russell as 'Elizabeth Kenny' in *Sister Kenny*
Jane Wyman as 'Ma Baxter' in *The Yearling*

GOLDEN GLOBE AWARDS – Rosalind Russell – *Sister Kenny*
NEW YORK – Celia Johnson – *Brief Encounter*
BOARD OF REVIEW – Anna Magnani – *Roma, Citta Aperta (Open City)*

The early favourite for the year's Best Actress honours was Olivia de Havilland. In May she starred in the melodrama *To Each His Own* as a woman who rediscovers her illegitimate son in wartime London, a role turned down by Ginger Rogers (NYT "may now take her exalted place alongside Helen Hayes, Ruth Chatterton and Bette Davis as a tragic heroine … her performance is extraordinarily fine"; V "superb"). Soon after she earned further praise for her portrayal of English novelist Charlotte Brontë in *Devotion* (V "expert"). Towards the end of the year, however, her performance as twins involved in a murder mystery in *The Dark Mirror* was slammed by critics. The New York Times said she "does nothing that will add to her stature as an actress." Variety complained that she "can't make her roles come to life" and that "she comes up with two-ply wooden characterizations."

Having been nominated unsuccessfully in the supporting category in 1939 and as Best Actress two years later (when she lost the Oscar to her younger sister Joan Fontaine), de Havilland was desperate to win an Academy Award. Noting the success of Joan Crawford the previous year she hired the same publicist and began campaigning for her performance in *To Each His Own* to be rewarded.

Also mounting a strong campaign was David O. Selznick who wanted to secure a nomination for his wife, previous winner Jennifer Jones, as the promiscuous and fiery half-caste in his expensive Western *Duel in the Sun*. Although critics had given her performance decidedly mixed reviews (NYT "strangely uneven … gives occasional glints of the pathos of loneliness and heartbreak, but mostly she has to pretend to be the passion-torn child of nature in the loosest theatrical style"; V "extremely capable"; TT "stylized") Jones had the advantage of another performance that year which was well-received: her first comic turn in *Cluny Brown* (V "excellent").

1946

Despite the campaigns, neither actresses were rewarded with any of the prestigious end of year critics' accolades in the months leading up to the Academy Awards.

On 18 December 1946, the NBR made history when it named Italian actress Anna Magnani as the year's Best Actress for her acclaimed performance in the realist war drama *Roma, Citta Aperta (Open City)* (NYT "profound"; V "top performance"; TT "extremely well-acted"). It was the first time a major American acting prize had gone to a performer in a foreign-language film (neither the Academy nor the New York critics would give a prize to a foreign-language performance until 1961).

Nearly two weeks later, on the sixth ballot, the New York critics chose English actress Celia Johnson as their choice as the year's Best Actress for her performance as a housewife tempted to have an affair in David Lean's popular British romantic drama *Brief Encounter* (NYT "gives a consuming performance ... she is naturally and honestly disturbing with her wistful voice and large, sad saucer-eyes"; V "terrific"). De Havilland, who led after the first ballot, finished as runner-up.

At the Golden Globes, Rosalind Russell, who had also received support during the New York voting, emerged as the winner for her portrayal of Sister Elizabeth Kenny, the Australian nurse who pioneered a treatment for infantile paralysis in the biopic *Sister Kenny* (NYT "plays the title character with tremendous vitality and warmth"; V "one of the best performances in her luminous film career"; TT "an admirable performance, sincere and authoritative"). It was the first of her record five Globe victories.

When the Academy Award nominations were announced de Havilland, Johnson, Jones and Russell were all included on the list of contenders. Magnani was overlooked. Included instead was Jane Wyman in the family drama *The Yearling* (her first nomination) (NYT "compels credulity and sympathy"; V "capital"; TT "admirable").

Performers passed over for Oscar consideration included: previous winner Ingrid Bergman as a spy in the espionage thriller *Notorious* (NYT plays "with surprising and disturbing clarity ... there is rich and real emotion expressed by Miss Bergman in her role, and the integrity of her nature as she portrays it is the prop that holds the show"; V "Bergman's best job to date"; TT "persuasive"); the previous year's winner Joan Crawford in *Humoresque* (NYT "violently emoting"); Lana Turner in *The Postman Always Rings Twice* (NYT "remarkably effective"); Gene Tierney in the Best Picture nominee *The Razor's Edge* (NYT "spectacularly deficient"); Loretta Young in *The Stranger* (V "particularly effective" in an "exceptionally strong performance"); Irene Dunne in *Anna and the King of Siam* (NYT "plays the fabled governess briskly and winsomely"; V "superb"; TT "a little too pettish and peevish"); Eleanor Parker in a remake of the drama *Of Human Bondage* (V "excellent"); Barbara Stanwyck in *The Strange Love of Martha Ivers* (NYT "playing to the hilt ... [but] her characterization of Martha is more on a one-dimensional plane"); Rita Hayworth for her iconic role in *Gilda*; Phyllis Calvert as a woman with a split personality in the British thriller *Madonna of the Seven Moons* (NYT "plays a tricky role extremely well"); Ann Todd in *The Seventh Veil* (NYT "restrained and sensitive"; V "fine"); and Françoise Rosay in the 1942 Swiss film *Une Femme Disparaît (Portrait of a Woman)* (NYT "brilliant" and "impressive" in "four disparate roles").

Most surprising, however, was the exclusion of rising Hollywood newcomer Dorothy McGuire for her lauded performance as a mute servant targeted by a serial killer in the thriller *The Spiral Staircase* (NYT "gives a remarkably lucid performance", "McGuire is to be heartily commended for her adventurousness and the high degree of resourcefulness with which she tackled the demanding and little used art of pantomime"; V her "stature as an actress will be increased by her performance"; SMH "creditable acting").

Despite failing to collect any of the three other end of year Best Actress prizes, de Havilland was still the favourite for the Academy's prize.

At the Oscar ceremony, the previous year's Best Actor winner Ray Milland opened the envelope and declared de Havilland the winner of the statuette. She told the audience at the Shrine Auditorium in Los Angeles, "I feel humble, too, as well as proud", and then thanked all those involved in the making of *To Each His Own*.

De Havilland was nominated twice more during the next three years, and in 1949, she went one better than her younger sister and claimed a second Best Actress trophy from the Academy for her portrayal of Catherine Sloper in *The Heiress*.

1946

BEST SUPPORTING ACTOR

ACADEMY AWARDS
Charles Coburn as 'Alexander Gow' in *The Green Years*
William Demarest as 'Steve Martin' in *The Jolson Story*
Claude Rains as 'Alexander Sebastian' in *Notorious*
• **Harold Russell as 'Homer Parrish' in *The Best Years of Our Lives***
Clifton Webb as 'Elliott Templeton' in *The Razor's Edge*

GOLDEN GLOBE AWARDS – Clifton Webb – *The Razor's Edge*

An amateur actor won the Academy Award for Best Supporting Actor in 1946. Harold Russell, a veteran who had lost both his hands in the war, claimed the Oscar for playing a returning veteran in William Wyler's *The Best Years of Our Lives* (NYT "incredibly fine": NYDN "a remarkable performance"). Russell also won a special award for his performance, making him the only person to collect two statuettes for the same performance.

Russell's victory resulted in popular character actor Claude Rains' fourth defeat in just eight years in the Supporting Actor category. Rains was nominated (for the final time) for his performance as a Nazi agent in Alfred Hitchcock's post-war espionage thriller *Notorious* (NYT "Rains' shrewd and tense performance is responsible for much of the anguish that the situation creates"; SMH "polished"). He had been considered the frontrunner for the award.

Also outpolled by Russell were: the 1943 Supporting Actor Oscar winner Charles Coburn, who had received his third (and final) nomination in five years for playing a great-grandfather in *The Green Years* (NYT "plays the swag-bellied old rascal with a beautifully fustian air but laces into his comicality a great of moving sentiment … his bearded and brummagemed performance in this role will be remembered for a long time"); Golden Globe winner Clifton Webb, who was mentioned for the second time in three years for his turn as a pompous socialite in *The Razor's Edge* (NYT "crisply amusing"); and William Demarest, who made the Oscar list (for the only time) as Al Jolson's friend and mentor in *The Jolson Story* (NYT "Demarest is truculent and tickling as an old burlesque partner of the star"). Just two years earlier Demarest had been a shock omission for a trio of comedies including Preston Sturges' *Hail the Conquering Hero*.

Left out of Oscar consideration were: previous Best Actor Oscar winner Charles Laughton as a stage idol tricked into helping an aspiring actress in *Because of Him* (NYT "magnificent"); both previous three-time Best Supporting Actor winner Walter Brennan (NYT "completely characteristic") and Victor

Mature as Doc Holliday (NYT "soundly played") in John Ford's *My Darling Clementine*; both Lionel Barrymore (NYT "almost a caricature") and Henry Travers (NYT "a little too sticky for our taste"; HRp "magnificent") in Frank Capra's Christmas tale *It's a Wonderful Life*; one of the previous year's nominees Michael Chekhov for his comic turn in *Specter of the Rose* (NYT "striking"); both the late Philip Merivale (NYT "excellent – cold and dignified and severe") and Alexander Knox (NYT "a winning performance") in *Sister Kenny*; Herbert Marshall in *The Razor's Edge* (NYT "wan"); Peter Lorre in *The Chase* (NYT "excellent"); Broderick Crawford as a police officer in *The Black Angel*; Edward G. Robinson in *The Stranger* (NYT "is well restrained"); Leon Ames as the district attorney in *The Postman Always Rings Twice* (V "splendid"); Roger Livesey in *A Matter of Life and Death (Stairway to Heaven)* (NYT "magnificent"); Arthur Kennedy as Bramwell Brontë, the drunken poet-painter brother of the Brontë sisters, in *Devotion* (V "a standout"); Kirk Douglas in *The Strange Love of Martha Ivers* (NYT "playing to the hilt … convincing); and Roland Culver in *To Each His Own* (NYT "superb").

1946

BEST SUPPORTING ACTRESS

ACADEMY AWARDS
Ethel Barrymore as 'Mrs Warren' in *The Spiral Staircase*
• **Anne Baxter as 'Sophie Nelson' in *The Razor's Edge***
Lillian Gish as 'Laura Belle McCanles' in *Duel in the Sun*
Flora Robson as 'Angelique Buiton' in *Saratoga Trunk*
Gale Sondergaard as 'Lady Thiang' in *Anna and the King of Siam*

GOLDEN GLOBE AWARDS – Anne Baxter – *The Razor's Edge***

At just twenty-three years of age Anne Baxter won the Golden Globe and Oscar as Best Supporting Actress for her performance as a young alcoholic in *The Razor's Edge* (NYT "wallows in debauchery and pathos"; V "personal hit"; TT "brilliant"). The unexpected win propelled Baxter to a series of significant roles, and just four years later she was a Best Actress nominee for *All About Eve*.

Baxter outpolled four highly regarded actresses: previous winner Ethel Barrymore (her second nod) as a widowed invalid in *The Spiral Staircase* (NYT "always interesting even though her role as a cantankerous invalid is hardly deserving of her vast talents"; TT "magnificent"; SMH "creditable acting"); previous winner Gale Sondergaard (her second mention) as the King's first wife in *Anna and the King of Siam* (V "commanding"; TT "a lovely performance"); Lillian Gish, the great star of American silent films receiving her only Oscar nomination, as a cattle baron's wife in *Duel in the Sun* (NYT "no better – nor worse – than the script allows"); and the great English theatre actress Flora Robson, also receiving her only Oscar recognition, as the servant of a fortune hunter in *Saratoga Trunk* (NYT "monotonous").

Overlooked for Academy consideration were: Lauren Bacall in *The Big Sleep* (NYT "plays the older of the daughters languidly … [she] is a dangerous looking female, but she still hasn't learned to act"; TT "excellent"); Constance Collier as the aunt in *Kitty* (NYT "excellent in a small but incisive role"); Lizabeth Scott in *The Strange Love of Martha Ivers* (NYT "has some pretty silly-sounding lines and her performance generally lacks conviction"); and Leopoldine Konstantin in *Notorious* (NYT "a splendid touch of chilling arrogance").

Also bypassed were four actresses in Best Picture nominees: both previous Best Actress nominee Myrna Loy (NYDN "enchanting") and previous Oscar winner Teresa Wright (NYT "a lovely, quiet performance"; NYDN "excellent") in *The Best Years of Our Lives*; Donna Reed in *It's a Wonderful Life* (NYT "remarkably poised and gracious"); and Renée Asherson as Princess Katherine of France in *Henry V* (NYT "very lovely and gracefully piquant").

1947

BEST PICTURE

ACADEMY AWARDS
The Bishop's Wife
  (Goldwyn, RKO Radio, 105 mins BW, 16 Feb 1948, 5 noms)
Crossfire
  (RKO Radio, 86 mins BW, 22 Jul 1947, $2.5m, 5 noms)
• *Gentleman's Agreement*
  (20th Century Fox, 118 mins BW, 11 Nov 1947, $3.9m, 8 noms)
Great Expectations
  (Rank-Cineguild, 118 mins BW, 22 May 1947, $2.0m, 5 noms)
Miracle on 34th Street
  (20th Century Fox, 96 mins BW, 2 May 1947, 4 noms)

GOLDEN GLOBE AWARDS – *Gentleman's Agreement*
BRITISH ACADEMY AWARDS
  (Best Film) – *The Best Years of Our Lives*
  (Best British Film) – *Odd Man Out*
NEW YORK – *Gentleman's Agreement*
BOARD OF REVIEW – *Monsieur Verdoux*

Two years after the Best Picture Academy Award was won by a drama about alcoholism, two films about another important issue in US society were the early frontrunners for Best Picture honours. Both Elia Kazan's *Gentleman's Agreement* and Edward Dmytryk's surprise box office hit *Crossfire* were strong indictments of anti-Semitism. *Gentleman's Agreement* starred Gregory Peck as a journalist who pretends to be Jewish in order to research an article on discrimination against Jews (NYT "a sizzling film"; V "brilliant and powerful film", "impressive"; TT "intelligent") while *Crossfire* centred on the murder of a Jewish man by a US army soldier (NYT "a frank and immediate demonstration of the brutality of religious bigotry", "grimly absorbing"; V "a frank spotlight on anti-Semitism" and "a hard-hitting film"). Both were included by the NYT on its list of the year's ten best films.

Towards the end of the year, however, the Oscar chances of *Crossfire* were hamstrung when Dmytryk and the film's producer Adrian Scott both refused to testify before the House Un-American Activities Committee hearings and were blacklisted. Despite nominations for the two men in the Best Picture and Best Director categories, they had little chance of claiming Academy honours. The effective exclusion of *Crossfire* left *Gentleman's Agreement* as the strong favourite for the Oscar. The film was named Best Picture by the New York critics, won the Golden Globe and earned more Oscar nominations that any other contender.

Also nominated for the Best Picture Oscar were: the popular melodrama *The Bishop's Wife* (NYT "superb"); the family film *Miracle on 34th Street* (NYT "a lively and heart-warming comedy"; V "one of the most appealing, heart-warming films to come out of Hollywood in many a day"); and *Great Expectations*, David Lean's film adaptation of the Charles Dickens novel, which finished as runner-up in New York (NYT "a perfect motion picture", "wonderful", "well-nigh perfect film"; HRv "a classic of the screen"; V "beautiful but lacks heart").

The consideration of *Great Expectations* by both the New York critics and the Academy was a testament to the increasingly strong presence of quality British movies in US cinemas. Also released in the US that year to critical acclaim were: the 1944 release *This Happy Breed*, also directed by Lean (NYT "absorbing and affecting"; V "needs drastic cutting" but still a "superior production"); *The Captive Heart* (NYT "impressive", "moving and wholly believable"); *Black Narcissus* starring Deborah Kerr (NYT "curiously fascinating", "an artistic accomplishment of no small proportions"; TT "a disappointment"); and Carol Reed's thriller *Odd Man Out*, which the British Academy in London chose as the winner of its inaugural Best British Film award (NYT "most intriguing"; V "art with a capital A"; SMH "compelling").

The end of the war also meant that more foreign-language films were being released in America. In 1947 critics hailed Vittorio de Sica's 1946 Italian drama *Sciuscia (Shoe Shine)* (NYT "one of the sharpest screen dramas produced in any country since the war"; V "superb acting" but "senselessly grim"), the Italian comedy *Vivere in Pace (To Live in Peace)* (NYT "wonderful", "among the fine motion pictures of our time"; V "sincere and poignant"), Julien Duvivier's 1946 French drama *Panique (Panic)* (NYT "vivid and disturbing", "thoroughly fascinating"; TT "a film which breaks out of the normal celluloid conventions") and *Ivan Groznyj I (Ivan the Terrible, Part One)* the first part of Sergei Eisenstein's planned trilogy about the Russian Tsar (NYT "one of the most imposing films ever made", "a film of awesome and monumental impressiveness"; V "will disappoint", "tiresome"). None were nominated for Best Picture but the Academy did introduce an annual Special Award for the year's best foreign-language film. The first recipient was *Sciuscia*.

Among the American films overlooked by the Academy was Charlie Chaplin's *Monsieur Verdoux* which had been named Best Picture by the NBR even though it had received mixed reviews and been a box office disaster (NYT "tediously slow ... those who go expecting to laugh at it may find themselves remaining to weep"; CIN "one of the most significant and unique post-war films" and "a landmark in the progress of the American screen"; Time "fascinating" and despite "serious shortcomings" still "one of the most notable films in years").

Also passed over were: *A Double Life* for which Ronald Colman won the Best Actor Oscar (NYT "rich, exciting"; V "nigh perfect", "distinguished"); John Ford's *The Fugitive* (NYT "strange and haunting ... one of the best films of the year"); *The Farmer's Daughter* for which Loretta Young won the Best Actress Oscar (NYT "a cheerful comedy-drama"); Elia Kazan's *Boomerang!* (NYT "a drama of rare clarity"; V "gripping, real-life melodrama"; TT "admirable"; SMH "compelling"); and the film noir *Out of the Past* (NYT "intensely fascinating for a time ... if only we had some way of knowing what's going on in the last half of this film, we might get more pleasure from it. As it is, the challenge is worth the try").

Despite a strong campaign by RKO, *Mourning Becomes Electra* was unable to overcome poor reviews (NYT "far from electric entertainment", "a static and tiresome show"; V "tolerably good" but "grim" and "unrelenting", "lacks much of the impact of the play"). The Academy did not include the film version of Eugene O'Neill's drama on the ballot for Best Picture.

Just as Variety had predicted, on Oscar night *Gentleman's Agreement* won the Academy Award as the year's Best Picture.

1947

BEST DIRECTOR

ACADEMY AWARDS
George Cukor for *A Double Life*
Edward Dmytryk for *Crossfire*
• **Elia Kazan for** *Gentleman's Agreement*
Henry Koster for *The Bishop's Wife*
David Lean for *Great Expectations*

GOLDEN GLOBE AWARDS – Elia Kazan – *Gentleman's Agreement*
NEW YORK – Elia Kazan – *Gentleman's Agreement* and *Boomerang!*
BOARD OF REVIEW – Elia Kazan – *Gentleman's Agreement* and
   Boomerang!

Two years after he was overlooked for his acclaimed directorial debut *A Tree Grows in Brooklyn*, Elia Kazan was the overwhelming favourite for the Best Director Oscar. He received his first mention for his anti-Semitism drama *Gentleman's Agreement*, the year's most nominated film (NYT "brilliant direction"). Earlier in the year he had also received positive notices for *Boomerang!* (NYT "sharp direction"). The NBR and the New York critics both awarded him their Best Director prizes for the two films. He also won the Golden Globe, for his handling of *Gentleman's Agreement*.

The runner-up to Kazan for the New York critics' accolade was Edward Dymtryk for the year's other lauded anti-Semitism drama *Crossfire* (NYT "has employed a slow, aggravatingly-set tempo and heavily-shaded pictorial style ... has worked for moods of ominous peril to carry to hot ferocity suggested in the script ... has handled most excellently a superlative cast"). Although he received an Oscar nomination, Dmytryk was a non-starter for the statuette. He refused to testify before the HUAC hearings into alleged communist activities and was blacklisted.

Finishing third in the New York voting had been previous Oscar winner John Ford for *The Fugitive*, but he did not make it onto the Academy's list of nominees (NYT "Ford has made *The Fugitive* a symphony of light and shade, of deafening din and silence, of sweeping movement and repose ... by this magnificent ordering of a strange, dizzying atmosphere, he has brewed a storm of implications of man's perils and fears in a world gone mad").

Also overlooked were: previous winner Michael Curtiz for the comedy *Life with Father* (NYT "expertly staged by the resourceful Michael Curtiz, who has made certain that none of the essential comedy is overdrawn"; HRp "outstanding"); Charlie Chaplin for *Monsieur Verdoux* (V "disjointed"); Zoltan

Korda for *A Woman's Vengeance* (NYT "visually forceful"); Jacques Tourneur for *Out of the Past* (NYT "made even more galvanic by a smooth realistic style … well and smartly directed"); Sergei Eisenstein for *Ivan Groznyj I (Ivan the Terrible, Part One)*; Julien Duvivier for *Panique (Panic)* (NYT "the brilliance of Duvivier's direction, his deceptively random accumulation of details and then his sudden, explosive demonstration of the viciousness and cruelty of a mob and the astonishment and torment of the hunted are of superior and adult quality"; TT "brilliant"); Vittorio de Sica for *Sciuscia (Shoe Shine)* (NYT "the direction of Vittorio De Sica reveals keen and sympathetic understanding of the nature of embittered, frustrated youth"); George Seaton for the Best Picture nominee *Miracle on 34th Street*; and Carol Reed for the thriller *Odd Man Out* (NYT "can be glowingly commended for his artistry"; Time "outstanding"; SMH "masterly direction").

Although Reed was passed over for consideration, British cinema was represented for the second year in a row by David Lean who was named for the Best Picture contender *Great Expectations* (NYT "superlatively sensitive direction"; HRv "directed with fine originality"). The other Oscar nominees were George Cukor for *A Double Life* (NYT "in his direction amply proves that he knows the theatre, its sights and sounds and brittle people") and Henry Koster for *The Bishop's Wife* (NYT directed "smoothly and with artful invention"; V "sympathetic direction").

On Oscar night Kazan won the Best Director Oscar. It was the seventh year in a row that the same film had won the Best Picture and Best Director Oscars and the fourth consecutive year that the same director had won accolades from the New York critics and the Academy. Kazan would collect a second Oscar and earn another four nominations from the Academy over the next twenty years. Dmytryk would never be nominated again.

1947

BEST ACTOR

ACADEMY AWARDS
• **Ronald Colman as 'Anthony John' in** *A Double Life*
John Garfield as 'Charley Davis' in *Body and Soul*
Gregory Peck as 'Phil Green' in *Gentleman's Agreement*
William Powell as 'Clarence Day' in *Life with Father*
Michael Redgrave as 'Orin Mannon' in *Mourning Becomes Electra*

GOLDEN GLOBE AWARDS – Ronald Colman – *A Double Life*
NEW YORK – William Powell – *Life with Father* **and** *The Senator was Indiscreet*
BOARD OF REVIEW – Michael Redgrave – *Mourning Becomes Electra*

The New York critics gave their Best Actor award to William Powell for his performances in the comedy *Life with Father* (NYT "even his voice, always so distinctive, has taken on a new quality, so completely has Mr Powell managed to submerge his own personality … not merely a performance; it is a character delineation of a high order and he so utterly dominates the picture that even when he is not on hand his presence is still felt"; HRp "just wonderful"; SMH "disappointing") and in the satire *The Senator was Indiscreet* (NYT "does about everything that a competent actor of farce comedy could do"). The runner-up was John Garfield for his performance as a young boxer in *Body and Soul* (NYT "a rattlingly good performance"; V "convincing").

The NBR, meanwhile, selected English actor Michael Redgrave for his turn in *Mourning Becomes Electra*, a film adaptation of the play by Eugene O'Neill (NYT "a good job").

All three made the Academy's list of nominees: Powell for the third (and final) time; Redgrave for the first (and only) time; and Garfield, having been repeatedly overlooked since being the unsuccessful favourite for the Best Supporting Actor Oscar in 1938, for the second (and final) time.

The frontrunners for the Academy Award, however, were the Golden Globe winner and the star of the year's most Oscar nominated film.

Ronald Colman won the Globe and earned his fourth (and final) nomination for his portrayal, in *A Double Life*, of a mentally unstable Shakespearian actor who comes to believe during a performance that he actually is Othello and murders his co-star (NYT "the only question is whether Mr Colman is more spectacular as the mentally distressed star of Broadway or as the bearded Venetian Moor"; V "Colman realizes on every facet of the demanding part in a performance that is flawless"; TT "disappointing").

189

For his performance as a journalist who pretends to be Jewish in order to research an article on anti-Semitism in *Gentleman's Agreement*, Gregory Peck received his third consecutive Best Actor nomination, equalling the record streaks of Spencer Tracy and Gary Cooper (NYT "crisply and agreeably played … a careful analysis"; V "unquestionably the finest performance of his career to date").

Overlooked by the Academy were: Robert Young as the police detective in the anti-Semitism drama *Crossfire* (NYT "a fine taut performance"; TT "admirable"); Charlie Chaplin in his box office failure *Monsieur Verdoux* (NYT "remarkably adroit"; V "Chaplin generates very little sympathy"; S&S "a stylized performance done with an elegance and brilliance yet unachieved in motion pictures"); previous winner Spencer Tracy as a rancher in *The Sea of Grass* (NYT his "austere performance" is "impressive and dignified"); Dana Andrews in *Boomerang!* (NYT "another sensitive job"; V "a top performance"; SMH "excellent"); Robert Mitchum as a detective in the film noir *Out of the Past* (NYT "magnificently cheeky and self-assured"); Cary Grant as an angel in the Best Picture nominee *The Bishop's Wife* (NYT "one of his most fluent and beguiling performances"); Nikolai Cherkasov in *Ivan Groznyj I (Ivan the Terrible, Part One)* (NYT & V "superb"), Michel Simon in *Panique (Panic)* (NYT "brilliant"); and, for their performances in British films, John Mills in *Great Expectations* (NYT "stands out … makes of this first-personal character such a full-bodied, gracious young man that Pip actually has more stature here than he has in the book"; HRv "a star performance" and "an extremely sensitive interpretation"); Robert Newton in *This Happy Breed* (NYT "brilliant"); and James Mason in *Odd Man Out* (NYT "a terrifying picture of a wounded man"; SMH "his greatest role").

By-passed for the second year in a row were Tyrone Power in *Nightmare Alley* (NYT "performing with considerable versatility and persuasiveness"), Henry Fonda in John Ford's *The Fugitive* (NYT "excellent … an agonized performance as the desperately bewildered priest") and Aldo Fabrizi as a peasant in the Italian comedy *Vivere in Pace (To Live in Peace)* (NYT "brilliant"; V "brilliant").

While many predicted a win for the popular young star Peck for his turn in the Best Picture frontrunner, Variety surprisingly predicted a win for the veteran star Colman.

On Oscar night, Variety was proven correct. Olivia de Havilland opened the envelope and revealed Colman to be the winner of the Best Actor Oscar. "I am very happy and very proud and very lucky," he told the audience at the Shrine Auditorium as he collected the statuette.

1947

BEST ACTRESS

ACADEMY AWARDS
Joan Crawford as 'Louise Howell' in *Possessed*
Susan Hayward as 'Angie Evans' in *Smash Up – the Story of a Woman*
Dorothy McGuire as 'Kathy Lacey' in *Gentleman's Agreement*
Rosalind Russell as 'Lavinia Mannon' in *Mourning Becomes Electra*
• **Loretta Young as 'Katrin Holstrom' in *The Farmer's Daughter***

GOLDEN GLOBE AWARDS – Rosalind Russell – *Mourning Becomes Electra*
NEW YORK – Deborah Kerr – *Black Narcissus* and *I See A Dark Stranger (The Adventuress)*
BOARD OF REVIEW – Celia Johnson – *This Happy Breed*

The year after earning an Oscar nomination for David Lean's *Brief Encounter*, English actress Celia Johnson was named Best Actress by the NBR for another Lean film, *This Happy Breed*, which she had actually made the year before her appearance in *Brief Encounter* (NYT "brilliant"; V "a masterful, poignant portrayal").

The New York critics, who had selected Johnson the previous year, gave their prize to Scottish actress Deborah Kerr for her performances in the war drama *I See A Dark Stranger (The Adventuress)* (NYT "clever and subtle characterization") and as a nun in *Black Narcissus* (NYT "brilliantly performed", "excellent").

Surprisingly, both women were overlooked by the Academy, who also passed over: Ida Lupino as a farmer in *Deep Valley* (NYT "well-acted … Lupino displays nice shadings of emotion and, in the early part, when she is required to speak haltingly, she manages to be quite convincing"); Jane Greer in *Out of the Past* (NYT "very sleek"); English actress Phyllis Calvert in her US film debut as a housekeeper's daughter in *Time Out of Mind* (NYT "impressive"); Anna Magnani in the 1946 Italian drama *Un Uomo Ritorna (Revenge)* (NYT "tremendous"); and Jessica Tandy in the courtroom drama *A Woman's Vengeance* (NYT "expertly accomplished", "brilliant").

The unexpected omission of both Johnson and Kerr left Rosalind Russell as the overwhelming favourite for the Academy Award for her performance as the cold-blooded daughter in *Mourning Becomes Electra* (NYT "never transmits the huge malevolence and the torment of the daughter's soul"; Time "fine", "notable"; MFB "is simply unequal to acting on this scale"). For her performance, Russell won the Golden Globe award for the second year in a row and received her third Oscar nomination in six years.

Nominated alongside Russell were previous winner Joan Crawford as a schizophrenic in *Possessed* (V "cops all thesping honors in this production with a virtuoso performance") and three first-time nominees: Susan Hayward as a nightclub singer who becomes an alcoholic when she sacrifices her career in favour of her husband's in *Smash Up – the Story of a Woman* (NYT "this film gives little evidence of sincerity … Hayward performs the boozy heroine with a solemn fastidiousness which turns most of her scenes of drunken fumbling and heebie-jeebies into off-key burlesque"); Loretta Young as a Swedish-American farmer's daughter who runs for Congress in *The Farmer's Daughter* (V "breezes through with finesse"; TT "acts very nicely"); and Dorothy McGuire as the prejudiced wife of a journalist in the Best Picture frontrunner *Gentleman's Agreement* (NYT "affectingly plays"; V "dramatically and emotionally compelling").

Russell hired the same publicist that helped Crawford and de Havilland to their Best Actress wins the previous two years and was confident of claiming the Oscar. Variety's straw poll of Academy members predicted that Russell would win easily ahead of a distant Hayward, followed, in order, by McGuire, Young and finally Crawford.

On Oscar night, Fredric March opened the evening's final envelope and announced one of the biggest upsets in the history of the Academy Awards. The Best Actress Oscar went to Young for her performance in a part that had been turned down by previous winners Ingrid Bergman and Olivia de Havilland as well as, ironically, by Russell. Young was so surprised, she even checked that her name really was inside the envelope before making her acceptance speech. "Up to now, this occasion has been for me a spectator sport. But I dressed, just in case!"

Apparently, Russell's chances of winning the Oscar were undermined by her overwhelming favouritism – voters felt that her victory was so certain that they could vote for the other nominees in sympathy – as well as by the unpopularity of the film in which she had appeared (NYT "a static and tiresome show"). Of the other four contenders, Young benefitted from an appealing part in a charming film, as well as from have also appeared in one of the year's Best Picture nominees, the popular melodrama *The Bishop's Wife* even though she had received mixed reviews for her turn (NYT "Weakness [in the cast] is only evident in Loretta Young's unctuousness as the bishop's wife … she is the one artificial, inconsistent and discordant note"; V "moving").

1947

BEST SUPPORTING ACTOR

ACADEMY AWARDS
Charles Bickford as 'Clancy' in *The Farmer's Daughter*
Thomas Gomez as 'Pancho' in *Ride the Pink Horse*
• **Edmund Gwenn as 'Kris Kringle' in *Miracle on 34th Street***
Robert Ryan as 'Montgomery' in *Crossfire*
Richard Widmark as 'Tommy Udo' in *Kiss of Death*

GOLDEN GLOBE AWARDS – Edmund Gwenn – *Miracle on 34th Street*

With his acclaimed turn in the popular Christmas film *Miracle on 34th Street* as a Macy's department store Santa Claus who might just be the real thing, Edmund Gwenn became the first man to win a Golden Globe and an Oscar as Best Supporting Actor (V "the best [performance] of his career"). Although he arguably had the film's leading role, the likeable Hollywood veteran had been the favourite for the Oscar in the weeks before the ceremony.

Gwenn's main rival was Richard Widmark, who earned his only nomination for his screen debut as a psychopath in the thriller *Kiss of Death* (NYT "Widmark runs away with all the acting honors"; V "the acting sensation of the piece").

Robert Ryan also earned his only nomination for playing a murderer, the sadistic and bigoted marine in *Crossfire* (NYT "frighteningly real"). He was among those considered for the New York critics' Best Actor prize. Also nominated were Thomas Gomez (his only mention) as a small-town carousel proprietor in the thriller *Ride the Pink Horse* and Charles Bickford (his second nod in five years) as the family butler in *The Farmer's Daughter*.

Overlooked for Oscar consideration were: Arthur Kennedy as an innocent man accused of murdering a minister in *Boomerang!* (NYT "convincing"); Pedro Armendáriz in *The Fugitive* (SMH "capable"); Kirk Douglas in *Out of the Past*; Gino Cavalieri as a priest in the Italian comedy *Vivere in Pace (To Live in Peace)* (V "superb"); and both previous Best Actor Oscar winner Charles Laughton as an elderly trial judge (NYT "a bit too much flutter and flourish"; V "a revealing portrait"; TT "magnificent"; MFB "brilliant") and Leo G. Carroll as an old family solicitor (NYT "superlatively sardonic") in Alfred Hitchcock's courtroom drama *The Paradine Case*.

John Garfield was also overlooked for his supporting performance in the Best Picture winner *Gentleman's Agreement* (NYT "too mechanical"; V "a natural", "admirable"), but was mentioned in the Best Actor category for *Body and Soul*.

BEST SUPPORTING ACTRESS

ACADEMY AWARDS
Ethel Barrymore as 'Lady Sophie Horfield' in *The Paradine Case*
Gloria Grahame as 'Ginny Tremaine' in *Crossfire*
• **Celeste Holm as 'Anne Detrie' in *Gentleman's Agreement***
Marjorie Main as 'Ma Kettle' in *The Egg and I*
Anne Revere as 'Mrs Green' in *Gentleman's Agreement*

GOLDEN GLOBE AWARDS – Celeste Holm – *Gentleman's Agreement*

The winners of the Best Supporting Actress Oscar in 1944 and 1945 were both contenders for the prize once again in 1947. Rather surprisingly, Ethel Barrymore received her third nomination in the category in just four years for her brief appearance as the emotional wife of a trial judge in Alfred Hitchcock's courtroom drama *The Paradine Case* (NYT "entirely too little intelligence is in Ethel Barrymore's skits as [the judge's] balmy wife": MFB "brilliant") while Anne Revere earned her third nomination in five years for playing the kindly mother of a journalist in the year's Best Picture Oscar winner *Gentleman's Agreement*. Revere had also appeared in the supporting role of the mother of a boxing champion in *Body and Soul*.

Nominated alongside them were three first-time nominees: Gloria Grahame as a lonely nightclub floozie in the drama *Crossfire* (NYT "believably brazen and pathetic as a girl of the streets"); Marjorie Main as a farmer's long-suffering and hard-working wife in the comedy *The Egg and I* (NYT together Kilbride and Main "do contribute some bits of rustic spoof but mostly are used for nothing more original than old-time bumpkin burlesque"); and Celeste Holm as a magazine fashion editor in *Gentleman's Agreement* (V "excellent").

Overlooked were: Ann Todd as a trial lawyer's loyal and understanding wife in *The Paradine Case* (NYT "attractively anguished"; SMH "intelligent study"); Martita Hunt as Miss Havisham in *Great Expectations* (NYT "neither space nor words are sufficient to praise adequately"); Edna Best as the housekeeper in *The Ghost and Mrs Muir* (NYT "gives by far the best performance [in the film]"); both Kathleen Byron (NYT "plays the unfortunate Sister Ruth with a careful shading of emotion that bespeaks a talented artist ... a truly magnificent performance") and Jean Simmons (TT "an extremely clever study") in *Black Narcissus*; Mildred Natwick in *A Woman's Vengeance* (NYT "superior"); both Signe Hasso (NYT "remarkably and charmingly nimble") and Shelley Winters in *A Double Life* (NYT "remarkably and charmingly nimble"); Martha Ryer in *Monsieur Verdoux*; Maria Campi, in her only film appearance, as the dowdy fortune-teller in *Sciuscia (Shoe Shine)* (V "superb"); and Ave Ninchi as the distraught wife in *Vivere in Pace (To Live in Peace)* (V "brilliant").

Holm won the Golden Globe and Variety correctly predicted that she would also collect the Oscar. "Thank you for letting this happen," she told the audience at the Shrine Auditorium in Los Angeles. "I'm happy to be part of an industry that can create so much understanding in a world that needs it so much." She was the first actress to win the Best Supporting Actress Globe and Oscar for the same performance and over the next three years she would be nominated in the category twice more.

Of the other nominees, Revere would never again make the Academy's lists and neither would Main, although she would reprise her Oscar-nominated role in a whole series of hugely popular films. Barrymore was recognised a fourth and final time just two years later, while Grahame would win the statuette in 1952.

BEST PICTURE

ACADEMY AWARDS
• *Hamlet*
  (Rank, Two Cities, 155 mins BW, 29 Sep 1948, $3.2m, 7 noms)
Johnny Belinda
  (Warner Bros., 102 mins BW, 14 Sep 1948, $4.6m, 12 noms)
The Red Shoes
  (Rank-Archers, Eagle-Lion, 133 mins, 22 Oct 1948, $2.2m, 5 noms)
The Snake Pit
  (20th Century Fox, 108 mins BW, 13 Nov 1948, $4.1m, 6 noms)
The Treasure of the Sierra Madre
  (Warner Bros., 126 mins BW, 7 Jan 1948, $2.3m, 4 noms)

GOLDEN GLOBE AWARDS – *Johnny Belinda* and *The Treasure of the Sierra Madre*

BRITISH ACADEMY AWARDS

(Best Film)	(Best British Film)
Crossfire	• *The Fallen Idol*
The Fallen Idol	*Hamlet*
• *Hamlet*	*Oliver Twist*
Monsieur Vincent	*Once a Jolly Swagman*
The Naked City	*The Red Shoes*
Paisa (Paisan)	*Scott of the Antarctic*
Quattro Passi Fra le Nuvole	*The Small Voice*
(Four Steps in the Clouds)	(The Hideout)

NEW YORK – *The Treasure of the Sierra Madre*
BOARD OF REVIEW – *Paisa (Paisan)*

In 1946, the Academy presented Laurence Olivier with a Special Award for his achievements as producer, director and star of *Henry V* thus all but ensuring the Best Picture Oscar was not won by a foreign film. Two years later Olivier's film version of *Hamlet* earned acclaim from critics and enjoyed a long run in US cinemas (NYT "magnificent", "brilliant"; V "a masterpiece", "picture-making at its best"; Time "admirable"; S&S "excellent"). Named Best Picture at the 1948 Venice Film Festival, *Hamlet* finished as runner-up for the New York critics' top award and was recognised by the Academy in seven categories including Best Picture, Director and Actor.

Olivier's Shakespearian drama, however, was not the only British film to meet with Oscar approval. Unexpectedly nominated for the Academy's top accolade was also Michael Powell and Emeric Pressburger's ballet fantasy *The Red Shoes* (NYT "there has never been a picture in which the ballet and its special, magic world have been so beautifully and dreamily presented ... one you must see"). It was the first time that two foreign films had been included in the Best Picture short-list.

The NBR passed over all the year's lauded British and American films to give their Best Picture award to the Italian film *Paisa (Paisan)*, a collection of vignettes about life in wartime Italy (NYT "a milestone in the expressiveness of the screen"; V "a film that must rank near the great foreign pictures of all time"). The film was also named Best Foreign Film by the New York critics.

Other acclaimed foreign-language films released in the US that year were: Carl Dreyer's 1943 drama about witchcraft in 17th century Denmark, *Vredens Dag (Day of Wrath)* (NYT "handsome but dull"; V "tedious to the extreme"; S&S "the most distinguished piece of cinema to appear on our screen since the war"; NYer "powerful", "one of the best [films] ever made"); *Les Maudits (The Damned)* (NYT "taut, wholly believable and absorbing"); *La Symphonie Pastorale* (NYT "intense, disturbing"); the 1947 Mexican drama *La Perla (The Pearl)*; and Maurice Cloche's biopic about St Vincent de Paul, *Monsieur Vincent* (NYT "remarkably vivid"). The Academy presented Cloche's film with a Special Award for outstanding foreign-language film.

The New York critics named *The Treasure of the Sierra Madre* as the year's Best Picture by just a single vote over *Hamlet*. Although acclaimed by critics (NYT "original ... fascinating ... a searching drama"; V "a distinguished work", "radically different", "compelling"; Time "one of the best things Hollywood has done", "magnificent"; TT "too long"), the film was not a success at the box office.

The frontrunner for the Academy's top award was *Johnny Belinda*, an acclaimed and popular melodrama about a deaf-mute woman (V "sombre, tender, moving"). At the Golden Globes, *Johnny Belinda* shared the Best Picture award with *The Treasure of the Sierra Madre*, but heading into the Oscars it led the field with twelve nominations, nearly twice as many as *Hamlet*.

The final nominee for the Oscar was *The Snake Pit*, a melodrama about a woman in a psychiatric hospital (NYT "a true, illuminating presentation ... although it is frequently harrowing, it is a fascinating and deeply moving film"; V "a standout"; HRp "compelling"; MFB "powerful and gripping").

Producer Walter Wanger campaigned strongly for his expensive biopic *Joan of Arc* starring Ingrid Bergman. Although mentioned in seven categories, the poorly reviewed film was not a Best Picture nominee (NYT "a stupendous film

... [that] fails to come fully to life"; MFB a "failure"). Wanger was presented an honorary Oscar as a consolation prize.

Also passed over were: the post-war drama *The Search* (NYT "an absorbing and gratifying emotional drama", "vivid and convincing"; V "superb"; S&S & MFB "moving"); the thriller *Key Largo* (HRp "electrifying"; V "tense ... hard-hitting"); *Force of Evil* (NYT "a dynamic crime-and-punishment drama, brilliantly and broadly realized"); *A Foreign Affair* (NYT "a sharp, shrewd and sophisticated comedy"; V "a witty satire"); *I Remember Mama* (NYT "should prove irresistible"; V "deeply moving nostalgia"); *Letter from an Unknown Woman* (NYT an "obvious onslaught on the heart-strings"; V "distinguished"; SMH "by no means an outstanding picture"; TT "moving"); and the thriller *The Naked City*, which was a surprise nominee for the Best Film BAFTA (NYT "the drama is largely superficial, being no more than a conventional 'slice of life' – a routine and unrevealing episode in the everyday business of the cops ... studiously over-written and even contrived").

Variety predicted an easy win for *Johnny Belinda* with its main rival thought to be *The Treasure of the Sierra Madre* (for the previous four years the New York prize-winner had collected the Oscar). The surprise winner, however, turned out to be *Hamlet*. It was the first time in the Academy's history that a foreign production had won the Best Picture Oscar.

1948

BEST DIRECTOR

ACADEMY AWARDS
• **John Huston for** *The Treasure of the Sierra Madre*
Anatole Litvak for *The Snake Pit*
Jean Negulesco for *Johnny Belinda*
Laurence Olivier for *Hamlet*
Fred Zinnemann for *The Search*

GOLDEN GLOBE AWARDS – John Huston – *The Treasure of the Sierra Madre*

DIRECTORS GUILD AWARD
(1948/49)
Howard Hawks – *Red River*
Anatole Litvak – *The Snake Pit*
• **Joseph L. Mankiewicz –** *A Letter to Three Wives*
Fred Zinnemann – *The Search*

NEW YORK – John Huston – *The Treasure of the Sierra Madre*
BOARD OF REVIEW – Roberto Rossellini – *Paisa (Paisan)*

The Best Director category at the Academy Awards included five first-time nominees. Having been overlooked two years earlier Laurence Olivier was mentioned for *Hamlet* (SMH "fine direction"), but he was considered only an outside chance as he had also been nominated in the Best Actor category for the same film and was favoured to win in that category. Fred Zinnemann was nominated for *The Search* (NYT "brilliant"; MFB "natural and exciting"), but he too was a longshot because his film had not been included in the Best Picture category. Anatole Litvak made the Academy's list (for the only time) for the melodrama *The Snake Pit* (NYT "sure and rhythmic throughout"; V "adroit" direction) in the same year that he had directed the suspense drama *Sorry, Wrong Number* (MFB "brilliant"). The stars of both his films were nominated as Best Actress and he was seen as a dark horse for the Best Director prize.

A serious contender for the award was Jean Negulesco for *Johnny Belinda* which was the year's most Oscar nominated film and the Best Picture frontrunner (NYT "able direction"). The overwhelming favourite for the Best Director award, however, was John Huston, the only American nominee. Huston had earned praise from critics for both the thriller *Key Largo* (NYT "Huston has certainly done a great deal to tighten and speed a still overcrowded story ... with remarkable filming and cutting, Mr Huston had notably achieved a great deal of interest and tension in some rather static scenes ... he has also got stinging performances out of most of his cast") and the drama *The Treasure of the Sierra Madre* (NYT "trenchant and fascinating"; Time "establishes himself in the top rank of contemporary moviemakers"). It was for the latter that he won the Best Director Golden Globe and the accolade from the New York critics (he narrowly out-polled Olivier).

The inaugural prize from the DGA, which was awarded for a non-calendar year period, was presented to Joseph L. Mankiewicz for his 1949 release *A Letter to Three Wives* ahead of three other finalists for 1948 films: Litvak, Zinnemann and Howard Hawks, who was overlooked by the Academy, for the hit Western *Red River* (NYT "has filled it with credible substance and detail, with action and understanding, humor and masculine ranginess ... has made it look raw and dusty ... he has also got several fine performance out of solidly masculine cast").

Italian director Roberto Rossellini was chosen as Best Director ahead of Huston by the NBR for his acclaimed film *Paisa (Paisan)*, but was overlooked by the Academy (NYT "Rossellini constructs a terrifying picture of the delusion, the irony, the horribleness of strife"). He was the first NBR winner to have been left out of consideration for the Oscar.

Also by-passed were: Carl Dreyer for *Vredens Dag (Day of Wrath)* (S&S "Dreyer is a master of the art of the film"; NYer "superb" direction); George Stevens for *I Remember Mama* (V "expert direction"); John Ford for *Fort Apache* (NYT "masterful direction"); Jules Dassin for *The Naked City* (NYT "accomplished); Max Ophüls for *Letter from an Unknown Woman* (TT "directing with uncommon skill"; MFB "sensitive"); and, once again, the British collaborative team of Michael Powell and Emeric Pressburger for the Best Picture nominee *The Red Shoes* (NYT "seems to have the construction and flow of a romantic dance").

On Oscar night, Olivier won the Best Actor Oscar and *Hamlet* was named Best Picture. As predicted by Variety, however, the Best Director award went to Huston. Another winner that night for *The Treasure of the Sierra Madre* was Huston's father, Walter Huston, who won the Best Supporting Actor award. Nearly forty years later John Huston earned a fourth nomination as Best Director for the gangster film *Prizzi's Honor* his daughter, Anjelica Huston, won Best Supporting Actress that year for her performance in the same film.

1948

BEST ACTOR

ACADEMY AWARDS
Lew Ayres as 'Dr Robert Richardson' in *Johnny Belinda*
Montgomery Clift as 'Ralph Stevenson' in *The Search*
Dan Dailey as 'Skid Johnson' in *When My Baby Smiles at Me*
• **Laurence Olivier as 'Prince Hamlet of Denmark' in** *Hamlet*
Clifton Webb as 'Lynn Belvedere' in *Sitting Pretty*

GOLDEN GLOBE AWARDS – Laurence Olivier – *Hamlet*
NEW YORK – Laurence Olivier – *Hamlet*
BOARD OF REVIEW – Walter Huston – *The Treasure of the Sierra Madre*

John Huston narrowly outpolled Laurence Olivier to win the New York critics' Best Director award but in the Best Actor vote, it was Olivier who won by a small margin ahead of Huston's father, Walter Huston.

Olivier was rewarded for his performance as William Shakespeare's tragic Danish Prince in *Hamlet* (NYT "outstanding"; Time "in its subtlety, variety, vividness and control, Olivier's performance is one of the most beautiful ever put on film"; SMH "beautiful acting", "unfaltering genius"). It was Olivier's second New York critics' Best Actor award in just three years having previously won for another Shakespearean role, the title character in *Henry V*.

Huston, who had won the New York critics' award in 1936, was considered for his portrayal of an old gold prospector in *The Treasure of the Sierra Madre*. He was named Best Actor by the NBR, and at the Golden Globes both he and Olivier won awards – Huston was named Best Supporting Actor while Olivier won as Best Actor.

At the Oscars, Huston was nominated for the supporting award (which he won) and Olivier earned his fourth Best Actor nomination in a decade.

The other main contender was expected to be Huston's co-star, Humphrey Bogart. His performance in *The Treasure of the Sierra Madre* was hailed by The New York Times as "expert" and "perhaps the best and most substantial [work] that he has ever done." Bogart, however, was a shock omission from the Academy's list.

Having been overlooked for his turn as the young solider in the 1929/30 Best Picture Oscar winner *All Quiet on the Western Front*, Lew Ayres received a nomination (his only one) for playing the gentle doctor who helps a pregnant deaf-mute rape victim in the year's most nominated film, *Johnny Belinda* (NYT "makes a credibly humble young doctor").

Also nominated was 28-year old Montgomery Clift for his screen debut as a young American soldier who helps a lost boy in post-war Nuremberg in *The Search* (NYT "superb", "precisely the right combination of intensity and casualness"; MFB "powerful", "dynamic naturalism"). Clift had also starred in the box office hit *Red River* (NYT "Clift has our admiration as the lead and leathery kid").

The two surprise nominees came from films directed by Walter Lang: musical star Dan Dailey as an alcoholic comedian in *When My Baby Smiles at Me* (NYT "romps and capers with accustomed breeziness and charm ... he's the one refreshing thing about the show"); and Clifton Webb, who received his third nomination in five years, for playing a babysitter in the comedy *Sitting Pretty* (NYT "the material is handled dexterously ... a student of the fine shades of kidding will find a lot to admire in Mr Webb"; SMH "magic").

In addition to Bogart, overlooked in favour of these nominees were: John Garfield in *Force of Evil* (NYT the director "was very fortunate in having John Garfield play the young lawyer ... sentient underneath a steel shell, taut, articulate – he is all good men gone wrong"; S&S "remarkable"); John Wayne in *Red River* (NYT "surpasses himself in this picture"); previous winner Fredric March in the euthanasia drama *Live Today for Tomorrow* (NYT "superb"); Joseph Cotten in *Portrait of Jennie* for which he was the winner of the Best Actor prize at the 1949 Venice Film Festival (NYT "morbidly solemn"; V "a top performance"); Pedro Armendáriz in the 1947 Mexican drama *La Perla (The Pearl)* (NYT "beautifully acted"; V "beautiful performance"); Osvaldo Valenti in the title role of the 1943 Italian historical *Enrico IV (Henry IV)* (V "extraordinary bravura thesping", "passionate and compelling"); Pierre Blanchar in *La Symphonie Pastorale* (NYT "brilliant" and "subtle" as "one of the most difficult characters ever shown on the screen"); and Pierre Fresnay, both in *Le Corbeau (The Raven)* (V "brilliant"), and as St Vincent de Paul in *Monsieur Vincent* (NYT "fine", "haunting"; V "masterful"; TT "perfect").

Arguably, the most surprising omission after Bogart was that of Austrian actor Anton Walbrook for his turn as the dictatorial director of the National Ballet Company in the Best Picture nominee *The Red Shoes* (NYT "winning ... a wonderful performance": V "flawless").

With Bogart excluded from the category, the favourite for the award was Olivier, whose Best Actor chances two years earlier for *Henry V* had been undermined by the Academy's decision to present him with a Special Award. On Oscar night, Olivier lost in the Best Director category to John Huston, but his portrayal of the troubled prince in *Hamlet* won him the Best Actor statuette. His win came nearly a decade since his wife, Vivien Leigh, had won the Best Actress Oscar for *Gone with the Wind*. Olivier was not at the ceremony to collect his statuette in person.

1948

BEST ACTRESS

ACADEMY AWARDS
Ingrid Bergman as 'Joan of Arc' in *Joan of Arc*
Olivia de Havilland as 'Virginia Cunningham' in *The Snake Pit*
Irene Dunne as 'Mama' in *I Remember Mama*
Barbara Stanwyck as 'Leona Stevenson' in *Sorry, Wrong Number*
• **Jane Wyman as 'Belinda McDonald' in *Johnny Belinda***

GOLDEN GLOBE AWARDS – Jane Wyman – *Johnny Belinda*
NEW YORK – Olivia de Havilland – *The Snake Pit*
BOARD OF REVIEW – Olivia de Havilland – *The Snake Pit*

For only the second time, the five actresses short-listed for the Best Actress Oscar were previous nominees (the scenario would not occur again until 1994). The early favourite was previous winner Olivia de Havilland for her lauded performance as a woman in a psychiatric hospital in Anatole Litvak's *The Snake Pit*, a role turned down by Ginger Rogers (NYT "a brilliant, heart-rendering job", "excellent"; V "rises to new distinction" with "a memorable performance"; S&S "unforgettable characterisation" which "would surely be the most outstanding piece of film acting in any year"; HRp "one of the greatest performances we have ever seen on screen or stage"; MFB "perfect ... never falters once"). For her portrayal, de Havilland won the NBR prize and New York critics' award in only the group's second unanimous vote. In 1949, she also won the Best Actress honour at the Venice Film Festival for her performance.

The other frontrunner for the Oscar was Jane Wyman as a deaf-mute rape victim in the popular drama *Johnny Belinda*, which was the year's most nominated film. The critics had praised her performance (NYT "sensitive and poignant performance", "brings superior insight and tenderness to the role", "plays her role in a manner which commands compassion and respect"; V "personal success" in "a daring role"; TT "distinguished") and she was a popular figure in Hollywood. She had recently also become a figure of sympathy after suffering a miscarriage and then, during filming of *Johnny Belinda*, separating from her husband, actor and future US President Ronald Reagan. At the Golden Globe Awards, Wyman was named Best Actress.

Another popular nominee – and, for many, a sentimental choice for the Oscar – was Irene Dunne who earned her fifth (and final) mention from the Academy for her turn as a Norwegian mother in the nostalgic *I Remember Mama* (NYT "a beautiful job ... has the strength and vitality, yet the softness, that the role requires"; V "in holding down the most demanding role of her career, she earns new honors as an actress of outstanding versatility").

Also nominated were Barbara Stanwyck (her fourth and final nomination) as a bedridden heiress in another film directed by Litvak, *Sorry, Wrong Number* (NYT "a quite elaborate job"), and previous winner Ingrid Bergman. The popular Swedish star was a surprise inclusion following poor reviews for her appearances in both Lewis Milestone's *Arch of Triumph* (SMH "has to struggle to convince") and Walter Wanger's extravagant *Joan of Arc* (NYT "has no spiritual quality"; V "convincing", "vivid"; MFB "too insipid and sentimental"). It was for playing the title role in the latter that she was included on the Oscar ballot.

Unlike Bergman, previous winner Vivien Leigh was unable to overcome poor reviews for her performance in *Anna Karenina* (NYT "Leigh is a pretty sad disappointment"). Similarly, the previous year's Best Actress favourite, Rosalind Russell, had her Oscar hopes dashed by negative reviews of her performance as an actress playing Hedda Gabler in the tragedy *The Velvet Touch*.

Despite a huge campaign and a contrasting role in the Bing Crosby musical *The Emperor Waltz* (NYT "magnificent", "a sweet job of farce") previous winner Joan Fontaine, the younger sister of de Havilland, was unable to secure a nomination for her acclaimed turn in *Letter from an Unknown Woman*, a film which she had produced herself (V "splendid"; SMH "adroit"; TT "beautifully conveyed", "nowhere in her performance is there any suggestion of artificiality"; S&S "very touching"; MFB "a tender performance").

Also overlooked were: the 1947 Venice Film Festival Best Actress winner Anna Magnani for *L'Onorevola Angelina (Angelina)* (NYT "most impressive and awesome"; MFB "magnificent"); previous winner Jennifer Jones for *Portrait of Jennie* (V "compelling"); Michèle Morgan as a blind girl in *La Symphonie Pastorale* (NYT "brilliant", "an exquisite piece of art"); and both Jean Arthur as a Congresswoman (NYT "excellent") and Marlene Dietrich as a Berlin nightclub singer (NYT "excellent" and "fascinating") in the comedy *A Foreign Affair*.

On Oscar night, it was Wyman who outpolled de Havilland and the other nominees to win the Best Actress Oscar. It was the seventh year in a row that the New York winner had not been rewarded with the Oscar. That streak, however, would be ended by de Havilland the very next year.

BEST SUPPORTING ACTOR

ACADEMY AWARDS
Charles Bickford as 'Black McDonald' in *Johnny Belinda*
José Ferrer as 'the Dauphin of France' in *Joan of Arc*
Oscar Homolka as 'Uncle Chris' in *I Remember Mama*
• **Walter Huston as 'Howard' in *The Treasure of the Sierra Madre***
Cecil Kellaway as 'Horace' in *The Luck of the Irish*

GOLDEN GLOBE AWARDS – Walter Huston – *The Treasure of the Sierra Madre*

Time magazine hailed Walter Huston's performance as a gold prospector in *The Treasure of the Sierra Madre* as "his best job in a lifetime of grand acting." In The New York Times, Bosley Crowther said Huston played his character "with such humor and cosmic gusto that he richly suffuses the picture with human vitality and warmth". Later the paper praised Huston further for his part as the kindly father in *Summer Holiday* (NYT "magnificently sapient and adroit").

At the end of the year Huston's turn in *The Treasure of the Sierra Madre* earned him the Best Actor prize from the NBR and a Best Supporting Actor Golden Globe. He also finished runner-up for the New York critics' Best Actor prize. He was an overwhelming favourite for the Oscar at his fourth nomination, and on the same night as his son won the Best Director honour, Huston won the Academy Award for Best Supporting Actor.

The nominees outpolled by Huston were: Charles Bickford, who received his third nomination in just six years for playing the fisherman father of Jane Wyman's character in *Johnny Belinda* (NYT "good"); Oscar Homolka, who made the list (for the only time) for reprising his Broadway role as the mischievous uncle in *I Remember Mama* (NYT "gives to it all the bluff and blunder that was in this decidedly 'hammy' gent"; V "memorable"; TT "an uproarious performance"); José Ferrer for his screen debut as the Dauphin in *Joan of Arc* (NYT "electric"; S&S "provides the film's only moments of strength"); and Cecil Kellaway as a leprechaun in *The Luck of the Irish* (NYT "played by Cecil Kellaway with considerable affection")

Surprisingly Richard Haydn was overlooked for his performances as the neighbour in *Sitting Pretty* (NYT "magnificently obnoxious"; V "a gem of a performance as suburban snoop and prissy gossiper") and as the Emperor Franz Joseph in the musical *The Emperor Waltz* (NYT "Hadyn is cute as the emperor"). Another glaring omission was Ralph Richardson as the title character's husband in *Anna Karenina* (NYT "emphatic and superior", "a beautiful piece of illustration"; V "masterly yet uneven").

Also overlooked were: Edward G. Robinson as the gangster in *Key Largo* (NYT "Robinson's performance is an expertly timed and timbred scan of the vulgarity, corruption and egoism of a criminal man"; V "a standout"); Ivan Jandl as the lost child in *The Search* (NYT "unquestionably the remarkable performance a little Czech lad named Ivan Jandl as the principal figure in the drama is vital to the spirit of the whole ... [he] has such tragic expression in his slight frame, such poetry in his eyes and face, and such melting appeal in his thin voice that he is the ultimate embodiment of the sorrow-inflicted child"; S&S "a performance of extraordinary pathos"); Thomas Gomez in *Force of Evil* (NYT "does a fine, tense job as the small-time brother of the tough guy"); Felix Aylmer as Polonius in *Hamlet* (NYT "fine work"; Time "it is hard to imagine better work"); Frank Morgan in *Summer Holiday*; Raymond Burr in *Pitfall* (NYT "sinister and fascinating"; V "excellent"); Rex Ingram in *Moonrise* (V "stands out"); and both Mark Stevens as the husband (NYT "Stevens is gentle as her husband – a notably hard role to play": V "excellent") and Leo Genn as the caring doctor in *The Snake Pit* (NYT "remarkably fine": MFB "convincing").

Alec Guinness' memorable portrayal of Fagin in *Oliver Twist* would not be eligible for Academy Award consideration until the film's release in the United States three years later.

1948

BEST SUPPORTING ACTRESS

ACADEMY AWARDS
Barbara Bel Geddes as 'Katrin' in *I Remember Mama*
Ellen Corby as 'Aunt Trina' in *I Remember Mama*
Agnes Moorehead as 'Aggie McDonald' in *Johnny Belinda*
Jean Simmons as 'Ophelia' in *Hamlet*
• **Claire Trevor as 'Gaye Dawn' in *Key Largo***

GOLDEN GLOBE AWARDS – Ellen Corby – *I Remember Mama*

In the reviews of Laurence Olivier's *Hamlet*, film critics praised both Eileen Herlie as Queen Gertrude (NYT "vibrant"; V "special praise is due"; Time "profoundly exciting job"; SMH "brilliant") and Jean Simmons as Ophelia (NYT "luminous"; V "sensitive"; Time "genuine", "gives every one of her lines the bloom of poetry"; SMH "marvellous"). At the Venice Film Festival, Simmons won the Best Actress award and, a few months later, she received an Oscar nomination. Herlie was overlooked.

Also nominated were: Barbara Bel Geddes as the literary daughter (V "a tour de force") and Ellen Corby as one of the sisters (V "superbly played"; TT "stands out") in *I Remember Mama*; Agnes Moorehead, who earned her third nod in just seven years, as the stern aunt in *Johnny Belinda* (NYT "good"); and Claire Trevor as an alcoholic former singer and gangster's moll in *Key Largo* (TT "superb", claims the "major honors").

Corby was honoured with the Golden Globe award, but the Oscar went to Trevor, a popular actress who had first been nominated for an Oscar over a decade earlier.

Surprisingly overlooked were both Elsa Lanchester as an eccentric painter in *The Big Clock* (NYT "truly delicious"; V "particularly superb") and previous nominee Beulah Bondi as an old lady who imagines herself to be wealthy in the Best Picture nominee *The Snake Pit* (HRp "outstanding").

Also by-passed were: Helen Craig as a nurse in *The Snake Pit* (NYT "good, tough performance"); Angela Lansbury in *State of the Union*; Jane Wyatt in *Pitfall* (NYT "excellent and altogether natural"); both Aline MacMahon as the American army bureaucrat (MFB "powerful") and Jarmila Novotna as the lost boy's mother in *The Search*; and Line Noro in *La Symphonie Pastorale* (NYT "remarkably human").

1949

BEST PICTURE

ACADEMY AWARDS
• *All the King's Men*
 (Columbia, 109 mins BW, 8 Nov 1949, 7 noms)
Battleground
 (M-G-M, 118 mins BW, 20 Jan 1950, $5.0m, 6 noms)
The Heiress
 (Paramount, 115 mins BW, 6 Oct 1949, 8 noms)
A Letter to Three Wives
 (20th Century Fox, 103 mins BW, 20 Jan 1949, 3 noms)
Twelve O'Clock High
 (20th Century Fox, 132 mins BW, 26 Jan 1950, $3.2m, 4 noms)

GOLDEN GLOBE AWARDS
• *All the King's Men*
Come to the Stable

BRITISH ACADEMY AWARDS

(Best Film)	(Best British Film)
Berliner Ballade	*Kind Hearts and Coronets*
(The Ballad of Berlin)	*Passport to Pimlico*
• *Ladri di Biciclette*	*The Queen of Spades*
(Bicycle Thieves)	*A Run for Your Money*
Ostatni Etap	*The Small Back Room*
(The Last Stage)	• *The Third Man*
The Set-Up	*Whisky Galore!*
The Third Man	
The Treasure of the Sierra Madre	
The Window	

NEW YORK – *All the King's Men*
BOARD OF REVIEW – *Ladri di Biciclette (Bicycle Thieves)*

Two years after the Best Picture Academy Award was won by Elia Kazan's drama about anti-Semitism *Gentleman's Agreement*, four notable films addressed the issue of racial discrimination and violence in America – and all were acclaimed by critics (three of them appeared on The New York Times list of the year's ten best films).

The most high-profile was Kazan's box office hit *Pinky*, a drama about a young African-American woman who passes as white (NYT "vivid, revealing and emotionally intense; V "engrossing and dramatic"; HRp "brilliantly compelling").

The other three were: Clarence Brown's *Intruder in the Dust*, about a Southern town's reaction to the lynching of an African-American (NYT "a brilliant stirring film" ... the year's "pre-eminent picture and one of the great cinema dramas of our time"; TT "exciting"; MFB "gripping" and "impressive"); Mark Robson's *Home of the Brave*, about a racially-motivated persecution within the US army (NYT "a film of emotional impact as well as strong intellectual appeal"; V "hits hard with utter credibility"); and Alfred L. Werker's *Lost Boundaries*, about an African-American couple who pass as whites (NYT "one of the most effective pictures that we are likely to have this year ... one of the many bitter aspects of racism in our land is exposed with extraordinary courage, understanding and dramatic power".)

Despite strong campaigns for *Pinky* and *Intruder in the Dust* – which was the runner-up for the Best Picture accolade in New York – all four films were shut out of consideration for the year's top Academy Award. *Pinky* was the only one to receive any nominations at all. The following year, the British Academy included *Intruder in the Dust* in the field of Best Film contenders.

The other major omission from the Academy's list was Vittorio de Sica's Italian drama *Ladri di Biciclette (Bicycle Thieves)* (NYT "brilliant and devastating" S&S "the crowning example of the Italian renaissance", V "superb"; MFB "a film of rare humanity and sensibility"). The film was named Best Picture by both the NBR and the British Academy, but the Academy in Hollywood nominated it only for Best Writing. The Board of Governors subsequently voted to award the film a Special Oscar as the year's best foreign-language film.

A year after a foreign-made film had won the Best Picture Oscar for the first time, the Academy shortlisted five American films, overlooking such foreign movies as: the Polish holocaust drama *Ostatni Etap (The Last Stage)* (NYT "uncompromising", "powerful"); Carol Reed's *The Fallen Idol*, which had been the second runner-up for the New York critics' Best Picture award (NYT "brilliant"; TT "outstanding"); and David Lean's *The Passionate Friends (One Woman's Story)* (V "in the top rank of class British productions").

The British comedy *Passport to Pimlico* is now regarded as a classic and earned strong praise from critics in the United Kingdom (MFB "genuinely funny", "too much cannot be said in praise of this film"). Its awards prospects in the United States were sadly compromised, however, by the edited form in which it was originally shown to American audiences. "We have a strong suspicion that some of the picture's charm was lost in the injudicious cutting that was done to shorten it for this side [of the Atlantic]," wrote Bosley Crowther when he reviewed the picture for The New York Times.

1949

The year's most nominated film was the costume drama *The Heiress*, a screen version of Augustus and Ruth Goetz's theatrical adaptation of the novel 'Washington Square' by Henry James (NYT "one of the most handsome, intense and adult dramas of the year"; V "a class production"). Also nominated were: the political drama *All the King's Men* (NYT "a rip-roaring film ... the picture bounces from raw-boned melodrama into dark psychological depths"; V "smashing, dramatically-compelling ... one of the most gripping films of the year"; Life "the most exciting film to come out of Hollywood this year"; MFB "more conspicuous for scope and worthiness of intention than for inspiration"); the World War Two army drama *Battleground*, which went on to become the second biggest box office hit of 1950 (NYT deserves "the highest commendation that could be handed to any war film"; S&S "inferior sort of film"; TT "commendable"); the World War Two air force drama *Twelve O'Clock High* (NYT & V both "a topflight drama"; S&S "a failure"); and Joseph L. Mankiewicz's comedy *A Letter to Three Wives* (NYT "interesting", "sophisticated"; V a "standout in every aspect"; Time "a bright, unusual comedy"; MFB "good entertainment").

Surprisingly, Golden Globe nominee *Come to the Stable* received seven nominations from the Academy but was not included in the Best Picture race (V "a drama of considerable charm"; MFB "deplorable"). Similarly, the boxing drama *Champion* (HRp "compelling"; V "stark, realistic") received six nominations but was not considered for the Best Picture Oscar.

Other American films passed over were: *Sands of Iwo Jima*, for which Republic had campaigned strongly (NYT "has undeniable moments of greatness ... Republic tried hard to make a film that would do full credit to the United States Marine Corps ... the effort wasn't altogether successful"); *Command Decision* (TT "the most adult and responsible film about the war yet to be produced by Hollywood"); *The Stratton Story* (V "a heart-warming dramatic saga"); Jules Dassin's *Thieves' Highway* (NYT "first-rate"); the BAFTA nominee *The Set-Up* (V "compact and suspenseful"); and *We Were Strangers* (V "suspenseful"). Alfred Hitchcock's poorly reviewed *Under Capricorn* was also ignored (NYT "an overlong overlabored essay on the torments of conscience and love"; V "overlong and talky").

Despite having one nomination less than *The Heiress*, Robert Rossen's drama *All the King's Men* was the favourite for the Academy's top honour having claimed Best Picture accolades at the Golden Globes and from the New York critics' circle.

On Oscar night, although Rossen lost the Best Director Oscar, the Best Picture Academy Award went to *All the King's Men*.

1949

BEST DIRECTOR

ACADEMY AWARDS
• **Joseph L. Mankiewicz for** *A Letter to Three Wives*
Carol Reed for *The Fallen Idol*
Robert Rossen for *All the King's Men*
William Wellman for *Battleground*
William Wyler for *The Heiress*

GOLDEN GLOBE AWARDS
• **Robert Rossen** – *All the King's Men*
William Wyler – *The Heiress*

DIRECTORS GUILD AWARD
(1948/49)
Howard Hawks – *Red River*
Anatole Litvak – *The Snake Pit*
• **Joseph L. Mankiewicz** – *A Letter to Three Wives*
Fred Zinnemann – *The Search*

DIRECTORS GUILD AWARD
(1949/50)
Carol Reed – *The Third Man*
Mark Robson – *Champion*
• **Robert Rossen** – *All the King's Men*
Alfred L. Werker – *Lost Boundaries*

NEW YORK – **Carol Reed** – *The Fallen Idol*
BOARD OF REVIEW – **Vittorio de Sica** – *Ladri di Biciclette (Bicycle Thieves)*

Both the National Board of Review and the New York Film Critics Circle awarded their Best Director prizes to non-American directors for their handling of foreign films. The NBR gave their prize to Italian director Vittorio de Sica for *Ladri di Biciclette (Bicycle Thieves)* (NYT "has artfully wrapped it [all] into a film that will tear your heart, but which should fill you with warmth and compassion"; MFB "extraordinary") while British director Carol Reed was voted Best Director in New York for his drama *The Fallen Idol* (NYT "directed in brilliant style"; V "unmistakably a director's picture"; S&S "excellent"). The Academy overlooked de Sica but nominated Reed (for the first time).

1949

Also nominated were: William Wyler (for a record seventh time) for the literary drama *The Heiress* (NYT "Wyler has taken this drama and has made it into a motion picture that crackles with allusive life and fire"); William Wellman (for the second time) for the popular war drama *Battleground* (NYT "a tremendous job"); and, each for the first time, the first two winners of the DGA award – Joseph L. Mankiewicz for *A Letter to Three Wives* (NYT "cleverly evolves an interesting cross-sectioned picture of the small-town younger-married set ... as writer as well as director, he has capably brought forth a film which has humor, scepticism, satire and gratifying romance"; MFB "competent") and Robert Rossen for *All the King's Men* (NYT "has assembled in this starkly unprettified film a piece of pictorial journalism that is remarkable ... all of these things, Mr Rossen, as director, has pictured stunningly"). Both Mankiewicz and Rossen were also nominated for the Best Screenplay Oscar.

Omitted from the category were: the New York runner-up Clarence Brown for *Intruder in the Dust* (NYT "powerfully pieced together ... in Mr Brown's brilliant techniques"); previous winner Elia Kazan for *Pinky* (TT sets a "high standard"); DGA nominee Alfred L. Werker for *Lost Boundaries*; DGA nominee Mark Robson for both *Champion* (HRp "imaginative direction") and *Home of the Brave* (NYT "intelligently directed"); Henry King for Best Picture nominee *Twelve O'Clock High*; Henry Koster for *Come to the Stable* (V "directed with great sensitivity"); John Huston for *We Were Strangers*; Robert Wise for *The Set-Up* (V "skillful direction"); Fred Zinnemann for *Act of Violence* (NYT "smart direction", V "knowing direction"); Roy Boulting for *Fame is the Spur* (V "first-rate" direction); David Lean for *The Passionate Friends (One Woman's Story)* (V "masterly direction"); George Stevens for *Edward, My Son* (V "skillful direction"); and the late Sam Wood for both *Command Decision* and the baseball biopic *The Stratton Story* (NYT "fine direction").

Having won the Golden Globe, Rossen was the favourite to win the Best Director Oscar. *All the King's Men* was named Best Picture, but in a major surprise Mankiewicz collected both the Best Screenplay and Best Director Oscars. It was the first time that the New York critics' circle and Academy had disagreed on their choices for Best Director since 1943. Interestingly, Mankiewicz had not received a single vote in the balloting by the New York critics.

The following year, Mankiewicz repeated his double Oscar win and also claimed the Best Picture Academy Award.

1949

BEST ACTOR

ACADEMY AWARDS
• **Broderick Crawford as 'Willie Stark' in** *All the King's Men*
Kirk Douglas as 'Midge Kelly' in *Champion*
Gregory Peck as 'Gen. Frank Savage' in *Twelve O'Clock High*
Richard Todd as 'The Scot' in *The Hasty Heart*
John Wayne as 'Sgt. John M. Stryker' in *Sands of Iwo Jima*

GOLDEN GLOBE AWARDS
• **Broderick Crawford** – *All the King's Men*
Richard Todd – *The Hasty Heart*

NEW YORK – **Broderick Crawford** – *All the King's Men*
BOARD OF REVIEW – **Ralph Richardson** – *The Fallen Idol* and *The Heiress*

For his acclaimed performance as a corrupt politician (apparently based on Louisiana Governor Huey Long) in *All the King's Men*, Broderick Crawford, an actor who had previously played mostly smaller roles in gangster films and Westerns, won both the New York Film Critics Circle award and the Golden Globe, before receiving the Best Actor Oscar (NYT "concentrates tremendous energy into every delineation he plays … he draws a compelling portrait, in two dimensions, of an egomaniac"; V "a standout" with "one of the most dynamic character studies the screen has glimpsed"; Esq "colorful and sympathetic"). Although he won the statuette over a strong field of acclaimed nominees and made a notable appearance in *Born Yesterday* the following year, Crawford never received a second Oscar nomination from the Academy.

Gregory Peck received his fourth Best Actor nomination in just five years as an air force bombing group commander in the war drama *Twelve O'Clock High* (NYT deserves "high and particular praise"; S&S "a lack of depth in the principal character"; V "just about his best work to date"). His portrayal subsequently earned him the 1950 Best Actor award from the New York critics'.

Kirk Douglas was mentioned on the Oscar ballot for the first time for his turn as a boxer in *Champion* (NYT "good"; V "makes the character live"; HRp "forceful"; TT "admirable"; MFB "impressive"). He had also appeared that year as the kindly schoolteacher in *A Letter to Three Wives*.

Also mentioned by Oscar voters was John Wayne for his performance as a Marine sergeant in the war drama *Sands of Iwo Jima* (NYT "especially honest and convincing"; V "a powerful portrait"; HRp "personal triumph"). Like

Douglas, Wayne had benefitted from having given another acclaimed performance during the year: he had earned praise for his turn in John Ford's Western *She Wore a Yellow Ribbon.*

The final nominee was Irish actor Richard Todd, who was named for the only time, for his portrayal of a doomed Scottish soldier in *The Hasty Heart* (NYT "deeply touching"; MFB "commendable").

The glaring omission from the Academy's list of nominees was English actor Ralph Richardson. He had been commended by critics for both his leading performance as the household servant suspected of murder in Carol Reed's British thriller *The Fallen Idol* (NYT "superb", "fine"; V "masterly portrayal") and his supporting turn as the domineering father in the Best Picture nominee *The Heiress.* For the two portrayals, he was named Best Actor by the NBR and finished as runner-up for the New York critics' award. The Academy, however, nominated him only in the supporting category for his work on *The Heiress.*

Juano Hernandez, who finished in third place in the voting for the New York critics' Best Actor prize, was also overlooked for his performance as the elderly black man accused of shooting a white man in the anti-racism drama *Intruder in the Dust* (NYT "the stanch and magnificent integrity that Mr Hernandez displays is his carriage, his manner and expression, with never a flinch in his great self-command, is the bulwark of all the deep compassion and ironic comment in this film"; V "standout"; TT "the true strength of the film"; S&S "strong").

Edward G. Robinson was also left out of consideration for his work as a ruthless financier who manipulates his four sons for his own ends in the drama *House of Strangers* (V "especially vivid"). His performance won him the Best Actor prize at the Cannes Film Festival.

Others passed over for consideration included: James Edwards as the persecuted African-American soldier in *Home of the Brave* (NYT "a finely tempered job"; V "always believable"; S&S "impassioned"); Robert Ryan as a former boxing champion in *The Set-Up* (V "carrying off top honors in a moving portrayal"); John Garfield a revolutionary in Cuba in the political thriller *We Were Strangers* (S&S "remarkable"; V "highly convincing"); previous winner James Stewart as Chicago White Sox pitcher Monty Stratton in the biopic *The Stratton Story* (NYT "it is almost impossible to imagine anyone else playing the role"; V "exceptional" in "one of his most versatile performances"); previous winner James Cagney as a psychopathic gangster in *White Heat* (NYT "brilliant"; V "authentic"); Richard Conte in the mobster drama *Thieves' Highway* (NYT "superb"); Michael Redgrave as a rising politician in the British film *Fame is the Spur* (V "grand"); previous winner Spencer Tracy in *Edward, My* Son (V "sterling" in "a forceful portrayal"; MFB "little short of magnificent"); and Lamberto Maggiorani in the acclaimed Italian film *Ladri di Biciclette (Bicycle Thieves)* (NYT "superb"; V "magnificently touching").

1949

BEST ACTRESS

ACADEMY AWARDS
Jeanne Crain as 'Patricia "Pinky" Johnson' in *Pinky*
• **Olivia de Havilland as 'Catherine Sloper' in *The Heiress***
Susan Hayward as 'Eloise Winters' in *My Foolish Heart*
Deborah Kerr as 'Evelyn Boult' in *Edward, My Son*
Loretta Young as 'Sister Margaret' in *Come to the Stable*

GOLDEN GLOBE AWARDS
• **Olivia de Havilland – *The Heiress***
Deborah Kerr – *Edward, My Son*

NEW YORK – Olivia de Havilland – *The Heiress*

Months out from the Oscars, it seemed on paper that seven previous Best Actress Oscar winners would dominate the field for the prize again in 1949. Nominations seemed possible for Jennifer Jones in *Madame Bovary*, Ingrid Bergman in *Under Capricorn*, Bette Davis in *Beyond the Forest*, Joan Crawford in *Flamingo Road*, Olivia de Havilland in *The Heiress*, Greer Garson in *That Forsythe Woman* and Loretta Young in *Come to the Stable*. As each film was released, however, the chances of most of these actresses were undermined by negative reviews or poor box office returns. The exceptions were Crawford, de Havilland and Young. Although MFB considered Crawford's turn as "one of the best performances in recent years" the Academy overlooked her. Included on the list however, were both de Havilland (her fifth and final mention) as the repressed, naive heroine in *The Heiress* (NYT "beautifully played"; V "an acting tour de force"; TT "remarkable"; MFB "a highly expert performance") and Young (recognised for a second and final time) as a nun trying to secure land for a children's hospital in *Come to the Stable* (NYT "less suggestive of reality than [she is of a] theatrical type ... beatific and sublime; her face is perpetually beaming and her words are perpetually sugar-edged"; V "sure, underplaying role").

A major campaign helped secure a second nomination in three years for rising star Susan Hayward as an unmarried mother in *My Foolish Heart* (NYT "the casting of Susan Hayward as this lady is a bit off the beam ... hard to believe"; V "her performance is a gem [which] displays a positive talent for capturing reality"). Also nominated, each for a first time, were Scottish actress Deborah Kerr as the mother in *Edward, My Son* (NYT "affectingly played"; V "displays remarkable ability"; TT "seldom more than a promising sketch"; MFB "little short of magnificent") and Jeanne Crain as a young African-American nurse who passes as white in *Pinky* (NYT "successfully channels resentment against bitter experiences"; V "brings proper dignity and sincerity to her role, although she's not always convincing"; HRp "superb").

Surprisingly overlooked was English theatre star Edith Evans, who was the runner-up for the Best Actress award from the New York critics for her first leading role as the widow who will not leave her home in *Dolwyn (The Last Days of Dolwyn)* (NYT "remarkable depth and definition, color and character are got by this exquisite actress into this rich and reasoned role"; V "sincere" in "a dominating but not aggressive performance"; MFB "superb").

Also left out of consideration for the Oscar were: June Allyson in *The Stratton Story* (NYT "affecting"); Ann Todd in *The Passionate Friends (One Woman's Story)*, a film directed by her husband, David Lean (V "rises to new heights" with "a flawless portrayal"); Joan Bennett in *The Reckless Moment*; Googie Withers in *It Always Rains on Sunday* (NYT "expert performance"); Valentina Cortese in *Thieves' Highway* (NYT "superb"); and Mai Zetterling in *The Girl in the Painting* (NYT a "convincing portrayal"). Previous winner Jennifer Jones, whose performance in *Madame Bovary* Variety had dismissed as merely "competent", was overlooked for her better-reviewed turn in *We Were Strangers* (V "excellent", "effective and altogether convincing").

The year after being unanimously voted the year's Best Actress by the New York critics for *The Snake Pit*, de Havilland became the first person to win a second consecutive acting award from the group when she won for *The Heiress*. She subsequently won the Golden Globe and was picked as the favourite for the Oscar by Variety. The NBR elected not to bestow a Best Actress accolade that season.

At the Academy's annual ceremony, de Havilland won her second Oscar. She was the first actress to win honours from both the New York critics and the Academy in the same year since her younger sister Joan Fontaine in 1941. Accepting her statuette she told the audience, "Your award for *To Each His Own* I took as an incentive to venture forward. Thank you for this very generous assurance that I have not failed to do so."

1949

BEST SUPPORTING ACTOR

ACADEMY AWARDS
John Ireland as 'Jack Burden' in *All the King's Men*
• **Dean Jagger as 'Maj. Harvey Stovall' in *Twelve O'Clock High***
Arthur Kennedy as 'Connie Kelly' in *Champion*
Ralph Richardson as 'Dr Austin Sloper' in *The Heiress*
James Whitmore as 'S/Sgt. Kinnie' in *Battleground*

GOLDEN GLOBE AWARDS
David Brian – *Intruder in the Dust*
• **James Whitmore – *Battleground***

For the first time since 1937, all the Best Supporting Actor contenders were first-time Oscar nominees: John Ireland as a journalist in *All the King's Men*; Dean Jagger as the adjutant in *Twelve O'Clock High* (V "standout"); Arthur Kennedy as the crippled brother of a boxer in *Champion* (NYT "dour"; HRp "a touching portrait"); Ralph Richardson as the stern father in *The Heiress* (NYT "rich and sleek performance"; V "grand"; TT "commanding"; MFB "finely calculated ... entirely satisfactory and believable"); and James Whitmore as a soldier in *Battleground* (NYT "magnificent"). The frontrunners were Whitmore, winner of the Golden Globe, and Richardson, who had won the NBR Best Actor prize and finished as the runner-up in New York for both *The Heiress* and *The Fallen Idol* (in which he was the lead actor).

Surprisingly, the Academy overlooked the performance of David Brian as the lawyer in *Intruder in the Dust* (NYT "excellent") even though he had been a nominee for the Golden Globe. Also passed over were: Paul Stewart as the hard-bitten boxing manager in *Champion* (NYT "most convincing"; HRp "a masterpiece of subtle, restrained playing"); Gilbert Roland as a Cuban revolutionary in *We Were Strangers* (V "excellent"); Paul Douglas in *A Letter to Three Wives* (V a "standout" in a "fine film debut"); Sydney Greenstreet in *Flamingo Road* (V "powerful"; MFB "brilliant"); Richard Conte in *House of Strangers* (V "excellent"); Richard Hylton in *Lost Boundaries* (MFB "sensitive"); and Robert Keith in *My Foolish Heart*.

Producer Darryl F. Zanuck campaigned heavily for a win by Jagger, and shortly before the ceremony Variety declared him to be the favourite. When Claire Trevor opened the envelope on Oscar night, it was indeed Jagger's name inside.

1949

BEST SUPPORTING ACTRESS

ACADEMY AWARDS
Ethel Barrymore as 'Miss Em' in *Pinky*
Celeste Holm as 'Sister Scolastica' in *Come to the Stable*
Elsa Lanchester as 'Miss Potts' in *Come to the Stable*
• **Mercedes McCambridge as 'Sadie Burke' in *All the King's Men***
Ethel Waters as 'Dysey Johnson' in *Pinky*

GOLDEN GLOBE AWARDS
Miriam Hopkins – *The Heiress*
• **Mercedes McCambridge – *All the King's Men***

Former radio actress Mercedes McCambridge earned mixed reviews for her screen debut as a rising politician's secretary in *All the King's Men* (NYT "picturesque but vagrant"; V "compelling", "registers strongly"). She nonetheless won the Golden Globe and the Oscar. The Academy honoured her ahead of two pairs of actresses nominated for performances in the same films.

Nominated for Elia Kazan's *Pinky* were previous winner Ethel Barrymore (her fourth and final Supporting Actress nomination in just six years) as the dying Southern matriarch (NYT "brilliantly commanding and expressive of conventional sentiment") and Ethel Waters as the hard-working grandmother (NYT "endows this gentle lady with tremendous warmth and appeal"; HRp "a wonderfully conceived characterization"; MFB "beautifully played"). A decade after Hattie McDaniel had won the Best Supporting Actress prize, Waters was only the second African-American performer to be nominated for an Oscar.

Nominated for *Come to the Stable* were previous winner Celeste Holm as a tennis-playing French nun (NYT "a bit too starry-eyed for comfort and for credibility") and Elsa Lanchester, the wife of previous Best Actor winner Charles Laughton, as an eccentric painter (V "excellent").

Overlooked were: Edith Evans in *Queen of Spades*, her first film role (NYT "wonderful", V "outstanding"; S&S "fantastic"; MFB "beautifully acted"); Golden Globe nominee Miriam Hopkins in *The Heiress* (NYT "delightful"); Lucille Ball in *Easy Living* (NYT "an attractive performance"); Agnes Moorehead in *The Stratton Story* (MFB "a beautiful performance of calm and restraint"); Flora Robson in *Saraband* (NYT "runs off with the acting honors"); Denise Darcel in *Thunder in the Pines* (V "takes the acting honors with a really excellent interpretation"); both Margaret Wycherly (V "quietly effective") and Virginia Mayo (NYT "excellent") in *White Heat*; and both Janet Leigh (NYT "tortured performance") and previous winner Mary Astor in *Act of Violence*.

BEST PICTURE

ACADEMY AWARDS
• *All About Eve*
   (20th Century Fox, 138 mins BW, 14 Oct 1950, $2.9m, 14 noms)
Born Yesterday
   (Columbia, 103 mins BW, 26 Dec 1950, $4.1m, 5 noms)
Father of the Bride
   (M-G-M, 92 mins BW, 16 Jun 1950, $4.0m, 3 noms)
King Solomon's Mines
   (M-G-M, 103 mins, 24 Nov 1950, $5.6m, 3 noms)
Sunset Boulevard
   (Paramount, 110 mins BW, 10 Aug 1950, $2.3m, 11 noms)

GOLDEN GLOBE AWARDS
All About Eve
Born Yesterday
Cyrano de Bergerac
Harvey
• *Sunset Boulevard*

BRITISH ACADEMY AWARDS

(Best Film)	(Best British Film)
• *All About Eve*	**• *The Blue Lamp***
La Beauté du Diable	*Chance of a Lifetime*
(Beauty and the Devil)	*Morning Departure*
Intruder in the Dust	*Seven Days to Noon*
The Men	*State Secret*
On the Town	*The Wooden Horse*
Orphee (Orpheus)	

NEW YORK – *All About Eve*
BOARD OF REVIEW – *Sunset Boulevard*

Two films about ageing actresses were the frontrunners for Best Picture accolades in 1950.

In *All About Eve*, Bette Davis played a middle-aged New York theatre star threatened by a newcomer. Adapted and directed by Joseph L. Mankiewicz, the winner of both the Best Director and Best Screenplay Oscars the previous year, the film was a hit with both audiences and critics when it was released in October. In The New York Times, Bosley Crowther called it "a withering satire

– witty, mature and world-wise" that was "dazzling and devastating" in its mockery of Broadway theatre and its stars, while in London, The Times labelled it a "savage, realistic, cynical film". There were some dissenting voices, however. Esquire considered it "somewhat tedious" while the Monthly Film Bulletin concluded that *All About Eve* was "ultimately a hollow film".

Released two months earlier, *Sunset Boulevard*, recounted a young Hollywood writer's encounter with a former silent film star, played by Gloria Swanson. It was co-written and directed by Billy Wilder, the winner of the Best Director and Screenplay Oscars in 1945. In The New York Times, Thomas M. Pryor called it a "clever compound of truth and legend … which quickly casts a spell over an audience and holds it enthralled" and "a great motion picture". The film was met by almost universal praise from critics on both sides of the Atlantic (S&S "Hollywood craftsmanship at its smartest and at just about its best"; MFB "fascinating").

At the end of the year the two films split the critics' prizes. *Sunset Boulevard* was named Best Picture by the NBR, but then finished as runner-up to *All About Eve* in New York. Mankiewicz's drama took the east coast prize with just one round of voting.

Both films were nominated for the Golden Globe Award along with an English-language film version of *Cyrano de Bergerac* and the popular comedies *Born Yesterday* (NYT "one of the best pictures of the year"; V "bright, biting comedy") and *Harvey* (NYT "a charmingly fanciful farce"), both big screen adaptations of hit Broadway plays.

Surprisingly overlooked, despite a Best Director nod for John Huston, was the acclaimed crime drama *The Asphalt Jungle* which had finished third in the New York critics' voting (NYT "one of the most clever, taut and suspenseful crime melodramas ever made"; V "hard-hitting"; HRp "striking" and "breathtaking and suspenseful").

Although the winner of the New York Critics Circle's Best Picture accolade had gone on to win the Golden Globe Award for the previous six years, the Hollywood Foreign Press Association passed over *All About Eve* and presented their award to *Sunset Boulevard*.

When the Academy's nominations were announced, however, *All About Eve* became the strong favourite for the prestigious golden statuette with an unprecedented fourteen Oscar nominations in twelve categories. *Sunset Boulevard*, meanwhile, received eleven nominations. Both films were included in the Best Picture category along with *Born Yesterday* and two surprise choices: the comedy *Father of the Bride* (NYT "wonderful") and the action adventure film *King Solomon's Mines*, which was the year's third most popular film at the US box office (NYT "there is more than a trace of outright hokum in this thriller

... but there is also an ample abundance of scenic novelty and beauty to compensate").

As had been the case at the Golden Globes, *The Asphalt Jungle* was overlooked for a Best Picture nod by the Academy even though Huston was nominated for Best Director. Despite a nomination for director Carol Reed, the thriller *The Third Man* was also by-passed even though it had won the Palme d'Or at the 1949 Cannes Film Festival and the BAFTA as Best British Film (NYT "extraordinarily fascinating"; V "absorbing"; MFB "impressive"; TT "excellent").

Other omissions were: the drama *In A Lonely Place* (NYT "a superior cut of melodrama"); the Best Film BAFTA nominee *The Men*, about paraplegic war veterans (NYT "a fine and arresting film drama"; V "sensitive, moving"; S&S "remarkable"); *Three Came Home*, about women in a Japanese PoW camp (NYT "one of the strongest [films] of the year"); Disney's animated fairy tale *Cinderella* (NYT "Mr Disney and his craftsmen have brilliantly splashed upon the screen a full-blown and flowery animation of the perennially popular fairy tale"); the 1949 British black comedy *Kind Hearts and Coronets* (V "sophisticated comedy entertainment"; MFB "exceedingly funny"); the Italian film *Cuore (Heart and Soul)* (V "touching and compelling"); and the French film *Au-dela des Grilles (The Walls of Malapaga)* (NYT "a picture of strength and eloquence") which received a Special Academy Award as the year's best foreign-language film (NYT "a picture of strength and eloquence", "forceful"; V "a pulsating drama").

Variety predicted a win for Mankiewicz's Broadway satire and on Oscar night *All About Eve* indeed won the Best Picture award along with five other Oscars. Wilder's Hollywood satire collected three statuettes.

In London, the British Academy agreed with its Hollywood counterpart and named *All About Eve* as the year's Best Picture. Surprisingly, *Sunset Boulevard* did not even make the list as a nominee. The Best British Film award, meanwhile, went to *The Blue Lamp*, a hugely popular thriller about the hunt for a policeman's murderer which The Times had considered to be a warm tribute to the police force but one that lacked realistic characters. When the film was released in the United States by Warner Bros. in early 1951, Bosley Crowther echoed that appraisal in The New York Times calling it "warm and affectionate".

At the 1951 Cannes Film Festival, the jury overlooked *All About Eve* for the Palme d'Or, even though the film did screen in competition at the festival. Instead, Mankiewicz's drama was awarded a special prize.

1950

BEST DIRECTOR

ACADEMY AWARDS
George Cukor for *Born Yesterday*
John Huston for *The Asphalt Jungle*
• **Joseph L. Mankiewicz for *All About Eve***
Carol Reed for *The Third Man*
Billy Wilder for *Sunset Boulevard*

GOLDEN GLOBE AWARDS
George Cukor – *Born Yesterday*
John Huston – *The Asphalt Jungle*
Joseph L. Mankiewicz – *All About Eve*
• **Billy Wilder – *Sunset Boulevard***

DIRECTORS GUILD AWARD
(1949/50)
Carol Reed – *The Third Man*
Mark Robson – *Champion*
• **Robert Rossen – *All the King's Men***
Alfred L. Werker – *Lost Boundaries*

DIRECTORS GUILD AWARD
(1950/51)
John Huston – *The Asphalt Jungle*
• **Joseph L. Mankiewicz – *All About Eve***
Vincente Minnelli – *An American in Paris*
Billy Wilder – *Sunset Boulevard*

NEW YORK – Joseph L. Mankiewicz – *All About Eve*
BOARD OF REVIEW – John Huston – *The Asphalt Jungle*

Joseph L. Mankiewicz, the surprise winner of the Best Director Academy Award the previous year, was favoured to win the statuette again in 1950 for his handling of *All About Eve* which had earned a record fourteen nominations. In the lead up to the Oscars, his work on the film earned him the Best Director accolades from both the New York critics and the DGA (his second prize from the Guild).

Mankiewicz was nominated for the Golden Globe Award along with George Cukor for *Born Yesterday* and John Huston, who won the NBR prize and finished runner-up in the New York critics' circle voting, for the drama *The Asphalt Jungle* (NYT "brilliantly realistic"; HRp "masterly"). The winner, however, was Billy Wilder for *Sunset Boulevard* (NYT "masterly direction").

All four Golden Globe nominees were short-listed by the Academy (Cukor for the fourth time, previous winner Wilder for a third time and Huston and Mankiewicz, the winners over the previous two years, each for the second time). The fifth place in the list of Oscar nominees went to Carol Reed who was mentioned – for the second year in a row – for the British thriller *The Third Man* (NYT "top credit must go to Mr Reed for molding all possible elements into a thriller of super consequence … and especially must he be credited with the brilliant and triumphant device of using the music of a zither as the sole musical background in this film"; V "painstaking direction", "lives up to his high reputation").

Overlooked were: Vincente Minnelli for *Father of the Bride* (NYT "deft directorial hand"); previous winner Michael Curtiz for *The Breaking Point* (NYT "commanding"); Fred Zinnemann for *The Men* (V "masterful" direction); and René Clément for *Au-dela des Grilles (The Walls of Malapaga)*, winner of a Special Academy Award for Best Foreign-Language Film (NYT "excellent"; V "excellent direction").

Although acclaimed by critics, the chances of Huston and Reed were limited by the exclusion of their films from the Best Picture category. No director had won the Best Director statuette when his film had been overlooked for the top award since the second Academy Awards in 1928/29. With the New York and DGA prizes under his belt and his film's unprecedented tally of nominations, Mankiewicz was a strong favourite.

On Oscar night, he made history when he collected both the Best Director and Best Screenplay Oscars for the second year in a row.

BEST ACTOR

ACADEMY AWARDS
Louis Calhern as 'Oliver Wendell Holmes' in *The Magnificent Yankee*
• **José Ferrer as 'Cyrano de Bergerac' in *Cyrano de Bergerac***
William Holden as 'Joe Gillis' in *Sunset Boulevard*
James Stewart as 'Elwood P. Dowd' in *Harvey*
Spencer Tracy as 'Stanley T. Banks' in *Father of the Bride*

GOLDEN GLOBE AWARDS

(Drama)

(Comedy/Musical)

Louis Calhern
  – The Magnificent Yankee
• **José Ferrer**
  – Cyrano de Bergerac
James Stewart *– Harvey*

• **Fred Astaire *– Three Little Words***
Dan Dailey
  – When Willie Comes Marching Home
Harold Lloyd *– Mad Wednesday*

NEW YORK – Gregory Peck *– Twelve O'Clock High*
BOARD OF REVIEW – Alec Guinness *– Kind Hearts and Coronets*

The war drama *Twelve O'Clock High* opened in Los Angeles in late December 1949 and eared four Academy Award nominations, including a nod for Gregory Peck as Best Actor. The film did not, however, play in cinemas in New York until a month later and, subsequently, was not considered by the New York critics for prizes until the end of 1950, at which time they gave their Best Actor accolade to Peck. This unusual situation meant that, for the first time, the New York winner was not eligible for the year's other accolades. Furthermore, the third placed performance in the voting was not in consideration for the Best Actor Oscar either. For his performances as various members of an aristocratic family in the British comedy *Kind Hearts and Coronets*, Alec Guinness polled third in New York and was named Best Actor by the NBR. Because he had supporting roles, however, he was not a contender for the Best Actor Oscar.

    The New York critics' vote, however, did present one major candidate – Puerto Rican actor José Ferrer, who was a popular Broadway star and who had been Billy Wilder's original choice for Ray Milland's 1945 Best Actor Oscar-winning role in *The Lost Weekend*. Ferrer was the New York runner-up for his portrayal of the title character in an English-language film version of Edmond Rostand's play *Cyrano de Bergerac* (NYT "plays the famous large-nosed hero with eloquence and grace"; V "an outstanding achievement"; TT "no other actor could have made more" of the part; MFB "falls short at all the vital moments").

1950

At the Golden Globe Awards the main acting prizes were divided, for the first time, into separate awards for Drama and for Comedy or Musical. Ferrer won the Globe (Drama) for *Cyrano de Bergerac* ahead of James Stewart, who was considered for his performance as a man accompanied everywhere by a six foot tall invisible rabbit in *Harvey* (NYT "utterly beguiling"; MFB "mannered") and Louis Calhern, who was nominated for his portrayal of the famous judge Oliver Wendell Holmes in *The Magnificent Yankee* (NYT "fine", "a warm and appealing characterization"; V "virtually a tour de force"). The Globe (Comedy/Musical) was won by Fred Astaire for portraying vaudeville dancer and magician Bert Kalmar in *Three Little Words* (NYT "polished performance").

The Academy nominated all three of the Globe (Drama) nominees. Twelve years after his last mention previous winner Spencer Tracy also made the list for *Father of the Bride* (NYT "delightful acting"; TT "one of the best performances in his long career"; MFB "a virtuoso performance"). William Holden was also included as the struggling Hollywood writer in *Sunset Boulevard* (NYT "excellent", "the finest acting of his career", he "never falters"; V "exceptionally fine", a "standout job"; MFB "an extremely difficult part beautifully played").

The Academy overlooked all three of the Globe (Comedy/Musical) nominees – winner Astaire, Dan Dailey in *When Willie Comes Marching Home* (NYT "at the top of his comic form"; MFB "clever and engaging") and silent film legend Harold Lloyd in *Mad Wednesday*, a revised version of *The Sins of Harold Diddlebocker* which had briefly screened in just three US cities in 1947.

Gregory Peck, who had been nominated four times over the previous five years, was passed over for *The Gunfighter* (NYT a "fine performance"; V "perfectly portrays the title role"; MFB "does not come very vividly to life"). Also unrecognised were: previous winner Humphrey Bogart in the independent film *In A Lonely Place* (NYT "in top form … plays the role for all its worth"); previous winner Robert Donat in the British drama *The Winslow Boy* (NYT "a sparkling performance"); John Garfield in *The Breaking Point* (S&S "impressive"; MFB "firm, incisive"), Jean Gabin in *Au-dela des Grilles (The Walls of Malapaga)* (NYT "excellent"; V "strong"); and Italian actor-director Vittorio de Sica in *Cuore (Heart and Soul)* (NYT "impeccable"; V "gains new laurels for his thesping"). Another notable oversight was young Broadway sensation Marlon Brando whose film debut as a paraplegic war veteran in *The Men* had polarised critics (NYT "vividly real, dynamic and sensitive"; V "fails to deliver"; TT "adequate"; MFB plays "powerfully and movingly").

Variety predicted that Ferrer would narrowly outpoll Holden for the award and when the big night came, Helen Hayes opened the envelope and declared Ferrer the winner. Unable to attend the ceremony because he was appearing in a play in New York, Ferrer told the Academy via radio link, "I consider it a vote of confidence and an act of faith and believe me, I'll not let you down."

BEST ACTRESS

ACADEMY AWARDS
Anne Baxter as 'Eve Harrington' in *All About Eve*
Bette Davis as 'Margo Channing' in *All About Eve*
• **Judy Holliday as 'Billie Dawn' in *Born Yesterday***
Eleanor Parker as 'Marie Allen' in *Caged*
Gloria Swanson as 'Norma Desmond' in *Sunset Boulevard*

GOLDEN GLOBE AWARDS
(Drama)

(Comedy/Musical)

Bette Davis – *All About Eve*

Spring Byington – *Louisa*

Judy Holliday – *Born Yesterday*

• **Judy Holliday – *Born Yesterday***

• **Gloria Swanson**
  – *Sunset Boulevard*

Betty Hutton – *Annie Get Your Gun*

NEW YORK – Bette Davis – *All About Eve*
BOARD OF REVIEW – Gloria Swanson – *Sunset Boulevard*

Only three actresses received votes from the New York critics for the Best Actress award in 1950: Bette Davis, for playing an ageing theatre star in *All About Eve* (NYT "excellent", for "probably the best [performance] of her career" she "merits an Academy award"; NYDN "superb"; V "Davis, persuasive and generous, incisive and impossible, builds Margo up, shot by shot, scene by scene, into a very complete person"; S&S "splendid"; Esq "an extra-special performance"; MFB "believable" and "magnificent"); Judy Holliday, for reprising her stage success as a squeaky-voiced dumb blonde in the comedy *Born Yesterday* (NYT "wonderful" and "priceless"; TT "masterly" in the drawing of "a complete portrait"; S&S she "stood out as an actress able to achieve a rare combination of high comedy and genuine pathos"; MFB "brilliant"); and former silent film star Gloria Swanson, who had only made one film in the previous fifteen years, for her performance as a deluded former silent movie star planning a comeback in *Sunset Boulevard* (NYT a "tour de force", "it is inconceivable that anyone else might have been considered for the role"; Esq "nothing short of sensational"; MFB "magnetic" and "powerful").

On the first ballot the New York critics could not separate Davis and Holliday who each received seven votes. On subsequent ballots, with the third-placed Swanson eliminated, Davis managed to narrowly outpoll Holliday and claim her first (and only) New York Best Actress award. The NBR, meanwhile, declared Swanson to be the Best Actress of the year.

1950

At the Golden Globe awards, the fortunes of the three contenders were reversed with the two New York runners-up receiving awards and Davis finishing empty handed. Swanson won the Globe for Best Actress (Drama), and Holliday claimed the Globe for Best Actress (Comedy or Musical) after being nominated, rather curiously, in both categories.

When the Oscar nominations were announced, previous winner Davis became the first person to receive an eighth nomination for acting, while Swanson, who had been nominated for a performance in a silent film in the very first year of the Oscars, made the list of nominees for the third time. Holliday was recognised by the Academy for the first (and only) time.

Also nominated was Eleanor Parker who won the Best Actress prize at the 1950 Venice Film Festival and earned her first Oscar mention for her portrayal of a frightened girl transformed into a bitter and cynical woman by her experience as a prison inmate in *Caged* (NYT "a creditable and expressive performance"; V "strong portrayal"; TT "manages the metamorphosis with astonishing sensitiveness and control"; MFB "extremely well-acted"). Surprisingly, the other nominee was the 1946 Supporting Actress winner Anne Baxter for her (arguably supporting) performance as the rising star in *All About Eve* (NYDN "superb"). The inclusion of Baxter alongside Davis was the first time two women had been nominated as Best Actress for the same film.

Baxter's unexpected nomination came ahead of other acclaimed performances: Claudette Colbert in *Three Came Home* (NYT "a beautifully modulated display of moods and passions"; V "superbly acted", "a thumping performance"); Katharine Hepburn in *Adam's Rib*; Teresa Wright in *The Men* (V "the best performance of her filmatic career"); Golden Globe nominee Spring Byington in *Louisa* (NYT "plays it with deliciously venturesome bounce"; V "delightful"); Margaret Sullavan in *No Sad Songs for Me*, her first film in seven years (NYT "carries off a difficult role"; V "powerfully moving", "a standout"); Gloria Grahame in *In A Lonely Place* (NYT "a smoldering performance"); Valentina Cortese as the lovelorn Italian village girl in *The Glass Mountain* (NYT "sensitive, poised and wholly convincing"; V a "standout"; MFB "outstanding"); and Isa Miranda as the waitress in *Au-dela des Grilles (The Walls of Malapaga)* (NYT "subtle"; V "superb").

Davis was certain that her performance in *All About Eve* would bring her the record third Oscar that she so coveted. However, on Oscar night it was Holliday who was honoured by the Academy. It may have been a different outcome had Holliday also been nominated, as she was at the Golden Globes, in the supporting category for her performance as another dumb blonde in *Adam's Rib*. In such circumstances, Holliday may have won the Best Supporting Actress statuette and left the way clear for Davis to triumph as Best Actress.

Davis later received the Best Actress award at the 1951 Cannes Film Festival.

BEST SUPPORTING ACTOR

ACADEMY AWARDS
Jeff Chandler as 'Cochise' in *Broken Arrow*
Edmund Gwenn as 'William "the Skipper" Miller' in *Mister 880*
Sam Jaffe as 'Doc Riedenschneider' in *The Asphalt Jungle*
• **George Sanders as 'Addison DeWitt' in *All About Eve***
Erich von Stroheim as 'Max von Mayerling' in *Sunset Boulevard*

GOLDEN GLOBE AWARDS
• **Edmund Gwenn – *Mister 880***
George Sanders – *All About Eve*
Erich von Stroheim – *Sunset Boulevard*

In the 1949 British black comedy *Kind Hearts and Coronets* Alec Guinness played eight members of an aristocratic family who are murdered by a young man determined to come into an inheritance. In Britain, S&S praised him for "eight brilliant sketches" and MFB said he "shows his power as a character actor." When the film was released in the United States the following year, Variety enthusiastically called his turn "flawless acting" and an "individual acting triumph." In The New York Times, Bosley Crowther commented that Guinness was "so deft in his impersonations ... that with this one film he should garner three or four awards for fine support." While Guinness earned further plaudits from critics for his supporting performance as a newspaper editor in the British comedy *A Run for Your Money* (NYT "superbly underplayed"), it was for his roles in *Kind Hearts and Coronets* that he was named Best Actor by the NBR and finished third in the voting for the New York prize. Surprisingly, Guinness was not considered for the Golden Globe award and soon after became the first winner of the NBR award to be overlooked for an Oscar nomination by the Academy.

Seventy-five-year-old Edmund Gwenn won his second Best Supporting Actor Golden Globe for his performance as a counterfeiter in *Mister 880* (NYT "charming"; V "a great performance"). He also became the oldest man to that date to be nominated for an Oscar for acting when he was included on the Academy's list of nominees for the second time, just three years after his victory for *Miracle on 34th Street*.

Also short-listed by the Academy were the two other Globe nominees: George Sanders as the cynical theatre critic in *All About Eve* and actor-director Erich von Stroheim as the devoted butler in *Sunset Boulevard* (NYT "excellent"; V "delivers with excellent restraint"). Sam Jaffe also made the list as a criminal mastermind obsessed with young women in *The Asphalt Jungle*, a role for which he had won the Best Actor prize at the 1950 Venice Film Festival (NYT "does wonders"). The final nominee was Jeff Chandler as the peace-loving Native American leader in *Broken Arrow* (NYT "in his enthusiasm to treat the Indian with politeness and respect, Delmer Daves, the director, brought forth red men who act like denizens of the musical comedy stage … Chandler carries himself with the magnificence of a decathlon champion at the Olympic Games and speaks with the round and studied phrasing of the salutatorian of a graduating class").

In addition to Guinness, other acclaimed performances overlooked by the Academy were: Louis Calhern (one of the year's Best Actor nominees) for his supporting turn as a crooked lawyer in *The Asphalt Jungle* (NYT "exceptional"); both Japanese actor Sessue Hayakawa (NYT "a rare accomplishment") and Patric Knowles (NYT "excellent"; V "superbly acted") in *Three Came Home*; English comedian Alastair Sim in Alfred Hitchcock's *Stage Fright* (NYT & V both a "standout"); Mexican-American Lalo Rios as the fugitive in *The Lawless* (NYT "a most touching demonstration of fright and anguish in remarkably few scenes"); African-American Sidney Poitier as the doctor unjustly accused in *No Way Out* (NYT "a fine, sensitive performance"; V "splendid"); Leslie Banks as the stern father in *Madeline* (V "powerful"); Everett Sloane as the doctor in *The Men* (MFB "excellent"); Dirk Bogarde as a young criminal in the British drama *The Blue Lamp* (TT "admirable"); and both Trevor Howard (MFB "particularly good") and Orson Welles (MFB "magnetic") in Carol Reed's acclaimed thriller *The Third Man*.

On the big night, Gwenn was unable to repeat his Globe win and collect his second Oscar. Instead the statuette went to Sanders for *All About Eve*. He was the only one of the film's five nominated performers to receive an Oscar.

None of the five nominees were ever included on the Academy's lists again, however the overlooked Guinness later received the Best Actor Oscar and four other nominations in the acting and writing categories.

BEST SUPPORTING ACTRESS

ACADEMY AWARDS
Hope Emerson as 'Evelyn Harper' in *Caged*
Celeste Holm as 'Karen Richards' in *All About Eve*
• **Josephine Hull as 'Veta Louise Simmons' in *Harvey***
Nancy Olson as 'Betty Schaefer' in *Sunset Boulevard*
Thelma Ritter as 'Birdie' in *All About Eve*

GOLDEN GLOBE AWARDS
Judy Holliday – *Adam's Rib*
• **Josephine Hull – *Harvey***
Thelma Ritter – *All About Eve*

Judy Holliday received nominations for the Best Actress and Best Supporting Actress Golden Globe Awards for her acclaimed performances as dumb blondes in *Born Yesterday* and *Adam's Rib*, respectively. The Academy rewarded her with the Best Actress Oscar for *Born Yesterday* but did not include her in the list of nominees in the supporting category for *Adam's Rib* (NYT "a simply hilarious representation of a dumb but stubborn dame … her perfect New Yorkisms, her blank looks, her pitiful woes are as killingly funny – and as touching – as anything we've had in farce this year"; V "a better realization doesn't seem possible"; MFB "remarkable").

Also overlooked by the Academy were: Barbara Bel Geddes in *Panic in the Streets* (S&S "a beautiful performance"; MFB "most touching and sensitive"); Florence Desmond in *Three Came Home* (NYT "superb"); Jean Hagen in *The Asphalt Jungle* (V & HRp a "standout"); Sybil Thorndike in Alfred Hitchcock's *Stage Fright* (NYT a "standout"; V "excellent"; TT "responsible for the film's funniest moments"); Australian-born actress Marie Lohr in the British film *The Winslow Boy* (V "faultless"); Agnes Moorehead as the warden in *Caged* (NYT "splendid"); and Phyllis Thaxter in *The Breaking Point*.

While Moorehead was passed over, one of her co-stars in *Caged*, Hope Emerson, earned a nomination for her portrayal of the sadistic prison matron (NYT "vicious and inexorable as the Amazonian, corrupt guard"; MFB "extremely well-acted").

Sixty-five-year-old Josephine Hull, the winner of the Golden Globe, was included for reprising her stage role as the daffy sister in *Harvey* (NYT "plays Elwood's sister with such hilarious confusion and daft concern that she brings quite as much to the picture as does Mr Stewart"; TT "after an opening phase of overacting, settles down to give a spirited performance"; MFB "over-stagey"), while previous winner Celeste Holm was mentioned for the third (and final) time in just four years for playing the best friend of a Broadway star in *All About Eve* (MFB "exceptionally accomplished").

Also nominated for *All About Eve* was Globe nominee Thelma Ritter, who received her first mention for her role as a Broadway star's maid and dresser (NYT "screamingly funny"). Ritter also earned praise as a pregnant juror in *Perfect Strangers* (V "a gem of characterization").

The unexpected nominee was Nancy Olson for her lauded performance as the aspiring screenwriter in *Sunset Boulevard* (NYT "beautifully portrayed", "excellent"; V "splendid").

Hull was a respected theatre actress who only appeared in five films during her career: *After Tomorrow* and *Careless Lady* in 1932, Frank Capra's macabre 1945 comedy *Arsenic and Old Lace* as one of the murderous old sisters, *Harvey*, and *The Lady from Texas* in 1951. Despite having made only these occasional forays into film, Hull was embraced by the Academy who rewarded her turn in *Harvey* with the Oscar.

1951

BEST PICTURE

ACADEMY AWARDS
• *An American in Paris*
  (M-G-M, 113 mins, 9 Nov 1951, $4.5m, 8 noms)
Decision Before Dawn
  (20th Century Fox, 119 mins BW, 21 Dec 1951, 2 noms)
A Place in the Sun
  (Paramount, 122 mins BW, 28 Aug 1951, $3.5m, 9 noms)
Quo Vadis
  (M-G-M, 171 mins, 23 Feb 1951, $10.5m, 8 noms)
A Streetcar Named Desire
  (Feldman, Warner Bros., 122 mins BW, 19 Sep 1951, $4.2m, 12 noms)

GOLDEN GLOBE AWARDS
(Drama)
Bright Victory
Detective Story
• *A Place in the Sun*
Quo Vadis
A Streetcar Named Desire

(Comedy/Musical)
• *An American in Paris*

BRITISH ACADEMY AWARDS
(Best Film)
An American in Paris
The Browning Version
Detective Story
Domenica d'Argosto (Sunday in August)
Édouard et Caroline
  (Edward and Caroline)
Fourteen Hours
Froken Julie (Miss Julie)
The Lavender Hill Mob
The Magic Box
The Man in the White Suit
No Resting Place
Red Badge of Courage
• *La Ronde (Roundabout)*
The Small Miracle
The Sound of Fury
A Place in the Sun
White Corridors

(Best British Film)
The Browning Version
• *The Lavender Hill Mob*
The Magic Box
The Man in the White Suit
No Resting Place
The Small Miracle
White Corridors

1951

NEW YORK – *A Streetcar Named Desire*
BOARD OF REVIEW – *A Place in the Sun*

The Hollywood Foreign Press and the NBR both awarded their Best Picture prizes to George Stevens' *A Place in the Sun*, an adaptation of Theodore Dreiser's novel, 'An American Tragedy' (NYT "a work of beauty, tenderness, power and insight"; V "distinguished"; TT "powerful"; MFB "rewarding and exciting"). The New York critics, meanwhile, honoured Elia Kazan's *A Streetcar Named Desire*, a film version of the acclaimed play by Tennessee Williams (NYT "throbs with passion and poignancy ... you must see it", "the best film of the year"; V "absorbing"). Both dramas were among the year's top ten earners at the box office and were considered the frontrunners for the Academy's major award. *A Streetcar Named Desire* topped the list of Oscar nominees with twelve mentions, followed by *A Place in the Sun* with nine. Variety predicted that *A Streetcar Named Desire* would collect all four acting awards, but *A Place in the Sun* would claim Best Picture and Best Director.

The year's third most commercially successful release, the Golden Globe (Comedy/Musical) winner *An American in Paris* was also nominated for the Oscar (NYT "beguiling and refreshing"; V "imaginative"; MFB "merely a good musical"). Also nominated for both the Globe and the Oscar despite mixed reviews was the epic historical *Quo Vadis*, which eventually finished as the second most popular film of 1952 at the North American box office (NYT "a staggering combination of cinema brilliance and sheer banality" containing both "visual triumphs" and "a hackneyed romance"; V "a super-spectacle"; MFB a "lavish but dull spectacle"). Following a strong campaign by 20th Century Fox, the other Oscar nominee was the war drama *Decision Before Dawn* (NYT "a taut, exciting spy drama").

The inclusion of *Decision Before Dawn* was something of a surprise and came ahead of several highly favoured contenders: Globe nominee *Bright Victory* (NYT "inspiring"; V "very distinguished"); Globe nominee *Detective Story* (NYT "absorbing"; V "a cinematic gem"; TT "little more than a melodramatic box of tricks manipulated with considerable technical skill"); John Huston's adventure romance *The African Queen* (NYT "there is rollicking fun and gentle humor in this outlandish [film]"; V "engrossing"; MFB "a misfire", "much too long"); Billy Wilder's *The Big Carnival [aka Ace in the Hole]* (NYT "a sordid and cynical drama ... something of a dramatic grotesque ... a masterly film [but] badly weakened by a poorly constructed plot"); and *Death of a Salesman*, a film version of the lauded Arthur Miller play (NYT "in every respect, this transference to the motion picture form enhances the episodic structure and the time-ranging nature of the play"). *Death of a Salesman* won more Golden Globes than any other film that year, and yet was overlooked for both the Best Picture Globe and the Best Picture Oscar.

Other omissions were: the New York runner-up Jean Renoir's *The River* (NYT "a haunting reverie … sweet and beguiling"); the popular musical *Show Boat* (NYT "magnificent"); *Fourteen Hours* (NYT "remarkable", a "superior American film"; V "gripping"; MFB "exciting"); Alfred Hitchcock's *Strangers on a Train* (NYT "Hitchcock again is tossing a crazy murder story in the air and trying to con us into thinking that it will stand up without support"; V "topnotch"); David Lean's 1948 British film *Oliver Twist* (NYT "a superb piece of motion picture art"); *Red Badge of Courage* (NYT "a major achievement that should command attention for years and years"; V "a curiously moody, arty study"); the BAFTA winner *La Ronde (Roundabout)* (TT "artificial" but "elegantly sophisticated"); and the Palme d'Or winner and New York critics' Best Foreign Film winner *Miracolo a Milano (Miracle in Milan)* (NYT "riotously comic" and "lively entertainment"; V "outstanding").

While Akira Kurosawa's *Rashomon* won the Academy's Special Award for Best Foreign-Language Film, it was not eligible for Oscar consideration in other categories until the following year once it had played in Los Angeles cinemas.

The Best Picture Oscar winner in 1951 was a major upset. Neither *A Streetcar Named Desire*, which won three Oscars in the acting categories, nor *A Place in the Sun*, which won the Best Director award, emerged with the Academy's top accolade. Instead, the winner was Vincente Minnelli's *An American in Paris*, only the second colour film to win the Best Picture Oscar. As The New York Times commented the morning after the ceremony: *"An American in Paris* scored one the biggest upsets in Oscar history by being named the best picture of 1951 and winning seven other honors."

BEST DIRECTOR

ACADEMY AWARDS
John Huston for *The African Queen*
Elia Kazan for *A Streetcar Named Desire*
Vincente Minnelli for *An American in Paris*
• **George Stevens for *A Place in the Sun***
William Wyler for *Detective Story*

GOLDEN GLOBE AWARDS
• **Laslo Benedek – *Death of a Salesman***
Vincente Minnelli – *An American in Paris*
George Stevens – *A Place in the Sun*

DIRECTORS GUILD AWARD
Alfred Hitchcock – *Strangers on a Train*
Vincente Minnelli – *An American in Paris*
• **George Stevens – *A Place in the Sun***

NEW YORK – Elia Kazan – *A Streetcar Named Desire*
BOARD OF REVIEW – Akira Kurosawa – *Rashomon*

For the literary adaptation *A Place in the Sun* (NYT "expert direction") George Stevens led the vote for the New York critics' prize after the first round. He eventually lost, however, to Elia Kazan, who received his second New York award in five years for the stage-to-screen version of *A Streetcar Named Desire*.

When Stevens received a nomination for the Golden Globe Award but the New York winner was overlooked, he was favoured to emerge victorious over both Vincente Minnelli for *An American in Paris* (NYT "candor and charm invade the picture under Vincente Minnelli's helpful wand") and Laslo Benedek for *Death of a Salesman* (NYT "Laslo Benedek's direction is commendable all the way"; MFB "shows a firm, sympathetic touch"). However, while the two Golden Globe trophies for Best Picture went to *A Place in the Sun* and *An American in Paris*, the Best Director award surprisingly went to Benedek, whose film had not even been short-listed as a Best Picture contender by the Hollywood Foreign Press Association.

It was not until the Directors Guild of American handed out their annual prizes, that Stevens finally emerged as a winner.

Both Stevens and Kazan were nominated by the Academy (each for the second time). Also mentioned were: Globe nominee Minnelli; previous winner

William Wyler (earning a record eighth nod) for *Detective Story* (TT "remarkably successful"); and John Huston (his third mention in four years) for *The African Queen* (NYT "merits credit"). Huston had also been praised by critics for his handling of *Red Badge of Courage* (NYT "magnificent").

The unexpected exclusion of Benedek made him the first winner of the Golden Globe for Best Director to be snubbed by the Academy.

Also overlooked were: Anatole Litvak (TT "exceptional skill") and Mervyn LeRoy for Best Picture nominees *Decision Before Dawn* and *Quo Vadis* respectively; DGA nominee Alfred Hitchcock for *Strangers on a Train*; David Lean for *Oliver Twist* (NYT "brilliant"); Jean Renoir for *The River*; Vittorio de Sica for *Miracolo a Milano (Miracle in Milan)*; Mark Robson for *Bright Victory* (NYT "a superior job"; V "sensitive and sympathetic" direction); and Billy Wilder for the controversial drama *The Big Carnival [Ace in the Hole]* (NYT "the director has done a spectacular job of visioning the monstrous vulgarity of mob behavior").

Variety predicted that Stevens would receive the Best Director award and on Oscar night he was indeed honoured with his first Academy Award as Best Director. He won again five years later.

1951

BEST ACTOR

ACADEMY AWARDS
• **Humphrey Bogart as 'Charlie Allnut' in** *The African Queen*
Marlon Brando as 'Stanley Kowalski' in *A Streetcar Named Desire*
Montgomery Clift as 'George Eastman' in *A Place in the Sun*
Arthur Kennedy as 'Larry Nevins' in *Bright Victory*
Fredric March as 'Willy Loman' in *Death of a Salesman*

GOLDEN GLOBE AWARDS
(Drama)   (Comedy/Musical)
Kirk Douglas – *Detective Story*   Bing Crosby
Arthur Kennedy – *Bright Victory*   – *Here Comes the Groom*
• **Fredric March**   • **Danny Kaye – *On the Riviera***
   – *Death of a Salesman*   Gene Kelly – *An American in Paris*

NEW YORK – Arthur Kennedy – *Bright Victory*
BOARD OF REVIEW – Richard Basehart – *Fourteen Hours*

Marlon Brando had been a sensation during the 1947/8 Broadway season for his performance in the original production of Tennessee Williams' play 'A Streetcar Named Desire'. When, at age twenty-six, he reprised his role in Elia Kazan's film version, he impressed most film critics and became the favourite for the end of year Best Actor awards (NYT "brilliant"; V "performs unevenly"; TT "all too convincing"; S&S "creates a figure of frightening power"; MFB "outstandingly good ... a superbly dominating, vigorous and primitive performance"). Surprisingly, however, he received none of the major accolades. Brando won neither the NBR award nor the New York critics' prize (he was runner-up) and was overlooked for even a nomination for the Golden Globe Award (Drama) by the Hollywood Foreign Press Association.

The NBR gave their Best Actor prize to Richard Basehart for his performance as the man threatening to jump from a high-rise building in the drama *Fourteen Hours* (NYT "does a startling and poignant job").

The New York critics, meanwhile, voted for Arthur Kennedy as their choice as Best Actor of the year for his portrayal of a blind war veteran in *Bright Victory* (NYT an "excellent performance", "played with extraordinary perception"; V "makes the character very real and understandable").

The Golden Globe (Drama) was won by Hollywood veteran Fredric March as the failed travelling salesman in *Death of a Salesman*, a film version of the Arthur Miller play (NYT "outstanding"; V "one of the great film performances of the year"; TT there is "a certain monotony" about his performance; MFB a "performance of great integrity"). March's portrayal subsequently also won the Best Actor accolade at the 1952 Venice Film Festival.

The other Globe candidates were NY critics' winner Kennedy and Kirk Douglas as a NYC police detective in the drama *Detective Story* (NYT "forceful and emotionally expressive"). Earlier in the year Douglas had also earned praise as the unscrupulous newspaper reporter in the box office disappointment *The Big Carnival [Ace in the Hole]* (NYT "in his sure-fire portrayal of this character, Mr Douglas is superb, full of arrogance and the cruelty of the desperately insecure").

March was subsequently honoured as the first man to receive a fifth Best Actor Oscar nomination. Kennedy received his second mention, as did both Montgomery Clift as a social climber in *A Place in the Sun* (NYT "full, rich, restrained and, above all, generally credible and poignant"; V a "wonderfully shaded and poignant performance"; MFB "as nearly perfect as one could ask"), and Humphrey Bogart as the old riverboat captain in *The African Queen* (V "has never been better"; S&S "brilliant"; NYer "remarkable"). Completing the list was Brando, who earned his first nomination.

For the second year in a row the NBR winner was overlooked with Basehart left out of consideration. Surprisingly Globe nominee Douglas was also by-passed as were: Paul Douglas as the kindly police officer in *Fourteen Hours* (NYT "takes the honors"); previous winner James Cagney as an alcoholic in *Come Fill the Cup* (V "scores dramatically"; MFB "a sensitive and thoroughly convincing performance"); Gene Kelly in the musical *An American in Paris*; and both Robert Walker (NYT "as the diabolic villain is a caricature of silken suavity") and Farley Granger (NYT "plays the terrified catspaw as though he were constantly swallowing his tongue") in the Alfred Hitchcock thriller *Strangers on a Train*.

Many of the year's most notable omissions, however, were foreigners. The Academy's Best Actor nominees were all American for the first time since 1934.

British actors overlooked included: Cannes Film Festival winner Michael Redgrave as the unpopular teacher on the verge of retirement who unexpectedly wins the admiration of a student in *The Browning Version* (NYT "beautifully acted", "superb"; V "a performance which never falters"; MFB "a performance of considerable distinction"); Alec Guinness as Fagin in David Lean's *Oliver Twist*, a film adaptation of the novel by Charles Dickens (NYT "vastly clever"; MFB "excellent"); Richard Attenborough as a gangster in *Brighton Rock*, a crime thriller released in North America as *Young Scarface* (NYT "Attenborough is blistering as the criminal"); James Mason as Field Marshal Rommel in *The Desert Fox*; and Alastair Sim as the title character in *Scrooge (A*

Christmas Carol) (NYT "is precisely the dour and crabbed creature that he is in the memorable tale").

Also passed over were the non-English-language performances of Pierre Fresnay in *Dieu a Besoin des Hommes (God Needs Men)* (NYT "a powerful performance") and Francesco Golisano in *Miracolo a Milano (Miracle in Milan)* (NYT "infectiously appealing", "a grand job").

Despite failing to garner any of the end of year accolades and refusing to mount a campaign, Brando was considered the frontrunner for the Oscar. When Greer Garson opened the envelope on Oscar night, however, she revealed what The New York Times later called a "surprise choice" – the winner was Bogart. Unsuccessfully nominated for *Casablanca* and unexpectedly overlooked for a nod for *The Treasure of the Sierra Madre*, the fifty-two-year old Bogart had campaigned strongly for the award. It was the only Best Actor statuette he received during his career.

The following year the British Academy included Bogart and March and the overlooked Fresnay and Golisano among the nominees for its inaugural Best Foreign Actor award. In the end, however, they were all outpolled by Brando for his performance as the Mexican revolutionary Emiliano Zapata in *Viva Zapata!*, a portrayal for which he was once again unsuccessfully nominated for the Oscar.

1951

BEST ACTRESS

ACADEMY AWARDS
Katharine Hepburn as 'Rose Sayer' in *The African Queen*
• **Vivien Leigh as 'Blanche DuBois' in** *A Streetcar Named Desire*
Eleanor Parker as 'Mary McLeod' in *Detective Story*
Shelley Winters as 'Alice Tripp' in *A Place in the Sun*
Jane Wyman as 'Louise Mason' in *The Blue Veil*

GOLDEN GLOBE AWARDS
(Drama)   (Comedy/Musical)
Vivien Leigh   • **June Allyson –** *Too Young to Kiss*
 – *A Streetcar Named Desire*
Shelley Winters – *A Place in the Sun*
• **Jane Wyman –** *The Blue Veil*

NEW YORK – Vivien Leigh – *A Streetcar Named Des*ire
BOARD OF REVIEW – Jan Sterling – *The Big Carnival [Ace in the Hole]*

Three of the four principals from the Broadway production of Tennessee Williams' play 'A Streetcar Named Desire' were cast in Elia Kazan's film version. The exception was Jessica Tandy, who was replaced in the role of the fragile and vain faded southern belle, Blanche DuBois, by English actress Vivien Leigh. Winner of an Oscar over a decade earlier for playing the role of a feisty southern belle in *Gone with the Wind*, Leigh had played DuBois in the London production of Williams' play.

Leigh's performance was acclaimed by most critics and she was rewarded with her second New York Film Critics Circle Best Actress prize as well as the Best Actress accolade at the Venice Film Festival (NYT "haunting … brilliant"; V "compelling"; TT a "triumph"; S&S "a polished, professional performance" but "over-calculated [and] lacking inner compulsion"; MFB "her performance is too exterior, too synthetic, for pathos").

The NBR gave their award to Jan Sterling as the cold-hearted, sarcastic wife in Billy Wilder's hard-hitting drama *The Big Carnival* (originally released as *Ace in the Hole*) (NYT "fills with venom the role of the victim's trampish wife"; MFB "a subtly vicious and sullen performance").

At the Golden Globe awards Leigh was a nominee for Best Actress (Drama) alongside the actress whom she had outpolled for the NY prize: Shelley Winters as the young factory worker murdered by an ambitious social climber in *A Place in the Sun* (NYT "never been better"; V "wonderfully shaded and poignant"; MFB "admirable").

Leigh had been expected to triumph at the Golden Globe Awards as well, however in a big surprise, the trophy went to the third nominee: Jane Wyman, who collected her second Globe as a self-sacrificing nanny in the tear-jerker *The Blue Veil* (V "outstanding"; TT "Wyman makes Louise a person rather than a bundle of abstract virtues. There is something perhaps a little too careful, a little too consistent, in her acting ... but it is an admirable performance nevertheless"; MFB "too calculated").

The three Globe nominees were recognised by the Academy – Winters for the first time; previous winner Leigh for the second (and final) time; and previous winner Wyman for the third time in just six years. Nominated for the fifth time for her lauded performance as the spinster sister of a murdered missionary in *The African Queen* was previous winner Katharine Hepburn (NYT "played with her crisp flair for comedy"; TT "a tour de force"; S&S "brilliant"; NYer "remarkable"; MFB "wonderful"). Unexpectedly, the Academy snubbed NBR winner Sterling and rounded out their short-list by nominating Eleanor Parker for what was really just a supporting part in *Detective Story*. Her performance as the detective's wife had not earned glowing reviews, indeed Bosley Crowther in The New York Times for example had felt she was the weakest part of the film. "In the performance of this business," he wrote, "every member of the cast rates a hand, with the possible exception of Eleanor Parker". Crowther considered her miscast and her performance "conventional". It was her second consecutive Oscar nomination.

In addition to Sterling, Academy members overlooked were: Golden Globe (Comedy/Musical) winner June Allyson as a pianist pretending to be a child prodigy in *Too Young to Kiss*; Elizabeth Taylor as the society girl in *A Place in the Sun* (NYT "a shaded, tender performance"; V "poignant"); and twenty-year-old Leslie Caron in the Best Picture winner *An American in Paris* (NYT "the picture takes on its glow of magic when Miss Caron is on the screen ... all things are forgiven when Miss Caron is on the screen. When she is on with Mr Kelly and they are dancing, [the film] is superb").

Despite Wyman's upset win at the Globes, on Oscar night, as predicted by Variety, Leigh claimed her second Best Actress Academy Award. Her victory came just three years after her husband, Laurence Olivier, had won the Best Actor Oscar. She repeated her win for *A Streetcar Named Desire* in London the following year, receiving the British Academy's Best British Actress award.

Jessica Tandy, the actress who had originated the role of Blanche DuBois on Broadway, won the Best Actress Oscar nearly forty years later for the part of a very different southern lady in *Driving Miss Daisy*.

1951

BEST SUPPORTING ACTOR

ACADEMY AWARDS
Leo Genn as 'Petronius' in *Quo Vadis*
• **Karl Malden as 'Mitch' in *A Streetcar Named Desire***
Kevin McCarthy as 'Biff Loman' in *Death of a Salesman*
Peter Ustinov as 'Emperor Nero' in *Quo Vadis*
Gig Young as 'Boyd Copeland' in *Come Fill the Cup*

GOLDEN GLOBE AWARDS – Peter Ustinov – *Quo Vadis*

Upon the release in November 1951 of the expensive epic *Quo Vadis*, The New York Times film critic Bosley Crowther, harshly condemned Peter Ustinov's portrayal of the unstable Roman Emperor Nero. "Mr Ustinov's mouthing and screaming, if halved, might be durable," he wrote, "As it is, they become the most monotonous and vexing things in the film." Variety's reviewer was similarly unimpressed, dismissing the performance as "scenery-chewing." Despite such negative reviews, Ustinov won the Best Supporting Actor Golden Globe Award and received his first nomination from the Academy.

Four other first-time nominees were also recognised by the Academy: Leo Genn as a Roman nobleman in *Quo Vadis*; Gig Young as an alcoholic youth in *Come Fill the Cup* (V a "standout"); and both Karl Malden (V "excellent") and Kevin McCarthy (NYT "disturbingly shifty") for reprising their acclaimed Broadway performances as the sensitive lover in *A Streetcar Named Desire* and as one of the sons in *Death of a Salesman*, respectively.

The shock omission from the category was Oskar Werner as the German turncoat in *Decision Before Dawn* (NYT "remarkable", "commanding"; MFB "sensitive"; TT "makes the story plausible and exciting"). Also overlooked were: Howard de Silva in *Fourteen Hours* (NYT "excellent"); James Gleason in *Come Fill the Cup* (V "standout"); and William Hartnell in *Brighton Rock (Young Scarface)* (NYT "fine").

On Oscar night, the strongly favoured Malden won the Academy Award. Three years later he was nominated a second time, once again for a role in an Elia Kazan film. Malden served as the President of the Academy of Motion Picture Arts and Sciences from 1989 until 1992.

1951

BEST SUPPORTING ACTRESS

ACADEMY AWARDS
Joan Blondell as 'Annie Rawlins' in *The Blue Veil*
Mildred Dunnock as 'Linda Loman' in *Death of a Salesman*
Lee Grant as 'the shoplifter' in *Detective Story*
• **Kim Hunter as 'Stella Kowalski' in *A Streetcar Named Desire***
Thelma Ritter as 'Ellen McNulty' in *The Mating Season*

GOLDEN GLOBE AWARDS
Lee Grant – *Detective Story*
• **Kim Hunter – *A Streetcar Named Desire***
Thelma Ritter – *The Mating Season*

In *Death of a Salesman*, Mildred Dunnock reprised her Broadway role of the wife of the failed salesman and earned praise from critics (NYT & V "superb"; TT "touching"; MFB "performance of great integrity"). At the end of the year she finished third in the voting for the New York critics' Best Actress award.

Surprisingly, however, she was not nominated for the Golden Globe Award. Short-listed ahead of her were: Lee Grant as the shoplifter in *Detective Story* (NYT "a standout"); Kim Hunter, also reprising a role she had originated on Broadway, in *A Streetcar Named Desire* (V "excellent"; MFB "outstandingly good"); and Thelma Ritter as a mother-in-law in *The Mating Season* (NYT "rips into this character with gusto"). The award was won by Hunter.

Dunnock and all three Globe nominees were recognised by the Academy. Also named was Joan Blondell as the fading musical actress who hires a nanny in *The Blue Veil*.

Surprisingly, Agnes Moorehead, who had already been unsuccessfully nominated three times over the previous decade, was overlooked as the distraught mother in *Fourteen Hours* (NYT "brilliantly effective"; V & MFB "excellent"). Also passed over were Marilyn Monroe in *As Young as You Feel* (NYT "superb") and Laura Elliott for her brief turn as the murder victim in Alfred Hitchcock's *Strangers on a Train* (NYT "stands out").

As Variety correctly predicted, Golden Globe winner Hunter repeated her win at the Oscar ceremony. Only a few years after receiving the statuette, her career was unfairly interrupted when she was named as a communist sympathiser and blacklisted. Lee Grant, whose performance in *Detective Story* was awarded the Best Actress prize at the Cannes Film Festival in 1952, also became a victim of the blacklist. While Grant won an Oscar in 1975, Hunter never again made the Academy's list of nominees.

BEST PICTURE

ACADEMY AWARDS
• *The Greatest Show on Earth*
   (DeMille, Paramount, 152 mins, 10 Jan 1952, $12.0m, 5 noms)
High Noon
   (Kramer, United Artists, 85 mins BW, 24 Jul 1952, $3.4m, 7 noms)
Ivanhoe
   (M-G-M, 106 mins, 31 Jul 1952, $7.0m, 3 noms)
Moulin Rouge
   (Romulus, United Artists, 119 mins, 23 Dec 1952, $5.0m, 7 noms)
The Quiet Man
   (Argosy, Republic, 129 mins, 21 Aug 1952, $3.2m, 7 noms)

GOLDEN GLOBE AWARDS
(Drama)
Come Back, Little Sheba
• *The Greatest Show on Earth*
The Happy Time
High Noon
The Thief

(Comedy/Musical)
Hans Christian Anderson
I'll See You In My Dreams
Singin' in the Rain
Stars and Stripes Forever
• *With a Song in My Heart*

BRITISH ACADEMY AWARDS
(Best Film)
The African Queen
Angels One Five
The Boy Kumasenu
Carrie
Casque d'Or (Golden Marie)
Death of a Salesman
Limelight
Mandy
Miracolo a Milano (Miracle in Milan)
Los Olvidados (The Young and the Damned)
Outcast of the Islands
Rashomon
The River
Singin' in the Rain
• *The Sound Barrier (Breaking the Sound Barrier)*
A Streetcar Named Desire
Viva Zapata!

(Best British Film)
Angels One Five
Cry, the Beloved Country
Mandy
Outcast of the Islands
The River
• *The Sound Barrier*
   (Breaking the Sound Barrier)

1952

"*High Noon* is a cinch to win the trophy as Best Picture of the year" wrote Variety just prior to the Oscar ceremony. *High Noon* was an allegorical criticism of the House Committee on Un-American Activities (HUAC) hearings into alleged communist activities in the Hollywood film-making community. It took the form of a Western in which a sheriff on the verge of retirement must stand alone against a gang of murderous outlaws as the townsfolk desert him. Gary Cooper played the lead and Fred Zinnemann directed. The film was hailed by critics (NYT "a thrilling and inspiring work of art" and "a rare and exciting achievement"; V "excellent"; TT "a highly intelligent film") and was one of the ten most successful films of the year at the box office. It was named Best Picture by the New York critics, was runner-up for the top prize from the NBR and was a Golden Globe nominee. The Academy recognised it with seven nominations.

Although both had been surprisingly overlooked for the Golden Globe, the two other main contenders for the Best Picture Oscar were: *The Quiet Man*, John Ford's popular romantic comedy starring John Wayne and Maureen O'Hara which was set in Ireland and had been selected by the NBR as the year's Best Picture (NYT a "vigorous and rollicking comedy"; V "excellent"); and *Moulin Rouge*, a biopic starring José Ferrer as the French artist Henri de Toulouse-Lautrec, directed by John Huston (NYT "brilliantly illustrative"). Both films equalled the seven Oscar nominations of *High Noon*.

The Academy's other two Best Picture nominees were both box office hits. Cecil B. DeMille's lauded circus extravaganza *The Greatest Show on Earth*, which was the year's biggest box office attraction and the surprise winner of the Golden Globe (Drama) Award (NYT a "lusty triumph of circus showmanship and movie skill", "a piece of entertainment that will delight movie audiences for years"; V "a smash"; MFB "cannot conceal an almost heroic lack of imagination"); and *Ivanhoe*, a lavish M-G-M historical adventure romance film that finished as the year's third most popular film (NYT "brilliantly colored tapestry of drama and spectacle"; V "a picture that cannot miss", "a spectacular feast").

The surprise inclusion of *Ivanhoe* came ahead of several more acclaimed films, most notably the popular musical and Globe nominee *Singin' in the Rain* and Akira Kurosawa's *Rashomon*, which had won the Special Oscar for Best Foreign-Language Film the previous year and now become eligible for the Academy's competitive arts and technical achievement awards (NYT "an artistic achievement"; S&S "one of the most stimulating and extraordinary pictures made anywhere in the world since the end of the war"; MFB "masterly and fascinating").

Two other notable omissions were: *Los Olvidados (The Young and the Damned)*, Luis Buñuel's controversial drama about the criminal activity of poverty-stricken juveniles in the slums of Mexico City (NYT "a brutal and unrelenting picture"; MFB "brilliant"); and David Lean's *The Sound Barrier (Breaking the Sound Barrier)*, an acclaimed British drama about a man's quest to design and build the world's first supersonic aircraft (NYT "excellent", "a film of pictorial excitement and truly poetic eloquence", "wonderfully beautiful and thrilling"; V "technically, artistically and emotionally, this is a topflight British offering", "a fine piece of entertainment"). *The Sound Barrier* was the first film honoured with both the Best Film and Best British Film awards by the British Academy.

Surprisingly ineligible for Oscar consideration because it never played in a theatre in Los Angeles until 1972 was Charlie Chaplin's lauded *Limelight*, a semi-autobiographical drama about an ageing clown (NYT "a brilliant weaving of comic and tragic strands"; TT "fascinating"). The Times said that it was "conspicuously absent" from the list of Oscar nominees.

Also overlooked were: Golden Globe nominee *Come Back, Little Sheba*, for which Shirley Booth won the Best Actress Oscar (NYT "poignant and haunting"; V "compelling", "a potent piece of screen entertainment"); Golden Globe nominee *The Happy Time* (NYT "it's not the tender film – the mellow and understanding picture – of a boy's growing up that it could be"; V "unusually good" and "almost constantly entertaining"); surprise Golden Globe (Comedy/Musical) winner *With a Song in My Heart*, a biopic about crippled singer Jane Froman; Joseph L. Mankiewicz's thriller *Five Fingers* (NYT "first-rate"; V "good, if somewhat overlong"); the British comedy *The Lavender Hill Mob* (V "another comedy winner"; MFB "bright and entertaining"); and the British drama *Cry, the Beloved Country*, about racial divisions in South Africa (V "very moving").

Despite the acclaim for *High Noon*, the only black and white Best Picture nominee that year, the Academy chose a safer and less controversial candidate. At the RKO Pantages Theatre in Los Angeles, Mary Pickford opened the envelope on Oscar night and announced to the astonished audience that the Academy's choice as Best Picture of the year was DeMille's circus epic *The Greatest Show on Earth*. It was the sixth time in a decade that the same film had won the Golden Globe and the Oscar. More significantly, it was the second year in a row that the Academy's top honour had gone to a hugely successful, large-scale, colour production that had not earned any nominations in the acting categories. Two other films that had been unrecognised in the acting categories would be honoured with the Best Picture Academy Award by the end of the decade.

It is likely that the enormous popularity of DeMille's circus spectacle was the factor that helped it to claim the Best Picture Oscar ahead of both the politically controversial *High Noon* and the popular and uncontroversial *The Quiet Man* for which John Ford won the Best Director statuette ahead of both DeMille for *The Greatest Show on Earth* and Zinnemann for *High Noon*.

Surprisingly, neither *The Greatest Show on Earth*, *The Quiet Man* nor *High Noon* were the year's most honoured film at the Academy Awards. Emerging from the night with a tally of five Oscar statuettes from six nominations, including the awards for Best Screenplay and Best Supporting Actress, was Vincente Minnelli's *The Bad and the Beautiful*, a drama about an ambitious Hollywood producer (V "excellent"; TT "instead of satire there is false sentiment"). The film had not even been nominated for the Best Picture or Best Director Oscars. It had also been by-passed for Best Picture consideration at the Golden Globes. The following year, however, *The Bad and the Beautiful* was among the British Academy's Best Film nominees.

BEST DIRECTOR

ACADEMY AWARDS
Cecil B. DeMille for *The Greatest Show on Earth*
• **John Ford for *The Quiet Man***
John Huston for *Moulin Rouge*
Joseph L. Mankiewicz for *Five Fingers*
Fred Zinnemann for *High Noon*

GOLDEN GLOBE AWARDS
• **Cecil B. DeMille – *The Greatest Show on Earth***
Richard Fleischer – *The Happy Time*
John Ford – *The Quiet Man*

DIRECTORS GUILD AWARD
Charles Crichton – *The Lavender Hill Mob*
• **John Ford – *The Quiet Man***
Joseph L. Mankiewicz – *Five Finge*rs
Fred Zinnemann – *High Noon*

NEW YORK – Fred Zinnemann – *High Noon*
BOARD OF REVIEW – David Lean – *The Sound Barrier (Breaking the Sound Barrier)*

Second-time nominee Fred Zinnemann became the favourite to win the Best Director Oscar for his politically controversial Western *High Noon* after he received the Best Director Award from the New York critics' (NYT "brilliant"; MFB "expert").

Zinnemann's competition for the Oscar statuette were: previous winner John Ford, nominated for a fifth and final time, for *The Quiet Man* (TT "well directed"); previous winner Joseph L. Mankiewicz, earning his third nod in four years, for *Five Fingers*; previous winner John Huston, receiving his fourth nomination in five years, for *Moulin Rouge* (V "Huston's direction is superb"); and Cecil B. DeMille for *The Greatest Show on Earth*. It was the only time that legendary DeMille ever appeared on the ballot for the Best Director Oscar.

Surprisingly overlooked was the NBR winner David Lean for the British drama *The Sound Barrier (Breaking the Sound Barrier)* (V "bold and imaginative"; TT "brilliant").

Also passed over were: the 1951 NBR winner Akira Kurosawa for *Rashomon* (NYT "brilliant"); the 1951 Cannes winner Luis Buñuel for *Los Olvidados (The*

1952

Young and the Damned) (TT "brilliantly" directed); DGA nominee Charles Crichton for the British comedy *The Lavender Hill Mob*; Daniel Mann for *Come Back, Little Sheba* (V "great sensitivity"); Henry Koster for *My Cousin Rachel* (V "fine direction"); and William Wyler for *Carrie*.

Due to a technicality, Charlie Chaplin was ineligible for *Limelight* (NYT "cinema artistry"). Although released in select arthouse cinemas across North America that year, the film did not play in a cinema in Los Angeles (a requirement for Oscar qualification) until 1972.

Zinnemann's early status as the Oscar frontrunner looked increasingly shaky at the awards seasons unfolded. The Directors Guild gave their prestigious accolade to Ford while the Hollywood Foreign Press Association chose to fête DeMille. All three men, it seemed, had a realistic chance of taking home the Academy statuette.

On Academy Awards night, it was the Guild which proved to be the best indicator of Oscar fortune. It's brief but flawless record was kept intact when Olivia de Havilland revealed the winner of the Best Director Academy Award to be John Ford for *The Quiet Man*. It was his fourth statuette in less than twenty years. He remains the only person to have won the Best Director Oscar on four occasions.

BEST ACTOR

ACADEMY AWARDS

Marlon Brando as 'Emiliano Zapata' in *Viva Zapata!*
• **Gary Cooper as 'Marshal Will Kane' in *High Noon***
Kirk Douglas as 'Jonathon Shields' in *The Bad and the Beautiful*
José Ferrer as 'Henri de Toulouse-Lautrec' in *Moulin Rouge*
Alec Guinness as 'Henry Holland' in *The Lavender Hill Mob*

GOLDEN GLOBE AWARDS

(Drama)
Charles Boyer – *The Happy Time*
• **Gary Cooper – *High Noon***
Ray Milland – *The Thief*

(Comedy/Musical)
Danny Kaye
   – Hans Christian Anderson
• **Donald O'Connor**
   – *Singin' in the Rain*
Clifton Webb
   – Stars and Stripes Forever

BRITISH ACADEMY AWARDS

(Foreign Actor)
Humphrey Bogart – *The African Queen*
• **Marlon Brando – *Viva Zapata!***
Pierre Fresnay
   – Dieu a Besoin des Hommes
   (God Needs Men)
Francesco Golisano
   – Miracolo a Milano
   (Miracle in Milan)
Fredric March – *Death of a Salesman*

(British Actor)
Jack Hawkins – *Mandy*
James Hayter
   – The Pickwick Papers
Laurence Olivier – *Carrie*
Nigel Patrick – *The Sound Barrier*
   (Breaking the Sound Barrier)
• **Ralph Richardson**
   – *The Sound Barrier*
   (*Breaking the Sound Barrier*)
Alastair Sim – *Folly to be Wise*

NEW YORK – **Ralph Richardson** – ***The Sound Barrier (Breaking the Sound Barrier)***
BOARD OF REVIEW – **Ralph Richardson** – ***The Sound Barrier (Breaking the Sound Barrier)***

For the first time since 1936 the winner the of the New York Film Critics Circle's Best Actor Award did not appear on the Academy's list of nominees. Ralph Richardson was overlooked for his acclaimed performance as an aeroplane manufacturer determined to build the first supersonic aircraft in the British drama *The Sound Barrier (Breaking the Sound Barrier)* (NYT "cannot tell you how impressively Mr Richardson shows not only the passion and concentration of a rich and famous builder of planes but the almost fanatic absorption of a man in the challenge of space"; V "superbly played"; TT "extraordinary skill"; MFB "clever but too stylized and theatrical"). The Academy's exclusion of Richardson was even more surprising given that he had earned the British Academy's inaugural award for Best British Actor and had also received the Best Actor prize from the NBR for the second time. It was the third year in a row that the NBR winner had gone unrecognised by the Academy.

The other major omission from the Academy's list was the New York runner-up, Charlie Chaplin, for his performance as an ageing clown in his semi-autobiographical *Limelight*. The New York Times had said "Chaplin's own performance in the leading role runs a gamut from deep and haunting pathos to the grandest, most artful burlesque." Variety had praised him for a "tour de force" that was both "magnificent" and "compelling." As the film had not screened in a Los Angeles cinema, however, Chaplin was ineligible for Oscar consideration.

Others passed over by the Academy were: John Wayne in *The Quiet Man*; Burt Lancaster as the alcoholic husband in *Come Back, Little Sheba* (NYT "excellent", "should not be overlooked"; V "a fine job"; TT "extraordinary"); Laurence Olivier as an actress' married lover in *Carrie* (NYT "haunting" in "a genuine portrait"; V "never quite fits the role"; S&S "played with a fine suppressed force and feeling"; MFB "a notable achievement"); James Mason as a spy in *Five Fingers* (NYT "superb" in an "elegant performance"); Michael Gough as an Irish tinker who kills a man in *No Resting Place* (NYT "superb"); both Golden Globe (Comedy/Musical) winner Donald O'Connor (V a "standout") and Gene Kelly (NYT "runs away, of course, with the dancing") in the musical *Singin' in the Rain*; previous winner Robert Donat as the British cinema pioneer William Friese-Greene in *The Magic Box* (NYT "a superlative job"; V "superbly acted", "excellent"); the late African-American actor Canada Lee as a priest in South Africa in the British drama *Cry, the Beloved Country* (NYT "splendid" in "a profoundly moving job"; V "restrained and underplayed", "a rich, heart-warming portrayal"; MFB "strained, theatrical"); and Cary Grant in the comedy *Monkey Business*.

Despite the exclusion of Richardson, a British actor was nominated for the Best Actor Oscar. Conspicuously overlooked in 1950 for his supporting performances in the black comedy *Kind Hearts and Coronets*, Alec Guinness received his first mention from the Academy for his performance as a bank clerk who plans a massive gold heist in the 1951 British comedy *The Lavender Hill*

Mob (NYT "wickedly droll" and "deliciously adroit"; V "shines", "at his best"; MFB "excellent").

The previous year's unsuccessful Best Actor favourite Marlon Brando earned his second consecutive nomination for his portrayal of the Mexican revolutionary leader Emiliano Zapata in *Viva Zapata!*, a portrayal for which he was honoured at the Cannes Film Festival and won the inaugural Best Foreign Actor Award from the British Academy (NYT "not at his best … his acting of a baffled, tongued-tied Indian does not carry too much force … but when this dynamic young performer is speaking his anger or his love for a fellow revolutionary, there is power enough in his portrayal"; S&S "fine, deeply felt"; MFB "superbly vigorous and sensitive").

Kirk Douglas also garnered his second nomination for playing an ambitious Hollywood producer in *The Bad and the Beautiful* (NYT "plays the fellow with all that arrogance in the eyes and jaw that suggests a ruthless disposition covering up for a hurt and bitter soul"; V "scores").

Previous winner José Ferrer somewhat surprisingly made the Academy's list for the third (and final) time for his impersonation of the artist Henri de Toulouse-Lautrec in *Moulin Rouge*, even though it had been poorly received by film critics (NYT "a mere façade … his acting, which is done very largely with his bodily poses and his eyes, does little more, in their limited employment, than ditto the absurdity and pathos of this façade"; MFB "mannered, monotonous and unsympathetic").

Finally, another previous winner, Gary Cooper, received his fifth (and final) Oscar nomination for his performance as a U.S. marshal abandoned by the inhabitants of a small frontier town to face a gang of outlaws alone in *High Noon* (NYT "at the top of his form"; V "an unusually able job"; TT "one of the best performances of his long career"; MFB "excellent").

Cooper received the Globe (Drama) award for his performance in *High Noon* and Variety correctly predicted that he would repeat his win at the Academy Awards. It was Cooper's second Best Actor Oscar having won eleven years earlier for *Sergeant York*.

1952

BEST ACTRESS

ACADEMY AWARDS
• **Shirley Booth as 'Lola Delaney' in** *Come Back, Little Sheba*
Joan Crawford as 'Myra Hudson' in *Sudden Fear*
Bette Davis as 'Margaret Elliot' in *The Star*
Julie Harris as 'Frankie Adams' in *The Member of the Wedding*
Susan Hayward as 'Jane Froman' in *With a Song in My Heart*

GOLDEN GLOBE AWARDS
(Drama)
• **Shirley Booth**
   – *Come Back, Little Sheba*
Joan Crawford – *Sudden Fear*
Olivia de Havilland
   – *My Cousin Rachel*

(Comedy/Musical)
• **Susan Hayward**
   – *With a Song in My Heart*
Katharine Hepburn – *Pat and Mike*
Ginger Rogers – *Monkey Business*

BRITISH ACADEMY AWARDS
(Foreign Actress)
Edwige Feuillère – *Olivia*
Katharine Hepburn – *Pat and Mike*
Judy Holliday – *The Marrying Kind*
• **Simone Signoret**
   – *Casque d'Or (Golden Marie)*
Nicole Stéphane
   – *Les Enfants Terrible*
   (*The Strange Ones*)

(British Actress)
Phyllis Calvert – *Mandy*
Celia Johnson – *I Believe in You*
• **Vivien Leigh**
   – *A Streetcar Named Desire*
Ann Todd – *The Sound Barrier*
   (*Breaking the Sound Barrier*)

NEW YORK – Shirley Booth – *Come Back, Little Sheba*
BOARD OF REVIEW – Shirley Booth – *Come Back, Little Sheba*

At age forty-five, respected stage actress Shirley Booth made her film debut in *Come Back, Little Sheba* reprising her Tony Award-winning performance as a housewife trapped in a failed marriage. The New York Times praised her for "a great piece of character revelation" commenting that "enough cannot be said for the excellence of the performance Miss Booth gives." Variety said she was "wonderful" and that she was "certain to be among the major contenders when the annual Academy Awards screen honors are voted on." In Britain, S&S considered her "stunning" and "outstanding" while The Times wrote "the acting honours unquestionably go to Miss Shirley Booth" and MFB called her "extraordinary." At the end of the year Booth made a clean sweep of the major Best Actress accolades collecting prizes from both the NBR and the New York critics as well as the Golden Globe (Drama) and the Academy Award. She was the second thespian, after Ray Milland in 1945, to be so honoured. Like Milland, she was also subsequently recognised at the Cannes Film Festival – she won the Best Actress award in 1953. The Academy Award win made Booth the first person to win an Oscar in the major acting categories for a debut screen performance.

Overshadowed by Booth's acclaimed performance were lauded portrayals by several other actresses. Recognised by the Academy were: previous Oscar winner Bette Davis, who became the first person to receive a ninth Academy Award nomination in the acting categories for her performance as a former award-winning Hollywood actress in *The Star* (NYT "eloquent and sure"; V "a strong performance"; S&S "remarkable"; MFB "a wonderful bravura display"); previous winner Joan Crawford as a playwright who realises her new, younger husband is planning to kill her in the thriller *Sudden Fear* (NYT "a truly professional performance"; V "scores"); Golden Globe (Comedy/Musical) winner Susan Hayward for her impersonation of singer Jane Froman in *With a Song in My Heart* (NYT "one would not call her performance either subtle or restrained"; V "first-rate"); twenty-seven-year old Julie Harris for reprising her Broadway success as a twelve-year-old girl growing up in the deep South in *The Member of the Wedding* (NYT "skillful"; V "compelling").

Also recreating her stage role in *The Member of the Wedding* was Ethel Waters. She too earned praise from critics (V "splendid"; S&S "radiant performance") but was listed by Columbia as a candidate for the supporting prize so as to not compete with Harris. She went unrecognised in either category.

The surprise omission of the year was previous Oscar winner and Globe nominee Olivia de Havilland in *My Cousin Rachel* (V "commanding"). Also overlooked were: previous winner Jennifer Jones in *Carrie* (V "one of the brightest performances of her career"); previous Oscar winner and BAFTA nominee Judy Holliday in the comedy *The Marrying Kind* (NYT "beautifully textured"; MFB "brilliantly done"); previous Oscar winner Katharine Hepburn in *Pat and Mike*, a performance for which she was both a Globe and BAFTA nominee; Marilyn Monroe in *Don't Bother to Knock* (V "excellent"); BAFTA nominee Ann Todd in *The Sound Barrier (Breaking the Sound Barrier)* (NYT "impassioned performance"); Anna Neagle as Florence Nightingale in *Lady with a Lamp* (V "a sincerely moving study"); BAFTA nominee Nicole Stéphane in *Les Enfants Terribles (The Strange Ones)* (V "brilliant"; TT "very well acted"); and BAFTA winner Simone Signoret in *Casque d'Or (Golden Marie)* (NYT "notably conveys the hard-bitten poignancy required"; V "a standout"; TT "a generous performance").

1952

BEST SUPPORTING ACTOR

ACADEMY AWARDS
Richard Burton as 'Philip Ashley' in *My Cousin Rachel*
Arthur Hunnicutt as 'Uncle Zeb' in *The Big Sky*
Victor McLaglen as 'Red Will Danaher' in *The Quiet Man*
Jack Palance as 'Lester Blaine' in *Sudden Fear*
• **Anthony Quinn as 'Eufemio Zapata' in *Viva Zapata!***

GOLDEN GLOBE AWARDS
Kurt Kasznar – *The Happy Time*
• **Millard Mitchell – *My Six Convicts***
Gilbert Roland – *The Bad and the Beautiful*

For his performance in the prison drama *My Six Convicts*, Millard Mitchell won the Golden Globe as Best Supporting Actor (NYT "runs off with the acting honors"; V "stand-out"). Mitchell outpolled nominees Gilbert Roland for his high-profile part in *The Bad and the Beautiful* (NYT "performs with proper motions"), and Kurt Kasznar for his reprisal of his Broadway performance as one of the uncles in *The Happy Time* (NYT "farcical performing" by the entire cast; V "a delight"; MFB "excellent").

Unexpectedly, Mitchell became the first Best Supporting Actor Globe winner to be overlooked for an Oscar nod. Both Kasznar and Roland were snubbed as well as were: previous winner Barry Fitzgerald as the marriage broker in *The Quiet Man* (NYT "superb"); Eddie Albert as a travelling salesman in *Carrie* (V "excellent"); Sidney Poitier as a clerical worker in the British drama *Cry, the Beloved Country* (NYT "splendid"); and Claude Dauphin as the cruel gang leader in *Casque d'Or (Golden Marie)* (TT "a brilliant portrait").

The Academy instead chose to nominate a previous Best Actor Oscar winner and four first-time contenders. Seventeen years after he had won Best Actor for John Ford's *The Informer*, Victor McLaglen made the ballot for his appearance in John Ford's *The Quiet Man* (NYT "fine"; V "excellent"). Also in contention were: Arthur Hunnicutt in the Western *The Big Sky* (NYT "outstanding"; V "a standout"); Jack Palance as the young husband planning to murder his wife in *Sudden Fear* (V "fails to impress"); Anthony Quinn as the brother of a Mexican revolutionary in *Viva Zapata!*; and Welshman Richard Burton as the young aristocrat in *My Cousin Rachel* (NYT "perfect"; V "creates a strong impression"; TT "his acting has purpose and personality").

Prior to the Oscar ceremony Variety declared Burton the strong favourite for the Academy's honour. On the night, however the upset winner was Quinn.

1952

BEST SUPPORTING ACTRESS

ACADEMY AWARDS
• **Gloria Grahame as 'Rosemary Bartlow' in *The Bad and the Beautiful***
Jean Hagen as 'Lina Lamont' in *Singin' in the Rain*
Colette Marchand as 'Marie Charlet' in *Moulin Rouge*
Terry Moore as 'Marie Buckholder' in *Come Back, Little Sheba*
Thelma Ritter as 'Clancy' in *With a Song in My Heart*

GOLDEN GLOBE AWARDS
Mildred Dunnock – *Viva Zapata!*
Gloria Grahame – *The Bad and the Beautiful*
• **Katy Jurado – *High Noon***

Mexican actress Katy Jurado won the Golden Globe for her performance as the hero's former lover in *High Noon* (MFB "excellent"). In a major shock, however, she was overlooked by the Academy becoming the first recipient of the Best Supporting Actress Golden Globe Award to be passed over for an Oscar nomination.

African-American stage star Ethel Waters was another notable omission from the list of Oscar contenders for her performance as the old cook in *The Member of the Wedding*, a role she had previously played on Broadway (NYT "glows with a warmth of personality and understanding that transmits a wonderful incidental concept of the pathos of the transient nurse"; V "splendid"; S&S "radiant performance"). Although arguably a co-leading role, Columbia pushed for Waters to be considered in the supporting category (where she had been a nominee three years earlier) so as not to have her in competition with co-star, Julie Harris. While Harris earned a Best Actress nomination from the Academy, Waters was left off the ballot entirely.

Also overlooked were: Globe nominee Mildred Dunnock for *Viva Zapata!*; both Edith Evans as Lady Bracknell (NYT "genius"; V "distinguished"; MFB "magnificent") and Margaret Rutherford as Miss Prism (NYT "plays in an expertly bumbling style"; V "distinguished") in a British film version of *The Importance of Being Earnest*, from the play by Oscar Wilde; and Danielle Darrieux as the exiled Polish countess in the espionage thriller *Five Fingers* (NYT "magnificently poised and efficient … she is as stirring but elusive as an indescribably elegant perfume").

All the Academy Award nominees for the Best Supporting Actress statuette were American for the third year in a row. The unexpected nominees were Colette Marchand as a prostitute in *Moulin Rouge* (NYT "does a quick but excruciating job of revealing the sharp, metallic spirit and the helpless weaknesses of the gutter girl") and Terry Moore as the young boarder in *Come Back, Little Sheba* (NYT "strikes precisely the right note"). Thelma Ritter was included for the third consecutive year as the nurse of a crippled singer in *With a Song in My Heart* (NYT "conventionally amusing"; V "excellent") and Jean Hagen was recognised as the vain and squeaky-voiced silent movie star in the hit musical comedy *Singin' in the Rain* (NYT "an excellent farceuse"; V "first-rate").

The overwhelming favourite for the Oscar, however, was Gloria Grahame as the promiscuous Southern wife of a screenwriter in the melodrama *The Bad and the Beautiful* (MFB "very effective"). Grahame had also been lauded by critics as the girlfriend of the would-be murderous husband in the thriller *Sudden Fear* (NYT "excellent"; V "a hard-hitting performance") and she had appeared as the elephant trainer's girlfriend in the Best Picture Oscar winner *The Greatest Show on Earth* (NYT "smart playing"). It was Grahame's second nomination for the Best Supporting Actress Oscar and this time she proved successful.

Grahame never received another Oscar nod, although she was a strong contender for her role as Ado Annie Carnes in the musical *Oklahoma!* in 1955. In 2017, Annette Bening portrayed Grahame in the drama *Film Stars Don't Die In Liverpool* and received a BAFTA nomination for her performance.

BEST PICTURE

ACADEMY AWARDS

• *From Here to Eternity*
   (Columbia, 118 mins BW, 5 Aug 1953, $12.0m, 13 noms)
Julius Caesar
   (M-G-M, 120 mins BW, 4 Jun 1953, 5 noms)
The Robe
   (20th Century Fox, 135 mins, 16 Sep 1953, $36.0m, 5 noms)
Roman Holiday
   (Paramount, 118 mins BW, 27 Aug 1953, 10 noms)
Shane
   (Paramount, 118 mins, 24 Apr 1953, $9.0m, 6 noms)

GOLDEN GLOBE AWARDS – *The Robe*

BRITISH ACADEMY AWARDS

(Best Film)	(Best British Film)
The Bad and the Beautiful	*The Cruel Sea*
Come Back, Little Sheba	• *Genevieve*
The Cruel Sea	*The Heart of the Matter*
Due Soldi di Speranza	*The Kidnappers*
(Two Cents Worth of Hope)	*Moulin Rouge*
From Here to Eternity	
Genevieve	
The Heart of the Matter	
• *Jeux Interdits (Forbidden Games)*	
Julius Caesar	
The Kidnappers	
Lili	
The Medium	
Mogambo	
Moulin Rouge	
Nous Sommes tous des Assassins (We Are All Murderers)	
Le Petit Monde de Don Camillo (The Little World of Don Camillo)	
Roman Holiday	
Shane	
The Sun Shines Bright	

NEW YORK – *From Here to Eternity*
BOARD OF REVIEW – *Julius Caesar*

1953

In many ways the 1953 Best Picture winners echoed those of the previous year's awards season. For the second year in a row the New York critics selected an acclaimed drama directed by Fred Zinnemann: the war-time drama *From Here to Eternity* (NYT "brilliant", "towering and persuasive", "a shining example of truly professional movie-making"; V "outstanding") and for the second year in a row Zinnemann's Oscar frontrunner was ignored by the NBR in favour of another lauded contender: Joseph L. Mankiewicz's *Julius Caesar*, an expensive film version of William Shakespeare's classic political tragedy (NYT "stirring and memorable"; V "a triumphant achievement"; TT "tremendous and remarkable"). And for the second year in a row, the New York and NBR winners were both passed over at the Golden Globes in favour of the year's box office champ: Henry Koster's biblical epic *The Robe*, the first CinemaScope release (NYT "less compelling than the process by which it is shown ... essentially a smashing display of spectacle [but] an unwavering force of personal drama is missed in the size and length of the show, and a full sense of spiritual experience is lost in the physicalness of the display"; TT "spectacular extravagance").

Several factors, however, differed from the previous year. Unlike the previous year's *High Noon*, *From Here to Eternity* was not politically controversial. Furthermore, while *High Noon* had been a respectable box office success (it finished in the top ten films at the box office in 1952), *From Here to Eternity* took in three times as much money to finish as the second most successful release of the year. In addition, while Zinnemann was again nominated as Best Director, both Koster and Mankiewicz were overlooked. Notably, the last film to win the Best Picture Oscar without a nomination for its director had been over two decades earlier in 1931/32. And finally, *From Here to Eternity* received thirteen nominations, nearly twice the number garnered by *High Noon*. As a result, Zinnemann's war drama was the overwhelming favourite for the Oscar over a field of contenders that included both *Julius Caesar* and *The Robe*.

The other two films nominated for the Best Picture Academy Award were the Western *Shane*, the year's third-biggest commercial success (NYT "magnificent", "a powerful and moving film"; TT "a Western with style") and the popular romantic comedy *Roman Holiday*, which had been the runner-up for the New York critics' circle Best Picture accolade (NYT "contrived" but "with laughs that leave the spirit soaring"; V "a winner").

The surprise omission from the Best Picture category at the Academy Awards was the musical *Lili*, which had been nominated in six other categories and which was a nominee for the Best Film BAFTA in London (NYT "ingenuous"; "exceptionally adroit and tasteful").

Also overlooked were: Elia Kazan's drama *Man on a Tightrope* (NYT "powerful", "arresting"); Billy Wilder's comedy-drama about men in a prisoner-of-war camp in Nazi Germany, *Stalag 17* (NYT "suspenseful, disturbing and rousing", "one of the year's most smashing films"); Fritz Lang's crime drama *The Big Heat* ("a tense and eventful crime show … a hot one"); the Lutheran Church-funded historical biopic *Martin Luther* (NYT "powerful", "truly monumental"); and the BAFTA nominated French-language comedy *Le Petit Monde de Don Camillo (The Little World of Don Camillo)* (NYT "charming … there may be guileless simplicity and calculated comedy in this folk tale, but, thanks to M. Duvivier and all his company, it makes up into a cheerful and wholesome film").

Ineligible for Best Picture Oscar consideration was René Clément's acclaimed French film *Jeux Interdits (Forbidden Games)*. Winner of the 1953 Best Film BAFTA as well as a Special Oscar the previous year as Best Foreign-Language Film, Clement's drama did not receive an Oscar-qualifying release in a Los Angeles cinema until the following year. Similarly, the BAFTA winner for Best British Film, the romantic comedy *Genevieve*, was also ineligible for Academy Award competition until the following year when it played in cinemas across North America for the first time.

On Oscar night, there was no major upset in the Best Picture category. As predicted by Variety, Zinnemann's *From Here to Eternity* was awarded the Academy's top prize. The Best Picture statuette was one of a record-equalling eight Oscars won by the film.

The success of *From Here to Eternity* at the prize-giving ceremonies in the United States resulted in a controversial decision by the Jury at the 1954 Cannes Film Festival to withdraw the film from competition and commend it with a statement of "special recognition" instead, thus denying the film the chance to win the Palme d'Or for which many had considered it a frontrunner.

1953

BEST DIRECTOR

ACADEMY AWARDS
George Stevens for *Shane*
Charles Walters for *Lili*
Billy Wilder for *Stalag 17*
William Wyler for *Roman Holiday*
• **Fred Zinnemann for *From Here to Eternity***

GOLDEN GLOBE AWARDS – Fred Zinnemann – *From Here to Eternity*

DIRECTORS GUILD AWARD
George Stevens – *Shane*
Charles Walters – *Lili*
Billy Wilder – *Stalag 17*
William Wyler – *Roman Holiday*
• **Fred Zinnemann – *From Here to Eternity***

NEW YORK – Fred Zinnemann – *From Here to Eternity*
BOARD OF REVIEW – George Stevens – *Shane*

For the first time the Academy nominated the same five directors has had been short-listed for the DGA prize: the previous year's unsuccessful favourite Fred Zinnemann was recognised for the Best Picture frontrunner *From Here to Eternity* (NYT "an expert directorial achievement"; V "solid"); Charles Walters for *Lili*, a musical romance on which he also served as choreographer; previous winner Billy Wilder for the war-time comedy-drama *Stalag 17*; previous winner and NBR winner George Stevens for the Western *Shane*; and previous winner William Wyler for the romantic comedy *Roman Holiday* (NYT "a credit to William Wyler's versatility"). Wyler made Academy history with a record ninth nomination in the Best Director category, but Zinnemann was the Oscar favourite following wins from the New York critics, the DGA and the HFPA.

Left out of consideration by both the Guild and the Academy were: Joseph L. Mankiewicz for *Julius Caesar* (V "one of his best direction jobs"); Elia Kazan for *Man on a Tightrope*; Carol Reed for *The Man Between*; Fritz Lang for *The Big Heat* (NYT "vivid" direction); George Cukor for *The Actress* (NYT "fine direction"); and Anthony Mann for *The Naked Spur*.

When Irene Dunne opened the envelope on Oscar night, there was no repeat of the previous year's upset. Zinnemann collected the golden statuette.

BEST ACTOR

ACADEMY AWARDS
Marlon Brando as 'Marc Antony' in *Julius Caesar*
Richard Burton as 'Marcellus Gallio' in *The Robe*
Montgomery Clift as 'Robert E. Lee Prewitt' in *From Here to Eternity*
• William Holden as 'Sefton' in *Stalag 17*
Burt Lancaster as 'Sgt. Warden' in *From Here to Eternity*

GOLDEN GLOBE AWARDS
(Drama) **Spencer Tracy – *The Actress***
(Comedy/Musical) **David Niven – *The Moon is Blue***

BRITISH ACADEMY AWARDS

(Foreign Actor)	(British Actor)
Eddie Albert – *Roman Holiday*	**• John Gielgud – *Julius Caesar***
• Marlon Brando – *Julius Caesar*	Jack Hawkins – *The Cruel Sea*
Van Heflin – *Shane*	Trevor Howard
Claude Laydu	– *The Heart of the Matter*
– *Journal d'un Curé de Campagne*	Duncan McRae – *The Kidnappers*
(Diary of a Country Priest)	Kenneth More – *Genevieve*
Marcel Mouloudji	
– *Nous Sommes tous des Assassins*	
(We Are All Murderers)	
Gregory Peck – *Roman Holiday*	
Spencer Tracy – *The Actress*	

NEW YORK – Burt Lancaster – *From Here to Eternity*
BOARD OF REVIEW – James Mason – *The Desert Rats* and *Face to Face*
    and ***Julius Caesar* and *The Man Between***

The New York Times called Spencer Tracy's portrayal of a cantankerous father in *The Actress* "magnificent" and a "triumph" and said it was "a performance that could fetch for Spencer Tracy another Academy award." Surprisingly, however, the Academy did not even nominate him. Tracy became the first winner of the Best Actor Golden Globe (Drama) to be left out of the Oscar race.

For the fourth year in a row the winner of the Best Actor prize from the NBR was also excluded from the Academy's list of contenders. James Mason had finished as second runner-up for the New York prize as Brutus in *Julius Caesar* (NYT "brilliantly acted"; V "excellent"; MFB "lacking") and had been honoured by the NBR for his performances in that film and three others: *The Man Between* (V "a vigorous portrayal"), *Face to Face* and *The Desert Rats*, in which he portrayed Field Marshal Rommel for the second time.

The major omission of the year, however, was that of Mason's co-star John Gielgud whose performance as Cassius in *Julius Caesar* had finished second in the voting for the New York critic's prize and won the British Academy's award for Best British Actor. Variety praised Gielgud's portrayal as "superb" and "a tour de force" and described it as "a performance worthy of an Academy Award." The New York Times considered Gielgud's turn a "rounded and subtle performance" that was "brilliantly acted." In Britain, S&S called his performance "superlative" while MFB labelled it "the film's best performance."

Others passed over for Oscar consideration were: the two stars of *Shane*, Alan Ladd and BAFTA nominee Van Heflin (NYT "outstanding"; V "sensitive performance"); BAFTA nominee Gregory Peck in *Roman Holiday* (NYT "delightful"); previous winner Clark Gable in *Mogambo* (NYT "beautifully commanding"); previous winner Fredric March in *Man on a Tightrope* (NYT "sensitive and moving"); Niall MacGinnis as the title character in the Lutheran Church-funded biopic *Martin Luther* (NYT "splendid"; V "magnificent"); and French comedian Fernandel in *Le Petit Monde de Don Camillo (The Little World of Don Camillo)* (NYT "much of the charm of the picture is due to Fernandel, who plays the priest with explosive gusto and infinite alteration of moods").

Although Gielgud and Mason were both overlooked for their performances in *Julius Caesar*, the Academy did recognise their American co-star, Marlon Brando (NYT "memorable", "brilliantly acted"; V "compelling" in "the performance of his career"; TT "effective"). His work was rewarded with his second consecutive British Academy Award as Best Foreign Actor and his third consecutive Best Actor Oscar nomination.

Also nominated by the Academy were: New York critics' winner Burt Lancaster (NYT "excellent"; MFB "honest and competent") and Montgomery Clift (NYT "another sensitive performance"; V "a sensitive, three-dimensional performance"; TT "works hard to make the character credible"; S&S "though miscast, plays [Prewitt] with his customary intelligence"; MFB "seems miscast") for *From Here to Eternity*; William Holden as a prisoner of war in *Stalag 17* (NYT "excellent"; MFB "quietly competent"); and Welsh actor Richard Burton in the popular epic *The Robe* (NYT "stalwart, spirited and stern"; V "particularly effective"; TT "commands respect").

Although *From Here to Eternity* was favoured to win the majority of awards for which it had been nominated, the presence of both Lancaster and Clift in the Best Actor category probably resulted in a split vote. As Variety correctly predicted the beneficiary was Holden. On Oscar night, he collected the Best Actor statuette for *Stalag 17*.

BEST ACTRESS

ACADEMY AWARDS
Leslie Caron as 'Lili Daurier' in *Lili*
Ava Gardner as 'Eloise Kelly' in *Mogambo*
• **Audrey Hepburn as 'Princess Ann' in *Roman Holiday***
Deborah Kerr as 'Karen Holmes' in *From Here to Eternity*
Maggie McNamara as 'Patty O'Neill' in *The Moon is Blue*

GOLDEN GLOBE AWARDS
(Drama) **Audrey Hepburn** – *Roman Holiday*
(Comedy/Musical) **Ethel Merman** – *Call Me Madam*

BRITISH ACADEMY AWARDS

(Foreign Actress)	(British Actress)
Shirley Booth	• **Audrey Hepburn**
– *Come Back, Little Sheba*	– ***Roman Holiday***
• **Leslie Caron** – *Lili*	Celia Johnson
Marie Powers – *The Medium*	– *The Captain's Paradise*
Maria Schell – *The Heart of the Matter*	

NEW YORK – Audrey Hepburn – *Roman Holiday*
BOARD OF REVIEW – Jean Simmons – *The Actress* and *The Robe* and
     Young Bess

The frontrunners for the year's major Best Actress accolades were a pair of 24-year old rising stars.

Jean Simmons received the Best Actress prize from the NBR and was unsuccessfully considered for the New York prize for three performances: as the schoolgirl determined to become a great stage actress in *The Actress* (V "perfect"); a Roman noblewoman in the Biblical epic *The Robe*, the year's box office champion (V "particularly effective"); and as a youthful Queen Elizabeth I of England in *Young Bess* (TT "comes out of a trying ordeal with considerable credit"). The New York Times believed that for her role in *The Actress* "she could merit an Oscar."

Audrey Hepburn, meanwhile, was honoured by the New York critics and won both the Golden Globe (Drama) and the BAFTA for Best British Actress for her portrayal of a European princess who longs to experience Rome as an ordinary tourist in the comedy *Roman Holiday* (NYT "delightful"; TT "it is to Miss Audrey Hepburn as the princess that the film belongs"; S&S "an engaging performance"). Although she had made brief appearances in other films, the role of Princess Ann in *Roman Holiday* was Hepburn's first starring role.

When the Oscar nominations were announced, Hepburn was included on the Academy's list for the first time, but Simmons was an unexpected omission. Also overlooked were: New York runner-up Anna Magnani in the 1951 Italian comedy *Bellissima* (NYT "a tour de force" … a "passionate display of emotions"); previous winner Joan Crawford in *Torch Song* (NYT "plays it to the hilt"; TT a "confident performance"); Globe (Comedy/Musical) winner Ethel Merman in the musical *Call Me Madam* (NYT "wonderful" and "dynamic" … she makes the film "bounce and zing with the vitality and freshness of a new type of show"); and Marilyn Monroe for the popular musical comedy *Gentleman Prefer Blondes*.

The surprise nominee was twenty-five-year old Maggie McNamara who received a nod as the provocative virgin in *The Moon is Blue*, a comedy which had defied the Production Code by addressing sexually-explicit subject matter and using previously taboo words (NYT "tends to be slightly annoying"; V makes "a good impression"; MFB "scores a distinct success").

The youngest nominee was twenty-two-year old Leslie Caron who earned her first Oscar nod as a homeless orphan employed in a circus puppet show in the romantic musical *Lili* (NYT "deserves admiration and praise" for a "touching characterization"; V "ingratiating"; TT "a performance by Miss Leslie Caron which is just right when it could so easily have been completely and disastrously wrong"; MBF a "delicious performance"; S&S "enchanting"). Caron's turn in *Lili* won her the BAFTA for Best Foreign Actress.

In the year that her husband Frank Sinatra won the Best Supporting Actor Oscar for *From Here to Eternity*, thirty-year old Ava Gardner was included on the Academy's list of nominees (for the only time) for playing a showgirl stranded in the African jungle in *Mogambo* (NYT "easily steals the show"; V "reveals a new ability for light comedy").

The fifth (and eldest) nominee was thirty-one-year old Deborah Kerr who was mentioned for the second time for playing the adulterous wife in the Best Picture frontrunner *From Here to Eternity*, a role which she had inherited when Joan Crawford backed out just prior to filming (NYT "excellent"). Kerr had also appeared that year as Portia in *Julius Caesar*.

Variety predicted that Hepburn would win easily and on Oscar night it was indeed her name inside the envelope. At the time, she was appearing on Broadway in 'Ondine' and so she attended the east coast part of the Oscar festivities at the NBC Century Theatre in New York. "This is too much," she humbly told the audience as she was presented with the Best Actress statuette.

Three days after the Academy Awards ceremony, Hepburn again outpolled Kerr to take home a Tony Award as the year's Best Actress in a Play.

BEST SUPPORTING ACTOR

ACADEMY AWARDS
Eddie Albert as 'Irving Radovich' in *Roman Holiday*
Brandon De Wilde as 'Joey Starrett' in *Shane*
Jack Palance as 'Jack Wilson' in *Shane*
• **Frank Sinatra as 'Private Angelo Maggio' in *From Here to Eternity***
Robert Strauss as 'Animal Stosh' in *Stalag 17*

GOLDEN GLOBE AWARDS – Frank Sinatra – *From Here to Eternity*

Singer turned actor Frank Sinatra was the overwhelming favourite for the Best Supporting Actor Oscar for his Golden Globe-winning performance as a rebellious soldier in the Columbia release *From Here to Eternity* (NYT "excellent"; V "scores a decided hit"; TT "an astonishingly lively portrait").

The other four nominees were all considered for performances in films produced and distributed by Paramount. Eleven-year old Brandon De Wilde earned a nomination as the young boy who hero-worships a passing drifter in the Western *Shane* (V "a standout") while Jack Palance received his second consecutive Best Supporting Actor Oscar nomination for his portrayal of a villainous gunfighter in the same film (V "impressive"). Robert Strauss made the Academy's list for reprising his Broadway turn as the prisoner of war obsessed with Betty Grable in the war-time comedy-drama *Stalag 17* (NYT "outstanding") while Eddie Albert was considered for his performance as the newspaper photographer in the romantic comedy *Roman Holiday* (NYT "excellent"; V "a major comedy contribution").

Overlooked for Oscar consideration were: Louis Calhern as the title character in *Julius Caesar* (V "a triumph" and "a tour de force"); twenty-one-year old Anthony Perkins for his screen debut in *The Actress* (V "impresses"); Mel Ferrer as the crippled puppeteer in the musical *Lili* (NYT a "touching characterization"; MFB "finely played"); both Lee Marvin (NYT "incisive") and Robert Keith ("excellent") in *The Wild One*; and dancer Tommy Rall in *Kiss Me Kate* (NYT "brings a lift where the picture needs it").

At the RKO Pantages Theatre on Oscar night, Mercedes McCambridge opened the envelope and announced that Sinatra had won an Academy Award. "If I start thanking everybody, I'll do a one-reeler," he joked to the audience. Sinatra's then wife, Ava Gardner, however, did not have the same luck: she lost the Best Actress category to Audrey Hepburn later in the evening.

The Oscar victory revitalised Sinatra's struggling acting career and he earned a second nomination from the Academy two years later.

1953

BEST SUPPORTING ACTRESS

ACADEMY AWARDS
Grace Kelly as 'Linda Nordley' in *Mogambo*
Geraldine Page as 'Angie Lowe' in *Hondo*
Marjorie Rambeau as 'Mrs Stewart' in *Torch Song*
• **Donna Reed as 'Alma' in *From Here to Eternity***
Thelma Ritter as 'Moe Williams' in *Pickup on South Street*

GOLDEN GLOBE AWARDS – Grace Kelly – *Mogambo*

Twenty-five-year old Hollywood newcomer Grace Kelly won her first Golden Globe and earned her first Oscar nomination for playing a sexually-repressed English woman on an African safari in the adventure romance *Mogambo*, but she had to wait another year before claiming a statuette from the Academy.

On Oscar night, the Best Supporting Actress trophy went to Donna Reed. Popular for her portrayals of devoted wives and mothers, such as in Frank Capra's *It's a Wonderful Life*, Reed was rewarded with an Oscar for shedding this image with a performance as a Hawaiian nightclub hostess in *From Here to Eternity* (NYT "polished and professional"). When Walter Brennan read her name out of the envelope she excitedly hurried to the stage and told the audience that "As wonderful as *From Here to Eternity* was, what's even more wonderful is *Eternity* to here!".

The other three nominees for the Best Supporting Actress Oscar were: Marjorie Rambeau as the mother of a neurotic musical star in *Torch Song* (NYT "competent"); Geraldine Page for her film debut as a rancher's wife in the Western *Hondo* (V "a sensitive portrayal"); and Thelma Ritter as an informer in *Pickup on South Street* (V "half-way convincing"). Ritter's nod was an unprecedented fourth consecutive mention in the category.

The most surprising omission was Jean Arthur for her final film role as a peace-loving frontier wife and mother in the Western *Shane* (NYT "good"). Also overlooked were: the previous year's winner Gloria Grahame in both Elia Kazan's *Man on a Tightrope* (NYT "excellent") and Fritz Lang's thriller *The Big Heat* (NYT "intriguingly casual as the renegade girlfriend of a crook"); Gabrielle Dorziat as the mother superior of a French orphanage in *Little Boy Lost* (NYT "exquisite acting", "subtle and brilliant"); previous winner Teresa Wright as the mother of an aspiring young actress in *The Actress* (V "one of her better portrayals"); and Ann Miller in *Kiss Me Kate* (NYT "is a splay of nimble legs and amusingly casual inclinations … brings a lift where the picture needs it").

BEST PICTURE

ACADEMY AWARDS

The Caine Mutiny
(Kramer, Columbia, 124 mins, 24 Jun 1954, $8.7m, 7 noms)

The Country Girl
(Perlberg-Seaton, Paramount, 104 mins BW, 17 Dec 1954, $6.9m, 7 noms)

• On the Waterfront
(Horizon, Columbia, 108 mins BW, 28 Jul 1954, $9.6m, 12 noms)

Seven Brides for Seven Brothers
(M-G-M, 103 mins, 22 Jul 1954, $4.7m, 5 noms)

Three Coins in the Fountain
(20th Century Fox, 102 mins, 12 May 1954, $5.0m, 3 noms)

GOLDEN GLOBE AWARDS

(Drama) **On the Waterfront**

(Comedy/Musical) **Carmen Jones**

BRITISH ACADEMY AWARDS

(Best Film)

*The Adventures of
    Robinson Crusoe*
The Caine Mutiny
Carrington, V.C.
The Divided Heart
Doctor in the House
Executive Suite
For Better, For Worse
Hobson's Choice
How to Marry a Millionaire
Jigokumon (Gate of Hell)
The Maggie
The Moon is Blue
On the Waterfront
Pane, Amore e Fantasia (Bread, Love and Dreams)
The Purple Plain
Rear Window
Riot in Cell Block 11
Romeo and Juliet
• Le Salaire de la Peur (The Wages of Fear)
Seven Brides for Seven Brothers

(Best British Film)

Carrington, V.C.
The Divided Heart
Doctor in the House
For Better, For Worse
• Hobson's Choice
The Maggie
The Purple Plain
Romeo and Juliet

1954

The New York Times said that it was "no surprise" when Elia Kazan's acclaimed drama *On the Waterfront* won the Best Picture Academy Award (NYT "uncommonly powerful, exciting and imaginative"; TT "a grim film which pulls no punches and makes no concessions"). Kazan's film, a gritty black-and-white drama about harbour unionists in New York City, had been named Best Picture by both the NBR and the New York critics and had won the Golden Globe (Drama). It had also received twelve Oscar nominations, nearly twice as many as any other film. Variety's strawpoll of Academy members had indicated that the film would receive more votes for Best Picture than the other four nominees combined.

On Oscar night, *On the Waterfront* equalled the record tally of eight Academy Awards and became the first film to win the Best Picture Oscar, a Best Picture Golden Globe and the Best Picture prizes from both the New York critics and the NBR.

The New York critics chose Kazan's drama on the very first ballot, but votes were also cast for three other contenders: *The Country Girl*, a lauded drama about an alcoholic actor and his wife, played by Bing Crosby and Best Actress Oscar winner Grace Kelly (NYT "excellent"; TT "a distinguished film"); *Romeo and Juliet*, a British-Italian film version of William Shakespeare's tragic romance that had won Best Picture at the 1954 Venice Film Festival (NYT "a brilliant and exciting action film … beautiful … the honors won by this picture at the film festival in Venice last fall were not bestowed unwisely"; V a "superlative production"); and the Best Picture Globe (Comedy/Musical) winner *Carmen Jones*, Otto Preminger's all African-American film version of Oscar Hammerstein's updating of the Bizet opera (NYT "a big musical shenanigan and theatrical tour-de-force"). Of these three contenders, only *The Country Girl* was included on the Academy's list of nominees.

The Academy also overlooked several acclaimed films that had been honoured by the British Academy, most notably the previous year's Best Picture BAFTA winner, René Clément's French film *Jeux Interdits (Forbidden Games)*, a drama about an orphan taken in by a French peasant family during World War Two which had also won the Best Picture prize at the 1952 Venice Film Festival as well as a Special Oscar from the Academy that year as Best Foreign-Language Film (NYT "shattering", "a brilliant and devastating drama", "powerful" and "haunting"; V "moving"). Also passed over were both the 1953 and 1954 Best British Film BAFTA winners: *Genevieve* (NYT "superior", "one of the funniest farce comedies in years"; V "a top-ranking comedy"; MFB "most enjoyable");

and David Lean's *Hobson's Choice*, which was the 1954 Berlin Film Festival's Best Picture winner (NYT "delightful and rewarding").

The remake of *A Star is Born*, with James Mason and Judy Garland in the roles originally played by Fredric March and Janet Gaynor in 1937, received six Oscar nominations, including mentions for both its stars, but was overlooked for the Best Picture award (NYT "one of the grandest heartbreak dramas that has drenched the screen in years").

Similarly, despite six nominations including a mention for Best Director, the romantic comedy *Sabrina* was by-passed for the top Oscar. The film had brought together the previous year's Best Actor and Best Actress Oscar winners, William Holden and Audrey Hepburn, as well as 1951 Best Actor Oscar winner Humphrey Bogart and 1945 Best Director Oscar winner Billy Wilder (NYT "the most delightful comedy-romance in years", "the year's outstanding achievement in romantic comedy"; V "a slick blend of heart and chuckles").

Other contenders overlooked by the Academy included: the thriller *Rear Window*, which had finished as the year's fifth most commercially successful release and for which Alfred Hitchcock had been included in the Best Director category (NYT "tense and exciting"; V "a tight, suspenseful show" and "an unusually good piece of murder mystery entertainment"); the melodrama *The High and the Mighty* for which William Wellman was a Best Director nominee (NYT "a bit on the synthetic side ... artificial and contrived ... [but] that is not to say it lacks excitement"); the prison drama *Riot in Cell Block 11*, a surprise nominee for the Best Film BAFTA (NYT "a realistic and effective combination of brawn, brains and heart"; V "a hard-hitting, suspenseful prison thriller"; TT "graphic, visually exciting"); the drama *Executive Suite* (V "a class drama", "a dramatically interesting motion picture"; TT "strong", "well-constructed" and "exciting" but "not altogether convincing"); Jacques Tati's French comedy *Les Vacances de Monsieur Hulot (Mr Hulot's Holiday)* (NYT "good, fast, wholesome fun", "vastly inventive and trenchantly pointed"); and Teinosuke Kinugasa's award-winning *Jigokumon (Gate of Hell)*, a lavish Japanese historical about twelfth century Samurai which won Oscars for Best Costume Design and Best Foreign-Language Film, as well as the New York critics' Best Foreign-Language Film award and the Palme d'Or at the 1954 Cannes Film Festival (NYT "exquisite ... somber and beautiful ... moving ... lovely ... the secret, perhaps, of its rare excitement is the subtlety with which it blends a subterranean flood of hot emotions with the most magnificent flow of surface serenity"; S&S "must be one of the most enthralling films ever made"; MFB "remarkable").

Unsurprisingly, the Academy also ignored the 16mm independent production *Salt of the Earth*, which was controversially banned by the US Congress shortly after its release on the grounds that it was subversive. The film was directed by Herbert J. Biberman, one of the blacklisted Hollywood Ten and husband of previous Best Supporting Actress Oscar winner Gale Sondergaard (who had been blacklisted herself in 1951).

Alongside *The Country Girl* and *On the Waterfront*, and ahead of all these lauded films, the Academy nominated three of the year's ten biggest box office successes: the naval drama *The Caine Mutiny*, starring Humphrey Bogart and Jose Ferrer (NYT "though somewhat garbled, is a vibrant film"; V "highly recommendable ... topgrade"; TT "a respectable rather than memorable film"; MFB "excellent and intelligent"); the musical *Seven Brides for Seven Brothers* (NYT "a wholly engaging, bouncy, tuneful and panchromatic package ... skillfully blends a warm and comic yarn with strikingly imaginative choreography and a melodic score several notches above standard": V "a happy, hand-clapping, foot-stomping, country type of musical"); and, most unexpectedly, *Three Coins in the Fountain*, the CinemaScope romance filmed on location throughout Italy which had received mostly negative reviews from critics (NYT "clearly a film in which the locale comes first"; TT "obvious and laboured"). It was the second year in a row that the Academy had shortlisted a successful CinemaScope feature despite poor reviews.

The Academy's questionable selection of *Three Coins in the Fountain* was highlighted by the film's absence from any of the other major categories. Its only other nominations were for Best Cinematography (Color) and for Best Song. The film had not featured in the voting for any of the other major end-of-year accolades for Best Picture.

Although *On the Waterfront* made a clean sweep of all the major Best Picture plaudits in the United States, across the Atlantic in London it was outpolled for the Best Film BAFTA by Henri-Georges Clouzot's *Le Salaire de la Peur (The Wages of Fear)*, a French-language drama which was notably overlooked the following year by the Academy in Hollywood.

BEST DIRECTOR

ACADEMY AWARDS
Alfred Hitchcock for *Rear Window*
• **Elia Kazan for *On the Waterfront***
George Seaton for *The Country Girl*
William Wellman for *The High and the Mighty*
Billy Wilder for *Sabrina*

GOLDEN GLOBE AWARDS – Elia Kazan – *On the Waterfront*

DIRECTORS GUILD AWARD
Alfred Hitchcock – *Rear Window*
• **Elia Kazan – *On the Waterfront***
George Seaton – *The Country Girl*
William Wellman – *The High and the Mighty*
Billy Wilder – *Sabrina*

NEW YORK – Elia Kazan – *On the Waterfront*
BOARD OF REVIEW – Renato Castellani – *Romeo and Juliet*

Previous Oscar winner Elia Kazan was the overwhelming favourite for the year's Best Director Academy Award after he received several major end-of-year accolades and earned his third nomination from the Academy in eight years for the drama *On the Waterfront* (NYT "moviemaking of a rare and high order"; V "a penetrating job"). He received his third Best Director prize from the New York critics and his second Golden Globe from the Hollywood Foreign Press Association before collecting his first award from the DGA. Kazan made it a clean sweep of the major end of year Best Director accolades on Academy Awards night when he received his second golden statuette at the NBC Century Theatre in New York.

Also nominated for both the DGA accolade and the Oscar were: previous winner Billy Wilder, who made the list for the fifth time with his second consecutive nod, for the romantic comedy *Sabrina* (NYT "credit, above all, Mr Wilder, for it is unerring sense of form, his fluency with the picture, his 'feel' for the realistic look, his dramatic use of popular music and his wonderfully hardgrained comic style that makes *Sabrina* a picture to be cherished as a real and lasting joy"); William Wellman, who earned his third (and final) mention, for the melodrama *The High and the Mighty* (NYT "Wellman directs it with the vigor and snap he's always shown ... Wellman is thoroughly and capably at home and he makes all such business in this picture have a direct effect on the nerves"); George Seaton, who was recognised for the only time in his career for the drama *The Country Girl* (NYT "directed with a hand as firm as iron"); and Alfred Hitchcock, who was nominated for the fourth time for the thriller *Rear Window*, which had finished as the year's fifth most commercially successful release (NYT "When he takes on a stunt of this sort he may be counted on to pull it with a maximum of build-up to the punch, a maximum of carefully tricked deception and incidents to divert and amuse. This time he does it with precision."). That same year, Hitchcock had also directed *Dial M for Murder* (NYT "a technical triumph"). It was the second year in a row that the Academy nominated the same five directors short-listed for the DGA prize.

Overlooked for the Oscar were: the National Board of Review winner Renato Castellani for the British-Italian film version of *Romeo and Juliet* (NYT "Castellani has framed a brilliant and exciting action film"); Edward Dmytryk for the Best Picture nominee *The Caine Mutiny*; Otto Preminger for the musical *Carmen Jones* (V "Preminger has directed with a deft touch"); blacklisted director Herbert J. Biberman for the banned drama *Salt of the Earth*; René Clément for *Jeux Interdits (Forbidden Games)* (NYT "has fused a powerful drama"; V "excellent"); Jacques Tati for *Les Vacances de Monsieur Hulot (Mr Hulot's Holiday)* (NYT "goes in for wild invention"); Robert Bresson for *Journal d'un Curé de Campagne (Diary of a Country Priest)* (NYT "his cinema technique is brilliant"); and Teinosuke Kinugasa for the Japanese drama *Jigokumon (Gate of Hell)* (NYT "how Teinosuke Kinugasa, who wrote the screen play and directed this film, has achieved such extraordinary emotional impact is a matter of true wizardry").

BEST ACTOR

ACADEMY AWARDS

Humphrey Bogart as 'Capt. Queeg' in *The Caine Mutiny*
• **Marlon Brando as 'Terry Malloy' in *On the Waterfront***
Bing Crosby as 'Frank Elgin' in *The Country Girl*
James Mason as 'Norman Maine' in *A Star is Born*
Dan O'Herlihy as 'Robinson Crusoe' in *The Adventures of Robinson Crusoe*

GOLDEN GLOBE AWARDS

(Drama) **Marlon Brando – *On the Waterfront***
(Comedy/Musical) **James Mason – *A Star is Born***

BRITISH ACADEMY AWARDS

(Foreign Actor)	(British Actor)
Neville Brand – *Riot in Cell Block 11*	Maurice Denham
• **Marlon Brando**	*– The Purple Plain*
– *On the Waterfront*	Robert Donat – *Lease of Life*
José Ferrer – *The Caine Mutiny*	John Mills –*Hobson's Choice*
Fredric March – *Executive Suite*	• **Kenneth More**
James Stewart	**– *Doctor in the House***
– The Glenn Miller Story	David Niven – *Carrington, V.C.*
	Donald Wolfit – *Svengali*

NEW YORK – Marlon Brando – *On the Waterfront*
BOARD OF REVIEW – Bing Crosby – *The Country Girl*

Critics raved about Marlon Brando's performance as a former boxer in Elia Kazan's *On the Waterfront*. The New York Times said he was "uncommonly revealing" in "a shatteringly poignant portrait" and Variety thought he was "spectacular" in "a fascinating, multi-faceted performance." In London, The Times commented that he set "a remarkable standard in acting" with "a performance of unusual power." Although his portrayal of Napoleon in *Desiree* was less well-received later in the year, Brando was the overwhelming favourite for the end of year Best Actor accolades. For his work in *On the Waterfront*, Brando was named Best Actor by the New York critics for the first time, won his first Golden Globe, and received his third consecutive BAFTA as Best Foreign Actor. The Academy recognised him in the Best Actor category for a record fourth consecutive year and observers predicted that he would finally collect the statuette.

1954

Previous winner Humphrey Bogart received a third (and final) nomination for his performance as an unstable naval captain who drives his crew to mutiny in the year's second most commercially successful film, *The Caine Mutiny* (NYT mannered but "sound"; V "almost certain to make an Oscar bid"; TT "outstanding"; S&S "brilliant"; MFB "extremely well played"). A contrasting role in *Sabrina* (NYT "incredibly adroit") probably helped give Bogart the edge over his co-stars in *The Caine Munity*, previous Oscar winner José Ferrer (V "compelling") and Van Johnson (NYT "excellent").

Contrasting performances also helped secure a nomination for National Board of Review champion and previous Oscar winner, Bing Crosby. In the same year that he starred in the biggest box office success, the musical *White Christmas*, Crosby earned mixed praise from critics for playing the straight dramatic role of an alcoholic former star in *The Country Girl* (NYT "it is truly Mr Crosby's appearance and performance as the has-been thespian who fights and is helped back to stardom that hits the audience right between the eyes … it is Mr Crosby who merits particular praise … deserves all the kudos he will get"; V "masterly", "exceptionally well performed"; TT "not altogether satisfactory"; MFB "never really conveys the character's essential weaknesses and torment"). For his performance, Crosby earned his third (and final) mention from the Academy. Interestingly, he was the first NBR Best Actor winner nominated by the Academy since 1949.

Also nominated for playing an alcoholic former star was James Mason in the remake of *A Star is Born* (NYT "gets performances from Miss Garland and Mr Mason that make the heart flutter and bleed"; S&S "performance is finely calculated"; MFB "admirable"). Mason, who had been overlooked the previous year for several lauded performances, was the first winner of the Best Actor Golden Globe (Comedy/Musical) to be included on the Academy's list of contenders. Mason was nominated for recreating the role of Norman Maine for which Fredric March had received a Best Actor nomination in 1937. Ironically, March was one of the year's surprise omissions from the category.

The surprise nominee was Dan O'Herlihy in the bilingual Mexican film *The Adventures of Robinson Crusoe* (NYT "does a good straight job of playing the hermit hero, without getting inside the man"; MFB "perfect").

Although nominated for the Best Foreign Actor BAFTA for his performance in *Executive Suite*, previous winner March was overlooked for the Oscar (NYT "adroit"; V "a standout performance ... will be remembered"; TT "a closely observed portrait of an unlikeable man"). Also passed over for Oscar consideration were: previous winner Charles Laughton in David Lean's *Hobson's Choice* (NYT "distinguished"; V "richly overplays every major scene"; TT "too emphatic"; MFB "fails"); previous winner James Stewart both as the photographer in Alfred Hitchcock's *Rear Window* (NYT "first-class"; V "fine"; MFB "polished") and as the late Glenn Miller in *The Glenn Miller Story*, for which he was a BAFTA nominee (V a "topflight performance"); previous winner Spencer Tracy as a cattle rancher in *Broken Lance* (NYT "Tracy's delineation of the stern, white-haired beef tycoon is artistic"; V "finely handled characterization"); Kirk Douglas in *Act of Love* (NYT "exceedingly good", a "masterful job"); BAFTA nominee Neville Brand in *Riot in Cell Block 11* (NYT "outstanding"); Gregory Peck in *The Purple Plain* (V "superb"); Harry Belafonte in *Carmen Jones* (V "extremely convincing"); previous winner Robert Donat as the dying vicar in *Lease of Life* (NYT "touching"; V "dominates ... with appealing sincerity"; MFB "an earnest, careful, rather theatrically shaded performance"); and Claude Laydu as a troubled young priest in *Journal d'un Curé de Campagne (Diary of a Country Priest)* (NYT "impressive", he "gives such a sense of general suffering that he is literally painful to watch").

Brando had been the favourite for the Oscar in 1951 for Kazan's *A Streetcar Named Desire* but had been outpolled in an upset by Bogart. He had then been unsuccessfully nominated in 1952 for *Viva Zapata!* and in 1953 for *Julius Caesar*. On Oscar night, Brando finally won his first Best Actor Academy Award for Kazan's *On the Waterfront*. Nearly twenty years later, he would win a second statuette for *The Godfather*.

1954

BEST ACTRESS

ACADEMY AWARDS
Dorothy Dandridge as 'Carmen Jones' in *Carmen Jones*
Judy Garland as 'Vicki Lester' in *A Star is Born*
Audrey Hepburn as 'Sabrina Fairchild' in *Sabrina*
• **Grace Kelly as 'Georgie Elgin' in *The Country Girl***
Jane Wyman as 'Helen Phillips' in *Magnificent Obsession*

GOLDEN GLOBE AWARDS
(Drama) **Grace Kelly – *The Country Girl***
(Comedy/Musical) **Judy Garland – *A Star is Born***

BRITISH ACADEMY AWARDS

(Foreign Actress)
Shirley Booth – *About Mrs Leslie*
• **Cornell Borchers**
  – *The Divided Heart*
Judy Holliday – *Phffft!*
Grace Kelly – *Dial M for Murder*
Gina Lollobrigida
  – *Pane, Amore e Fantasia*
  (Bread, Love and Dreams)

(British Actress)
Brenda de Banzie
  – *Hobson's Choice*
Audrey Hepburn – *Sabrina*
Margaret Leighton
  – *Carrington, V.C.*
Noelle Middleton
  – *Carrington, V.C.*
• **Yvonne Mitchell**
  – *The Divided Heart*

NEW YORK – Grace Kelly – *The Country Girl* and *Dial M for Murder* and *Rear Window*
BOARD OF REVIEW – Grace Kelly – *The Country Girl* and *Dial M for Murder* and *Rear Window*

A year after winning the Best Supporting Actress Golden Globe and earning her first Oscar nomination, Grace Kelly appeared as the glamorous leading lady in two Alfred Hitchcock thrillers – *Dial M for Murder* (NYT "does a nice job of acting the wife's bewilderment, terror and grief") and *Rear Window* (NYT "fascinating"; V "fine"). However, it was for appearing as the plain and embittered wife of an alcoholic former singer attempting a comeback in *The Country Girl* that Kelly earned the praise of critics (NYT "intense, perceptive acting"; V "exceptionally well performed"; TT "throughout is in beautiful control"; MFB "miscast"). Over the course of the awards season Kelly became only the third person to receive all four of the year's major accolades: the NBR award, the New York critic's prize, the Golden Globe (Drama) and the Academy Award. The sweep had been previously achieved by Ray Milland in 1945 and Shirley Booth in 1952.

Despite both the New York and NBR prizes and the Golden Globe, Kelly was not an overwhelming favourite for the Oscar. The other major contender for the statuette was New York runner-up and Golden Globe (Comedy/Musical) winner Judy Garland. The former child star, who had starred in *The Wizard of Oz* in 1939, received her first Oscar nomination for her performance in the remake *A Star is Born* (NYT "gets performances from Miss Garland and Mr Mason that make the heart flutter and bleed ... Garland is excellent in all things"; MFB "triumphs on all levels"). Garland recreated the role of rising star Vicki Lester for which the first Best Actress Oscar winner, Janet Gaynor, had earned a nomination in 1937. While Kelly had claimed the critics' prizes and the Globe, many observers believed that the popular and respected Garland would nonetheless be rewarded with the Best Actress Oscar for her many years in the industry.

Another strong contender for the Academy Award was Dorothy Dandridge for her acclaimed portrayal in the musical *Carmen Jones* (NYT "theatrical tour de force"; V "fine"; S&S "perfect"; TT "makes [Carmen] entirely credible and endows her with an abundance of life, a challenging, dangerous personality"; MFB "fine", "maintains the right hedonistic note throughout"). Dandridge was only the third African American performer nominated for an Academy Award and was the first to be included in the lead acting categories – the others were winner Hattie McDaniel in 1939 and nominee Ethel Waters in 1949, both in the Best Supporting Actress category.

The remaining nominees were the previous year's winner Audrey Hepburn as the chauffeur's daughter in the romantic comedy *Sabrina* (NYT "sweetly bewitching ... wonderful"; TT "delights") and previous winner Jane Wyman, who earned her fourth (and final) mention, as a wealthy, blind widow in the tear-jerker *Magnificent Obsession* (NYT "refreshingly believable throughout"; V "expert"; MFB "manages to convince"). Wyman's role had been played by Irene Dunne in the original 1935 version.

Overlooked for consideration were: previous winner Judy Holliday as an actress who embarks on a major self-promotion campaign in the comedy *It Should Happen to You* (NYT "brilliantly droll"); French actress Dany Robin in the romantic drama *Act of Love* (NYT "exceedingly good", a "masterful job"); Japanese star Machiko Kyo in *Jigokumon (Gate of Hell)* (NYT "electrifying"); and Italian actress Gina Lollobrigida in *Pane, Amore e Fantasia (Bread, Love and Dreams)* for which she was a nominee for the Foreign Actress BAFTA (NYT "does a grand job of playing the graceless gamin ... there is in her performance a suggestion of poignancy"; V "steals the proverbial show with her best performance to date, an instinctive, animal portrayal of the town hooligan").

Unsurprisingly, the Academy also ignored the acclaimed performance of Mexican actress Rosaura Revueltas in *Salt of the Earth*, the controversial American film which was banned by the US Congress shortly after its release because of its alleged subversive communist message (NYT "dynamic").

Although the film now considered a classic with a cult following, the Western *Johnny Guitar* was panned by critics upon its release and so the Academy unsurprisingly ignored the lead performance by previous winner Joan Crawford (NYT "as sexless as the lions on the public library steps and as sharp and romantically forbidding as a package of unwrapped razor blades ... let's put it down as fiasco"; V "it proves the actress should leave saddles and levis to someone else").

Variety's straw-poll of Academy members indicated that the contest between Garland and Kelly was too close to call, until the last week of voting during which Kelly apparently edged ahead.

On Oscar night, Kelly attended the ceremony, but Garland was in hospital having given birth to her son, Joey Luft, just two days earlier. William Holden, revealed that the winner was his co-star in *The Country Girl*, Grace Kelly. "The thrill of this moment prevents me from saying exactly what I feel," she told the Academy.

Despite coming so close to Oscar glory, Garland didn't make another film for six years. She received a second Oscar nomination in 1961 as Best Supporting Actress for *Judgment at Nuremberg*, but was again unsuccessful. Her daughter, Liza Minnelli, won the Best Actress Oscar in 1972, three years after Garland's death.

The year after her Oscar triumph, Kelly retired from the screen (after making just fourteen films in five years) to marry Prince Rainier III of Monaco. She never made another film, turning down all offers to make a comeback, most notably from Hitchcock who wanted to her to play the title role in *Marnie* in the early 1960s.

1954

BEST SUPPORTING ACTOR

ACADEMY AWARDS
Lee J. Cobb as 'Johnny Friendly' in *On the Waterfront*
Karl Malden as 'Father Barry' in *On the Waterfront*
• **Edmond O'Brien as 'Oscar Muldoon' in *The Barefoot Contessa***
Rod Steiger as 'Charley Malloy' in *On the Waterfront*
Tom Tully as 'Capt. Devriess' in *The Caine Mutiny*

GOLDEN GLOBE AWARDS – Edmond O'Brien – *The Barefoot Contessa*
BOARD OF REVIEW – John Williams – *Dial M for Murder* and *Sabrina*

"When supporting nominations come up at Academy Awards time, certain to command attention will be Tom Tully's delightful old salt, Captain Devriess," wrote Variety in its review of *The Caine Mutiny*. When the Oscar candidates were announced eight months later in mid-February, Tully was indeed mentioned for his portrayal of a retiring naval captain in the box office hit.

Also nominated were three actors for their performances in Elia Kazan's Best Picture favourite *On the Waterfront*: Lee J. Cobb earned his first nomination for playing a union racketeer (NYT "effective"; V "fine"; MFB "overplays"); Rod Steiger received his first mention for his turn as the corrupt lawyer brother of a former boxer (NYT "excellent"); and, three years after winning the Best Supporting Actor Oscar for his role in another Kazan drama, Karl Malden was named for a second time for his portrayal of a priest (V "fine"; MFB "overplays"). It was the first time since 1935 that three performances in the same film had been shortlisted by the Academy in the same category.

The final nominee was the Golden Globe winner Edmond O'Brien, for his portrayal of a Hollywood press agent in Joseph L. Mankiewicz's *The Barefoot Contessa* (NYT "brilliant"; TT "mention must be made of the brilliant impression of a publicity agent contributed by Mr Edmond O'Brien").

Overlooked by the Academy were: John Williams, the inaugural winner of the NBR's Best Supporting Actor award, for his work in both Alfred Hitchcock's thriller *Dial M for Murder* (NYT "thrilling") and Billy Wilder's romantic comedy *Sabrina* (NYT "witty"); John Mills in *Hobson's Choice* (NYT "superb", "hilariously revealing"); Emile Meyer as the warden in *Riot in Cell Block 11* (V "a standout performance"); and Louis Calhern in *Executive Suite* (V "effective").

As well as claiming the Globe, O'Brien finished third in the voting for the New York critics' Best Actor award, and Variety predicted a close race between him and Cobb. On Oscar night, it was O'Brien who emerged with the Best Supporting Actor Oscar. He received a second nomination a decade later.

1954

BEST SUPPORTING ACTRESS

ACADEMY AWARDS
Nina Foch as 'Erica Martin' in *Executive Suite*
Katy Jurado as 'Senora Devereaux' in *Broken Lance*
• **Eva Marie Saint as 'Edie Doyle' in *On the Waterfront***
Jan Sterling as 'Sally McKee' in *The High and the Mighty*
Claire Trevor as 'May Hoist' in *The High and the Mighty*

GOLDEN GLOBE AWARDS – Jan Sterling – *The High and the Mighty*
BOARD OF REVIEW – Nina Foch – *Executive Suite*

Two years after she was unexpectedly left off the Academy's list of Best
Supporting Actress nominees for her Golden Globe-winning performance in
High Noon, Mexican actress Katy Jurado received her only Oscar nomination
for her portrayal of the Native American wife of an ageing cattle baron in the
Western *Broken Lance* (V "one of the film's better points").

Also nominated were: Nina Foch, who won the inaugural NBR Supporting
Actress prize, for her performance as the grief-stricken secretary in *Executive
Suite* (V "a performance that commands professional respect"); both Golden
Globe Award winner Jan Sterling as a fading beauty en route to an arranged
marriage (V "standout") and previous winner Claire Trevor as a wealthy older
woman (V "standout") in the melodrama *The High and the Mighty*; and Eva
Marie Saint, who made the list (for the only time), for playing the girlfriend of a
former boxer in *On the Waterfront* (NYT "gives tenderness and sensitivity to
genuine romance").

A Best Supporting Actress Oscar nominee for the previous four years in a
row, Thelma Ritter was overlooked for her part as the smart-talking
physiotherapist in Alfred Hitchcock's *Rear Window*. Also overlooked were:
June Allyson in *The Glenn Miller Story* (NYT "gives magic warmth to the
film"); Pearl Bailey in the musical *Carmen Jones* (NYT "unrestrainedly broad";
V "stands out", "scoring a particular triumph"); and Brenda de Banzie as the
spirited eldest daughter in *Hobson's Choice* (NYT "superb"; V "captures top
femme honors"; TT "a beautiful performance").

Despite the NBR and Globe wins of Foch and Sterling, the strong favourite
for the Oscar proved to be the winner. Saint had polled third in the voting for the
New York critics' Best Actress award, and in Hollywood topped the supporting
category to win the coveted statuette. Pregnant at the time of Oscar ceremony
she joked to the audience "I think I might have the baby right here!".

BEST PICTURE

ACADEMY AWARDS

Love is a Many–Splendored Thing
(Twentieth Century Fox, 102 mins, 18 Aug 1955, 8 noms)
• *Marty*
(Hecht–Lancaster, United Artists, 91 mins BW, 11 Apr 1955, $2.0m, 8 noms)
Mister Roberts
(Warner Bros., 123 mins, 30 Jul 1955, $8.5m, 3 noms)
Picnic
(Columbia, 115 mins, 11 Feb 1956, $6.3m, 6 noms)
The Rose Tattoo
(Paramount, 117 mins BW, 12 Dec 1955, 8 noms)

GOLDEN GLOBE AWARDS

(Drama) *East of Eden*
(Comedy or Musical) *Guys and Dolls*
(Outdoor Drama) *Wichita*

BRITISH ACADEMY AWARDS

(Best Film)
Bad Day at Black Rock
Carmen Jones
The Colditz Story
The Dam Busters
East of Eden
The Ladykillers
Marty
The Night My Number Came Up
The Prisoner
• *Richard III*
Shichinin no Samurai (Seven Samurai)
Simba
La Strada
Summertime

(Best British Film)
The Colditz Story
The Dam Busters
The Ladykillers
The Night My Number Came Up
The Prisoner
• *Richard III*
Simba

NEW YORK – *Marty*
BOARD OF REVIEW – *Marty*

In May 1955, two American films were honoured with prizes at the Cannes Film Festival. *East of Eden*, Elia Kazan's highly anticipated follow–up to the previous

1955

year's Best Picture Oscar winner *On the Waterfront*, was presented with a special prize as Best Dramatic Picture. More significantly, the independent movie *Marty* won the coveted Palme d'Or, becoming the first American film to be so honoured at the festival. This victory followed the controversy of the previous year in which Fred Zinnemann's 1953 Best Picture Oscar winner, *From Here to Eternity*, had been dropped from competition by the festival's jury because of the number of awards it had already received in the United States. Although given a citation of "special recognition", the film was denied the chance to win the Palme d'Or for which it had been favoured.

Adapted from a telemovie, *Marty* was a low–budget drama starring Ernest Borgnine which had been modestly successful at the box office. The New York Times described it as "a warm and winning film," while Variety called it "an enjoyable experience." *East of Eden*, meanwhile, was an adaptation of the last section of a John Steinbeck novel. It was a much bigger commercial success even though it had not been as universally embraced by critics (NYT "there is energy and intensity but little clarity and emotion in this film"; V "powerfully somber dramatics … it is a tour de force for the director's penchant for hard-hitting forays with life").

The biggest hit feature of the year was the comedy *Mister Roberts* (only the Cinerama travelogue film *Cinerama Holiday* grossed more). Starring Henry Fonda and James Cagney, *Mister Roberts* was also among the most acclaimed with The New York Times labelling it as "strikingly superior entertainment" in turns "hilarious" and "wonderfully sentimental and touchingly perceptive".

Another of the best reviewed films of the year was the British thriller *The Prisoner*, which starred Alec Guinness as a cardinal held political prisoner in a communist country (NYT a "grim and gripping drama", "one of the best of the year"). Also praised by critics were: the pseudo-Western *Bad Day at Black Rock*, starring Spencer Tracy (NYT "interesting" but "smacks of being contrived"; V "gripping"; TT "rich in atmosphere and suspense"); the musical *Guys and Dolls* starring Marlon Brando, which was the highest grossing film of 1956; the musical *Oklahoma!* (NYT "a production that magnifies and strengthens all the charm it had upon the stage … [matches] in vitality, eloquence and melody any musical this reviewer has ever seen"); *A Man Called Peter* (NYT "a surprising and extraordinary film"); Henri-Georges Clouzot's French thriller *Les Diaboliques (The Fiends)* (NYT "one of the dandiest mystery dramas that has shown here in goodness knows when … the writing and the visual construction are superb, and the performances by top-notch French actors on the highest level of sureness and finesse"; TT a "masterpiece … one of the best conceived, directed and acted films of its kind ever to be made"); and the Italian drama *Umberto D* (NYT "truly extraordinary ... an utterly heart-breaking picture"; TT "one of the outstanding films of our time"; MFB "quite unique poetic power").

At the end of the year all of the above-mentioned films were included on The New York Times' annual top ten list with the exception of *East of Eden*.

The New York critics' circle gave their top prize to *Marty* with *Mister Roberts* finishing the voting as runner-up. The circle jointly named *Umberto D* and *Les Diaboliques* as Best Foreign–Language Film. The NBR also honoured *Marty*, naming it as the year's best American film while selecting the British drama *The Prisoner* as Best Foreign Film. Although released in New York City in 1955, *The Prisoner*, *Les Diaboliques* and *Umberto D* all opened in Los Angeles the following year making them contenders for that year's Oscars.

While *East of Eden* did not figure in the voting by the New York critics, Warner Bros.' Oscar hopes for Kazan's film were kept alive when it won the Golden Globe (Drama).

At the very end of the year, *Picnic* entered Best Picture contention when Columbia hastily arranged a qualifying run in Los Angeles for the adaptation of William Inge's successful play. The move worked. When the Oscar nominations were announced, *Picnic* was among the nominees for the top award.

Marty and *Mister Roberts* were also nominated, but despite a Best Director nod for Kazan, *East of Eden* was left off the ballot paper. It became the first winner of the Golden Globe (Drama) not nominated for the Best Picture Oscar.

Also missing were all the year's acclaimed foreign films as the Academy went with five American nominees for the seventh year in a row. Perhaps most notable among those excluded was *Le Salaire de la Peur (The Wages of Fear)*, which won Best Picture awards at the Cannes and Berlin Film Festivals in 1953 and from the British Academy in 1954.

The other Oscar nominees were *The Rose Tattoo* (V "realistic") and the melodrama *Love is a Many–Splendored Thing* (NYT "elaborately sentimental" with an "impotent screenplay"). These two films tied with *Marty* as the most nominated of the year but the directors of each were snubbed for nominations in the Best Director category which severely undermined the chances of either collecting the Best Picture statuette. Also, *Marty* was the only Best Picture contender nominated for the screenplay awards. Despite Warner Bros.' high hopes for *Mister Roberts*, the film only received three nominations, missing out on Best Actor and Best Director nods. As a result, *Marty*, which had won the top prizes from both the New York critics and the NBR, was the overwhelming Oscar favourite. On the big night, *Marty* duly won the Best Picture statuette.

Marty was not able to continue its winning streak in London, however. Although nominated as Best Picture by the British Academy it lost to a British film that would be an Oscar contender the following year: Laurence Olivier's *Richard III*. The film version of the great Shakespeare historical was only the second film to win both the Best Film and Best British Film BAFTAs.

1955

BEST DIRECTOR

ACADEMY AWARDS
Elia Kazan for *East of Eden*
David Lean for *Summertime*
Joshua Logan for *Picnic*
• **Delbert Mann for *Marty***
John Sturges for *Bad Day at Black Rock*

GOLDEN GLOBE AWARDS – Joshua Logan – *Picnic*

DIRECTORS GUILD AWARD
John Ford and Mervyn LeRoy – *Mister Roberts*
Elia Kazan – *East of Eden*
Joshua Logan – *Picnic*
• **Delbert Mann – *Marty***
John Sturges – *Bad Day at Black Rock*

NEW YORK – David Lean – *Summertime*
BOARD OF REVIEW – William Wyler – *The Desperate Hours*

In its review of *Marty*, Variety commented that director Delbert Mann "deserves a large share of the credit for its overall excellence". The film was Mann's feature film directorial debut, although he had directed various television movies, including the 1953 telemovie from which *Marty* had been adapted.

Also making his solo feature film directorial debut was Joshua Logan, an experienced theatre director who had previously co–directed a film in 1938. Logan helmed *Picnic*, a big-screen adaptation of one of the plays that he had directed on Broadway. His efforts were lauded by The New York Times which declared the "characters come alive again through his directorial artistry".

One of Logan's previous Broadway credits was the original stage production of 'Mister Roberts'. It too was translated to the big screen in 1955 as a big-budget Warner Bros. release starring Henry Fonda (reprising his Broadway success) and James Cagney. Oscar-winning director John Ford began work on the project, but was replaced part-way through filming by Mervyn LeRoy when Ford became ill. Both men were credited for their work and were jointly nominated for the DGA accolade. *Mister Roberts* was one of the year's biggest money-earners at the box office.

Praised in film reviews during the year were: Nicholas Ray for *Rebel Without a Cause* (NYT "[the Cinema-Scope slickness] battles at times with the realism in the direction of Nicholas Ray"); the previous year's Oscar winner Elia Kazan for *East of Eden* (V "a tour de force"); previous winner William Wyler for *The Desperate Hours*; previous Best Actor Oscar winner Charles Laughton for his directorial debut *The Night of the Hunter* (NYT "a clever and exceptionally effective job"); John Sturges for *Bad Day at Black Rock* (NYT "patient, methodical pacing"); David Lean for *Summertime* (NYT directed "with magnificent feeling and skill"); Otto Preminger for both *The Court–Martial of Billy Mitchell* and *The Man with the Golden Arm*; Daniel Mann for *The Man from Laramie* (NYT "fierce and steady direction"); and Henri-Georges Clouzot for the drama *Le Salaire de la Peur (The Wages of Fear)*.

At the end of the year the critics groups favoured experienced directors. Wyler was named Best Director by the NBR and then runner–up (along with Preminger) to Lean for the New York critics' prize. As the Academy Awards drew closer, however, the emerging talents moved into favour. Logan won the Golden Globe and Mann picked up the prize from the DGA, which was beginning to establish an excellent track–record as an Oscar indicator.

Both Mann and Logan were nominated by the Academy and they were the only nominees whose films were among the Best Picture contenders. The previous year's winner, Kazan, was again nominated as was Sturges who was mentioned (for the only time) for *Bad Day at Black Rock*. The only change the Academy made from the list of Guild finalists was the inclusion of New York winner Lean ahead of the joint efforts of Ford and LeRoy. The NBR winner Wyler, already omitted from the DGA's list, was also overlooked by the Academy and would have to wait another year to earn his tenth nomination. The year after he had been snubbed for *Carmen Jones*, Preminger was again absent from the list of Oscar candidates.

The DGA win and Best Picture expectations for *Marty* made Mann the firm favourite for the Best Director Oscar. On the big night in Hollywood, he indeed proved to be the Academy's choice. He was the first director to win the golden statuette for his feature debut.

BEST ACTOR

ACADEMY AWARDS
• **Ernest Borgnine as 'Marty Piletti' in** *Marty*
James Cagney as 'Martin Snyder' in *Love Me or Leave Me*
James Dean as 'Cal Trask' in *East of Eden*
Frank Sinatra as 'Frankie Machine' in *The Man with the Golden Arm*
Spencer Tracy as 'John J. Macreedy' in *Bad Day at Black Rock*

GOLDEN GLOBE AWARDS
(Drama) **Ernest Borgnine** – *Marty* and **James Dean** – *East of Eden*
(Comedy/Musical) **Tom Ewell** – *The Seven Year Itch*

BRITISH ACADEMY AWARDS

(Foreign Actor)	(British Actor)
• **Ernest Borgnine** – *Marty*	Alfie Bass – *The Bespoke Overcoat*
James Dean – *East of Eden*	Alec Guinness – *The Prisoner*
Jack Lemmon – *Mister Roberts*	Jack Hawkins – *The Prisoner*
Toshiro Mifune	Kenneth More – *The Deep Blue Sea*
– Shichinin no Samurai	• **Laurence Olivier** – *Richard III*
(Seven Samurai)	Michael Redgrave
Takashi Shimura	*– The Night My Number Came Up*
– Shichinin no Samurai	
(Seven Samurai)	
Frank Sinatra – *Not as a Stranger*	

NEW YORK – Ernest Borgnine – *Marty*
BOARD OF REVIEW – Ernest Borgnine – *Marty*

The Palme d'Or win by *Marty* drew a great deal of attention to its star, Ernest Borgnine, who was mainly known for playing thugs such as in the 1953 Best Picture Oscar winner *From Here to Eternity*. His performance in *Marty*, said The New York Times, "is a beautiful blend of the crude and the strangely gentle and sensitive". Variety, meanwhile, lauded him for "a performance that will be recalled next time thespian awards are distributed." Borgnine collected acting prizes from the New York critics and the NBR as well as the Golden Globe (Drama) on his way to earning a nomination from the Academy (the only one he ever received).

The success of American cinema at the Cannes Festival was not limited to *Marty*. Previous Oscar winner Spencer Tracy was awarded the Best Acting citation for his critically acclaimed portrayal of a one-armed war veteran investigating a mystery in the pseudo–Western *Bad Day at Black Rock* (NYT "sturdy and laconic"; TT "a performance up to his own high standards"; MFB "quietly authoritative"). The Academy named him in the Best Actor category for a record–equalling fifth time for his performance.

Widely tipped for a Best Actor nomination but overlooked was Henry Fonda's reprisal of his Tony Award-winning portrayal of the title character in *Mister Roberts*. "Fonda is Mr Roberts," wrote The New York Times, "a beautifully lean and sensitive characterization, full of dignity and power." Fonda's omission from the list of Oscar nominees was the year's biggest shock. Spencer Tracy told reporters, "It was a blatant omission on the part of the Academy to leave Henry Fonda out of the running. He was great in *Mister Roberts*."

Also overlooked were: Golden Globe (Musical/Comedy) winner Tom Ewell in *The Seven Year Itch* (NYT "adroitly played"); Richard Todd in *A Man Called Peter*, a biopic of Peter Marshall, the Scottish clergyman who became the U.S. Senate chaplain (NYT brings "a fervour and eloquence to his acting that fairly lifts him right out of the large screen"; V "a masterful job"; TT "the best performance of his career"); previous winner Fredric March in *The Desperate Hours* (V "powerful"); Charles Vanel in *Le Salaire de la Peur (The Wages of Fear)* (NYT "played intensely"); and previous winner William Holden, who starred in two of the year's Best Picture nominees, *Love is a Many–Splendored Thing* and *Picnic* (NYT "miscast"). For the first time since 1950 Marlon Brando was not on the Academy's list. His turn in the box office hit musical *Guys and Dolls* was also overlooked.

Although the film is now considered a masterpiece, Charles Laughton's *The Night of the Hunter* was a commercial failure upon its release. Critics were unsure of what to make of it and the Academy, unsurprisingly, ignored it entirely, including the lead performance by Robert Mitchum which has come to be highly-regarded by historians (NYT "plays the murderous minister with an icy unctuousness that gives you the chills.").

Nominations were instead awarded to previous winner James Cagney for his portrayal of a gangster in *Love Me or Leave Me* (NYT "Cagney's verve and virtuosity makes the character sufferable"; MFB "monotonous"); previous Supporting Actor Oscar winner Frank Sinatra for playing a heroin addict in Otto Preminger's controversial *The Man with the Golden Arm* (NYT "plausible"); and the late teen-idol James Dean whose turn in *East of Eden* had divided critics (NYT mimics Marlon Brando's style in "a clumsy display"; V "seems required to play his lead character as though he were straight out of a Marlon Brando mold, although he has a basic appeal that manages to cut though"). Dean also appeared that year in the popular teen drama *Rebel Without a Cause* (V "very effective"). Dean's untimely death partly resulted in his performance in *East of Eden* sharing the Golden Globe (Drama) prize with Borgnine, and earning him the first of two consecutive posthumous Oscar nominations as Best Actor.

On the New York critics' first ballot, Borgnine and Sinatra tied with four votes each, one ahead of BAFTA nominee Alec Guinness as the cardinal placed on trial in *The Prisoner*, a film released in Los Angeles early the following year and thus eligible for the 1956 Oscars (NYT "Guinness's talent [as a dramatic actor of rare competence] is brilliantly and movingly revealed"; V "flawless"; MFB "soberly convincing"). After subsequent ballots, Borgnine emerged with the prize. The accolade from the east coast, along with the Best Picture nomination for *Marty*, made him the favourite for the Oscar and he duly out-polled Sinatra to win the Academy Award. He was the second man to win all four of the major Best Actor accolades (Ray Milland had been the first a decade earlier). Despite another half a century in front of the camera, he was never again in an Oscar race.

In London, Borgnine was also named Best Foreign Actor by the British Academy. He outpolled: the year's Best Supporting Actor Oscar-winner Jack Lemmon for *Mister Roberts*; Dean in *East of Eden*; Sinatra as a medical student in the box office hit *Not as a Stranger*; and both Toshiro Mifune and Takashi Shimura in Akira Kurosawa's *Shichinin no Samurai (Seven Samurai)*. The two Japanese actors were eligible for Oscar consideration the following year, but neither received nominations.

Guinness and his co-star Jack Hawkins were both nominated for the Best British Actor prize in London, but they lost to Laurence Olivier for his portrayal of the title character in *Richard III*. The following year, Olivier would receive an Oscar nomination for his performance but both Guinness and Hawkins would be overlooked.

BEST ACTRESS

ACADEMY AWARDS
Susan Hayward as 'Lillian Roth' in *I'll Cry Tomorrow*
Katharine Hepburn as 'Jane Hudson' in *Summertime*
Jennifer Jones as 'Han Suyin' in *Love is a Many–Splendored Thing*
• **Anna Magnani as 'Serafina Delle Rose' in *The Rose Tattoo***
Eleanor Parker as 'Marjorie Lawrence' in *Interrupted Melody*

GOLDEN GLOBE AWARDS
(Drama) **Anna Magnani – *The Rose Tattoo***
(Comedy/Musical) **Jean Simmons – *Guys and Dolls***

BRITISH ACADEMY AWARDS

(Foreign Actress)
• **Betsy Blair – *Marty***
Dorothy Dandridge – *Carmen Jones*
Judy Garland – *A Star is Born*
Julie Harris – *I am a Camera*
Katharine Hepburn – *Summertime*
Grace Kelly – *The Country Girl*
Giulietta Masina – *La Strada*
Marilyn Monroe – *The Seven Year Itch*

(British Actress)
• **Katie Johnson – *The Ladykillers***
Margaret Johnston – *Touch and Go*
Deborah Kerr
 – *The End of the Affair*
Margaret Lockwood
 – *Cast a Dark Shadow*

NEW YORK – Anna Magnani – *The Rose Tattoo*
BOARD OF REVIEW – Anna Magnani – *The Rose Tattoo*

Sixteen years after first playing the role in *The Private Lives of Elizabeth and Essex*, Bette Davis starred as Queen Elizabeth I of England in *The Virgin Queen*. Variety said that her "strong and colourful performance" was "the major strength of the film" while MFB called her turn "remarkable." After her loss for *All About Eve* in 1950, Davis desperately wanted to win a third Oscar, but the prestige role did not even earn for her a mention.

Critics raved about Vivien Leigh's performance in *The Deep Blue Sea* (NYT "exquisite ... superbly adroit emotional acting"; V "a faultless, prize–winning performance") which was her first film appearance since winning her second Oscar for *A Streetcar Named Desire*. Surprisingly, she too was overlooked.

Also passed over for consideration were Yvonne Mitchell and Cornell Borchers who, respectively, had won the Best British Actress and Best Foreign Actress BAFTAs the previous year in *The Divided Heart* (V "stirring performances" by both actresses). The Academy also overlooked: Julie Harris in *East of Eden* (V "gives her particular style to an effective portrayal"; TT "excellent"); and Golden Globe (Comedy/Musical) winner Jean Simmons in *Guys and Dolls*.

While Davis and Leigh were passed over, two other previous winners were nominated. Katharine Hepburn was named for playing an old maid in *Summertime* (NYT "clever") while Jennifer Jones received her fifth (and final) nomination for playing a doctor in the romantic melodrama *Love is a Many–Splendored Thing* (V film's success due to Jones' "accomplishment in a very difficult part").

The New York Times noted "there was real surprise" at the nomination of Eleanor Parker for her turn as Marjorie Lawrence, the Australian singer stricken with polio, in *Interrupted Melody* (NYT "no one can take from Miss Parker the full credit for the emotional power she brings to the scenes of agonizing self–torment that come later in the film"; V "deftly shaded"; MFB "somewhat strained"). Few had expected her to make the list ahead of Davis and Leigh.

Hepburn and Jones had been contenders for the New York critics' prize but were defeated on the first ballot by Anna Magnani, who triumphed with the role in *The Rose Tattoo* which Tennessee Williams had written specifically for her. It was Magnani's first English–language film and garnered very strong reviews (NYT "ardent and intense"; V "spellbinding"; TT "superb"). In addition to the New York prize, Magnani won the NBR Best Actress prize and the Golden Globe (Drama). When she was nominated for the Oscar, she was favoured to win, but faced a challenger who entered the race at the last minute.

Although not released until after the New Year, M-G-M arranged a brief qualifying run for *I'll Cry Tomorrow* in which Susan Hayward played the role of singer Lillian Roth. Variety wrote "there will be professional and critical acclaim for Susan Hayward's smash portrayal of the alcoholic who came back – a performance that can't miss being a major Academy contender." Hayward was recognised by the Academy for the fourth time for a portrayal described by The New York Times as "thoroughly authentic and convincing, shattering and sad."

Magnani had the momentum of several critics' prizes, but was appearing in her first Hollywood film. Hayward, on the other hand, had been a major Hollywood star for years, had three times missed out on an Oscar and was the star of what became one of the five biggest box office successes of 1956. Prior to the awards the Variety poll tipped Magnani to win and on Oscar night it was her name in the envelope. For the second year in a row an actress had swept the four major Best Actress accolades. Hayward lost again to Magnani at the 1956 British Academy Awards, but was honoured at the 1956 Cannes Film Festival.

BEST SUPPORTING ACTOR

ACADEMY AWARDS
Arthur Kennedy as 'Barney Castle' in *Trial*
• **Jack Lemmon as 'Ensign Frank Thurlowe Pulver' in *Mister Roberts***
Joe Mantell as 'Angie' in *Marty*
Sal Mineo as 'Plato' in *Rebel Without a Cause*
Arthur O'Connell as 'Howard Bevans' in *Picnic*

GOLDEN GLOBE AWARDS – Arthur Kennedy – *Trial*
BOARD OF REVIEW – Charles Bickford – *Not as a Stranger*

At one point, it seemed like Charles Bickford would finally win an Oscar. Having been nominated unsuccessfully three times in just six years during the 1940s, his critically acclaimed portrayal of an ailing country doctor in the second half of the box office smash *Not as a Stranger* was rewarded with the Best Supporting Actor prize from the NBR (V "comes near to stealing the picture"). Despite the accolade, however, Bickford was snubbed by the Academy.

Instead, the golden statuette went to Jack Lemmon, who received his first Oscar nomination for what was arguably a leading role in one of the year's other big money-earners, *Mister Roberts* (NYT "a broad delineation of the amorous misfit"; V "a big hit").

Lemmon won his first Oscar over a field of strong candidates. Arthur Kennedy had received positive reviews and won the Golden Globe for his portrayal of a communist lawyer in *Trial* (TT his performance is "staggering in its strength and cleverness"). His nomination was his third in six years, and came in the same year in which he had also been praised for the Western *The Man from Laramie* (NYT "played with authority and vividness"). Also nominated were: Joe Mantell as the best friend in *Marty* (MFB "outstanding"); seventeen-year-old Sal Mineo as one of the kids in *Rebel Without a Cause* (V "stands out"); and Arthur O'Connell for reprising his stage role in *Picnic*.

As well as overlooking Bickford, the Academy passed over: Lee Marvin as a saxophone-player in *Pete Kelly's Blues*; Raymond Massey as the father in *East of Eden*; Louis Calhern as one of the teachers in *Blackboard Jungle* (V "reads all of the forlorn bitterness of a life–beaten man into his cynical teacher"); and Kenneth More in *The Deep Blue Sea* (NYT a "giddy performance").

Although some observers believed sentiment would deliver the Oscar to Hollywood veteran Kennedy at his third nomination, the Oscar went to Lemmon's portrayal of Ensign Pulver in *Mister Roberts*.

1955

BEST SUPPORTING ACTRESS

ACADEMY AWARDS
Betsy Blair as 'Clara Schnyder' in *Marty*
Peggy Lee as 'Rose Hopkins' in *Pete Kelly's Blues*
Marisa Pavan as 'Rosa Delle Rose' in *The Rose Tattoo*
• **Jo Van Fleet as 'Kate' in** *East of Eden*
Natalie Wood as 'Judy' in *Rebel Without a Cause*

GOLDEN GLOBE AWARDS – Marisa Pavan – *The Rose Tattoo*
BOARD OF REVIEW – Marjorie Rambeau – *A Man Called Peter* and *The View from Pompey's Head*

Columbia wanted to mount a Best Supporting Actress campaign for Rosalind Russell for her acclaimed performance in *Picnic* (NYT "uneven [but] powerful and genuinely moving"; V "Russell is a standout, moving in her plea for marriage, amusing as she pretends indifference to men and pitiable in her whiskey–inspired outburst"). Russell had been a star for twenty years and had been unsuccessfully nominated as Best Actress three times. Credited in *Picnic* as "co–starring", she considered herself a leading lady and refused to allow Columbia to promote her for supporting actress accolades.

With Russell out of the running, Betsy Blair became a major contender for *Marty* (NYT "wonderfully revealing"; V "impressive in her finely etched delineation of the sensitive school teacher"; MFB a "wholly believable and closely observed portrait"). Nominated alongside her were: seventeen-year-old Natalie Wood as a troubled teenager in *Rebel Without a Cause*; Marisa Pavan as the daughter in *The Rose Tattoo* (NYT "good … gives this picture a quality of utter authenticity"); singer Peggy Lee in *Pete Kelly's Blues* (V "scores a personal hit"); and Broadway star Jo Van Fleet for her film debut as the brothel–madam mother in *East of Eden* (MFB "impressive").

Overlooked were: Betty Field in *Picnic* (V "restrained but perceptive"); Margaret Hayes in *Blackboard Jungle* (V "simply great"); Lillian Gish in *The Night of the Hunter* (V "shows great skill"; MFB "marvellously moving"); and Marjorie Rambeau in *A Man Called Peter* (V "priceless").

Rambeau was named Best Supporting Actress by the NBR while Pavan won the Golden Globe. Just prior to the Oscar ceremony, however, Variety's straw–poll of Academy members indicated that Van Fleet was the frontrunner even though she had refused to conduct a campaign. On the night, Van Fleet became the third actress in five years to win an Oscar for a film directed by Elia Kazan. In London, meanwhile, Blair won the Best Foreign Actress BAFTA for *Marty*.

BEST PICTURE

ACADEMY AWARDS
• *Around the World in 80 Days*
  (Todd, United Artists, 175 mins, 17 Oct 1956, $23.1m, 8 noms)
Friendly Persuasion
  (Allied Artists, 137 mins, 25 Nov 1956, 6 noms)
Giant
  (Warner Bros., 201 mins, 10 Nov 1956, $12.0m, 10 noms)
The King and I
  (20th Century Fox, 133 mins, 29 Jun 1956, $8.5m, 9 noms)
The Ten Commandments
  (DeMille, Paramount, 220 mins, 5 Oct 1956, $34.2m, 7 noms)

GOLDEN GLOBE AWARDS
(Drama)
• *Around the World in 80 Days*
Giant
Lust for Life
The Rainmaker
War and Peace

(Comedy/Musical)
Bus Stop
• *The King and I*
The Opposite Sex
The Solid Gold Cadillac
Teahouse of the August Moon

BRITISH ACADEMY AWARDS
(Best Film)
Amici per la Pelle (Woman in the Painting)
Baby Doll
The Battle of the River Platte
Le Défroqué (The Unfrocked One)
• *Gervaise*
Guys and Dolls
The Killing
The Man Who Never Was
The Man with the Golden Arm
Picnic
Poprigunya (The Grasshopper)
Reach for the Sky
Rebel Without a Cause
Sommarnattens Leende (Smiles of a Summer Night)
A Town Like Alice
The Trouble with Harry
War and Peace
Yield to the Night

(Best British Film)
The Battle of the River Platte
The Man Who Never Was
• *Reach for the Sky*
A Town Like Alice
Yield to the Night

1956

The increasing number of televisions in American homes by the mid-1950s had a major impact on feature film production in Hollywood. The studios attempted to attract audiences back to cinemas with a form of entertainment that the new box in the living room could not provide – large screen, colour epics with big-name movie stars. The biggest and longest of these new cinematic spectacles was Cecil B. DeMille's biblical epic *The Ten Commandments*, starring Charlton Heston as Moses (NYT "a moving story of the spirit of freedom", "a rather handsome romance"; V "too long" but still "extremely impressive"; S&S "more monumental than spectacular"). It ran for over three and a half hours and topped the box office in 1957. By the end of its cinematic run it was the highest grossing film released since *Gone with the Wind*.

The other major releases of the year – in descending order of running time – were: King Vidor's three and a half hour literary adaptation *War and Peace* starring Henry Fonda and Audrey Hepburn (NYT "oddly mechanical and emotionally sterile ... the war scenes are as massive, colorful and exciting as anything of this sort we've ever seen ... but, alas, the human stories that Tolstoy told so significantly in the book are sketchy and inconsequential, despite the time devoted to them"; V "a rich contribution to the art form", "an entertainment and educational force"; S&S "flat and overcast"); George Stevens' Texan epic *Giant* starring Elizabeth Taylor, Rock Hudson and James Dean (NYT "tremendously vivid", "staggering", "for all its complexity, is a strong contender for the year's top-film award"; V "excellent"); the adventure film *Around the World in 80 Days* starring David Niven (NYT "a sprawling conglomeration of refined English comedy, giant-screen travel panoramics and slam-bang Keystone burlesque ... undeniably, quite a show"; V "a smash"; TT "too long"); Robert Rossen's historical *Alexander the Great* starring Richard Burton and Fredric March (NYT "sweeping and occasionally exciting"); William Wyler's Civil War family drama *Friendly Persuasion* starring Gary Cooper (NYT "a winning motion picture", "touching"; V "rewarding entertainment"); the musical *The King and I* starring Yul Brynner and Deborah Kerr (NYT "it is the pictorial magnificence of the appropriately regal production that especially distinguishes this film ... grand and moving"; V "pictorially exquisite, musically exciting and dramatically satisfying"; NYer "pretty and harmless"); the musical *Carousel* starring Gordon MacRae and Shirley Jones (NYT "stunning"); the comedy *Teahouse of the August Moon* starring Marlon Brando (NYT "a rambunctious farce"); Vincente Minnelli's biopic *Lust for Life* starring Kirk Douglas as

Vincent Van Gogh (V "unexciting"); John Ford's Western *The Searchers* starring John Wayne (NYT "a winner ... brashly entertaining"; V "somewhat disappointing"); and John Huston's expensive two hour film version of *Moby Dick* starring Gregory Peck (NYT "a rolling and thundering color film that is herewith devoutly recommended as one of the great motion pictures of our time ... space does not possibly permit us to cite all the things about this film that are brilliantly done or developed, from the strange, subdued color scheme employed to the uncommon faithfulness to details of whaling that are observed ... a remarkable job"; V "interesting more often than exciting"). These films dominated the US box office as well as the end of year Best Picture category accolades.

For the first time the New York critics selected a colour film as Best Picture of the year. *Around the World in 80 Days* was chosen on the second ballot over four other colour films: *Giant, The King and I, Lust for Life* and *Moby Dick.*

The NBR also gave their Best Picture prize to *Around the World in 80 Days* and the film was also honoured by the Hollywood Foreign Press Association with the Golden Globe for Best Picture (Drama).

The Globe for Best Picture (Comedy/Musical), meanwhile, was awarded to *The King and I*, which was the year's second biggest box office success after the 1955 release *Guys and Dolls.*

The King and I was included on the Academy's list of nominees along with the three biggest box office hits of 1957: *The Ten Commandments*, *Around the World in 80 Days* and *Giant*. Somewhat unexpectedly, the fifth Oscar contender was *Friendly Persuasion*, which was nominated ahead of the Golden Globe nominees *Lust for Life* and *War and Peace*, and the critically favoured *Moby Dick*. It was the first time that all the Best Picture candidates were colour.

The dominance of the Hollywood super-productions meant that many smaller colour films, black and white releases and foreign entrants were overshadowed. Notable omissions from the top Oscar category included: *Anastasia* starring Yul Brynner and Ingrid Bergman (NYT "notable ... proceeds as one strong complex of melodrama, mystery and romance ... splendid"; V "a wonderfully moving and entertaining motion picture"; TT "moving and memorable"); Globe nominee *The Rainmaker* starring Katharine Hepburn and Burt Lancaster (NYT "it is when the thing gets sentimental that the seams split and the fakery is laid bare"); Globe nominee *Bus Stop* starring Marilyn Monroe (NYT "swell"); Elia Kazan's *Baby Doll*, a drama written directly for the screen by Tennessee Williams (NYT "the major short-coming of Mr Williams' and Mr Kazan's film [is that] its people are virtually without character, content or consequence"; V "an explosive, provocative motion picture"); the widely praised British political drama *The Prisoner* (NYT "strong direction"; V "Glenville's studied direction is a technical achievement"; MFB "shows extreme accomplishment"); the French thriller *Les Diaboliques (The Fiends)* (NYT "one of the dandiest mystery dramas that has shown here in goodness knows when … the writing and the visual construction are superb, and the performances by top-notch French actors on the highest level of sureness and finesse"; TT a "masterpiece … one of the best conceived, directed and acted films of its kind ever to be made"); the Italian dramas *Umberto D* (NYT "truly extraordinary … an utterly heart-breaking picture"; TT "one of the outstanding films of our time"; MFB "quite unique poetic power") and *La Strada*, which won the Best Foreign-Language Film Oscar (NYT "strikingly realistic and yet genuinely tender and compassionate"); Akira Kurosawa's *Shichinin no Samurai (Seven Samurai)* (NYT "extraordinary", "cinema brilliance"; V "distinguished"; S&S "brilliant"); and *Richard III*, Laurence Olivier's latest film adaptation of one of William Shakespeare's history plays (V "a major contribution to motion pictures"; S&S "a very worthy and remarkable achievement"; MFB "brilliant").

The Academy also bypassed the science fiction thriller *Invasion of the Body Snatchers*. Although regarded decades later as a classic of American cinema, the film was dismissed at the time as cheap, sensationalist pulp entertainment. Variety, for example, described it as a "tense, offbeat piece of science-fiction" with "exciting" action but with a plot that was "occasionally difficult to follow" and a cast permitted "to overact in several sequences".

The month before the Oscar ceremony, the British Academy announced the winners of its annual awards. The Best Film category included *War and Peace*, but none of the Oscar candidates. The winner was *Gervaise*, a French drama directed by René Clément which was one of the candidates for the Academy's Best Foreign-Language Award and which would be eligible for the Best Picture Oscar the following year (S&S "a remarkable film").

The film with the most mentions from the Academy in Hollywood was *Giant* and following the DGA win by George Stevens, it was the frontrunner for the top prize. On the big night, however, while Stevens did collect his second Best Director statuette, the Best Picture Oscar went to the nominee with the best awards season track-record – *Around the World in 80 Days*.

Just two years after *On the Waterfront* had become the first film to win all four of the major American-based Best Picture accolades, *Around the World in 80 Days* repeated the sweep. The Best Picture Oscar was one of five statuettes won by *Around the World in 80 Days*. The film was released in Britain the following year, but was not even nominated for the British Academy's Best Picture award.

At the 1957 Cannes Film Festival, meanwhile, the unexpected Best Picture nominee, Wyler's *Friendly Persuasion*, became the second American film honoured with the Palme d'Or.

BEST DIRECTOR

ACADEMY AWARDS
Michael Anderson for *Around the World in 80 Days*
Walter Lang for *The King and I*
• **George Stevens for *Giant***
King Vidor for *War and Peace*
William Wyler for *Friendly Persuasion*

GOLDEN GLOBE AWARDS
Michael Anderson – *Around the World in 80 Days*
• **Elia Kazan – *Baby Doll***
Vincente Minnelli – *Lust for Life*
George Stevens – *Giant*
King Vidor – *War and Peace*

DIRECTORS GUILD AWARD
Michael Anderson – *Around the World in 80 Days*
John Huston – *Moby Dick*
Joshua Logan – *Bus Stop*
Daniel Mann – *Teahouse of the August Moon*
• **George Stevens – *Giant***
King Vidor – *War and Peace*
Robert Wise – *Somebody Up There Likes Me*
William Wyler – *Friendly Persuasion*

NEW YORK – John Huston – *Moby Dick*
BOARD OF REVIEW – John Huston – *Moby Dick*

The New York critics' circle and the NBR both the selected the same Best Director winner: John Huston for *Moby Dick* (NYT "Mr Huston and his technicians have done a remarkable job … this is the third time Melville's story has been put upon the screen. There is no need for another, because it cannot be done better, more beautifully or excitingly again"; MFB "wonderful control"). It was Huston's second prize from each group. The two directors previously honoured by both groups in the same year had both gone on to win the Oscar statuette so it was a major surprise when the Academy did not even nominate Huston. It was the fifth year in a row that the NBR winner had been excluded and only the third time the New York winner had been overlooked (the last time having been in 1938).

1956

Equally unexpected was the omission of Elia Kazan for *Baby Doll* (NYT "superb direction"; V "his greatest directing job to date"). Kazan had been the New York runner-up and had won a record third Golden Globe. He was only the second Globe winner left out of Best Director consideration at the Oscars.

The absence of Huston and Kazan marked the first time that both the Globe and New York winners were missing from the list of Best Director Oscar nominees. As a result, DGA prize-winner George Stevens was the frontrunner for the statuette. Stevens had won his second Guild award for *Giant* (NYT "Stevens and his able screen play-writers have contrived a tremendously vivid picture-drama ... and Mr Stevens has made it visual in staggering scenes of the great Texas plains and of passion-charged human relations that hold the hardness of the land and atmosphere"). It was his fourth time appearing on the ballot paper for the Best Director Oscar.

Also nominated were: Michael Anderson for *Around the World in 80 Days* (NYT "he has done a remarkable job") and Walter Lang for *The King and I* (NYT "it is got onto the screen with snap and vigor under the direction of Walter Lang"), each for the first and only time; William Wyler, for a record tenth time, for *Friendly Persuasion* (NYT "Wyler has brought forth a picture that is loaded with sweetness and warmth and as much cracker-barrel Americana as has been spread on the screen in some time ... what he achieves in this picture is acquaintance with solid characters whose lives are happily ordered by a simple morality and genuine love"); and King Vidor for *War and Peace* (NYT "unfolds with a ponderous rhythm ... oddly mechanical and emotionally sterile"). Nominated in the first year of the Oscars, Vidor's nomination was his fifth and last, and came nearly twenty years after he had last made the lists. Vidor was the only nominee not to have his film nominated as Best Picture.

The only director of a Best Picture nominee not included on the list was Cecil B. DeMille for *The Ten Commandments* (NYT "a rather handsome romance in Mr DeMille's best massive style"). Also overlooked were: previous winner John Ford for *The Searchers* (NYT "Ford hasn't lost his touch"); Federico Fellini for *La Strada* (NYT "has used his small cast, and, equally important, his camera, with the unmistakable touch of an artist"); Vincente Minnelli for *Lust for Life*; Laurence Olivier for *Richard III*; DGA nominee Joshua Logan for *Bus Stop*; DGA nominee Daniel Mann for *Teahouse of the August Moon*; Peter Glenville for *The Prisoner* (NYT "strong"; MFB "shows extreme accomplishment"); Henri-Georges Clouzot for *Les Diaboliques (The Fiends)* (NYT "superb") and Vittorio de Sica for *Umberto D* (NYT "nothing of his that has yet been seen here has had quite the pure simplicity and almost unbearable candor and compassion of his current *Umberto D*").

On Oscar night, Stevens was awarded his second Best Director Oscar in just six years. For the second time his victory came without a Best Picture win.

BEST ACTOR

ACADEMY AWARDS
• **Yul Brynner as 'King Tut of Siam' in *The King and I***
James Dean as 'Jett Rink' in *Giant*
Kirk Douglas as 'Vincent Van Gogh' in *Lust for Life*
Rock Hudson as 'Bick Benedict' in *Giant*
Laurence Olivier as 'King Richard III of England' in *Richard III*

GOLDEN GLOBE AWARDS
(Drama)
Gary Cooper – *Friendly Persuasion*
• **Kirk Douglas – *Lust for Life***
Charlton Heston
  – *The Ten Commandments*
Burt Lancaster – *The Rainmaker*
Karl Malden – *Baby Doll*

(Comedy/Musical)
Marlon Brando
  – *Teahouse of the August Moon*
Yul Brynner – *The King and I*
• **Cantinflas**
  – *Around the World in 80 Days*
Glenn Ford
  – *Teahouse of the August Moon*
Danny Kaye – *The Court Jester*

BRITISH ACADEMY AWARDS
(Foreign Actor)
Gunnar Björnstrand
  – *Sommarnattens Leende*
  (Smiles of a Summer Night)
James Dean – *Rebel Without a Cause*
Pierre Fresnay – *Le Défroqué (The Unfrocked One)*
William Holden – *Picnic*
Karl Malden – *Baby Doll*
• **François Périer – *Gervaise***
Frank Sinatra – *The Man with the Golden Arm*
Spencer Tracy – *The Mountain*

(British Actor)
• **Peter Finch – *A Town Like Alice***
Jack Hawkins – *The Long Arm*
Kenneth More – *Reach for the Sky*

NEW YORK – Kirk Douglas – *Lust for Life*
BOARD OF REVIEW – Yul Brynner – *Anastasia* and *The King and I* and
    The Ten Commandments

Yul Brynner appeared in three major films in 1956: the biblical epic *The Ten Commandments* as the Pharaoh Ramses, the melodrama *Anastasia*, and the year's second biggest box office success, the musical *The King and* I, in which he reprised his Tony Award-winning role as the King of Siam. The NBR named him Best Actor for all three films, but it was for *The King and I* that he earned the best reviews (NYT "unsurpassed", "excellent"; V "effective"; MFB "strong and sympathetic playing").

Brynner finished as the runner-up to Kirk Douglas for the New York prize. Douglas won the award for his portrayal of Vincent van Gogh in *Lust for Life* (NYT "striking", "superior" and "impressive"; TT "Douglas throws every ounce of his formidable personality into projecting his impression of an unbalanced, a gifted, a pathetic man"; NYer "succeeds most skillfully").

At the Golden Globe Awards, Douglas won the Drama award but, in a major upset, Brynner lost in the Comedy/Musical category. The award instead went to Mexican comic Cantinflas for *Around the World in 80 Days* (V "a standout"; TT "outstanding"). Despite the win, Cantinflas was overlooked by the Academy.

Of the ten Globe nominees the Academy mentioned only Douglas and Brynner, even though the other eight contenders included previous Oscar winner Gary Cooper in *Friendly Persuasion* (NYT "wonderfully spirited and compassionate"; V "an immense success"; MFB "likeable"), previous Best Supporting Actor Oscar winner Karl Malden in *Baby Doll* (V "superb"), previous Oscar winner Marlon Brando in *Teahouse of the August Moon* (V "excellent [in] a performance that establishes his thespic versatility") and Danny Kaye in *The Court Jester* (NYT "plays it adroitly").

Also absent from the Academy's list were: Richard Burton in *Alexander the Great* (NYT "serious and impassioned"); John Wayne in *The Searchers* (NYT "uncommonly commanding"); David Niven in *Around the World in 80 Days* (NYT "excellent"; V "perfect"); previous winner Fredric March in *The Man in the Gray Flannel Suit* (V "excellent"); both Alec Guinness (NYT "[his] talent is brilliantly and movingly revealed"; V "flawless"; MFB "soberly convincing") and Jack Hawkins (NYT "fine"; V "superb") in *The Prisoner*; Pierre Fresnay in *Le Défroqué (The Unfrocked One)* (V "his most complete composition to date"); Anthony Quinn in *La Strada* (NYT "excellent"); Carlo Battisti in *Umberto D* (NYT "perfect … never have we seen shame and torment so clearly revealed on a man's face"); and both Takashi Shimura (NYT "superb") and Toshiro Mifune (NYT "brilliant", "outstanding") in *Shichinin no Samurai (Seven Samurai)*.

Brynner was the favourite for the Oscar at his first nomination, ahead of Douglas, previous winner Laurence Oliver for his 1955 BAFTA winning turn in *Richard III* (NYT "brilliant", "tremendous"; V "classic, subtle playing of the deformed Richard") and both Rock Hudson (NYT "splendid" V "excellent") and the late James Dean (NYT "splendid"; V "an outstanding portrayal") in *Giant*. On Oscar night, Brynner won the Best Actor Oscar. "I hope this isn't a mistake," he told the audience, "because I won't give it back for anything in the world!"

BEST ACTRESS

ACADEMY AWARDS
Carroll Baker as 'Baby Doll Meighan' in *Baby Doll*
• **Ingrid Bergman as 'Anastasia' in *Anastasia***
Katharine Hepburn as 'Lizzie Curry' in *The Rainmaker*
Nancy Kelly as 'Christine Penmark' in *The Bad Seed*
Deborah Kerr as 'Anna Leonowens' in *The King and I*

GOLDEN GLOBE AWARDS

(Drama)
Carroll Baker – *Baby Doll*
• **Ingrid Bergman – *Anastasia***
Helen Hayes – *Anastasia*
Audrey Hepburn – *War and Peace*
Katharine Hepburn – *The Rainmaker*

(Comedy/Musical)
Judy Holliday
 – *The Solid Gold Cadillac*
• **Deborah Kerr – *The King and I***
Machiko Kyo
 – *Teahouse of the August Moon*
Marilyn Monroe – *Bus Stop*
Debbie Reynolds – *Bundle of Joy*

BRITISH ACADEMY AWARDS

(Foreign Actress)
Carroll Baker – *Baby Doll*
Eva Dahlbeck
 – *Sommarnattens Leende*
 (Smiles of a Summer Night)
Ava Gardner – *Bhowani Junction*
Susan Hayward – *I'll Cry Tomorrow*
Shirley MacLaine – *The Trouble with Harry*
• **Anna Magnani – *The Rose Tattoo***
Kim Novak – *Picnic*
Maria Schell – *Gervaise*

(British Actress)
Dorothy Allison – *Reach for the Sky*
Audrey Hepburn – *War and Peace*
• **Virginia McKenna**
 – *A Town Like Alice*
Jean Simmons – *Guys and Dolls*

NEW YORK – Ingrid Bergman – *Anastasia*
BOARD OF REVIEW – Dorothy McGuire – *Friendly Persuasion*

"Hold on to your chairs, everybody, and get set for a rattling surprise," wrote Bosley Crowther in The New York Times in September 1956, "Marilyn Monroe has finally proved herself an actress in *Bus Stop*. She and the picture are swell." The review praised Monroe for creating "a real character" and for playing her "expertly." Twentieth Century Fox decided not to mount a campaign for Monroe, however, and she was overlooked by the Academy.

Fox instead threw its support behind Deborah Kerr as the governess in the musical *The King and I* (NYT "excellent"; V "gives one of her finest performances", "skillfully conveyed"). Kerr was the runner-up for the New York Best Actress prize, won the Golden Globe (Comedy or Musical) and earned her third Oscar nod for the role. She also appeared in *Tea and Sympathy* (NYT "one of the most genuine and tender female characters we have seen on the screen in a long, long time") and the war romance *The Proud and Profane* (NYT "continuously interesting"; V "can't overcome the unconvincing script").

The favourite for the Oscar, however, was the actress who had outpolled Kerr to win her second New York award and become the first person to win a third Globe for acting: Ingrid Bergman. Condemned by moral organisations in the United States and ostracised by Hollywood in 1949 following her affair with director Roberto Rossellini, Bergman made a triumphant return to American cinema in *Anastasia* (NYT "moving" and "nothing short of superb" in "a beautifully molded performance, worthy of an Academy Award"; V "outstanding", "one of the greatest performances of the year").

Also nominated by the Academy were: previous winner and Globe nominee Katharine Hepburn in *The Rainmaker* (V "a winning job"; TT "at the top of her impressive form") and first-time nominees Nancy Kelly as the mother in *The Bad Seed* (V "outstanding"; MFB "a virtuoso study") and Carroll Baker as the tragic child bride in *Baby Doll* (V "superb" and "startling", "a top contender for this year's Academy Award"; TT "brilliant").

Surprisingly overlooked for the Globe and the Oscar was the NBR winner Dorothy McGuire in *Friendly Persuasion* (NYT "top honors ... wonderfully spirited and compassionate"). Also by-passed by the Academy were: previous winner Judy Holliday in *The Solid Gold Cadillac* (NYT "an incomparable performance"); Globe nominee Machiko Kyo in *Teahouse of the August Moon* (NYT "unsuited"); Elizabeth Taylor in *Giant* (NYT "splendid"; V "a surprisingly clever performance"); Giulietta Masina in *La Strada* (NYT "rare and acute perception", "expert"; MFB "remarkable"); and both Véra Clouzot (TT "plays to perfection") and Simone Signoret (TT "[her] best screen performance") in the French thriller *Les Diaboliques (The Fiends)*. The Academy also ignored the poorly reviewed performances of previous winners Jennifer Jones in *The Man in the Gray Flannel Suit* (V "faulty to a serious degree") and Globe and BAFTA nominee Audrey Hepburn in *War and Peace* (NYT "[her] amorous infatuations are represented without warmth").

On Oscar night, Bergman's return to Hollywood was crowned with a second Best Actress Oscar. She was not present to collect her statuette, however, as she was appearing in a play in Paris.

BEST SUPPORTING ACTOR

ACADEMY AWARDS
Don Murray as 'Bo Decker' in *Bus Stop*
Anthony Perkins as 'Josh Birdwell' in *Friendly Persuasion*
• **Anthony Quinn as 'Paul Gauguin' in *Lust for Life***
Mickey Rooney as 'Dooley' in *The Bold and the Brave*
Robert Stack as 'Kyle Hadley' in *Written on the Wind*

GOLDEN GLOBE AWARDS
Eddie Albert – *Teahouse of the August Moon*
• **Earl Holliman – *The Rainmaker***
Oscar Homolka – *War and Peace*
Anthony Quinn – *Lust for Life*
Eli Wallach – *Baby Doll*

BOARD OF REVIEW – Richard Basehart – *Moby Dick*

Surprisingly, the Academy overlooked both NBR winner Richard Basehart as Ishmael in *Moby Dick* (NYT "does right well") and Golden Globe winner Earl Holliman in *The Rainmaker*. Instead, three actors were included for co-leading roles: Don Murray for his debut in *Bus Stop* (NYT "a great deal is owed to Mr Murray"); Mickey Rooney in *The Bold and the Brave* (NYT "walks off with the show"; V "ably sells the part"); and Robert Stack in *Written on the Wind* (V "one of his best performances"). The only truly supporting performers in contention were Anthony Perkins in *Friendly Persuasion* (V "scores resoundingly"; TT "sensitive"; MFB "plays with melodramatic over-emphasis") and previous winner Anthony Quinn in *Lust for Life* (NYT "splendid"; V "competent").

As well as Basehart and Holliman, other supporting performances shut out of Oscar consideration included: Mel Ferrer in *War and Peace* (V "compelling"); Arthur O'Connell in *Bus Stop* (NYT "delightful"); Leo Genn in *Moby Dick* (NYT "excellent"); Globe nominee Eddie Albert as the psychiatrist in *Teahouse of the August Moon* (V "excellent"); Globe nominee Eli Wallach in *Baby Doll* (V "superb"); Jeffrey Hunter in *The Searchers* (NYT "wonderful"); Ed Begley in *Patterns*; the Golden Globe Best Actor (Comedy/Musical) winner Cantinflas in *Around the World in 80 Days* (V "a standout"; TT "outstanding"); Rod Steiger in *The Harder They Fall* (NYT "relentless"); and Paul Meurisse as the husband in *Les Diaboliques (The Fiends)* (NYT "tops").

Variety predicted that Stack would win the Oscar, but on Oscar night it was Quinn who scored his second upset in five years to again claim the statuette.

1956

BEST SUPPORTING ACTRESS

ACADEMY AWARDS
Mildred Dunnock as 'Aunt Rose Comfort' in *Baby Doll*
Eileen Heckart as 'Hortense Daigle' in *The Bad Seed*
• **Dorothy Malone as 'Marylee Hadley' in *Written on the Wind***
Mercedes McCambridge as 'Luz Benedict' in *Giant*
Patty McCormack as 'Rhoda Penmark' in *The Bad Seed*

GOLDEN GLOBE AWARDS
Mildred Dunnock – *Baby Doll*
• **Eileen Heckart – *The Bad Seed***
Marjorie Main – *Friendly Persuasion*
Dorothy Malone – *Written on the Wind*
Patty McCormack – *The Bad Seed*

BOARD OF REVIEW – Debbie Reynolds – *The Catered Affair*

Although eleven-year-old Patty McCormack's performance as the young killer in *The Bad Seed* had divided critics she was nominated for the Oscar, becoming the youngest actress to that date recognised by the Academy (NYT "unconvincing"; V "outstanding"; MFB "a performance of considerable originality and persuasiveness").

Also nominated were: McCormack's co-star in *The Bad Seed*, Golden Globe winner Eileen Heckart (NYT "badly confused"; V "terrific"; TT "moving"); Mildred Dunnock as the aunt of the young bride in *Baby Doll*; Dorothy Malone as a nymphomaniac in *Written on the Wind* (NYT "absurd"; V "hits a career high"; MFB "relies more on physical presence than acting ability"); and previous winner Mercedes McCambridge as a tough Texan rancher in *Giant* (NYT "excellent", "splendid"; V "occasionally stylized").

Surprisingly overlooked were: NBR winner Debbie Reynolds in *The Catered Affair*; Globe nominee Marjorie Main in *Friendly Persuasion*; and Ann Harding in *The Man in the Gray Flannel Suit* (V "a topnotch performance").

Perhaps the most unexpected omission from the list of candidates was previous Best Actress Oscar winner Helen Hayes for her portrayal of the Dowager Empress in *Anastasia* (NYT "excellent"; V "plays her difficult role to perfection", "deserves special mention"). Her supporting performance had earned Hayes a nomination for the Best Actress (Drama) Golden Globe.

On Oscar night, the winner turned out to be Malone, whose acceptance speech was so long that presenter Jack Lemmon has to interrupt her by raising his arm and pointing impatiently to his watch!

BEST PICTURE

ACADEMY AWARDS
- **The Bridge on the River Kwai**
  (Horizon, Columbia, 161 mins, 18 Dec 1957, $18.0m, 8 noms)
Peyton Place
  (Wald, 20th Century Fox, 162 mins, 12 Dec 1957, $12.0m, 9 noms)
Sayonara
  (Goetz, Warner Bros, 147 mins, 5 Dec 1957, $10.5m, 10 noms)
Twelve Angry Men
  (Orion-Nova, United Artists, 96 mins BW, 14 Apr 1957, 3 noms)
Witness for the Prosecution
  (Small-Hornblow, United Artists, 116 mins BW, 3 Dec 1957, 6 noms)

GOLDEN GLOBE AWARDS
(Drama)
- **The Bridge on the River Kwai**
Sayonara
Twelve Angry Men
Wild is the Wind
Witness for the Prosecution

(Comedy/Musical)
Don't Go Near the Water
- **Les Girls**
Love in the Afternoon
Pal Joey
Silk Stockings

BRITISH ACADEMY AWARDS
(Best Film)
The Bachelor Party
- **The Bridge on the River Kwai**
Celui qui Doit Mourir
  (He Who Must Die)
Un Condamné à Mort s'est
  Échappé ou le Vent Souffle où il Veut (A Man Escaped)
Edge of the City
Heaven Knows, Mr Allison
Pather Panchali (Song of the Road)
Paths of Glory
Porte des Lilas (The Gates of Paris)
The Prince and the Showgirl
The Shiralee
That Night!
3:10 to Yuma
The Tin Star
Twelve Angry Men
Windom's Way

(Best British Film)
- **The Bridge on the River Kwai**
The Prince and the Showgirl
The Shiralee
Windom's Way

1957

NEW YORK – *The Bridge on the River Kwai*
BOARD OF REVIEW – *The Bridge on the River Kwai*

The three most Oscar-nominated films of 1957 were all popular hits. Eventually, the three closed out the following year's North American box office as the three highest-grossing releases.

The most nominated film of the year was Joshua Logan's *Sayonara*, an acclaimed romantic tragedy about an American pilot, played by Marlon Brando, facing prejudice against his relationship with a Japanese actress during the Korean War (NYT a "beautiful, sentimental tale" and "a richly colorful film"; V "a picture of beauty and sensitivity" and "a major screen achievement"; TT "meanders slowly on with no outstanding incident"; S&S "monotonous"). The Academy honoured it with ten nominations, including a place on the ballot for Best Picture. The film finished 1958 as the third most commercially successful release at the box office.

Despite mixed reviews, *Peyton Place*, Mark Robson's film version of Grace Metalious' best-selling novel about the scandalous secrets hidden behind the seemingly perfect façade of an average American small town, surprisingly received nine mentions from the Academy (NYT "the interlocked dramas are put forth with strength and fascination – and comparative credibility – in this film"; V "something of a disappointment"; TT "unsuccessful"). It was the only Best Picture Oscar nominee not to have been in contention for the Golden Globe (Drama). *Peyton Place* was the second most popular film of 1958.

The overwhelming favourite for the Academy's top prize, however, with eight nominations, was *The Bridge on the River Kwai*, David Lean's lauded drama about British and American prisoners-of-war building a bridge for the Japanese during World War Two (NYT "exceptional", "magnificent", "a powerful personal drama" and "a tingling action thriller", "towering entertainment" that is "terrifically absorbing"; V "a gripping drama" and "an artistic triumph"). Released in mid-December, it went on to become the 1958 box office champion.

Also nominated for the Best Picture Oscar were two courtroom dramas: *Twelve Angry Men*, which starred Henry Fonda and had won the Best Picture award at the 1957 Berlin Film Festival (NYT "excellent ... forceful ... [a] taut, absorbing and compelling drama ... penetrating, sensitive and sometimes shocking"; V an "absorbing drama"; TT "a tense, taut, claustrophobic piece of work", "well-made"); and *Witness for the Prosecution*, an adaptation of a play by Agatha Christie which starred Charles Laughton and Marlene Dietrich and was directed by Billy Wilder (NYT "comes off extraordinarily well"; V "engaging"). All five of the Best Picture contenders also received nominations in the Best Director category; the first time in history that the two categories had so aligned.

At the time, the most glaring omission from the Academy's list of nominees was *A Hatful of Rain*, Fred Zinnemann's critically acclaimed drama about drug addiction. In The New York Times, Bosley Crowther had called it "a harrowing picture" that was "a striking, sobering film" and "forceful". Variety said it was "provocative and engrossing", while in Britain The Times called it "a masterpiece" and Sight & Sound magazine labelled it "powerful and compelling". At the end of the year, *A Hatful of Rain* was a major contender for the New York critics' Best Picture prize, but was passed over by the Hollywood Foreign Press Association and, subsequently, the Academy.

Over half a century later, leading film critics cite Stanley Kubrick's BAFTA nominated war drama *Paths of Glory* as the most egregious oversight by the Academy that year. Made independently with the backing of United Artists, the film garnered strong reviews from critics on both sides of the Atlantic (NYT "forthright" and "shattering"; TT "definite and brutal"; S&S "powerful", "impressive" and "brilliant", "not only a film of unusual substance but a powerfully realised and gripping work of art"), but failed to win support from Academy members in any category at the Oscars.

Other notable films overlooked for Oscar consideration were: John Huston's *Heaven Knows, Mr Allison* which, like the director's earlier release, *The African Queen*, was a war-time drama about a religious woman and a worldly man (NYT "stirring and entertaining"); Elia Kazan's *A Face in the Crowd* (NYT "sizzling and cynical exposure"); *The Great Man*, a hard-bitten behind-the-scenes drama about the television industry (NYT "smashingly brutal and generally intriguing"); the Golden Globe (Comedy/Musical) winner *Les Girls* (NYT "charming"; V "should rate prominent attention when the annual year-end accolades are passed around"); Billy Wilder's romantic comedy *Love in the Afternoon* (NYT "sophisticated comedy"; TT "at times funny" but "far too long"); René Clément's French drama *Gervaise*, a film version of Emile Zola's play which had won the Best Film BAFTA the previous year (NYT "deeply moving … one of the best the screen has offered this year"; S&S "remarkable"); Carl Dreyer's *Ordet (The Word)* (NYT "extraordinary", "both emotionally and intellectually the picture is hypnotic"); Ingmar Bergman's *Sommarnattens Leende (Smiles of a Summer Night)* (NYT "witty and cheerfully candid", "delightfully droll", "charming"); and BAFTA nominee *Un Condamné à Mort s'est Échappé ou le Vent Souffle où il Veut (A Man Escaped)*, a French drama about a secret service agent determined to escape from Gestapo imprisonment (NYT "a fine reflection of a cruel experience"; S&S "superb", "an extraordinary achievement").

The chances of several high-profile studio productions, meanwhile, were dashed by mixed to negative reviews from critics and poor box office returns. These included: M-G-M's *The Barretts of Wimpole Street*, Sidney Franklin's remake of his own 1934 Best Picture nominee, starring Jennifer Jones (NYT "another fine production of the old romance ... [a] handsome production"); David O. Selznick's remake of *A Farewell to Arms*, also with Jennifer Jones (NYT "a sense of deficiency and inconsequence emerges", "tedious"); Stanley Kramer's expensive historical *The Pride and the Passion*, starring Frank Sinatra, Cary Grant and Sophia Loren (NYT "an obvious appeal to popular taste" with "a casual disregard of plausibility" makes this "a turgid adventure yarn"); and, most notably, M-G-M's *Raintree County*, an historical epic starring Elizabeth Taylor and Montgomery Clift (NYT a poor script was "the fatal weakness of this costly, ambitious film", "tedious"; V "vague"; TT "a diffuse and rambling film"). By the time of its release following a lengthy and troubled production, *Raintree County*, was reportedly the most expensive movie ever made.

The Bridge on the River Kwai was the overwhelming favourite for the Best Picture Oscar. During the awards season, it was honoured with the top prizes from the New York critics and the NBR, won the Golden Globe (Drama) and in the month prior to the Oscars also received both the Best Film and Best British Film awards from the British Academy (it was an American-British co-production with an English director).

On Oscar night, *The Bridge on the River Kwai* claimed the Best Picture Academy Award to become the third film in four years to sweep the four major American-based end of year accolades. Meanwhile, *Peyton Place*, which had received nine nominations, went unrecognised on the night and consequently joined the 1941 release *The Little Foxes* as the most nominated film to that date to have failed to secure a single golden statuette.

BEST DIRECTOR

ACADEMY AWARDS
• **David Lean for *The Bridge on the River Kwai***
Joshua Logan for *Sayonara*
Sidney Lumet for *Twelve Angry Men*
Mark Robson for *Peyton Place*
Billy Wilder for *Witness for the Prosecution*

GOLDEN GLOBE AWARDS
• **David Lean – *The Bridge on the River Kwai***
Joshua Logan – *Sayonara*
Sidney Lumet – *Twelve Angry Men*
Billy Wilder – *Witness for the Prosecution*
Fred Zinnemann – *A Hatful of Rain*

DIRECTORS GUILD AWARD
• **David Lean – *The Bridge on the River Kwai***
Joshua Logan – *Sayonara*
Sidney Lumet – *Twelve Angry Men*
Mark Robson – *Peyton Place*
Billy Wilder – *Witness for the Prosecution*

NEW YORK – David Lean – *The Bridge on the River Kwai*
BOARD OF REVIEW – David Lean – *The Bridge on the River Kwai*

A decade after Elia Kazan had been the first person to claim all four major Best Director accolades, English director David Lean was awarded a clean sweep for *The Bridge on the River Kwai* (NYT "Lean has directed it so smartly and so sensitively for image and effect that its two hours and forty-one minutes seem no more than a swift, absorbing hour ... in addition to splendid performance, he has it brilliantly filled with atmosphere touched startlingly with humor, heart and shock"; V "expertly put together ... a superior job"). It was Lean's second prize from the NBR, his second accolade in three years from the New York critics' circle, and his first Golden Globe trophy.

Lean won the Globe ahead of New York runner-up Sidney Lumet for his directorial debut, *Twelve Angry Men* (NYT "expert") and three previous Globe winners: Joshua Logan for *Sayonara* (NYT "smartly controlled"); Billy Wilder for *Witness for the Prosecution* (NYT "splendid"); and Fred Zinnemann for *A*

Hatful of Rain (NYT "most effective … so directed by Mr Zinnemann that every concept and nuance of the story is revealed").

The Academy and the DGA made one change from the list of Globe nominees, mentioning Mark Robson for *Peyton Place* (V "beautifully directed") ahead of Zinnemann. It was the third time that the Oscar and Guild shortlists had precisely matched, and the first time that the Best Picture and Director Oscar nominees corresponded.

On Oscar night, Lean, who was in contention for the statuette for the fourth time, won his first Best Director Academy Award. He claimed a second statuette just five years later for *Lawrence of Arabia.*

As well as Globe nominee Zinnemann, the Academy overlooked several notable awards contenders, including: previous winner Elia Kazan for *A Face in the Crowd* (NYT "Kazan's staccato style eventually becomes a bit monotonous"); René Clément for the French drama *Gervaise* (NYT "Clement has put [Zola's novel] on the screen in a style of pictorial naturalism that has scarcely been matched since Erich von Stroheim's classic *Greed*"); Ingmar Bergman for the Swedish comedy *Sommarnattens Leende (Smiles of a Summer Night)* (NYT "Bergman skips us gaily through a mix-up of youthful and adult love affairs"); Stanley Kubrick for *Paths of Glory* (NYT "craftily directed"); previous Best Actor Oscar winner José Ferrer for *The Great Man* (NYT "a hard-boiled-reporter approach"); George Cukor for both the musical *Les Girls* (NYT "fine direction", "its cast of exquisite performers, under George Cukor's fine directorial hand, makes feminine ferocity about as charming as anyone could possibly want it to be") and the drama *Wild is the Wind*; John Sturges for *Gunfight at the OK Corral* (NYT "firmly directed"); and Cannes winner Robert Bresson for *Un Condamné à Mort s'est Échappé ou le Vent Souffle où il Veut (A Man Escaped)* (NYT "Bresson is an extraordinary artist … with a searching eye to detail, M. Bresson documents the enterprise, looking often at the face of the prisoner to comprehend his deliberate, desperate moods … an exceptional credit must be given the direction of M. Bresson").

1957

BEST ACTOR

ACADEMY AWARDS
Marlon Brando as 'Maj. Lloyd Gruver' in *Sayonara*
Anthony Franciosa as 'Polo' in *A Hatful of Rain*
• **Alec Guinness as 'Col. Nicholson' in *The Bridge on the River Kwai***
Charles Laughton as 'Sir Wilfrid Robarts' in *Witness for the Prosecution*
Anthony Quinn as 'Gino' in *Wild is the Wind*

GOLDEN GLOBE AWARDS

(Drama)
Marlon Brando – *Sayonara*
Henry Fonda – *Twelve Angry Men*
Anthony Franciosa – *A Hatful of Rain*
• **Alec Guinness**
   – *The Bridge on the River Kwai*
Charles Laughton
   – *Witness for the Prosecution*

(Comedy/Musical)
Maurice Chevalier
   – *Love in the Afternoon*
Glenn Ford
   – *Don't Go Near the Water*
David Niven – *My Man Godfrey*
Tony Randall
   – *Will Success Spoil
   Rock Hunter?*
• **Frank Sinatra – *Pal Joey***

BRITISH ACADEMY AWARDS

(Foreign Actor)
Richard Basehart – *Time Limit*
Pierre Brasseur – *Porte des Lilas*
   (The Gates of Paris)
Tony Curtis – *Sweet Smell of Success*
• **Henry Fonda – *Twelve Angry Men***
Jean Gabin – *La Traversée de Paris*
   (Four Bags Full)
Robert Mitchum
   – *Heaven Knows, Mr Allison*
Sidney Poitier – *Edge of the City*
Ed Wynn – *The Great Man*

(British Actor)
Peter Finch – *Windom's Way*
• **Alec Guinness**
   – *The Bridge on the River Kwai*
Trevor Howard – *Stowaway Girl*
Laurence Olivier
   – *The Prince and the Showgirl*
Michael Redgrave
   – *Time Without Pity*

NEW YORK – Alec Guinness – *The Bridge on the River Kwai*
BOARD OF REVIEW – Alec Guinness – *The Bridge on the River Kwai*

Seven years after naming Alec Guinness Best Actor for his performances in the comedy *Kind Hearts and Coronets*, the NBR presented him with a second prize for his portrayal of a British officer in a Japanese prisoner-of-war camp in the drama *The Bridge on the River Kwai* (NYT "memorable – indeed, a classic", "devastating" and "brilliantly revealing"; V "unforgettable" with "tremendous power and dignity"). Guinness also won the New York critics' prize and the Golden Globe.

The New York runner-up was Marlon Brando as an American pilot romantically involved with a Japanese actress during the Korean War in *Sayonara* (NYT Brando's performance "gives eccentricity and excitement to a richly colourful film .... Brando's offbeat acting of what could be a conventional role that spins what could be a routine romance into a lively and tense dramatic show"; V "outstanding"; TT "a performance which grows in sympathy and understanding as the film progresses until it is fully realized").

The Academy named Guinness for a second time and previous winner Brando for a fifth time in just seven years. Over twenty years since he was last recognised, previous winner Charles Laughton earned his third (and final) nod as an ailing defence lawyer in *Witness for the Prosecution* (NYT "first-rate", he "runs away with the show"; V "plays out the part flamboyantly and colorfully"). Anthony Franciosa, the husband of 1951 Best Actress nominee Shelley Winters, won Best Actor at the Venice Film Festival and earned his only Oscar nomination for reprising his Broadway role as the caring brother of a drug addict in *A Hatful of Rain* (NYT "a bit on the artificial side"; V "compelling" and "moving"; TT an "exquisite performance"). Franciosa had also appeared in Elia Kazan's *A Face in the Crowd* and *Wild is the Wind*. His co-star in the latter, Anthony Quinn, who had won a second Best Supporting Actor Oscar the previous year, was the fifth nominee as a Nevada rancher who marries his late wife's sister (NYT "is tossed about a great deal ... comical and cheerful at this point, at the next ponderous and churlish, then ugly and bad ... there is little consistency or sympathy in his character"; V "top grade performance").

Quinn was the only Oscar nominee not to have been a Globe candidate and his nomination came at the expense of Globe nominee Henry Fonda in the courtroom drama *Twelve Angry Men* (NYT "outstanding", "striking", "natural and effective" in "his most forceful portrayal in years"; TT "brilliantly acted"). Fonda was not, however, forgotten in London where he won the Best Foreign Actor BAFTA.

The other surprising omission was Franciosa's co-star in *A Hatful of Rain*, Don Murray in the role of the drug addict (NYT "is most impressive in the versatility with which he rings a junkie's baffling changes"; TT an "exquisite performance"; S&S "a restrained, even inhibited performance which remains unusual and effective throughout").

Also by-passed for Oscar consideration were: BAFTA nominee Robert Mitchum for *Heaven Knows, Mr Allison* (NYT "excellent"; V "remarkably good"; TT "spectacular"); both Anthony Perkins (NYT "excellent"; V "a remarkably sustained performance") and previous Best Supporting Actor Oscar winner Karl Malden (NYT "compelling") as a mentally fragile baseball player and his father in *Fear Strikes Out*; popular television star Andy Griffith in *A Face in the Crowd* (NYT "Griffith plays him with thunderous vigor"; S&S "amazing"); Sal Mineo in *Dino* (NYT "admirable"); both Burt Lancaster (NYT "efficient but largely restrained"; V "remarkable") and BAFTA nominee Tony Curtis (S&S "excellently conceived") in *Sweet Smell of Success*; previous winner James Cagney as actor Lon Chaney in *The Man of a Thousand Faces* (NYT "superlative"); Rod Steiger in *Across the Bridge* (NYT "a forceful and agonizing job"); Kirk Douglas in *Paths of Glory* (NYT "exudes tremendous passion"; V "excellent"; TT "authoritative"); previous winner Gary Cooper in *Love in the Afternoon* (NYT "superb", "delightful"); previous winner and BAFTA nominee Laurence Olivier in *The Prince and the Showgirl* (V "flawless"); BAFTA nominee Sidney Poitier in *Edge of the City* (V "turns in the most distinguished of his many first-rate characterizations"); previous winner Spencer Tracy in the comedy *Desk Set* (NYT "Under Walter Lang's relaxed direction, [Hepburn and Tracy] lope through this trifling charade like a couple of old-timers who enjoy reminiscing with simple routines"); Alastair Sim in *The Green Man* (NYT "masterful"); Henrik Malberg in *Ordet (The Word)* (NYT "magnificent"); and amateur performer François Leterrier in *Un Condamné à Mort s'est Échappé ou le Vent Souffle où il Veut (A Man Escaped)* (NYT "a sure, integrated performance").

Despite a strong campaign by Twentieth Century Fox, Academy members also overlooked Errol Flynn for his supporting role in *The Sun Also Rises* (NYT "Mr Flynn and the jovial Mr Albert fit their roles like gloves").

After Guinness added the Best British Actor BAFTA to his three American accolades he became an unbackable favourite for the Oscar. Even Laughton openly campaigned for Guinness to win the golden statuette, admitting that he had turned down the opportunity to play the role of Colonel Nicholson. "I never understood the part until I saw Guinness play it," he told reporters.

On the big night in Hollywood, Guinness won the Best Actor Academy Award. He was the second actor in three years to claim all the major end of year Best Actor accolades.

1957

BEST ACTRESS

ACADEMY AWARDS
Deborah Kerr as 'Sister Angela' in *Heaven Knows, Mr Allison*
Anna Magnani as 'Gloria' in *Wild is the Wind*
Elizabeth Taylor as 'Susanna Drake' in *Raintree County*
Lana Turner as 'Constance MacKenzie' in *Peyton Place*
• **Joanne Woodward as 'Eve' in *The Three Faces of Eve***

GOLDEN GLOBE AWARDS
(Drama)
Marlene Dietrich
  – *Witness for the Prosecution*
Deborah Kerr
  – *Heaven Knows, Mr Allison*
Anna Magnani – *Wild is the Wind*
Eva Marie Saint – *A Hatful of Rain*
• **Joanne Woodward**
  – *The Three Faces of Eve*

(Comedy/Musical)
Cyd Charisse – *Silk Stockings*
Taina Elg – *Les Girls*
Audrey Hepburn
  – *Love in the Afternoon*
• **Kay Kendall – *Les Girls***
Jean Simmons
  – *This Could Be the Night*

BRITISH ACADEMY AWARDS
(Foreign Actress)
Augusta Dabney – *That Night!*
Katharine Hepburn – *The Rainmaker*
Marilyn Monroe
  – *The Prince and the Showgirl*
Lilli Palmer
  – *Anastasia, Die Letzte Zarentochter*
  (Is Anna Anderson Anastasia?)
Eva Marie Saint – *A Hatful of Rain*
• **Simone Signoret – *Les Sorcières de Salem (The Witches of Salem)***
Joanne Woodward – *The Three Faces of Eve*

(British Actress)
Deborah Kerr – *Tea and Sympathy*
• **Heather Sears**
  – *The Story of Esther Costello*
Sylvia Syms
  – *Woman in a Dressing Gown*

NEW YORK – Deborah Kerr – *Heaven Knows, Mr Allison*
BOARD OF REVIEW – Joanne Woodward – *No Down Payment* and *The Three Faces of Eve*

A decade after she won her first New York Film Critics Circle Best Actress award for *Black Narcissus*, Deborah Kerr won her second prize from the circle for her performance as a nun on a Pacific island during the Second World War in *Heaven Knows, Mr Allison* (NYT "excellent"; V "apart from a few remarks the character and motivations of Deborah Kerr remain shrouded in mystery and she reveals very little of herself"). Kerr also appeared that year in the popular romance *An Affair to Remember*.

Runner-up for the New York award was Eva Marie Saint as the wife of a drug addict in *A Hatful of Rain* (NYT "the surest acting is done by Eva Marie Saint ... her portrait of the pregnant wife is tender, poignant, brave and haunting beyond words"; V "sensitive"; TT "exquisite performance").

The New York critics also cast votes for: Anna Magnani as the woman who marries her late sister's husband in *Wild is the Wind* (V "notable"); previous winner Audrey Hepburn in the comedy *Love in the Afternoon* (NYT "superb", "delightful"); Marilyn Monroe in *The Prince and the Showgirl* (NYT "Miss Monroe mainly has to giggle, wiggle, breathe deeply and flirt ... does not make the showgirl a person, simply another of pretty oddities"; S&S "a gentle performance"; "delightful"); and NBR winner Joanne Woodward as a housewife with a split personality in *The Three Faces of* Eve (NYT "stretches three ways convincingly"; V "excellent" in a "tour de force"; NYer "does well"). The NBR had also cited Woodward for her performance in *No Down Payment* (NYT "eminently believable").

At the Golden Globes, Woodward won the Best Actress (Drama) award ahead of Kerr, Magnani, Saint and Marlene Dietrich as the tough wife in *Witness for the Prosecution* (NYT "hits her high points"). Meanwhile, the Globe (Comedy/Musical) was won by English actress Kay Kendall for her turn in *Les Girls* (NYT "most lively and clever of 'Les Girls' is Miss Kendall, who leaps forth in this film as a formidable match for Beatrice Lillie as a light comedienne"; V "a truly blockbuster contribution").

In London, Monroe, Saint and Woodward were among the nominees for Best Foreign Actress, but the winner was Simone Signoret in *Les Sorcières de Salem (The Witches of Salem)*, a French film version of Arthur Miller's play 'The Crucible'. Signoret was eligible for Oscar consideration the following year. Kerr was a nominee for the Best British Actress award, for her role in the 1956 release *Tea and Sympathy*, but lost to Heather Sears for her supporting turn in *The Story of Esther Costello*.

The Academy nominated Kerr for the fourth time in just nine years (and for the second year in a row). Previous winner Magnani was mentioned for a second (and final) time and Woodward made her first appearance on the ballot. Previous Best Supporting Actress winner Saint, however, was a shock omission. Globe winner Kendall, Globe nominees Hepburn and Dietrich, and New York contender Monroe were also overlooked by Academy voters,

Also absent from the Oscar ballot were: the winner of the Best Actress prize at the 1956 Venice Film Festival, Maria Schell in *Gervaise* (NYT "beautifully, tragically played"; "matchless"); previous winner Jennifer Jones for the remakes of *The Barretts of Wimpole Street* in the role for which Norma Shearer earned a Best Actress nod in 1934 (NYT "quite handsome and credible") and *A Farewell to Arms* (NYT "studied"; V "never takes on real dimensions", "tends to go overboard on the dramatics"; TT "fails"); previous winner Katharine Hepburn in the comedy *Desk Set* (NYT "Under Walter Lang's relaxed direction, [Hepburn and Tracy] lope through this trifling charade like a couple of old-timers who enjoy reminiscing with simple routines"); Patricia Neal in Elia Kazan's *A Face in the Crowd* (NYT "plays [her] role capably"; S&S "amazing"); Jean Seberg, the young Iowa teenager who had been chosen in an international talent search for the role of Joan of Arc, in Otto Preminger's *Saint Joan* (NYT "unconvincing in a long, difficult and complex part"; S&S "gives the impression of trying desperately hard"); Giulietta Masina in *Le Notti di Cabiria (The Nights of Cabiria)* (NYT "touching").

Surprisingly nominated, each for the first time, were the former child star Elizabeth Taylor as a Southern belle in *Raintree County*, and Lana Turner as the mother of a troubled daughter in the small-town soap opera *Peyton Place* (NYT "plays remarkably well"). Neither had been Globe nominees or New York critics' prize contenders.

Many sections of the media expected the popular young star Taylor to win. If voting had not already closed, she may well have been carried to victory on a tide of sympathy when her husband Mike Todd, the producer of the previous year's Best Picture Oscar winner *Around the World in 80 Days*, was killed in a plane crash just four days before the Oscar ceremony.

As predicted by Variety, however, on Oscar night, Woodward was named the year's Best Actress. Wearing a homemade dress the 27-year old Hollywood newcomer thanked the audience admitting, "I've been daydreaming about this since I was nine years old." Her date to the ceremony was her new husband, Paul Newman, who would earn an Oscar of his own almost three decades later.

At the Venice Film Festival in 1958, Magnani received the Best Actress award for her Oscar-nominated performance in *Wild is the Wind*.

1957

BEST SUPPORTING ACTOR

ACADEMY AWARDS
• **Red Buttons as 'Sgt. Joe Kelly' in** *Sayonara*
Vittorio de Sica as 'Maj. Rinaldi' in *A Farewell to Arms*
Sessue Hayakawa as 'Col. Saito' in *The Bridge on the River Kwai*
Arthur Kennedy as 'Lucas Cross' in *Peyton Place*
Russ Tamblyn as 'Norman Page' in *Peyton Place*

GOLDEN GLOBE AWARDS
• **Red Buttons –** *Sayonara*
Lee J. Cobb – *Twelve Angry Men*
Sessue Hayakawa – *The Bridge on the River Kwai*
Nigel Patrick – *Raintree County*
Ed Wynn – *The Great Man*

BOARD OF REVIEW – Sessue Hayakawa – *The Bridge on the River Kwai*

Japanese actor Sessue Hayakawa became the first winner of the NBR award for Best Supporting Actor to be nominated for the Oscar. The NBR honoured him for his performance as the commandant of a Japanese prisoner-of-war camp in *The Bridge on the River Kwai* (NYT "superb"; V "solidly impressive"). Hayakawa was also a nominee for the Golden Globe.

Both the Globe and the Oscar, however, were won by Red Buttons as a US soldier who can't face being separated from his Japanese wife in *Sayonara* (NYT "excellent"; V "excellent" and "deeply moving").

The other three Globe candidates were all overlooked by the Academy: Lee J. Cobb in *Twelve Angry Men* (NYT "excellent"; TT "brilliantly acted"); Nigel Patrick in *Raintree County*; and Ed Wynn *in The Great Man* (NYT "excellent"; V "outstanding"). Others left out of Oscar consideration included: John Gielgud in *The Barretts of Wimpole Street* (NYT "brilliant"); Lloyd Nolan in *A Hatful of Rain* (V "topnotch portrayal"; S&S "excellent"); François Périer in both *Le Notti di Cabiria (The Nights of Cabiria)* (NYT "perfect") and *Gervaise* (NYT "brilliant"); Sidney Poitier in *Something of Value* (NYT "stirring"); George Macready in *Paths of Glory*; and Maurice Chevalier in *Love in the Afternoon* (NYT "adroit"; V "captivating").

The other nominees for the Oscar were: Italian actor-director Vittorio de Sica as an Italian medical officer in *A Farewell to Arms* (NYT "brings warmth and clarity to the character"); and both Russ Tamblyn as the shy boy (NYT "quietly moving") and Arthur Kennedy as the rapist in *Peyton Place*. De Sica had twice received the Best Foreign-Language Film Oscar.

1957

BEST SUPPORTING ACTRESS

ACADEMY AWARDS
Carolyn Jones as 'the existentialist' in *The Bachelor Party*
Elsa Lanchester as 'Miss Plimsoll' in *Witness for the Prosecution*
Hope Lange as 'Selena Cross' in *Peyton Place*
• **Miyoshi Umeki as 'Katsumi' in *Sayonara***
Diane Varsi as 'Allison MacKenzie' in *Peyton Place*

GOLDEN GLOBE AWARDS
Mildred Dunnock – *Peyton Place*
• **Elsa Lanchester – *Witness for the Prosecution***
Hope Lange – *Peyton Place*
Heather Sears – *The Story of Esther Costello*
Miyoshi Umeki – *Sayonara*

BOARD OF REVIEW – Sybil Thorndike – *The Prince and the Showgirl*

Variety predicted that Golden Globe winner Elsa Lanchester would narrowly win the Best Supporting Actress Oscar over Diane Varsi. Lanchester received her second nomination for playing the hen-pecking nurse in *Witness for the Prosecution* (NYT "delicious") while Varsi was mentioned for her performance as the rebellious teenager in *Peyton Place* (V "standout"; TT "admirable").

Also included on the Academy's list for her turn in *Peyton Place* was Hope Lange. She portrayed the rape victim who kills her assailant (NYT "a gentle and sensitive performance"; V "in top form", "exciting"; TT "admirable").

Carolyn Jones, later famous for her role as Morticia Addams on the television series 'The Addams Family', was a surprise nominee for her brief five-minute role in *The Bachelor Party* (NYT "good"; V "played with great vitality").

The surprise winner over this field of candidates, however, was Japanese actress Miyoshi Umeki as the tragic war bride of a US solider in *Sayonara* (V "charmingly simple"). Umeki was the first East Asian performer to win an Academy Award in the acting categories – and it would be over a quarter of a century before there was a second.

Overlooked by the Academy were: NBR winner Sybil Thorndike as the Dowager Queen in *The Prince and the Showgirl* (V "excellent"); Jean Anderson as a maid in *The Barretts of Wimpole Street* (NYT "excellent"); Joan Blondell in *Desk Set*; and twenty-one-year old Globe nominee and Best British Actress BAFTA winner Heather Sears for her film debut as the deaf and blind girl in the British melodrama *The Story of Esther Costello* (V "remarkable", "poignant acting of rare quality, sensitive and compelling").

1958

BEST PICTURE

ACADEMY AWARDS
Auntie Mame
(Warner Bros., 143 mins, 4 Dec 1958, $9.0m, 6 noms)
Cat on a Hot Tin Roof
(Avon, M-G-M, 108 mins, 20 Sep 1958, $6.1m, 6 noms)
The Defiant Ones
(Kramer, United Artists, 97 mins BW, 24 Sep 1958, 9 noms)
• **Gigi**
(Freed, M-G-M, 119 mins, 15 May 1958, $6.7m, 9 noms)
Separate Tables
(Hecht-Hill-Lancaster, United Artists, 100 mins BW, 18 Dec 1958, 7 noms)

GOLDEN GLOBE AWARDS

(Drama)	(Comedy)	(Musical)
Cat on a Hot Tin Roof	• **Auntie Mame**	*Damn Yankees*
• **The Defiant Ones**	*Bell, Book and Candle*	• **Gigi**
Home Before Dark	*Indiscreet*	*South Pacific*
I Want to Live!	*Me and the Colonel*	*Tom Thumb*
Separate Tables	*The Perfect Furlough*	

BRITISH ACADEMY AWARDS

(Best Film)	(Best British Film)
Aparajito	*Ice Cold in Alex*
Cat on a Hot Tin Roof	*Indiscreet*
The Defiant Ones	*Orders to Kill*
Ice Cold in Alex	• **Room at the Top**
Indiscreet	*Sea of Sand*
Letjat Zhuravli	
(The Cranes are Flying)	
No Down Payment	
Le Notti di Cabiria (The Nights of Cabiria)	
Orders to Kill	
• **Room at the Top**	
Sea of Sand	
The Sheepman	
Smultronstället (Wild Strawberries)	
The Young Lions	

NEW YORK – *The Defiant Ones*
BOARD OF REVIEW – *The Old Man and the Sea*

1958

The Academy's list of nominees for Best Picture of 1958 was comprised of all three of the year's Golden Globe winners, one of which was also the New York critics' champion, and two of the unsuccessful Globe (Drama) nominees, one of which was also the runner-up for the New York Film Critics Circle prize.

The Golden Globe (Drama) was won by *The Defiant Ones*, Stanley Kramer's acclaimed anti-racism drama starring Sidney Poitier and Tony Curtis as a pair of escaped convicts, one African American and the other a bigoted white, who are hand-cuffed together (NYT "a remarkably apt and dramatic visualization of a social idea" and "a fast and exciting melodrama"; V "a raw, powerful film"; S&S "disturbing and occasionally brilliant"). *The Defiant Ones* had earlier been named Best Picture by the New York critics and was a Best Film nominee at the British Academy Awards.

Outpolled for the Globe (Drama) were: *Cat on a Hot Tin Roof*, a film version of Tennessee Williams' familial drama starring Paul Newman and Elizabeth Taylor, which was also a Best Film BAFTA nominee (NYT "a ferocious and fascinating show"; V "an intense, important motion picture"); *Home Before Dark*, starring Jean Simmons as a woman re-adjusting to life after suffering a nervous breakdown; *I Want to Live!*, a dramatisation of the life of petty criminal Barbara Graham who was executed in California for her alleged involvement in the death of a disabled woman, for which Susan Hayward won the Best Actress Oscar and Robert Wise received a Best Director nomination (NYT "arresting"; V "overwhelming"); and *Separate Tables*, an ensemble piece about the various inhabitants of an English coastal boarding house, for which David Niven won the Best Actor Oscar (V "provocative and intelligent"). In the New York critics' voting for Best Picture, *Separate Tables* had finished as the runner-up to *The Defiant Ones*.

The winner of the Golden Globe (Comedy) was *Auntie Mame*, which starred Rosalind Russell as the eccentric title character in a lavish adaptation of the novel by Patrick Dennis. The film was a popular hit and became the most successful movie at the North American box office in 1959. Among the other nominees were: *Indiscreet*, a British romantic comedy starring Ingrid Bergman and Cary Grant, which was nominated for both of the Best Film prizes at the British Academy Awards in London; and *Me and the Colonel*, a satire for which Danny Kaye collected the Golden Globe for Best Actor (Comedy).

In the Best Picture (Musical) category, the Globe was presented to *Gigi*, a lavish M-G-M production of Colette's popular story about a young French girl becoming a courtesan (NYT "stylish" and "charming entertainment"; V "destined for a global boxoffice mopup … 100% escapist fare"). *Gigi* reunited Vincente Minnelli and Leslie Caron, the director and one of the stars of the 1951 Best Picture Oscar winning musical *An American in Paris*. Among the other nominees for the trophy was *South Pacific*, a film version of the Rodgers and

Hammerstein musical, which had been one of the top ten box office successes of the year (V "compelling").

When the Academy revealed its lists of nominees on 23 February 1959, ten days prior to the announcement of the Globe winners, Kramer's anti-racism drama *The Defiant Ones* and Minnelli's musical *Gigi* were the most honoured contenders of the year with nine nominations apiece, including mentions in both the Best Picture and Best Director categories.

Also nominated for the top prize were *Auntie Mame, Cat on a Hot Tin Roof* and *Separate Tables*. Despite a Best Director nod for Robert Wise, the acclaimed drama *I Want to Live!* was excluded from consideration for the Best Picture Oscar.

Also shut-out of contention for the Academy's top accolade, despite a Best Director nomination, was *The Inn of the Sixth Happiness*, a drama directed by Mark Robson. The film starred Ingrid Bergman as an English missionary in China who led a group of children to safety prior to the outbreak of the Second World War (V "unduly overlong").

To some observers, the most surprising omission was that of *The Old Man and the Sea*, an adaptation of Ernest Hemingway's novel about an ageing fisherman, played by Spencer Tracy. It was the first NBR Best Picture winner to be absent from the Oscar shortlist since 1949.

Also by-passed for both Globe and Oscar consideration were: the Western *The Big Country*, directed by William Wyler and starring Gregory Peck as a reformed gunfighter caught between feuding cattle barons (NYT "conventional"); *The Brothers Karamazov*, an expensive and highly-anticipated adaptation of Dostoyevsky's family tragedy, starring Yul Brynner as the eldest son, which had been poorly received by critics (NYT "a large splash of vigorous drama"; TT "a tedious and interminable exercise"); *The Young Lions*, a BAFTA nominated war drama starring Marlon Brando as a Nazi soldier questioning his beliefs and Montgomery Clift as a young Jewish American soldier; *The Goddess*, a drama about a young woman determined to become a Hollywood star, written by Paddy Chayefsky and based on the life of Marilyn Monroe (NYT "a shattering but truly potent film"); and *The Horse's Mouth*, a British comedy-drama starring Alec Guinness as an eccentric painter (NYT "the picture is a triumph").

Both the Academy and the Hollywood Foreign Press Association also ignored two American releases which have since come to be regarded as classics of the twentieth century. *Touch of Evil*, Orson Welles' dark drama about a narcotics officer and a corrupt policeman in a seedy Mexican border town, was taken out of Welles' control prior to release and subjected to significant changes by its producer. Cuts were made, sequences re-ordered and additional material inserted after being shot by another director. The original release version of the film was not well received by critics (NYT "the lasting impression of this film is effect rather than substance"; V "ultimately flounders") and the movie's reputation largely rests on a partially restored edit made available on DVD in the late 1990s. At the time of its release, meanwhile, Alfred Hitchcock's *Vertigo*, which has appeared atop some critics' polls as the greatest film ever made, was regarded as confounding, flawed or merely sleek entertainment (NYT "clever [but] devilishly far-fetched ... there is a big hole – a big question-mark – at a critical point. It will stop you, if you're a quick thinker. But try not to be and enjoy the film"; V "uneven ... the film's first half is too long and too slow ... it's questionable whether that much time should be devoted to what is basically only a psychological murder mystery").

With the Academy nominating five American productions for the Best Picture statuette, the year's best foreign-language releases were again overlooked. Glaring omissions included: Jacques Tati's French comedy *Mon Oncle (My Uncle)*, which won the Best Foreign-Language Oscar (TT "expressive and original"; S&S "brilliant": SMH "awarded top place here for the thousands of bits of sly, twinkling, unforced inventions that keep it inexhaustibly on the chuckle"); Ingmar Bergman's low-budget 1957 Swedish drama *Det Sjunde Inseglet (The Seventh Seal)* (NYT "a piercing and powerful contemplation of the passage of man upon this earth ... essentially intellectual, yet emotionally stimulating ... rewarding [and] provocative"; TT "extraordinary" and "highly sophisticated"; S&S "a revelation"; FQ "a triumph"); Satyajit Ray's 1955 Indian drama *Pather Panchali (Song of the Road)*; and *Les Sorcières de Salem (The Witches of Salem)*, a 1957 French film version of Arthur Miller's play 'The Crucible' starring Simone Signoret in a BAFTA-winning performance and Yves Montand (NYT "powerful and compelling"; V "a cumbersome, plodding affair").

In Hollywood, the contest for Oscar honours between *The Defiant Ones* and *Gigi* was resoundingly won by Minnelli's musical – it won every award for which it was nominated earning an unprecedented nine statuettes, including Best Picture. The next year *Ben-Hur* went two better and claimed eleven Oscars. The epic also outpolled *Gigi* to claim the Best Film BAFTA that year.

In London, the British Academy gave both Best Film and Best British Film to the drama *Room at the Top*, a drama which would be among the Best Picture Oscar contenders the following year.

BEST DIRECTOR

ACADEMY AWARDS
Richard Brooks for *Cat on a Hot Tin Roof*
Stanley Kramer for *The Defiant Ones*
• **Vincente Minnelli for *Gigi***
Mark Robson for *The Inn of the Sixth Happiness*
Robert Wise for *I Want to Live!*

GOLDEN GLOBE AWARDS
Richard Brooks – *Cat on a Hot Tin Roof*
Stanley Kramer – *The Defiant Ones*
Delbert Mann – *Separate Tables*
• **Vincente Minnelli – *Gigi***
Robert Wise – *I Want to Live!*

DIRECTORS GUILD AWARD
Richard Brooks – *Cat on a Hot Tin Roof*
Stanley Kramer – *The Defiant Ones*
• **Vincente Minnelli – *Gigi***
Mark Robson – *The Inn of the Sixth Happiness*
Robert Wise – *I Want to Live!*

NEW YORK – Stanley Kramer – *The Defiant Ones*
BOARD OF REVIEW – John Ford – *The Last Hurrah*

John Ford won the NBR Best Director award for his sentimental political drama *The Last Hurrah* and was among those who received support in the voting for the New York critics' prize (NYT "fine direction … Ford has put together a pungent pageant"). He was passed over, however, for both the Golden Globe Award and the DGA honour. Subsequently, he became the sixth NBR winner in just seven years to be overlooked by the Academy.

The Academy instead shortlisted the same five candidates as the Guild for the fourth time in six years: Vincente Minnelli, receiving his second nod, for the musical *Gigi* (NYT "Minnelli has marshaled a cast to give a set of performances that, for quality and harmony, are superb"; V "Minnelli's good taste in keeping it bounds"); Mark Robson, earning his second consecutive nomination, for *The Inn of the Sixth Happiness* (V "impressive"); Richard Brooks for *Cat on a Hot Tin Roof* ("driving direction"); Stanley Kramer for *The Defiant Ones* (NYT "while he is clawing out this message, Mr Kramer is also giving us a fast and exciting melodrama … by a pattern of crisp, direct cutting and jumping back and forth from the fugitives to their pursuers, he keeps the action moving"); and Robert Wise for *I Want to Live!* (NYT "sharp direction").

Overlooked by the Guild and the Academy were: Delbert Mann for *Separate Tables* (V "a sensitive and painstaking job"); previous winner William Wyler for *The Big Country*; Alfred Hitchcock for *Vertigo* (V ""through all this runs Hitchcock's directorial hand, cutting, angling and gimmicking with mastery); John Cromwell for *The Goddess* (NYT "beautifully directed"); Ronald Neame for *The Horse's Mouth* (NYT "has pointed and paced the whole thing grandly … deserves a grateful hand"); Ingmar Bergman for *Det Sjunde Inseglet (The Seventh Seal)* (NYT "Bergman hits you with it, right between the eyes"); Raymond Rouleau for *Les Sorcières de Salem (The Witches of Salem)*; Satyajit Ray for *Pather Panchali (Song of the Road)*; and Jacques Tati for *Mon Oncle (My Uncle)* (SMH "marvellous precision and consistency of style").

The frontrunners for the Oscar were Kramer and Minnelli, the directors of the year's two most Oscar-nominated films. Kramer had won the award from the New York critics while Minnelli had been presented with the Globe. When Minnelli was named by the DGA he became the strong Oscar favourite. In the nine years that the DGA had been handing out an award its honoree had always gone on to win the Academy Award.

On Oscar night, the DGA's faultless track record was preserved. Minnelli won the Best Director Academy Award.

1958

BEST ACTOR

ACADEMY AWARDS
Tony Curtis as 'John Jackson' in *The Defiant Ones*
Paul Newman as 'Brick Pollitt' in *Cat on a Hot Tin Roof*
• **David Niven as 'Maj. Pollock' in *Separate Tables***
Sidney Poitier as 'Noah Cullen' in *The Defiant Ones*
Spencer Tracy as 'the old man' in *The Old Man and the Sea*

GOLDEN GLOBE AWARDS

(Drama)
Tony Curtis – *The Defiant Ones*
Robert Donat
– *The Inn of the Sixth Happiness*
• **David Niven – *Separate Tables***
Sidney Poitier – *The Defiant Ones*
Spencer Tracy
– *The Old Man and the Sea*

(Comedy/Musical)
Maurice Chevalier – *Gigi*
Clark Gable – *Teacher's Pet*
Cary Grant – *Indiscreet*
Louis Jourdan – *Gigi*
• **Danny Kaye**
   – *Me and the Colonel*

BRITISH ACADEMY AWARDS

(Foreign Actor)
Marlon Brando – *The Young Lions*
Tony Curtis – *The Defiant Ones*
Glenn Ford – *The Sheepman*
Curt Jürgens
– *The Enemy Below* and
The Inn of the Sixth Happiness
Charles Laughton
– *Witness for the Prosecution*
Paul Newman – *Cat on a Hot Tin Roof*
• **Sidney Poitier – *The Defiant Ones***
Victor Sjöström – *Smultronstället (Wild Strawberries)*
Spencer Tracy – *The Last Hurrah*

(British Actor)
Michael Craig – *Sea of Sand*
Laurence Harvey – *Room at the Top*
• **Trevor Howard – *The Key***
I. S. Johar
   – *Harry Black and the Tiger*
Anthony Quayle – *Ice Cold in Alex*
Terry-Thomas – *Tom Thumb*
Donald Wolfit – *Room at the Top*

NEW YORK – David Niven – *Separate Tables*
BOARD OF REVIEW – Spencer Tracy – *The Last Hurrah* and *The Old Man and the Sea*

A contender for the Best Actor Academy Award emerged from each of the three major European film festivals.

1958

The Best Actor prize in Cannes was won by Paul Newman for his performance as a drifter who causes trouble when he decides to marry a local girl in *The Long Hot Summer* (NYT "Newman is best as the roughneck ... he could, if the script would let him, develop a classic character"). Later in the year Newman earned further praise as the troubled athlete in *Cat on a Hot Tin Roof* (NYT "resourceful and dramatically restrained"; FQ "a sensitive, subtle delineation").

In Venice, the Best Actor award was presented to Alec Guinness, the previous year's Best Actor Oscar winner, for his turn as an eccentric painter in *The Horse's Mouth* (NYT "Guinness plays with amazing clarity and zeal ... [a] brilliant performance ... the picture is a triumph – and it's all his ... remarkable", "one of the most incisive pictures of an artist ever made"; V "first-class"; S&S a "tour de force"; FQ "a rare comic achievement", "the performance must rate with his best"). Guinness had also adapted the screenplay from Joyce Cary's novel.

The Best Actor accolade in Berlin, meanwhile, was won by Sidney Poitier for his performance as one of the escaped prisoners in *The Defiant Ones* (NYT "stands out"; V "virtually flawless", "a cunning, totally intelligent portrayal"; NYer "solid").

Other candidates emerged when the end of year awards season began in the United States and Great Britain.

The NBR gave their award to Spencer Tracy for his performances as a politician mounting his final election campaign in *The Last Hurrah* (NYT "Tracy is at his best in the leading role") and as the Cuban fisherman in *The Old Man and the Sea* (NYT "a brave performance"; V "distinguished and impressive"; TT "the vital spark is missing"; FQ "a tour de force").

In New York, David Niven won the Best Actor prize for his portrayal of a sexual pervert masquerading as a retired officer in *Separate Tables* (NYT "starts weakly and gains strength"; V "one of the best performances of his career"). Guinness was the runner-up.

At the Golden Globes, Niven claimed the Best Actor (Drama) award ahead of Tracy, both Poitier and his co-star Tony Curtis (NYT "surprisingly good"; V "virtually flawless"; NYer "solid"), and the late Robert Donat for his final performance as the aged mandarin in *The Inn of the Sixth Happiness* (NYT "a standout"). It was Niven's second Globe and he became the first man to have won Best Actor trophies in both categories.

The British Academy, meanwhile, selected Poitier as the winner of its Best Foreign Actor award ahead of a group of nominees that included his co-star Curtis, Newman (for *Cat on a Hot Tin Roof*), Tracy (for *The Last Hurrah*) and Marlon Brando as a young German soldier who begins to question his Nazi beliefs in *The Young Lions* (NYT "sensitive"; "vital and interesting"; V "standout"; TT "fails altogether to carry through with his portrait").

The glaring omission of Guinness from the list of Globe nominees was repeated by the Academy – he was, however, nominated in the writing categories. Also passed over were: previous winner James Stewart in Alfred Hitchcock's thriller *Vertigo* (NYT "as usual, manages to act awfully tense in a casual way"; V "a startlingly fine performance"); previous winner Brando and his co-star in *The Young Lions*, Montgomery Clift (NYT "strangely hollow and lacklustre"; V "standout"; TT "never comes to terms with the part"); Orson Welles in *Touch of Evil* (NYT "obviously savors his dominant, colourful role"); Franchot Tone in *Uncle Vanya* (NYT "a thoughtful, sensitive and wholly striking portrayal"; V "excellent"); Frank Sinatra in *Some Came Running* (NYT "downright fascinating"; V "a top performance"); Max von Sydow in *Det Sjunde Inseglet (The Seventh Seal)* (NYT "excellent"; FQ "brilliant"); Yves Montand in *Les Sorcières de Salem (The Witches of Salem)* (NYT "outstanding"); Viktor Korshunov in *Pervyye Radosti (No Ordinary Summer)* (NYT "excellent"); and actor-director Jacques Tati in *Mon Oncle (My Uncle)*. A case could be made for the inclusion in the Best Actor category of Burl Ives for his portrayal of Big Daddy in *Cat on a Hot Tin Roof*, but M-G-M would not have wanted him competing against co-star Newman. Furthermore, Ives was already a strong chance for the Best Supporting Actor statuette for *The Big Country*.

In the end, the Academy nominated Newman (for *Cat on a Hot Tin Roof*), Tracy (for *The Old Man and the Sea*), Niven, and co-stars Poitier and Curtis. Poitier made history as the first African American man to be nominated for acting.

On Oscar night, Niven turned out to be the Academy's choice. He had been overlooked two years earlier for *Around the World in 80*, and was lauded by many for playing a controversial character. It was the first time that the Best Actor statuette had been presented to a foreigner for a third consecutive year. Niven's selection was controversial for some, however, as he had less than twenty minutes of screen time in an ensemble film.

BEST ACTRESS

ACADEMY AWARDS
• **Susan Hayward as 'Barbara Graham' in *I Want to Live!***
Deborah Kerr as 'Sybil Railton-Bell' in *Separate Tables*
Shirley MacLaine as 'Ginny Moorhead' in *Some Came Running*
Rosalind Russell as 'Mame Dennis' in *Auntie Mame*
Elizabeth Taylor as 'Maggie Pollitt' in *Cat on a Hot Tin Roof*

GOLDEN GLOBE AWARDS

(Drama)
Ingrid Bergman
   – The Inn of the Sixth Happiness
• **Susan Hayward – *I Want to Live!***
Deborah Kerr – *Separate Tables*
Shirley MacLaine
   – Some Came Running
Jean Simmons – *Home Before Dark*

(Comedy Musical)
Ingrid Bergman – *Indiscreet*
Leslie Caron – *Gigi*
Doris Day – *Tunnel of Love*
Mitzi Gaynor – *South Pacific*
• **Rosalind Russell – *Auntie Mame***

BRITISH ACADEMY AWARDS

(Foreign Actress)
Karuna Banerji – *Aparajito*
Ingrid Bergman
   – The Inn of the Sixth Happiness
Anna Magnani – *Wild is the Wind*
Giulietta Masina – *Le Notti di Cabiria*
   (The Nights of Cabiria)
Tatyana Samojlova – *Letjat Zhuravli*
   (The Cranes are Flying)
• **Simone Signoret – *Room at the Top***
Joanne Woodward – *No Down Payment*

(British Actress)
Hermione Baddeley
   – Room at the Top
Virginia McKenna
   – Carve Her Name with Pride
Elizabeth Taylor
   – Cat on a Hot Tin Roof
• **Irene Worth – *Orders to Kill***

NEW YORK – Susan Hayward – *I Want to Live!*
BOARD OF REVIEW – Ingrid Bergman – *The Inn of the Sixth Happiness*

The Oscar frontrunners were the two women who made awards history at the Golden Globes when they became the first to collect Best Actress trophies in both categories during their careers.

    Susan Hayward received her fifth (and final) Best Actress Oscar nomination for her portrayal of Barbara Graham, the petty criminal executed for her alleged involvement in the death of a disabled woman, in Robert Wise's anti-capital punishment drama *I Want to Live!* (NYT "superb", "she's never done anything so vivid or so shattering"; V "it is hard to think of any other star who could bring off this complex characterization"; TT "intelligent acting", she "makes Barbara something more than a symbol, an impersonal cause for argument"). Hayward won the New York critics' Best Actress prize and the Golden Globe Award in the drama category.

Rosalind Russell made the Oscar lists for the fourth (and final) time for reprising her Broadway triumph as a flamboyant eccentric in *Auntie Mame* (NYT "lets herself go with even more gushiness and grandeur of gesture than she did on the stage ... she succeeds in creating a creature that is as comically engrossing as a clown and yet possessed of surprising little pockets of tenderness that, every now and then, she suddenly opens and empties of a touching largess"; SMH "plays with tremendous zest ...[but] is sometimes not very subtle"). A winner of the Golden Globe for Drama in both 1946 and 1947, Russell equalled Ingrid Bergman's record tally of three Globes when she won as Best Actress in a Comedy or Musical for *Auntie Mame*.

The darkhorse contender for the Oscar was Deborah Kerr, mentioned by the Academy for the fifth time and a third year in a row, for playing a spinster in an English boarding house in *Separate Tables* (NYT "brilliant and true"; V "excellent").

Also included for consideration were: first-time nominee Shirley MacLaine in *Some Came Running* (NYT "overacted"; V "with her performance Miss MacLaine moves into the front row of actresses"); and, for the second year in a row, Elizabeth Taylor in *Cat on a Hot Tin Roof* (NYT "terrific"; V "has a major credit with her portrayal"; S&S "unable to convince"; FQ "persuasive and realistic"). Any sympathy vote for Taylor following the death of her husband, Oscar-winning producer Mike Todd, twelve months earlier had dissipated when it became known that she was involved with Eddie Fisher, the actor-singer who had been Todd's best man at his wedding to Taylor, and who was married to the popular actress Debbie Reynolds.

The surprise omission from the Academy's list was previous winner Ingrid Bergman, who had been nominated for both the Globe (Drama) for playing an English missionary in pre-war China in *The Inn of the Sixth Happiness* (V "impressively acted") and the Globe (Comedy/Musical) for playing a wealthy star in *Indiscreet* (V "delightful"; S&S "a sensitive, delicate performance"). For the dramatic role Bergman had also received the NBR Best Actress prize. Bergman was nominated in London by the British Academy Awards, but lost the Best Foreign Actress award to Simone Signoret who collected her third BAFTA for her role in *Room at the Top*. Signoret would claim the Oscar for her performance the following year.

Others overlooked were: Globe nominee Jean Simmons in *Home Before Dark* (NYT performs "very well"); Globe nominee Leslie Caron in *Gigi* (NYT "superb"; V "completely captivating and convincing"; TT "enchanting"); previous winner Shirley Booth in both *Hot Spell* and *The Matchmaker*; previous winner Anna Magnani as a Catholic nun running a school for underprivileged children in the Italian drama *Suor Letizia (The Awakening)* (NYT "interesting and touching"); the previous year's Best Actress Oscar winner Joanne Woodward in *The Long Hot Summer* (NYT "excellent"); Betsy Blair in *The Lovemaker* (NYT performed "extraordinarily well"); Kim Stanley as a girl who finds bittersweet stardom in Hollywood in *The Goddess* (NYT "brilliant"; TT "cunning"); Kim Novak in Alfred Hitchcock's thriller *Vertigo* (NYT "Novak is really quite amazing in dual roles"; V "Novak is interesting under Hitchcock's direction and nearer an actress than she was in either *Pal Joey* or *Jeanne Eagles*"); Kay Kendall in *The Reluctant Debutante* (NYT "professionally zany performance"); 1956 BAFTA winner Virginia McKenna in *A Town Like Alice* (NYT "forceful and believable"; TT "a most sensitive performance"); both 1957 BAFTA winner Simone Signoret (NYT "outstanding"; V "too subdued") and Mylène Demongeot (NYT "brilliant"; S&S "vivid") in *Les Sorcières de Salem (The Witches of Salem)*, a French adaptation of Arthur Miller's 'The Crucible'; and Roza Makagonova in the Russian film *Pervyye Radosti (No Ordinary Summer)* (NYT "excellent").

Perhaps stung by her spectacularly unsuccessful campaign for the Best Actress Oscar for *Mourning Becomes Electra* eleven years previously, Russell did not actively campaign for the Academy Award in 1958 for *Auntie Mame*, a decision which may have cost her. At the Academy Awards ceremony, it was Hayward who collected the Best Actress statuette at her fifth attempt.

BEST SUPPORTING ACTOR

ACADEMY AWARDS
Theodore Bikel as 'Sheriff Man Muller' in *The Defiant Ones*
Lee J. Cobb as 'Fyodor Karamazov' in *The Brothers Karamazov*
• **Burl Ives as 'Rufus Hannassey' in *The Big Country***
Arthur Kennedy as 'Frank Hirsh' in *Some Came Running*
Gig Young as 'Dr Hugo Pine' in *Teacher's Pet*

GOLDEN GLOBE AWARDS
Harry Guardino – *Houseboat*
• **Burl Ives – *The Big Country***
David Ladd – *The Proud Rebel*
Gig Young – *The Teacher's Pet*
Efrem Zimbalist Jr. – *Home Before Dark*

BOARD OF REVIEW – Albert Salmi – *The Bravados* and *The Brothers Karamazov*

Folksinger-turned-actor Burl Ives impressed critics with two indelible performances in 1958: as a feuding old cattle baron in the Western *The Big Country* (V "top-notch") and as Big Daddy in *Cat on a Hot Tin Roof* (NYT "superb … snorts and roars with gusto"; V "vibrant and convincing"; FQ "wonderful"). Ives had originated the role of Big Daddy on Broadway three years earlier, and although the big screen version of the Tennessee Williams play earned a Best Picture nod, it was for the Western that Ives won the Golden Globe and the Oscar.

The only other actor nominated for both prizes was Gig Young, as the psychologist best friend in *Teacher's Pet* (V "gives the picture its funniest moments").

The other Globe contenders were: Harry Gaurdino in *Houseboat* (V "outstanding"); eleven-year-old David Ladd in *The Proud Rebel* (NYT "astonishingly professional and sympathetic"); and Efrem Zimbalist Jr. in *Home Before Dark* (NYT "completely without revelation").

In contrast, the other Oscar candidates were: Theodore Bikel as the sheriff in *The Defiant Ones* (NYT "most impressive"; TT "deserves special mention"); Lee J. Cobb as the father in *The Brothers Karamazov* (V "walks away with the picture"); and Arthur Kennedy as the social-climbing brother in *Some Came Running*. Ives' victory on Oscar night left Kennedy as the first man to go unrewarded from five Academy Award nominations in the acting categories.

1958

Overlooked for both awards were: NBR winner Albert Salmi for both *The Bravados* and *The Brothers Karamazov*; Jack Carson in *Cat on a Hot Tin Roof* (S&S "compelling"; FQ "impressive"); Royal Dano in *Saddle the Wind* (NYT "superlatively affecting"); Clarence Derwent in *Uncle Vanya* (NYT "excellent Golden Globe nominee as Best Actor (Comedy/Musical) Maurice Chevalier in *Gigi* (V "well-nigh faultless"); BAFTA Best British Actor winner Trevor Howard as the captain of a tug boat in the Second World War in *The Key* (TT "completely real"; S&S "compelling"; FQ "excellent"); both Akim Tamiroff and Joseph Calleia in *Touch of Evil* (NYT both "excellent"); Bengt Ekerot in *Det Sjunde Inseglet (The Seventh Seal)* (NYT "excellent"); and Raymond Rouleau in *Les Sorcières de Salem (The Witches of Salem)* (NYT "excellent").

Previous Best Actor winner, the late Robert Donat, was also by-passed for his final performance as the aged mandarin in *The Inn of the Sixth Happiness* for which he had been a Best Actor Globe nominee (NYT "a standout"; TT the film's "obvious and pathetic weakness").

BEST SUPPORTING ACTRESS

ACADEMY AWARDS
Peggy Cass as 'Agnes Gooch' in *Auntie Mame*
• **Wendy Hiller as 'Miss Pat Cooper' in *Separate Tables***
Martha Hyer as 'Gwen French' in *Some Came Running*
Maureen Stapleton as 'Fay Doyle' in *Lonelyhearts*
Cara Williams as 'the woman' in *The Defiant Ones*

GOLDEN GLOBE AWARDS
Peggy Cass – *Auntie Mame*
• **Hermione Gingold – *Gigi***
Wendy Hiller – *Separate Tables*
Maureen Stapleton – *Lonelyhearts*
Cara Williams – *The Defiant Ones*

BOARD OF REVIEW – Kay Walsh – *The Horse's Mouth*

The Academy overlooked both the NBR winner, Kay Walsh in *The Horse's Mouth* (NYT "does a brilliant job"; V "overdoes her cockney role") and the Globe winner, Hermione Gingold in *Gigi* (NYT "elaborately humorous exhibition"; V "well-nigh faultless"). The omission of Gingold was particularly unexpected as only one Best Supporting Actress Golden Globe winner had been passed over before, and because *Gigi* was mentioned by Academy voters in nine other categories. Surprisingly, the film's star, Leslie Caron, was also snubbed as was the popular Maurice Chevalier. They too had been Golden Globe nominees.

The exclusion of Gingold was all the more curious given that the Academy nominated all of the other Globe candidates: Peggy Cass for reprising her Tony Award-winning Broadway role as the secretary in *Auntie Mame* (NYT "farcical and funny"); Wendy Hiller as a boarding house proprietress in *Separate Tables* (NYT "dignified, valiant and strong"; V "moving and touching"); Maureen Stapleton for her film debut as the wife of a crippled man in *Lonelyhearts* (V "proves a powerful character actress"); and Cara Williams as the lonely mother in *The Defiant Ones* (V "standout"). Included ahead of Gingold was Martha Hyer as the college tutor in *Some Came Running*.

In addition to Gingold, the Academy overlooked: Betty Lou Holland as the mother of a Hollywood star in *The Goddess* (NYT "fine and expressive"); previous winner Jo Van Fleet as the domineering mother in *The Sea Wall (This Angry Age)* (S&S a "tour de force"); both Janet Leigh and Marlene Dietrich (V "rather sultry and fun to watch") in *Touch of Evil*; Madeleine Sherwood in *Cat on a Hot Tin Roof* (S&S "compelling"; FQ "flawless"); Hope Lange a soldier's wife in *The Young Lions* (V "a sensitive performance"); and Pascale Petit as one of the hysterical girls in *Les Sorcières de Salem (The Witches of Salem)* (S&S "frightening").

On Academy Awards night, *Gigi* won all nine Oscars for which it was nominated. Had she been on the list, Gingold may well have been included in the film's clean sweep and won the Best Supporting Actress Oscar. As it was the statuette was presented to Hiller, whose win came twenty years after she had received her only previous nomination, in the Best Actress category in 1938 for her performance in *Pygmalion*.

The following year, Walsh earned a BAFTA nomination for Best British Actress for her performance in *The Horse's Mouth*.

BEST PICTURE

ACADEMY AWARDS

Anatomy of a Murder
(Preminger, Columbia, 160 mins BW, 2 Jul 1959, $5.5m, 7 noms)
• ***Ben-Hur***
(M-G-M, 212 mins, 18 Nov 1959, $38m, 12 noms)
The Diary of Anne Frank
(20th Century Fox, 180 mins BW, 18 Mar 1959, 8 noms)
The Nun's Story
(Warner Bros., 149 mins, 18 Jun 1959, $6.3m, 8 noms)
Room at the Top
(Romulus, Continental, 115 mins BW, 30 Mar 1959, 6 noms)

GOLDEN GLOBE AWARDS

(Drama)	(Comedy)	(Musical)
Anatomy of a Murder	*But Not for Me*	*The Five Pennies*
• ***Ben-Hur***	*Operation Petticoat*	*Li'l Abner*
The Diary of Anne Frank	*Pillow Talk*	• ***Porgy and Bess***
The Nun's Story	• ***Some Like It Hot***	*A Private's Affair*
On the Beach	*Who Was That Lady?*	*Say One for Me*

BRITISH ACADEMY AWARDS

(Film)	(British Film)
Anatomy of a Murder	*Look Back in Anger*
Ansiktet (The Magician)	*North West Frontier*
• ***Ben-Hur***	• ***Sapphire***
The Big Country	*Tiger Bay*
Compulsion	*Yesterday's Enemy*
Gigi	
Look Back in Anger	
Maigret tend un Piège (Inspector Maigret)	
North West Frontier	
The Nun's Story	
Popiól i Diament (Ashes and Diamonds)	
Sapphire	
Some Like It Hot	
Tiger Bay	
Yesterday's Enemy	

NEW YORK – *Ben-Hur*
BOARD OF REVIEW – *The Nun's Story*
SCREEN PRODUCERS GUILD – *Ben-Hur*

1959

The NBR began the major awards season in late December by giving its Best Picture prize to *The Nun's Story*, Fred Zinnemann's acclaimed and popular drama about a novice nun who renounces her vows. The film had been called "an amazing motion picture" by Bosley Crowther in The New York Times and "soaring and luminous" by Variety. Meanwhile, FQ said it was "a masterpiece" and "the best study of religious life ever made in the American cinema" while The Sydney Morning Herald called it a "distinguished production".

A few days later, the New York critics selected another critical and commercial success, *Ben-Hur*, M-G-M's expensive Roman epic (NYT "a remarkably intelligent and engrossing human drama"; V "a majestic achievement"; TT "powerful and impressive"; FQ "visually exciting film spectacle").

The runner-up for the New York prize was *Room at the Top*, a British drama which the previous year had received both the Best Film and Best British Film awards from the British Academy (NYT "strikingly effective … an engrossing picture"; S&S "compelling").

In February both *Ben-Hur* and *The Nun's Story* were nominated for the Best Picture (Drama) Golden Globe and the Best Picture Oscar. Also short-listed for both awards were: *Anatomy of a Murder* (NYT "magnificent"; V "forceful and enthralling"); and *The Diary of Anne Frank* (NYT "magnificent"; V "fine"; FQ "a film of great compassion and artistry", "unforgettable").

The only difference between the two lists of nominees was that *On the Beach* (NYT "deeply moving"; SMH "strong" but "uneven") was short-listed for the Globe while the Academy included *Room at the Top*. The latter was the first entirely British film nominated for the top Oscar since *Hamlet* in 1948.

All six of these films had been included by The New York Times on its annual list of the year's ten best, and all six had featured in the voting by the New York critics.

Ben-Hur was the year's most Oscar-nominated film with twelve nods and in early March, already well on the way to earning the top spot at the box office for 1960, the gladiator epic won the Globe (Drama) thus further consolidating its Oscar frontrunner status.

The other two Best Picture Globes went to acclaimed films overlooked by the Academy. The Globe (Comedy) went to Billy Wilder's popular farce *Some Like It Hot* (NYT "overlong, occasionally labored but often outrageously funny"; V "probably the funniest picture of recent memory … a whacky, clever, farcical comedy that starts off like a firecracker and keeps on throwing off lively sparks till the very end") while the Globe (Musical) was won by *Porgy and Bess*, a film adaptation of the acclaimed George Gershwin opera which had played on Broadway in 1935 (NYT "stunning, exciting and moving … a classic"; V "a handsome, intelligent and often gripping production").

1959

Ben-Hur gained further momentum for the Oscar later in the month when it was named Best Film by the British Academy. It outpolled a field of nominees that included: *Anatomy of a Murder*, *The Nun's Story*, the previous year's Best Picture Oscar winner *Gigi*, *Some Like It Hot*, and the year's Best British Film BAFTA winner *Sapphire* (NYT "absorbing", "a vivid illustration that something new and provocative can be added to the whodunit formula", "several interesting cuts above standard movie melodramas").

When the Academy Awards were handed out in early April, *Ben-Hur* was the overwhelming favourite. From its twelve nominations, the film bested the record nine statuettes won by *Gigi* the year before by collecting an unprecedented eleven Oscars, including the award for Best Picture of the year. Its record tally has yet to be broken and has been matched only twice – by *Titanic* in 1997 and *The Lord of the Rings: The Return of the King* in 2003.

Meanwhile, the Academy's Best Foreign-Language Oscar was won by the Cannes Film Festival Palme d'Or winner *Orfeu Negro (Black Orpheus)* (TT "an experience at once exhausting and exhilarating" but ultimately "unsatisfactory" since its "technical brilliance" is undermined by a lack of "genuinely personal response to the material").

Among the notable releases overlooked for the year's various Best Picture accolades were: Alfred Hitchcock's espionage thriller *North by Northwest* (NYT "suspenseful and delightful"; TT "consistently exciting and enjoyable"; S&S "thoroughly entertaining and suspenseful"); the popular battle-of-the-sexes comedy *Pillow Talk*, which had been a Globe nominee; *The Journey*, a drama about the 1956 Hungarian uprising (NYT "absorbing"); the courtroom drama *Compulsion* (NYT "exciting", "gripping" and "fascinating"; V "compelling, frank and exciting"); the British comedy *The Mouse That Roared* (NYT "a rambunctious satiric comedy"); François Truffaut's *Les Quatre Cents Coups (The 400 Blows)* (NYT "a small masterpiece", "striking", "smashingly convincing", "stunning"; FQ a "masterpiece"); and three acclaimed films by Swedish director Ingmar Bergman – the BAFTA nominee *Ansiktet (The Magician)*, *Nära Livet (Brink of Life)* (NYT "strikingly realistic") and *Smultronstället (Wild Strawberries)* which won Best Picture at the 1958 Berlin Film Festival (FQ "a great film").

BEST DIRECTOR

ACADEMY AWARDS
Jack Clayton for *Room at the Top*
George Stevens for *The Diary of Anne Frank*
Billy Wilder for *Some Like It Hot*
• **William Wyler for *Ben-Hur***
Fred Zinnemann for *The Nun's Story*

GOLDEN GLOBE AWARDS
Stanley Kramer – *On the Beach*
Otto Preminger – *Anatomy of a Murder*
George Stevens – *The Diary of Anne Frank*
• **William Wyler – *Ben-Hur***
Fred Zinnemann – *The Nun's Story*

DIRECTORS GUILD AWARD
Otto Preminger – *Anatomy of a Murder*
George Stevens – *The Diary of Anne Frank*
Billy Wilder – *Some Like It Hot*
• **William Wyler – *Ben-Hur***
Fred Zinnemann – *The Nun's Story*

NEW YORK – Fred Zinnemann – *The Nun's Story*
BOARD OF REVIEW – Fred Zinnemann – *The Nun's Story*

The Best Director award at the Cannes Film Festival was won by twenty-seven-year-old French film-maker François Truffaut for his directorial debut *Les Quatre Cents Coups (The 400 Blows)*, a drama about a young Parisian boy who turns to petty crime. The New York Times declared the film "brilliantly and strikingly reveals the explosion of a fresh creative talent in the directorial field."

At the Berlin Film Festival, Japanese film-maker Akira Kurosawa was named Best Director for his 1958 picture *Kakushi Toride no san Akunin (The Hidden Fortress)*, an historical drama about an independently-minded princess and her warrior-protector, while in Venice a special award was presented to Swedish director Ingmar Bergman for *Ansiktet (The Magician)*, a dark parable about the after-life.

While Kurosawa would not be eligible for Oscar consideration until 1962, both Truffaut and Bergman were in contention. Bergman was also eligible for *Nära Livet (Brink of Life)* (NYT "artful direction") and *Smultronstället (Wild*

Strawberries) (S&S "brilliantly constructed"). In the end both men were included by the Academy in the writing categories (Bergman for *Smultronstället*), but overlooked for their directorial efforts.

The frontrunners for the various end of year Best Director accolades were William Wyler for the historical epic *Ben-Hur*, which was the favourite for the Best Picture Oscar, and Fred Zinnemann for *The Nun's Story* (V "Zinnemann has achieved a pictorial sweep and majesty"; TT "most satisfying in his handling of two contrasting types of acting"; FQ "a major directorial achievement").

Zinnemann was honoured by the NBR (his first prize from the group) and by the New York critics who presented him with their accolade for the third time. Zinnemann was nominated for both the DGA prize and the Golden Globe, but in both cases he was outpolled by Wyler.

The Academy nominated Wyler for a record eleventh time and Zinnemann for a fourth time. Having featured in the voting in New York and been nominated for both the DGA award and the Globe, George Stevens received his fifth (and final) citation from the Academy for *The Diary of Anne Frank*, a dramatisation of the experience of a young Jewish girl and her family and friends hiding from the Nazis in an attic in Amsterdam (NYT "a superb job", "brilliant"). Previous winner Billy Wilder, passed over for the Globe but short-listed for the DGA prize, made the Academy's list for the seventh time for *Some Like It Hot*, a comedy starring Marilyn Monroe, Jack Lemmon and Tony Curtis, which was a hit at the box office (V "directed in masterly style", "directorial excellence"). The unexpected inclusion in the category was British director Jack Clayton, who had been the runner-up for the New York critics' prize for *Room at the Top*, but not a finalist for either the DGA plaudit or the Globe (NYT "discerning direction"; V "intelligent direction"). Clayton was the only Oscar nominee not to have previously collected a statuette.

The shock omission from the Academy's list of contenders was DGA and Globe nominee Otto Preminger for *Anatomy of a Murder*, a Best Picture nominee. Preminger had also handled the Globe (Musical) winner *Porgy and Bess*.

Also overlooked for Oscar consideration were: Globe nominee Stanley Kramer for *On the Beach* (NYT "brilliantly directed"); Richard Fleischer for *Compulsion* (V "expert direction"; TT "seldom wavers"); previous winner Joseph L. Mankiewicz for *Suddenly, Last Summer*; Alfred Hitchcock for *North by Northwest* (TT "an expert bit of film-making"); Douglas Sirk for the remake of *Imitation of Life*; and Basil Dearden for the BAFTA-winning anti-racism thriller *Sapphire*.

On Oscar night, Wyler collected his second Oscar as part of the *Ben-Hur* landslide. He received a twelfth and final nomination in 1965.

1959

BEST ACTOR

ACADEMY AWARDS
Laurence Harvey as 'Joe Lampton' in *Room at the Top*
• **Charlton Heston as 'Judah Ben-Hur' in *Ben-Hur***
Jack Lemmon as 'Jerry/Daphne' in *Some Like It Hot*
Paul Muni as 'Dr Sam Abelman' in *The Last Angry Man*
James Stewart as 'Paul Biegler' in *Anatomy of a Murder*

GOLDEN GLOBE AWARDS

(Drama)
Richard Burton – *Look Back in Anger*
• **Anthony Franciosa – *Career***
Charlton Heston – *Ben-Hur*
Fredric March – *Middle of the Night*
Joseph Schildkraut
    – *The Diary of Anne Frank*

(Comedy/Musical)
Clark Gable – *But Not for Me*
Cary Grant – *Operation Petticoat*
• **Jack Lemmon – *Some Like It Hot***
Dean Martin – *Who Was That Lady?*
Sidney Poitier – *Porgy and Bess*

BRITISH ACADEMY AWARDS

(Foreign Actor)
Zbigniew Cybulski
    – *Popiól i Diament*
    (Ashes and Diamonds)
Jean Desailly – *Maigret tend un Piège*
    (Inspector Maigret)
Jean Gabin – *Maigret tend un Piège*
    (Inspector Maigret)
• **Jack Lemmon – *Some Like It Hot***
Takashi Shimura – *Ikuru (To Live)*
James Stewart – *Anatomy of a Murder*

(British Actor)
Stanley Baker – *Yesterday's Enemy*
Richard Burton
    – *Look Back in Anger*
Peter Finch – *The Nun's Story*
Laurence Harvey – *Expresso Bongo*
Gordon Jackson
    – *Yesterday's Enemy*
Laurence Olivier
    – *The Devil's Disciple*
• **Peter Sellers – *I'm All Right Jack***

NEW YORK – James Stewart – ***Anatomy of a Murder***
BOARD OF REVIEW – Victor Sjöström – ***Smultronstället (Wild
    Strawberries)***

For only the second time, a foreign-language performance was honoured with
one of the major American-based end of year acting accolades. Thirteen years
after naming Anna Magnani for *Roma, Citta Aperta (Open City)*, the NBR gave
its Best Actor award to Swedish actor-director Victor Sjöström for playing an
elderly university professor in Ingmar Bergman's *Smultronstället (Wild*

Strawberries) (NYT "wonderfully warm and expressive", "real and sensitive and poignant"; S&S "superb"). The Academy, which was yet to nominate a foreign-language performance, overlooked Sjöström, and nominated the same five actors that had contested the Best Actor award in New York.

Twenty years after they first honoured him, the New York critics named James Stewart for a second time for his portrayal of a defence lawyer in *Anatomy of a Murder* (NYT "brilliantly revealed", "one of the finest performances of his career"; V "has his best role in years"). Stewart also won the Best Actor award in Venice for his work. It was Stewart's fifth and final mention from the Academy.

Also earning his fifth and final Oscar nomination was previous winner Paul Muni, who had been the runner-up in New York as a selfless Jewish doctor in *The Last Angry Man* (NYT "a canny performance"; V "superlative"; SMH "a superb portrait"). Muni's last nomination had been in 1937, and at sixty-four-years of age he was the oldest man yet considered for the Best Actor Oscar.

Included in the Best Actor category for the first time were: Laurence Harvey as a ruthless social-climber in the British drama *Room at the Top* (NYT "superb"; TT "builds up a consistent and persuasive portrait"); Charlton Heston as the Jewish prince who becomes a chariot racer in *Ben-Hur* (NYT "impressively delivers"; V "excellent"; TT "succeeds"); and 1955 Supporting Actor Oscar winner Jack Lemmon as the bass player who disguises himself as a woman to elude gangsters in *Some Like It Hot* (V "excellent", a "topnotch performance"). Lemmon was only the second Globe (Comedy/Musical) winner to be recognised by the Academy.

Surprisingly, the Academy's list only included two of the ten Golden Globe candidates. The Globe (Drama) winner Anthony Franciosa in *Career* (NYT "forceful"; V "convincing"), was only the second winner of the trophy to be snubbed by the Academy.

The most unexpected exclusion from the list of Oscar nominees, however, was previous Best Supporting Actor Oscar winner and Globe nominee Joseph Schildkraut for a reprisal of his stage portrayal of the father in *The Diary of Anne Frank* (NYT "moving" "his most sensitive presentation ... could not conceivably be surpassed"; V "marvellous", "there is not a false note in his performance"; FQ "perfect").

Other Globe nominees passed over for Oscar consideration included: Richard Burton in *Look Back in Anger* (FQ "electrifying"); previous winner Fredric March in *Middle of the Night* (NYT "isn't successful"); and Sidney Poitier in *Porgy and Bess* (NYT "sensitive and strong"; V "thoroughly believable").

Overlooked for both the Globe and the Oscar were: previous winner Yul Brynner in *The Journey* (NYT "sincere" and "skillful"); Henry Fonda in the

Western *Warlock* (NYT "excellent"; V "particularly fine"; TT "restrained and convincing"); Tony Curtis in *Some Like It Hot* (V "topnotch"; "excellent"); Cary Grant in *North by Northwest*; Nigel Patrick in *Sapphire* (NYT "excellent"); both Bradford Dillman (NYT "outstanding",; V "superb") and Dean Stockwell (NYT "outstanding" and "effective"; V "acted with skill"; FQ "superb") for their Cannes prize-winning performances in *Compulsion*; and Peter Sellers for his three comic portrayals in *The Mouse That Roared*. Sellers' BAFTA-winning turn in *I'm All Right Jack* would be eligible for Oscar consideration the following year.

In the absence of Franciosa and Schildkraut, Lemmon was favoured to win the Oscar ahead of Stewart. His frontrunner status was confirmed when he won the Best Foreign Actor award from the British Academy over a field that included his main rival.

On Oscar night, however, there was an upset. When Susan Hayward opened the envelope she announced that the winner was Heston (who hadn't even been a nominee in London). Heston had evidently been carried to victory by the sweeping success of *Ben-Hur* which won eleven statuettes, including Best Picture. He never made the Academy's list of nominees again.

1959

BEST ACTRESS

ACADEMY AWARDS
Doris Day as 'Jan Morrow' in *Pillow Talk*
Audrey Hepburn as 'Sister Luke' in *The Nun's Story*
Katharine Hepburn as 'Mrs Venable' in *Suddenly, Last Summer*
• **Simone Signoret as 'Georgie Elgin' in *Room at the Top***
Elizabeth Taylor as 'Catherine Holly' in *Suddenly, Last Summer*

GOLDEN GLOBE AWARDS

(Drama)
Audrey Hepburn – *The Nun's Story*
Katharine Hepburn
  – *Suddenly, Last Summer*
Lee Remick – *Anatomy of a Murder*
Simone Signoret – *Room at the Top*
• **Elizabeth Taylor**
  – *Suddenly, Last Summer*

(Comedy/Musical)
Dorothy Dandridge
  – *Porgy and Bess*
Doris Day – *Pillow Talk*
Shirley MacLaine – *Ask Any Girl*
• **Marilyn Monroe**
  – *Some Like It Hot*
Lilli Palmer – *But Not for Me*

BRITISH ACADEMY AWARDS

(Foreign Actress)
Ava Gardner – *On the Beach*
Susan Hayward – *I Want to Live!*
Ellie Lambeti – *To Telefteo Psemma*
  (The Final Lie)
• **Shirley MacLaine – *Ask Any Girl***
Rosalind Russell – *Auntie Mame*

(British Actress)
Peggy Ashcroft – *The Nun's Story*
• **Audrey Hepburn**
  – *The Nun's Story*
Yvonne Mitchell – *Sapphire*
Sylvia Sims – *No Trees in the Street*
Kay Walsh – *The Horse's Mouth*

NEW YORK – Audrey Hepburn – *The Nun's Story*
BOARD OF REVIEW – Simone Signoret – *Room at the Top*

In 1958, French actress Simone Signoret was named Best Foreign Actress by the British Academy for the third time in seven years. She won the accolade for her performance as the older mistress of a ruthless social climber in the acclaimed British film *Room at the Top* (NYT "superb performance"). The following year she was selected as Best Actress at the Cannes Film Festival. When the movie was released on the other side of the Atlantic, Signoret was named Best Actress by the NBR and finished runner-up for the New York critics' prize.

    The winner in New York was Belgian-born English actress Audrey Hepburn for her portrayal of a novice nun in *The Nun's Story* (NYT "fluent and luminous"; V "her finest performance" in "her most demanding film role"; FQ "a sincere and deeply moving portrait"; SMH "beautiful performance"). It was her second New York trophy.

The Oscar frontrunner, however, was English-born star Elizabeth Taylor. She outpolled both Hepburn and Signoret to win the Golden Globe (Drama) for her performance as the young woman on the verge of insanity in *Suddenly, Last Summer* (FQ "exceptionally perceptive"). It was the second year in a row that Taylor was an Oscar contender in a role written by Tennessee Williams – in 1958 she had been an Oscar nominee for playing Maggie in *Cat on a Hot Tin Roof*.

The Academy nominated all three actresses: Signoret for the first time, previous winner Hepburn for the third time, and Taylor for a third consecutive year. Also nominated, despite some negative reviews, was Taylor's co-star in *Suddenly, Last Summer*, previous Oscar winner and Globe nominee Katharine Hepburn (V "dominates"; TT "fails to take a definite line" with her character). As the woman who would rather see her niece lobotomised than face the truth about her son's gruesome death, Hepburn earned her sixth mention from the Academy. In a huge surprise, the other candidate was Globe nominee Doris Day, for her performance as an interior decorator sharing a telephone line with a casanova songwriter, in the romantic comedy *Pillow Talk* (NYT "played fiercely and smartly"; TT "a most professional performance"). Day was a popular singer and comedienne and *Pillow Talk* was a huge success at the box office, however few anticipated that she would be included as an Oscar contender.

The shock inclusion of Day came ahead of several notable performances including: Globe nominee Lee Remick as the wife who claims she was raped by the man her husband is accused of murdering in *Anatomy of a Murder* – a role that Lana Turner walked out on at the last minute (NYT ""treads beautifully a fine line between never-resolved uncertainties"); Globe nominee and Berlin Film Festival prize-winner Shirley MacLaine in the comedy *Ask Any Girl* (V "outstanding", "a performance that is a sheer delight, even topping her Academy Award nominated stint in *Some Came Running*"); Globe nominee Dorothy Dandridge in *Porgy and Bess* (NYT "a characterization that could be improved on"); Deborah Kerr in *The Journey*, a romantic drama set during the 1956 Hungarian uprising (NYT "a lustrous performance"); both Bibi Andersson (NYT "a touching portrait") and Ingrid Thulin (NYT "a masterly job") in Ingmar Bergman's *Nära Livet (Brink of Life)*; BAFTA nominee Ava Gardner in *On the Beach* (NYT "remarkably revealing"); child star Millie Perkins as the title character in *The Diary of Anne Frank*; and Lana Turner in the popular remake of *Imitation of Life* (V "outstanding").

The most glaring omission from the list of nominees, however, was the winner of the Best Actress (Comedy/Musical) Globe – Marilyn Monroe.

1959

Overlooked three years earlier for her acclaimed dramatic performance in *Bus Stop*, Monroe was again passed over by Academy voters, this time for her comic work as a ukulele player in a 1930s all-girl jazz band who dreams of marrying a millionaire in Billy Wilder's box office hit *Some Like It Hot* (NYT "contributes more assets than the obvious ones to this madcap romp ... proves to be the epitome of a dumb blonde and a talented comedienne").

In London, MacLaine was chosen as Best Foreign Actress by the British Academy for *Ask Any Girl* and Audrey Hepburn won her second Best British Actress award for *The Nun's Story*. Hepburn, however, was unable to repeat her win in Hollywood.

Twenty-five years after French-born Claudette Colbert won Best Actress for *It Happened One Night*, another French actress claimed the Academy Award. Signoret made history as the first actress in a non-American film to win the Best Actress statuette. Her victory signalled a massive change in her fortunes as until only a few months earlier she had been subject to a long-standing ban on her entering the United States due to her left-wing political activism. Her name appeared on the Academy's lists for a second time six years later.

1959

BEST SUPPORTING ACTOR

ACADEMY AWARDS
• **Hugh Griffith as 'Sheik Ilderim' in *Ben-Hur***
Arthur O'Connell as 'Parnell McCarthy' in *Anatomy of a Murder*
George C. Scott as 'Claude Dancer' in *Anatomy of a Murder*
Robert Vaughn as 'Chet Gwynn' in *The Young Philadelphians*
Ed Wynn as 'Albert Dussell' in *The Diary of Anne Frank*

GOLDEN GLOBE AWARDS
Fred Astaire – *On the Beach*
• **Stephen Boyd – *Ben-Hur***
Tony Randall – *Pillow Talk*
Robert Vaughn – *The Young Philadelphians*
Joseph N. Welch – *Anatomy of a Murder*

BOARD OF REVIEW – **Hugh Griffith – *Ben-Hur***

Best remembered today for his subsequent role in the TV series 'The Man from U.N.C.L.E.', Robert Vaughn was the only actor nominated for both the Golden Globe and the Oscar as Best Supporting Actor in 1959. He made the lists for his performance as a wealthy Korean war veteran accused of murder in *The Young Philadelphians* (NYT "striking").

Both prizes, however, were won by a cast member of the epic *Ben-Hur*. The Golden Globe was won by Stephen Boyd as Messala, while the Oscar went to Welsh actor Hugh Griffith as the Arab sheik (NYT "stand-out").

The other nominees for the Globe were: Fred Astaire as a cynical scientist in *On the Beach* (NYT "amazing"; V "excellent", "will attract considerable attention"); Tony Randall in *Pillow Talk* (NYT "no other could be more droll"); and Joseph N. Welch as the judge in *Anatomy of a Murder* (NYT "does an unbelievably professional job … he is delightful and ever so convincing"; V "tremendous").

The Academy meanwhile had considered Ed Wynn as the dentist hiding with the Frank family in *The Diary of Anne Frank*; and both Arthur O'Connell as a defence lawyer's alcoholic assistant and George C. Scott as the prosecution lawyer (NYT "makes the courtroom battle a deadly duel by offering himself as a skillful and unrelenting antagonist") in *Anatomy of a Murder*.

While Astaire was the most unexpected omission from the Academy's list, others overlooked included: Edward G. Robinson as the nagging brother in Frank Capra's *A Hole in the Head* (NYT "superb"); Joe E. Brown as the millionaire in *Some Like It Hot*; Anthony Perkins as the young lieutenant in *On the Beach* (NYT "excellent"); Orson Welles as a lawyer in *Compulsion*, for which he shared an ensemble acting award at the Cannes Film Festival (NYT film's "finest portrayal"; V "admirable"; TT "a tour de force"); Sammy Davis Jr in *Porgy and Bess*; BAFTA Best British Actor nominee Peter Finch in *The Nun's Story*; William Hartnell in the British comedy *The Mouse That Roared* (NYT "funny"); Earl Cameron as the brother of the slain girl in the British film *Sapphire* (NYT "effective and understanding; V "brings immense dignity to the role"); Gunnar Björnstrand as a surgeon in Ingmar Bergman's *Ansiktet (The Magician)* (NYT "brilliantly performed"); and Albert Rémy as the father in *Les Quatre Cents Coups (The 400 Blows)* (NYT "fine").

1959

BEST SUPPORTING ACTRESS

ACADEMY AWARDS
Hermione Baddeley as 'Elspeth' in *Room at the Top*
Susan Kohner as 'Sarah Jane Johnson' in *Imitation of Life*
Juanita Moore as 'Annie Johnson' in *Imitation of Life*
Thelma Ritter as 'Alma' in *Pillow Talk*
• **Shelley Winters as 'Mrs Van Daan' in *The Diary of Anne Frank***

GOLDEN GLOBE AWARDS
Edith Evans – *The Nun's Story*
Estelle Hemsley – *Take a Giant Step*
• **Susan Kohner – *Imitation of Life***
Juanita Moore – *Imitation of Life*
Shelley Winters – *The Diary of Anne Frank*

BOARD OF REVIEW – Edith Evans – *The Nun's Story*

Edith Evans won the NBR award for her performance in *The Nun's Story* and was subsequently nominated for the Golden Globe (NYT "powerfully plays"; FQ "superb"; SMH a "beautiful performance"). Despite this, she was overlooked by the Academy, as was her co-star Peggy Ashcroft who was a candidate in the Best Actress category at the British Academy Awards for her performance (FQ "superb").

Another Globe nominee passed over by the Academy was Estelle Hemsley as the understanding grandmother in *Take a Giant Step*, a role she had originated on Broadway in 1953 (V "warming"). Others left out of Oscar consideration were: Angela Lansbury in *Season of Passion*, a Hollywood version of the acclaimed Australian play 'Summer of the Seventeenth Doll' (V "brings a comic and sometimes sad dignity to bear"); Carolyn Jones as an agent in the Broadway drama *Career*; Eleanor Parker in *A Hole in the Head* (NYT "touching"); Diahann Carroll in *Porgy and Bess* (NYT "beautifully plays the young mother"); previous winner Eva Marie Saint in *North by Northwest*; BAFTA nominee Yvonne Mitchell in *Sapphire* (NYT "strong"); Katherine Squire in *The Story on Page One* (NYT "excellent"); both Billie Burke and Alexis Smith in *The Young Philadelphians*; and Claire Maurier in *Les Quatre Cents Coups (The 400 Blows)* (NYT "excellent").

For their respective roles as the African American maid and her daughter in the remake of *Imitation of Life*, Juanita Moore (V "played memorably") and

Hispanic actress Susan Kohner (V "a stirring portrayal"; TT "makes a powerful impression") were each nominated for the Globe and the Oscar.

Also included on both lists was Shelley Winters in *The Diary of Anne Frank* (V "vivid", "excellent").

Hermione Baddeley was recognised by the Academy for her brief part in *Room at the Top*, while Thelma Ritter was mentioned for the fifth time in a decade as the hung-over maid in *Pillow Talk* (NYT "no other could be more droll").

Kohner entered the Oscar vote with the momentum of the Globe win, while Ritter garnered sympathy for having gone unrewarded at four previous nominations. Kohner, however, was in competition with her co-star Moore. Furthermore, *Imitation of Life* and *Pillow Talk* were both Universal releases which perhaps diminished the chances of Kohner and Ritter.

On Oscar night, Winters received the Best Supporting Actress statuette. Just six years later she would become the first woman to win the prize a second time.

Index

Index

Index

Index

Index

Index

Index

Index

Index

Index

Index

Index

Index

Index

Index

Index

Index

Index

Index

Index

Index

Index

Index

Index

Index

Index

Index